A CULTURAL HISTORY
OF WOMEN

VOLUME 3

A Cultural History of Women
General Editor: Linda Kalof

Volume 1
A Cultural History of Women in Antiquity
Edited by Janet H. Tulloch

Volume 2
A Cultural History of Women in the Middle Ages
Edited by Kim M. Phillips

Volume 3
A Cultural History of Women in the Renaissance
Edited by Karen Raber

Volume 4
A Cultural History of Women in the Age of Enlightenment
Edited by Ellen Pollak

Volume 5
A Cultural History of Women in the Age of Empire
Edited by Teresa Mangum

Volume 6
A Cultural History of Women in the Modern Age
Edited by Liz Conor

A CULTURAL HISTORY OF WOMEN
IN THE RENAISSANCE

Edited by Karen Raber

BLOOMSBURY
LONDON • NEW DELHI • NEW YORK • SYDNEY

Bloomsbury Academic
An imprint of Bloomsbury Publishing Plc

50 Bedford Square
London
WC1B 3DP
UK

1385 Broadway
New York
NY 10018
USA

www.bloomsbury.com

Bloomsbury is a registered trade mark of Bloomsbury Publishing Plc

First published 2013
Reprinted 2013

© Karen Raber and contributors, 2013

Karen Raber has asserted her right under the Copyright, Designs and Patents Act, 1988, to be identified as Editor of this work.

All rights reserved. No part of this publication may be reproduced or transmitted in any form or by any means, electronic or mechanical, including photocopying, recording, or any information storage or retrieval system, without prior permission in writing from the publishers.

No responsibility for loss caused to any individual or organization acting on or refraining from action as a result of the material in this publication can be accepted by Bloomsbury or the author.

British Library Cataloguing-in-Publication Data
A catalogue record for this book is available from the British Library.

ISBN: HB: 978-0-8578-5099-7
Set: 978-1-8478-8475-6

Library of Congress Cataloging-in-Publication Data
A cultural history of women in the Renaissance / edited by Karen Raber.
    p. cm. — (A cultural history of women ; 3)
    Includes bibliographical references and index.
    ISBN 978-0-85785-099-7
 1. Women—History—Renaissance, 1450–1600. 2. Women—Europe—Social conditions.
I. Raber, Karen, 1961–
   HQ1148.C84 2013
   305.4209'024—dc23   2012036399

Typeset by Apex CoVantage, LLC, Madison, WI, USA.
Printed and bound in Great Britain

CONTENTS

Series Preface — vii
List of Illustrations — ix

Introduction — 1
Karen Raber

1 The Life Cycle — 25
Karen Raber and Stephanie Tarbin

2 Bodies and Sexuality — 45
Mara I. Amster

3 Religion and Popular Beliefs — 67
Megan L. Hickerson

4 Medicine and Disease — 95
Margaret Healy

5 Public and Private — 115
Danielle Clarke

6 Education and Work — 143
Meg Lota Brown and Kari Boyd McBride

7 Power — 163
Holly Hurlburt

8	Artistic Representation *Mary Rogers*	183
	NOTES	209
	BIBLIOGRAPHY	241
	CONTRIBUTORS	261
	INDEX	265

SERIES PREFACE

A Cultural History of Women is a six-volume series reviewing the changing cultural construction of women and women's historical experiences throughout history. Each volume follows the same basic structure and begins with an outline account of the major ideas about women in the historical period under consideration. Next, specialists examine aspects of women's history under eight key headings: the life cycle, bodies/sexuality, religion/popular beliefs, medicine/disease, public/private, education/work, power, and artistic representation. Thus, readers can choose a synchronic or a diachronic approach to the material—a single volume can be read to obtain a thorough knowledge of women's history in a given period, or one of the eight themes can be followed through time by reading the relevant chapters of all six volumes, thus providing a thematic understanding of changes and developments over the long term. The six volumes divide the history of women as follows:

Volume 1: A Cultural History of Women in Antiquity (500 B.C.E.–1000 C.E.)
Volume 2: A Cultural History of Women in the Middle Ages (1000–1500)
Volume 3: A Cultural History of Women in the Renaissance (1400–1650)
Volume 4: A Cultural History of Women in the Age of Enlightenment (1650–1800)
Volume 5: A Cultural History of Women in the Age of Empire (1800–1920)
Volume 6: A Cultural History of Women in the Modern Age (1920–2000+)

Linda Kalof, General Editor

LIST OF ILLUSTRATIONS

INTRODUCTION

Figure 0.1: Engraving after Gui. Vaughan's *Musick's Handmaid*, 1678. — 4

Figure 0.2: Woman milking cow (1547). — 15

Figure 0.3: Woman using a distaff, ca. 1675. — 18

CHAPTER 1

Figure 1.1: Jorg Breu, *The Nine Ages of Man*, c. 1540. — 26

Figure 1.2: Hans Baldung Grien, *The Three Ages of Woman and Death*, 1510. — 28

Figure 1.3: Hans Baldung Grien, *The Seven Ages of Woman*, 1544. — 30

Figure 1.4: Allegorical portrait of Elizabeth I, c. 1610, attributed to Marcus Gheerarts. — 42

CHAPTER 2

Figure 2.1: Title page, Helkiah Crooke, *Microcosmographia: A Description of the Body of Man* (1615). — 46

Figure 2.2: Title page, Richard Brathwaite, *The English Gentlewoman* (1631). 52

Figure 2.3: Title page, Barnabe Rich, *My Ladies Looking Glasse* (1616). 56

Figure 2.4: Title page, Thomas Middleton and Thomas Dekker, *The Roaring Girl* (1611). 60

CHAPTER 3

Figure 3.1: A skimmington. *Roxburgh Ballads*. 69

Figure 3.2: Detail, Pieter Breugel the Elder, *The Battle Between Carnival and Lent*, 1559. 70

Figure 3.3: Michelangelo Buonarotti, *Adam and Eve*. 75

Figure 3.4: Lucas Cranach the Elder, *Adam and Eve*. 75

Figure 3.5: Albrecht Dürer, woodcut, *Whore of Babylon*, 1497–98. 84

Figure 3.6: Frontispiece, *Babel and Bethel: or, The Pope in his Colours* (1679). 86

Figure 3.7: Hans Baldung Grien, *The Bewitched Groom*, 1544–45. 92

Figure 3.8: Hans Baldung Grien, *Three Witches*, 1514. 93

CHAPTER 4

Figure 4.1: Nude anatomical figure from a book of medical receipts. 96

Figure 4.2: Andreas Vesalius, *De Humani Corpore Fabrica*, illustration of a uterus. 97

Figure 4.3: Female anatomical figure, 1702. 100

Figure 4.4: A seated woman giving birth, 1583. 104

Figure 4.5: Depiction of Trotula of Salerno from a manuscript of the late twelfth or early thirteenth century. 107

Figure 4.6: A hospital ward in the Hotel Dieu. 110

LIST OF ILLUSTRATIONS xi

CHAPTER 5

Figure 5.1: *Tittle-Tattle: Or, the Several Branches of Gossipping*, c. 1640.   118

Figure 5.2: Dancers in a square. *Roxburgh Ballads*.   123

Figure 5.3: Tavern scene. *Roxburgh Ballads*.   132

CHAPTER 6

Figure 6.1: Title page, *The Accomplished Ladies Rich Closet* (1675), by Hannah Woolley.   147

Figure 6.2: *The Lesson*, drawing by Jacob Toorenvliet, 1650–1719.   150

Figure 6.3: Bathsua Makin (née Reginald), etching by William Marshall, after unknown artist, 1640s.   157

CHAPTER 7

Figure 7.1: *Christine de Pisan Presents Her Book to Isabella of Bavaria*, c. 1400.   176

Figure 7.2: Miniature portrait of Elizabeth I, Nicholas Hillyard.   178

CHAPTER 8

Figure 8.1: Alesso Baldovinetti, *Portrait of a Lady*, c. 1465.   185

Figure 8.2: Bartolomeo Veneto, *Portrait of a Lady*, c. 1525.   187

Figure 8.3: Leonardo da Vinci, *Lady with an Ermine* (Portrait of Cecilia Gallerani), c. 1490/1491.   191

Figure 8.4: Antonio Pisanello, medal of Cecilia Gonzaga (obverse), c. 1447.   194

Figure 8.5: Francesco Laurana, *Bust of Battista Sforza* (Duchess of Urbino), c. 1473.   196

Figure 8.6: Nineteenth-century cast after Francesco Laurana,
    Bust of a Lady (Ippolital Sforza?).   197

Figure 8.7: Sofonisba Anguissola, *Portrait of the Artist*, c. 1557.   199

Figure 8.8: Leonardo da Vinci, *Portrait of Isabella d'Este*
    (Marchioness of Mantua), c. 1500.   201

Figure 8.9: Francesco Bacchiacca, *Portrait of a Lady with
    Music Book*, c. 1530s.   204

Figure 8.10: Palma Vecchio, *Blonde Woman*, c. 1520.   206

Figure 8.11: Girolamo Savoldo, *Portrait of a Lady with the
    Attributes of St. Margaret*, c. 1530–40.   207

Introduction

KAREN RABER

Two young girls play chess while their younger sister and a nursemaid look on. Sofonisba Anguissola's *The Chess Game*, the cover image for this volume, is both an intimate portrait of a moment in her family's life and a distilled historical commentary on women's roles in Renaissance culture. Anguissola was raised by a wealthy noble father who gave his children, male and female, the benefits of an extensive education. Of all her siblings, Anguissola was the most talented as a painter, although all the children were given extensive training in the usual Renaissance humanist disciplines, including art, music, Latin, modern languages, rhetoric, as well as in domestic skills traditional for women. She became famous in her own age, given credit by that chronicler of the great painters Giorgio Vasari, for her talent, admired and encouraged by Michelangelo, approached and remembered by Van Dyck for her painterly advice. Her work consisted almost entirely of portraits, especially of her own family and of herself, because despite her talent, as a woman she was unable to gain the training that would have made her capable of large-scale multi-figure works typical of Renaissance art at the time.[1] Nevertheless, she served in a highly public role at the Spanish court, as court painter for Elisabeth of Valois, third wife of Philip II, and then for Philip's fourth queen, Anne of Austria. She married twice, but never gave up painting, and became famous for her unique style in portraits.

Anguissola thus embodies many of the period's contradictory attitudes toward women's place in Renaissance culture: the content of her education is a sign that for the Renaissance, literacy and moral reasoning were perceived as important not just for men, but for all members of civil society; thus, scholarship was no longer restricted to those destined for the professions. Yet attitudes toward women's place did not admit they might also become professionals, and so Anguissola was limited in her ability to practice her art. The body of her work indicates she was tenuously poised at the juncture of public and private spheres: she mastered an intimate, private form of painting that did not require the apprenticeship skills she lacked, yet she engaged in a very public court career that exploited her breadth of knowledge and even her diplomatic skills. She married, as a proper Renaissance woman was supposed to, but not until late in life—the first time to a spouse chosen for her by her patron, Philip of Spain, because it was assumed no woman of any age could or should function in the world without a husband, the second time for what seems like pure affection. Although Anguissola theoretically surrendered autonomy to both spouses (and King Philip) in obeisance to society's requirements for women, she never conceded to the dictates of marital conduct by giving up her vocation as an artist. Finally, while she was renowned during her lifetime, she suffered the fate of many Renaissance women by being almost forgotten by subsequent generations of scholars and artists, who assumed that women had no influence on or role in creating the high cultural artifacts of the Renaissance.

The compositional characteristics that distinguish Anguissola's *The Chess Game* also demonstrate the problem of women's complicated function as both subjects and objects of Renaissance ideologies of gender. The painting represents a world of women within the home, suggesting the comfort of sisterhood by excluding Anguissola's brother, Asdrubale, in favor of the female maid; this is a relatively hermetic domestic scene, then, eschewing elements of dynasty or hierarchy that appear in other family scenes of Anguissola's.[2] Instead of being formally posed, the four figures are relaxed, smiling at each other, gesturing to one another, a significant departure from most portraits of the period which show serious faces and demurely quiet limbs.[3] Familiar with the intricacies of dress and fashion, Anguissola offers exquisite detail of brocades and embroideries on the children in stark contrast to the nurse/servant's austere white head cover and collar. The combination of the informal moment and the attention to clothing might be imagined to mark the image as somehow unthreateningly "domestic," in contrast to the great panoramas of classical and biblical subjects undertaken by men. However, the girls are playing chess, a game which, despite being in some cases considered marginally acceptable for women to learn and play, involves its players in vicarious warfare, with complex moves that train its disciples in how to better negotiate the plots, politics, and strategies of a royal court. The girls' focus in the moment captured seems to be on each other, not the game itself, however, hinting that bonds of female society are what are at stake—yet the nursemaid's looming oversight of their activities hints at her possible anxiety that this game is too masculine an occupation for young women. Each of the girls is clearly individuated, especially the eldest, who holds the viewer's gaze; but at least three of the Anguissola sisters are missing. One of her sisters, Elena, became a nun, honoring the usual practice of sending at least one child into the Church; two others gave up their art upon marriage, when they also left their father's household. So despite the apparent unity of the sisterhood portrayed in the painting, and the emphasis on the individuation of the children, the Anguissola women's lives were no more their own than were the lives of other women like them, nor were they exempt from following women's communal paths in life. In Renaissance Italy's thoroughly patriarchal culture, artistic, intellectual, and other accomplishments were adornments for the sisters, but no substitutes for chastity and submission, both of which served to make women suitable for the institution of marriage.

Indeed, some critics have pointed out that women were subjected to intense cultural repositioning during the Renaissance that limited, rather than expanded, their opportunities and access to individual power. This dispute over women's place in Renaissance culture might be said to begin in the twentieth century with feminist responses to the claims of the founding "father" of cultural history, Jacob Burckhardt. Burckhardt saw the sweeping cultural transformations to which we now apply the term "Renaissance"—the rediscovery of classical texts, Humanism, the first glimmerings of the scientific revolution, artistic advances like the application of perspective in painting and architecture, the Reformation—as uniformly positive, and applicable to women. In 1860, Burckhardt wrote that Italian Renaissance women "stood on a footing of perfect equality with men."[4] Despite the apparent misogyny of so many Renaissance texts, Burckhardt still asserted that the education of well-born women was the same as that provided their male peers; he argued that "energy" and force of character were prized in women as much as in men. In the art and literature of the period, as well as in the salons and private rooms of aristocratic households, great women were celebrated for characteristics that might equally define a Renaissance general, including individuality, the appreciation of beauty, and intellectual accomplishment. Even courtesans participated in this grand flowering of mind and art among women. Only "young girls" were absent from the picture, perhaps cloistered in convents; yet Burckhardt can only speculate that they may have had "greater freedom of conversation" as a result of the cultural changes afoot.[5] Burckhardt would have viewed Anguissola as an example of his claims, since her unusual path in life does seem to demonstrate a new empowerment and valuation of women's individuality, energy, and accomplishment.

Burckhardt's view influenced generations of scholars, some of whom in turn celebrated the "great women" of early modern Europe for their accomplishments. Such accomplishments, although never quite as grand or world changing as those of men, were to these scholars nonetheless evidence that the Renaissance was in truth the birth of a modern, invigorated, triumphant Western culture that reversed the benighted ideologies and social trends of the moribund Middle Ages. Some early feminist scholars followed the gist of Burckhardt's argument, if not its tone or details: Juliet Dusinberre's 1975 *Shakespeare and the Nature of Women,* for instance, found that humanist and Puritan protestant philosophy authorized Shakespeare's portrayal of women's greater freedom, while Natalie Zemon Davis's early works on women and the family often suggested that women gained latitude in asserting themselves in the social sphere.[6] But in 1977 Joan Kelly asked a simple question—"Did Women Have a Renaissance?"—and found a quite different answer than had Burckhardt. The answer in her view was an emphatic "no": "Renaissance ideas on love and manners, more classical than medieval, and almost exclusively a male product,

FIGURE 0.1: Frontispiece, engraving, after Gui. Vaughan, *Musick's Handmaid*, 1678, *Roxburgh Ballads,* vol. 6.

expressed this new subordination of women to the interests of husbands and male-dominated kin groups and served to justify the removal of women from an 'unladylike' position of power and erotic independence."[7] Her essay has spawned as many responses, and as much controversy on both sides of the debate (and some sides that could not have been anticipated at the time it was first published), as Burckhardt's own magisterial work has done in subsequent generations. For Kelly, the rise of capitalism, changes in women's role within the household, and the expansion of patriarchy actually restricted women's authority and latitude for action in comparison with their opportunities in the Middle Ages. Following Kelly, feminist scholars rejected Burckhardt's happy picture of Renaissance women, and instead accounted for women's subjection to ideologies and institutions that privileged men. Linda Bamber announces in the introduction to her *Comic Women, Tragic Men* that she is reacting against a generation of feminist critics who credit Shakespeare with somehow rising above the misogyny of his culture; in Shakespeare's generic uses of women, Bamber finds unchallenged the ideological positioning of women as men's "other."[8] Christiane Klapisch-Zuber, in her study of Tuscan families, contends "[t]hat there was opportunity for real dialogue in the Tuscan household, an argument best supported by the speculations of a few well-intentioned humanists."[9] She demonstrates how women, although crucial in many symbolic and practical ways to Renaissance family life, were nevertheless marginalized and disempowered. Retha Warnicke analyzes the several generations of women who were supposed to have benefited from a humanist education, but finds that in general, those who enjoyed instruction with real academic content were few, whereas most education for women was designed to enforce a more thorough subjection within marriage.[10] A veritable explosion in print of feminist scholarship on the period during the 1980s and early 1990s—psychoanalytic, materialist, historicist—elaborated the picture of women's oppression in the sixteenth and seventeenth centuries.

However, in the process of enriching Kelly's counternarrative, feminist scholars and others began to further complicate it. As cultural studies continued to take account of class, national, and geographical differences; as scholars rescued the writings of women themselves, and investigated a broader array of social and cultural practices; as more critics explored the growth of crafts, and popular culture, or plumbed the nuances of theatrical practices, the question that most often seemed to direct their study was not did women *have* a Renaissance, but what *kinds* of Renaissance(s) did women have? That is, it became difficult to offer sweeping generalizations in the face of the many ways the Renaissance did or did not happen for diverse groups or individuals. The writers who have contributed their scholarship to this volume of *A Cultural History of Women* continue this process of creating a multivalent, multivocal version of women's Renaissance(s). In the sections that follow, I give a very limited overview of some aspects of women's experiences that should introduce a few of the overarching themes that emerge in the individual chapters of this volume.

Those experiences were in the first instance geographically and socially determined. It is fair to say, along with writers like Suzanne Hull, that women were generally expected to be "chaste, silent and obedient," but exactly how such prescriptions were put into effect depended greatly on particularities of geography, nation, religion, and class.[11] A Catholic convent in Italy could provide access to real power and self-determination for young women who did not wish to marry; their subjection to the authority of a ghostly "father" could challenge the practical hegemony of familial patriarchy, and their chastity could function as a kind of weapon against their oppression within a marriage. As we see in the case of Elena Anguissola, however, many of them may have had no real choice in whether they were fated for the convent or for marriage—that decision belonged in most cases to the male heads of families, who considered dynastic plans and financial burdens more than women's own vocations, and we have only a very few examples of women who defied parental choices in this matter.[12] Protestantism in England and Germany insisted on greater discipline in the service of a new definition of the pious family, which locked women into daily acts of submission to male authority. But some women who converted to the new religion used it as a tool to achieve authority within the house, and even a degree of public spiritual influence. Mediterranean countries saw women of Northern countries as having extraordinary freedom to walk abroad on the streets, conduct business, appear at theaters and other places of entertainment, and generally live a relatively public life if they so chose. The English traveler Fynes Moryson called England the "paradise of women" because "they use their women obsequiously," allowing women to move about freely, conduct household business, and socialize and generally act with relative freedom.[13] Yet the Catholic countries of southern Europe continued to offer women the chance to pursue vocations in monastic retreat: women could still emulate Saint Clare and other notable women who resisted their families' pressure to marry in favor of a life devoted to God. Northern travelers viewed the seclusion of most women in Catholic nations as lamentable for depriving society of a source of pleasure in women's company, but were also troubled by what they saw as the hypocrisy of red-light districts largely left unmolested. Granted that Moryson subscribed to many of the myths about Italian licentiousness, but he reports wonderingly on the Florentine courts of "honesty," which defended the rights of "Cortisans," who are even acknowledged by nobility: "the very Duke passing the streete will in honor putt of his hatt to some of them, and at publique Comedies Cortisans and Torchbearers enter freely, and pay nothing."[14]

In Moryson's own country, however, women, who were barred from nearly every profession, found themselves turning to the world's oldest: Elizabeth Holland, the madam of Holland House, catered to the sexual needs of the wealthier class of Englishmen, and fascinated readers who looked into her life story, published in 1632 in *Hollands Leaguer*, by Nicholas Goodman. Of course, both Elizabeth "Holland" and "Holland House" may merely be invented names that refer more to the reputation of Dutch women in England for sexual promiscuity—however "free" Englishwomen seemed to Europeans, the Dutch seemed yet more liberal to the English.

Class made all the difference to women who used sex to survive: Venice's Veronica Franco supported herself as a *cortegiana onesta* (honest courtesan), entertaining powerful men and composing poetry, while Diane de Poitiers, the recognized mistress of France's Henry II, nursed his wife Catherine de Medici when she fell ill, and supported the king's family in many ways, acting as a kind of household manager and secretary. At the other end of the spectrum were the poorest prostitutes. English readers of texts like Thomas Dekker's *Lantern and Candlelight* (1608) were titillated by descriptions of the exploits of loose women in London's suburbs, a virtual foreign country where young men were subjected to the "infection" of whoredom, bringing immorality back into the city with them. Thomas Harman's *A Caveat for Common Cursitors* (1567) introduces avid readers to "doxies," "kinchin-morts," "dells," "bawdy baskets," and other strange vagrant female life-forms. These women stole, conned, and sold themselves to survive, but imagined as part of a criminal underworld, they roused fear in many about the failure of social restraints on women's supposed nature as temptress and deceiver—not to mention fear of the "pox," syphilis.[15] Plays, ballads, and medical treatises all warned of this very real infection, the spread of which was attributed almost uniformly to women's agency, rather than men's. European Catholics occasionally attempted to remedy the lot of common prostitutes and fallen women of all classes by creating special houses, similar to convents, for them; Venice's Casa delle Zitelle, funded by wealthy women of the city, was created to provide an education and support for poor young girls who were at risk of becoming prostitutes, and ended up providing a unique community for the city's poor women.[16]

All nations and classes would have agreed with Thomas Overbury, who opines in his *Characters* (1622) that "A very Whore is a woman. She enquires out all the great meetings which are medicines for her itching [her lust]."[17] All women were suspected of sexual transgression by the very definition of their sex as daughters of Eve; but each nation and each class stratum had its own variant on how this "natural" licentiousness expressed itself and what its consequences were. The examples above of how women's behavior was constrained by religion, how defined by the work they were able to do—or were denied—and how they functioned as citizens should suggest the partial nature of any general statements about women I make in the related sections that follow below.

WOMEN'S POLITICAL AND LEGAL STATUS

In all countries of Europe, women were excluded from the general category of citizen, and had little or no political influence as a group. The English text *The Lawes Resolution of Womens Rights* (1632) connects women's political invisibility to original sin, which is punished by their subjection to men:

> Eve, because she had helped to seduce her husband, hath inflicted on her an especial bane: *in sorrow shalt thou bring forth thy children, they desires shall be subject to thy husband, and he shall rule over thee.* See here the reason of that which I touched before, that women have no voice in parliament. They make no laws, consent to none, they abrogate none.[18]

The text concludes that all women are "understood either married or to be married"—they are *femes coverts*, or covered women, who have no identity outside that given them by their fathers, husbands, or other male relatives. In Shakespeare's *Measure for Measure*, Duke Vincentio clarifies the situation when he tries to place the violated, but affianced Mariana: "Why you are nothing then, neither maid, widow nor wife?" Women's exclusion from political and legal status was considered part of a broader, God-given hierarchical order. Responding to what he saw as the disastrous and anomalous rule of women, John Knox announced in *The first blast of the trumpet against the monstrous regiment of women* (1558), "To promote a woman to bear rule, superiority, dominion or empire above any realm, nation or city is repugnant to nature, contumely to God, a thing most contrarious to his revealed will and approved ordinance, and finally it is the subversion of all good order, and all equity and justice."[19] If women were not supposed to have direct political or legal power, they might instead assert indirect influence, but only within significant limits. Baldassare Castiglione's *Book of the Courtier* devotes one of its four chapters to women's roles as courtiers. During the fictional discussion supposedly happening at the court of Urbino in 1507, Castiglione presents a variety of opinions on women's roles and virtues: according to one of the dialogue's participants, "no Court... can have any sightlinesse, or brightnesse in it, or mirth, without women," while others suggest that *sprezzatura,* or effortlessness that characterizes the male courtier's skills at every task, should in women be directed at making sure they never seem too masculine, despite their talents.[20] Some of the disputants believe courtly women should pursue all the activities of men, including sports, but overall the dialogue settles on chastity as women's highest virtue, and women's function as grease to the social wheels at court (especially through their place as objects of male love) as their highest achievement. The human models for perfect womanhood are the dialogue's instigator and director, Elisabetta Gonzaga, Duchess of Urbino, and her lady Emilia Pia, who also encourages and even at times controls the participants' discussion: both are social facilitators who minimally use their "power" over the men in the room, usually to calm hostilities with clever, but soothing, remarks. In sum, while women are lauded as important, their sphere of influence is different, their required behaviors dominated by the condition of their bodies and their reputations.[21] The fictional female courtier who emerges shares many qualities with Sofonisba Anguissola, who served (as does the fictional lady courtier created by the speakers in Castiglione's work) a great queen: Anguissola's active intellect stimulated by education, her facility with court politics, and her adventurous spirit were all summoned to the service of Elisabeth de Valois, a well-loved but largely powerless court figure.

Despite Castiglione's ambivalent portrait or the female courtier and Knox's absolute rejection of women's political authority, it is nevertheless fair to say that a number of individual women from all levels of society did assert themselves. England was ruled by two of Henry VIII's daughters, Mary and Elizabeth, and Scotland by Mary Stuart. France, where women were prevented by Salic law (codes evolved by the Salian Francs that dictated male inheritance) from ruling in their own right, nevertheless experienced several women who exerted substantial power as regents. Louise de Savoy, for instance, ruled in her son's place each time Francis I fought abroad (and was accused of financial malfeasance in his absence), while Catherine de Medici became regent for her underage son Charles IX, then advisor to her son Henry III after Charles's death. Meanwhile, women made claims in courts for inherited property, and even attempted to circumvent patrilineal inheritance laws: Anne Clifford, for example, was excluded from taking over the extensive estates of her family when her father died, although she was granted the title of Baroness of

Clifford. In 1649, after nearly a lifetime of fighting to regain control over the family properties, she succeeded, and by her death was the Dowager Countess of Dorset, Pembroke, and Montgomery. Elizabeth Hardwick, later Elizabeth Talbot, Countess of Shrewsbury, secured dynastic power for herself and her children, became the richest woman in England apart from the queen, and built Hardwick Hall, a prodigy house, as a monument to her own family. Elizabeth von Gorlitz of Luxembourg ruled the Duchy of Luxembourg from 1411 to 1443 by the simple fact of surviving her husband and all other heirs to the throne. Margaret of Austria governed the Netherlands for two lengthy periods during the sixteenth century, and with Louise of Savoy negotiated the Treaty of Cambrai, which ended the long battles between the Habsburgs and their enemies. The relative prominence of powerful women in the Renaissance suggests that material, demographic, political, and economic changes may have granted women some prospects where ideology did not.

The fundamental structure of governments in the Renaissance was patriarchal monarchy, based on and analogous to the family's patriarchal structure; this organization of political life was authorized by biblical examples, as we have already seen in T. E.'s account of women's exclusion from government and law. Robert Filmer's *Patriarcha* insisted, "I see not then how the children of Adam, or any man else can be free from subjection to their parents; and this subjection of children being the fountain of royal authority, by the ordination of God himself."[22] This line of thought had perhaps its most extreme expression in the speech James I made to Parliament in 1609 when he announced that "Kings are justly called Gods, for that they exercise a manner or resemblance of Divine power upon earth."[23] Of course, Filmer wrote his treatise during the civil war in England, a fact that by itself should suggest that the manifest necessity of patriarchal monarchy was not so clear to everyone. If, as many writers would have agreed, "A family is...a little Commonwealth...a school wherein first principles and the grounds of government and subjection are learned,"[24] then it could also be true that a monarch who violated the sanctity of the family or worked against its well-being could be vigorously attacked for those actions. In England, one justification for antagonisms toward Charles I and his rule in the 1640s was his willingness to arbitrarily interfere in his subjects' private lives. In 1641, the "gentlewomen and tradesmen's wives" of London submitted a petition to Parliament protesting royal interference:

> We thought it misery enough...but a few years since for some of our sex, by unjust divisions from their bosom comforts, to be rendered in a

manner widows, and the children fatherless, husbands were imprisoned from the society of their wives...and little infants suffered in their father's banishments...our present fears are, that unless the blood-thirsty faction of the Papists and prelates be hindered in their designs...[we] shall be exposed to that misery which is more intolerable...namely to the rage not of men alone, but of Devils incarnate."[25]

The invasion of the state into the sanctum of the family ends up creating a common bond among the women who suffer—now, no longer isolated individuals, they pursue a common political remedy. In a pamphlet arguing the English should not execute Charles I, Elizabeth Poole argued from the same analogical premises that undergird the appeal of the Puritan gentlewomen, but to opposite ends: "And although this bond is broken on his part, you never heard that a wife might put away her husband, as he is the head of her body...And accordingly you may hold the hands of your husband, that he pierce not your bowels with a knife or sword to take your life...Neither may you take his."[26] As Susan Amussen points out, basing the structure of government on patriarchal marriage and family raised more questions than it answered (for instance, as Poole suggests, what are the limits of a husband's power over his wife?), and gave women an experiential basis for understanding, and sometimes rebutting, arguments about certain forms of political action.[27] Despite the supposed biblical patriarchal justifications for women's disenfranchisement, then, women did find theoretical and practical ways of engaging with political power.

Having experienced religious conflict earlier than the English Puritans, European Protestants had already challenged the absolute nature of royal prerogative: Luther and Calvin both accepted absolute monarchy, but both also argued that men should obey God above other men, which opened the door for a few women to consider the related tyrannies of marriage. In France, Philippe Duplessis-Mornay, along with other political theorists, explored the idea that the forms and extent of government power came not from the Bible but from ancient legal precedents.[28] Women had their own versions of political theory: Jacqueline Broad and Karen Green take account of the less generically obvious ways in which women expressed their views on the purpose, origins, and power of the state, describing how authors like Christine de Pizan, Isotta Nogarola, and Laura Cereta debated in their writings the issue of women's civic roles. Shifting the focus of politics from official public office and action to the more fundamental, Aristotelian question of how the polis can promote virtue and the good of society, these women too saw the interrelatedness of marital-familial and political life. Cereta, for instance, "focus[ed] on the nature of the good life for women," and touched on the horrors of war, and its cyclical return to disrupt the lives of women and men.[29] While she remained an outward Catholic for the sake of her royal family, Marguerite de Navarre aided many Protestants with her patronage and protection; as sister to Francis I, King of France, she was powerful in her own right, and used that power to tamp down the rising religious hostilities that would explode into war after her death. Her *Heptameron* is comprised of a series of romance tales, many of which concern abuses of noble and royal power, especially those that challenge the sanctity of marital ties.

One of the most successful, but provocative, royal women in Renaissance history is surely England's Elizabeth I (1558–1603), who oversaw an unprecedented period of peace and prosperity, and proved herself an adept manipulator of male courtiers. Elizabeth's approach to power relied on a series of paradoxes: she remained a virgin, but exploited her sexualized image to confuse and control her subjects; she ruled alone, clearly violating the ideological positioning of women as inferior and submissive, yet implicitly embraced and defended patriarchy, never challenging the cultural belief that women are weak, physically and mentally feeble in comparison to men. She accepted the fiction of monarchical absolutism, yet deferred to Parliament where possible. (Her successors, James I and Charles I, could have taken a page from her book and had a better time of it—both failed to deliver on the supposed relief England should have felt at being ruled, at long last, by "proper" men.) Broad and Green note that Elizabeth capitalized on the conjugal model of sovereignty: "I am already bound to a husband, which is the kingdom of England," she assured Parliament in 1563 when they pressured her to marry.[30] Although she styled herself a prince, and called up images of Alexander and Caesar in her speeches, she did not deny her physical sex, but used it to her advantage. In her famous speech to the troops on the eve of combat with the Spanish Armada, she claimed she had "the weak and feeble body of a woman," but "the heart and stomach of a king."[31] Elizabeth's confusing strategies of rule, however, generated an enormous industry of literature, painting, and other arts, either from courtiers who were psychically tortured by her anomalous status and fickle behavior, or those who simply hoped to gain her favor. Elizabeth's court thus functioned as a wellspring of propaganda, nearly all of it directly or indirectly centering on her several incarnations as Flora (goddess of flowers and spring), Astraea (celestial virgin and harbinger of the return of the Golden Age), Urania (muse of astronomy and astrology), Diana (goddess of chastity), and so on. Castiglione's *Book of the Courtier* was still popular in Elizabethan England, but notably short on good advice for dealing with such an ambiguous and subtle female ruler for whom gender was simply—formidably—an instrument of state.

WOMEN AND RELIGIOUS CULTURE

Although the medieval Catholic Church generally limited women's participation in the creation of religious culture, women did have some clear opportunities for education, expression, and even a public life of a kind. Most obvious among the many contributions women made to religious life was their role as mystics and visionaries: Teresa of Avila, Julian of Norwich, Margeurite d'Oignt, and Hildegard von Bingen (to name just a few examples) all experienced their visions while cloistered from the world, while Angela of Foligno, Margery Kempe, and Birgitta of Sweden began life outside the auspices of a church order, but nevertheless gained notoriety and a degree of self-determination through their ecstatic visions. Even women whose revelations were part of a sanctioned religious experience within an order could find themselves in some friction with the authority of the church as an institution, but the idea that a rich spiritual life could include moments of prophecy and supernatural phenomena allowed some women to claim for themselves a mandate from heaven to influence others through speaking or writing about their mystical insights. Birgitta founded an order of her own, while Teresa was instrumental in reforming her Carmelite order. Margery Kempe dictated her life story despite being illiterate, claiming the approval of Julian, whose *Revelations of Divine Love* probably inspired Kempe, along with "Brigit's book," the *Revelations of Saint Birgitta*. Hildegard von Bingen founded two monasteries and wrote liturgical music, poems, and a morality play.

The Reformation in Europe, however, substantially changed the domain in which women were expected to exert influence. Protestants were no more inclined to allow women the latitude to become scholars, artists, or public figures than were Catholics; but the enclosed worlds of women, the convents, were not an option for Protestant women, whose assumed role was invariably that of wife and mother: "Protestantism...in theory at least, offered a more diminished role for women...than had medieval Catholicism."[32] Martin Luther himself married a former nun, Katharina von Bora, who managed his household and many aspects of his life, having been "kidnapped" from her monastery, along with eleven other sisters, at Luther's instigation. Their marriage was deeply affectionate, judging from Luther's many letters to her,[33] and she was clearly a great helpmeet in his busy, sometimes dangerous, career. Yet she had to make a sudden adjustment late in life to the demands of family, and while educated and clearly intelligent, she left no written works of her own. Where we know a great deal about even an illiterate mystic like Kempe, we know Katharina only as she is reflected in her husband's writings. The Puritan Englishwoman Lucy Hutchinson would articulate this ideal of invisibility in her *Memoir of the Life of Colonel Hutchinson*: "For she was thus a very faithful mirror, reflecting truly, though but dimly, his own glories upon him, so long as he was present; but she, that was nothing before his inspection gave her a fair figure, when he was removed, was only filled with a dark mist...So as his shadow, she waited on him everywhere."[34] Not only is Hutchinson's remark a concise version of the ideal relationship between husband and wife, it also articulates the supremacy of masculine spirituality in Protestant circles.

Such invisibility is not uniform among Protestant women, of course. Education, while no longer available to the few individual women who pursued it as a principal part of a monastic life, and less inflected with the goals of early Christian Humanism (which emphasized that "to be proper companions, women had to be learned"[35]), was perhaps more broadly important and available to Protestants, whose emphasis on individual knowledge of the scripture encouraged the creation of girls' schools. Luther himself established a "maiden school" in Wittenberg in 1533.[36] To be effective in cultivating a godly household, Protestant wives and mothers were expected to be literate, with a sound moral education; as Heide Wunder notes, once education was privileged as part of religious life for all, it could not easily be limited for women to domestic subjects, and so the Reformation might be seen as "the end of an epoch" in which only rich or cloistered women (and men) had access to scholarship.[37]

If Protestant women lost the advantages of the convent, where women could indulge in scholarship, the arts, and be valued for their profound spiritual exemplarity, they gained other platforms for action. The violent religious conflict that surged through European countries gave some Reformation women a significant public voice: Argula von Grumbach, for instance, wrote an angry attack on the University of Ingolstadt for prosecuting a young student for heresy. She is unapologetic about her sex, given the nature of her complaint: "What I have written to you is no woman's chit-chat, but the word of God; and (I write) as a member of the Christian Church against which the gates of Hell cannot prevail."[38] Luther himself approved: "That most noble woman, Argula von Stauffer [her maiden name], is there making a valiant fight, with great spirit, boldness of speech, and knowledge of Christ."[39] In 1546, the Englishwoman Anne Askew was arrested for heresy, tortured in the Tower of London, and burned at the stake. John Bale published her *Examinations*, an account

INTRODUCTION 15

of her sufferings for her belief, which was also later included in John Foxe's Protestant martyrology *Acts and Monuments* (1563).

WOMEN'S WORK

Theoretically, the only sanctioned work for women in the Renaissance was that related to marriage and family life—acting as a helpmeet to a husband, keeping house, and bearing children. Of course, as the subversive character Lucio in Shakespeare's *Measure for Measure* reminds the duke when he enumerates all the possible roles for women, in addition to being a maid, widow, or wife,

FIGURE 0.2: Woman milking cow (1547). Wellcome Collection, L0029211.

"she may be a punk" [whore]—an occupation that was indeed controversially available to women, but one that still retained links to the sexual labors that underwrote other sanctioned female roles.

However, the fact that women's work was largely domestic, linked to home and family, does not necessarily imply that it was entirely limited to the kind of housework we now associate with the home, and in practice many women did have what we might now call careers. For women of all classes, the household was a site of production, requiring skills in home-based industries including brewing, distilling, baking, the manufacture of textiles, and even basic medical arts. Further, for many women the parameters of "the domestic" had to be fairly wide, so much so that the term becomes almost meaningless: rural women helped with nearly every kind of farm labor on which the household's prosperity depended. Thus women gardened, milked cows, distilled spirits, and often joined their spouses—or simply supported themselves—in field work. Further, the boundary between household and public space could also be difficult to pin down when women who raised chickens, milked cows, baked bread, or mended and washed clothing sold their wares and labor in local markets.[40] English city comedies often revolved around the collapse of household and family spaces and functions, with the supposedly distinct shops, streets, and commercial activities undertaken by merchants' wives. Thomas Middleton and Thomas Dekker's *The Roaring Girl* places Mistress Openwork (a seamstress), Mistress Tiltyard (dealing in feathers), and Mistress Gallipot (an apothecary's wife) at their shops' thresholds, calling out for customers: "What is't you lack, gentlemen, what is't you buy?"[41] Whether their shops are an extension of domestic space or part of the public realm is finally impossible to determine.

The Renaissance, however, witnessed a significant transition from the recognition of women's physical and practical labor within the household to the marginalization of that labor.[42] Whether this transition was real or ideological (that is, whether women really were allowed to do less or were merely assumed and perceived to do less, due to different roles required in a new economy) is debatable; however, the eventual outcome of this process was the re-coding of most women's roles within the home as consumption based, rather than productive. Francesco Barbaro wrote in his *Of Wifely Duties* in 1416 that a wife's responsibility is to govern and protect the goods gained by her more far-ranging husband, for "what is the use of bringing home great wealth unless the wife will work at preserving, maintaining, and utilizing it?"[43] In Barbaro's view, wives have a crucial role in conserving and distributing household wealth. But by the seventeenth century, Joseph Swetnam was demonstrating his own wit at women's expense with his contribution to the *querelle des femmes*, the debate over women's nature, with the following opinions:

> He that gets a fair woman is like unto a Prisoner loaded with fetters of gold, for you shall not so oft kiss the sweet lips of your beautiful wife as you shall be driven to fetch bitter sighs from your sorrowful heart in thinking of the charge which cometh by her. For if you deny her of such toys as she stand not in need of, and yet is desirous of them, then she will quickly shut you out of the doors of her favor and deny you her person, and show herself as it were at a window playing upon you.
>
> Man must be at all the cost and yet live by the loss; a man must take all the pains, and women will spend all the gains. A man must watch and ward, fight and defend, till the ground, labor in the vineyard, and look what he gets in seven years: a woman will spread it abroad with a fork in one year, and yet little enough to serve her turn, but a great deal too little to get her good will.[44]

For Swetnam, women are only a drain on men's resources. While Swetnam's remarks represent the most misogynistic take on women's role with the household, they indicate a drastic change from Barbaro's perception of real value in women's contributions to household economy.

Women were also increasingly marginalized from the few official occupations they might have once entered, either through the closing of guilds to women members or through the professionalization of jobs that had once belonged primarily to women. Medieval guilds evolved to protect and organize practitioners of crafts; they controlled access through systems of apprenticeship, so that only licensed graduates of the guild system could legally work in a given field. Merry Wiesner describes "journeymen and poorer masters" of the guilds who felt threatened by the growth in the scale of production and marketing in the sixteenth and seventeenth centuries; gradually, guilds responded by restricting, then eliminating, women's ability to apprentice.[45] Midwives, traditionally women with special knowledge and experience in aiding childbirth (some with a sideline in medicines for sexual and fertility problems, as well as knowledge about contraception and abortion), had long dominated the birthing chamber, respected and compensated for their interventions in a domain where men seemed surplus to requirements. By the late seventeenth century, however, the increasing power of professionalized medical institutions and organizations was driving midwives out of

FIGURE 0.3: Woman using a distaff, ca. 1675. Wellcome Collection, L0042097.

practice. The new male doctors disparaged female midwives as superstitious, ignorant, and even dangerous—indeed, midwives and female folk-medicine purveyors were sometimes accused of witchcraft. One chapter of the *Malleus Maleficarum* (*Hammer of Witches*) is introduced by the statement, "That witches who are midwives in various ways kill the child conceived in the womb, and procure an abortion; or if they do not this, they offer new-born children to devils."[46]

A significant number of Renaissance women worked within homes that were not their own. Female servants were essential to the smooth running of larger households, and time in service was a natural part of many women's lives. There were advantages and dangers to household service: women servants were under constant supervision and suspicion for possible sexual indiscretions, and if assaulted or violated were often blamed and turned out of work. Isabella Whitney cautions in "An Order Prescribed by Is. W. to Two of her Young Sisters Serving in London":

> Your Masters gone to bed,
> your Mistresses at rest,
> Their daughters all with haste about
> to get themselves undrest.
> See that their plate be safe,
> and that no spoon do lack,
> See doors and windows bolted fast
> for fear of any wrack.
> help if need there be,
> to do some household thing:
> If not, to bed, referring you
> unto the heavenly King.[47]

Whitney repeatedly calls attention to the struggles, financial and emotional, that can afflict a young woman in service: to her sister Anne, she writes: "Had I a husband, or a house,/and all that longs thereto,/My self could frame about to rouse,/as other women do."[48] Without either, Whitney devotes herself to her pen, to writing—particularly to satires on greed and indifference to the suffering of the poor. But time spent in service could have real benefits, both material and emotional. Heide Wunder points out that girls sent out to service could "participate in a youth culture that provided a certain amount of freedom," female companionship, and eventually access to future spouses. Earning money for family or later for marriage was what usually motivated time spent working as a servant, and for a large number of women service was not a permanent job but a temporary stage of life.[49]

Upper-class women also served in households not their own, as did Anguissola in the Spanish court. Powerful rulers like Elizabeth I surrounded themselves with the women of noble families who provided friendship, entertainment, and personal care for the otherwise isolated queen; in return these women acted as ambassadors for male relatives seeking promotion at court.[50] While their labors generally furthered the interests of patriarchy by affirming women's place in smoothing the paths to men's advancement, following the pattern set by Castiglione's women who delight and entertain the men in *The Book of the Courtier*, a few women parlayed court careers into independent wealth or power, as noted above in the cases of the Englishwomen Elizabeth Hardwick and Anne Clifford.

Women also performed an important kind of ideological labor, whether they worked within or outside of the home. For example, one of the things we are witnessing in Joseph Swetnam's intensely misogynistic diatribes against women as consumers of men's wealth in the excerpts above is the articulation of a wider fear about the growth of an urban, mercantile, wage-based economy, in which men could no longer rely on traditional structures to guarantee masculine identity. Women became scapegoats for this threat. Gail Kern Paster argues that the representation of women as essentially fluid in body and character is a displacement of the anxieties felt by both sexes at new proto-capitalist forms of trade and accumulation. Seventeenth-century English city comedies like Ben Jonson's *Bartholomew Fair* stage the oozing, sweating, urinating, sexually promiscuous fluidity associated with women's bodies through figures like Ursula, the pig-woman, in whose tent can be found beer and pork, but also a ready toilet or trysting place.[51] Representations of women as "leaky vessels" (a version of Swetnam's "women will spend all the gains") gave an otherwise amorphous malaise a material (if soggy) target.

Even the apparently traditional functions of women associated with domestic work took on new dimensions in a changing Renaissance world. Michelle Dowd has analyzed the literary and dramatic representation of women's work in England during the seventeenth century, and finds religious influences, economic shifts in the labor economy, and demographic changes not only transformed the nature of women's work but allowed sometimes surprising new narratives about women's careers inside and outside the home.[52] As the labor market grew tighter, populations swelled, and the types of work available shifted gradually toward what we might call a proto-capitalist economy, which included a new role for international or colonial trade, with some forms of women's work disappearing or becoming unrecognizable (for instance, midwifery, as we have already noted, disappeared as a common career choice). When Shakespeare's *Twelfth Night* tells the story of two women in service—Viola, who serves the Duke of Illyria, albeit in men's clothing, and Maria, a maid in Olivia's household—who end up married off to appropriate men, the subtext is not just a fantasy of love, but an exploration of women's threat to social order within the noble household. Women as servants did not disappear, of course, but the fluidity of their movement into and out of service was increasingly halted, and service was made increasingly rigid to eliminate the potential that a servant might become anything else in her lifetime.[53] At the same time, the Protestant image of the godly household conferred divine status on housework, making it a form of worship; yet women's role as early childhood educators, much vaunted in Protestant treatises, invoked a degree of apprehension over their influence, and at the possibility for female agency involved. Women's work, then, was never done in the practical material sense, but, along with all aspects of women and gender, was endlessly contested in the representational works of the period.

CHAPTER DESCRIPTIONS

The individual chapters of this volume continue to elaborate the complex ways that the Renaissance situated women as a group, and their diverse responses to that cultural positioning. Karen Raber and Stephanie Tarbin give an overview of women's life cycle in Chapter One. Although life cycle depictions were common in early modern Europe, they largely focused on men's experiences; women's lives were assumed to follow a simpler schema, with stages determined by their relationship to men. This left many of the milestones in women's lives imperfectly articulated—was marriage, for instance, as or more important than menarche? When did a woman grow old? How did children, or the lack of them, make a difference to a woman's sense of status and progress through life? While most women internalized the ideological content of the life cycle, art and literature either ignored or challenged its assumed organization around marriage and reproduction.

Mara Amster writes that the pressure to create a "legible sexual female" body in poems, plays, and conduct literature of the period actually led to highly complex and contradictory textual representations of women's sexuality. In Chapter Two, Amster deals with the consequences of Renaissance women's imagined weakness of body and mind, which implied a lustful, sexually rapacious, wandering nature; since everything from patrilineal inheritance to male marital honor relied on women's chastity, the problem of women's sexual behavior became central to much of the period's popular literature. "Deciphering women's sexual identity" was one obsessive concern, precisely because those things that promised to allow men to "read" women failed to do so: women's words, blushes, gestures, modest clothing, even their supposed marital status could all be falsified, and so all were fundamentally flawed substitutes for what Othello calls "the ocular proof" of a chaste body.

Chapter Three concerns the way religious institutions and practices relied on representations of women. Megan Hickerson traces the governing principle of "dual classification," which dictates that all things are organized in hierarchized binaries of opposites; thus, men are perfect, active, and complete, while women are imperfect, passive, requiring government by a male. Even occasional inversions of these binaries, like those we find in charivaris and other festive events, only confirmed this idea of order by showing its chaotic opposite. The distinctions the Catholic Church drew between Eve and Mary followed this pattern, with the consequence that female sexuality (absent in the Virgin) was rejected, and non-virginal women consigned to repeat the sins of the flesh (Eve's fall) that doomed humankind in the first place. The Protestant Reformation did not, argues Hickerson, alter this basic misogyny. Although Protestants rejected celibacy, they replaced its definition of ideal masculinity with one founded on the general subjection of all women to all men. In fact, in anti-Catholic literature and art, Protestants assimilated male clergy to the model of unruly women who threatened God-sanctioned cosmic order, depicting them as effeminate and sexually suspect. Priests, witches, the anti-Christ—all these were manifestations of the "world turned upside down," confusing or erasing reliable gender categories and creating conceptual chaos.

In Chapter Four, Margaret Healy details the contradictory traditions and opinions on women's physiology. Assumed to be inferior to men in this, as in all areas, Renaissance medical authorities adopted the Aristotelian and Galenic model of women's "coldness," moistness, and weakness, which required that their reproductive organs be protected within the body. Beyond that difference, however, this model did not imagine substantial differences between men's genitalia and women's—the latter were usually depicted as inverted analogues to the former. Yet women were the vehicles of generation, the bearers of children, and as such could not be dismissed entirely from the reproductive schema. Menstruation became the "marker" of "intense anxiety" over the contradictions between women's physiological role and their constructed social position, a magnet for ritual, myth, and terrifying lore. The advent of Paracelsianism, which rejected the Galenic assimilation of the female body to the male paradigm, did allow for a degree of equality in accounts of conception and gestation; yet even Paracelsus concluded women had to be valued despite being "loathsome." Because of the profound anxieties attached to the female body, women physicians, midwives, and general practitioners, who had gained some sanction, even prominence, during the Middle Ages, were increasingly marginalized and demonized by the official world of the medical arts. Nevertheless, women continued to take responsibility for the care of others, rescripting their knowledge as part of the repertoire of appropriate "feminine" household skills.

Danielle Clarke deals with the unstable boundary between public and private worlds in Chapter Five. Advice books and sermons were adamant that women eschew public exposure, and began to more carefully map ideological aspects of women's symbolic and practical function in society onto the domestic/public divide. Yet Clarke qualifies the image some critics have offered of a rigid separation of spheres, as well as the predication of the whole concept of privacy on that distinction. She calls attention to the ways that model is influenced by nineteenth-century discourses about labor and gender, and she notes that it misses the complex blend of material and discursive changes taking place in the Renaissance. Women's "sphere," for instance, included many kinds of work and behavior that would later seem clearly "public," while the proper ordering of the domestic sphere became increasingly crucial in generating the individual subjects who would act in the public, social world. When the character of the good wife, her chastity, her education of her children, her proper submission to her husband are all building blocks for a whole array of public goals, how "private" could private life really be?

In Chapter Six, Meg Lota Brown and Kari Boyd McBride discuss women's education. Girls and boys were both expected to be educated to assume the roles proper to their station; education for girls of higher status could thus include a range of subjects typical of humanist education for boys—with the addition of training intended to enforce chastity, obedience, and other specifically "feminine" virtues. Male authors carefully prescribed programs of study for women, usually arguing against offering any material or skills that would either encourage women to agitate for more freedoms or violate strict codes of behavior. Yet women were sometimes encouraged to study widely, and some took advantage of more liberal attitudes to become genuinely learned. Unusually for critical discussions of education of the period, Brown and McBride give considerable attention not only to Christian attitudes toward education but also to Jewish arguments on the subject, reminding us that while there were significant religious differences between communities, their opinions on women's education were comparable.

Holly Hurlburt asks in Chapter Seven, "How might we understand 'power' in terms of the Renaissance woman?" As her questions suggests, the term is flexible and expansive. Hurlburt notes the fact of the extraordinary number of women rulers in the period, but also their ability to represent themselves as powerful figures through the instruments of state propaganda. Indeed, access to cultural technologies allowed women to answer the inevitable backlash when women became political players. However, women also exercised power through their accepted and theoretically powerless roles within family and household: when wives, widows, and mothers of any social class took charge of family finances, oversaw estates, patronized the arts, contributed to charity, or negotiated their children's marriages, they exercised informal power within the culture, often leaving extensive representational evidence of themselves in the process.

The final chapter of the volume deals with women's role in Renaissance art. Regarding portraits of women in the period, Mary Rogers argues that they do not necessarily convey only conservative patriarchal ideals. Although women were part of a culture of display, which could explain the growth in the visibility of women in portraiture, that role did not preclude their seizing the opportunity for self-expression. Rogers's careful qualification that only very few women could exploit the changes that marked the Renaissance to "forge new identities" brings us back to the example of Sofonisba Anguissola. A rare departure from the norm, yet no permanent threat to the conventions governing women at the time, she did not radically transform the world of art or retain her celebrity in the ensuing centuries—but the Renaissance did transform her life and work.

CHAPTER ONE

The Life Cycle

KAREN RABER AND STEPHANIE TARBIN

Men and women "play many parts" during a lifetime, opines Shakespeare's Jacques in *As You Like It*: from the "mewling and puking infant," to the old man, "sans teeth, sans eyes, sans taste, sans everything," men live through seven ages, or seven "acts" in the play of life.[1] The idea that human lives followed a natural cycle already had a long history by the time Shakespeare took up the theme. The Sphinx's riddle for Oedipus in Sophocles's play in the fifth century B.C.E. belongs to this tradition: what walks on four legs at dawn, two at noon, and three at sunset? asks the Sphinx, and Oedipus answers "man." The "Ages of Man" topos was thus a well-known scheme, drawing on classical roots but thoroughly elaborated by medieval scholars who divided the human life into as few as three and up to as many as twelve or more life stages. Although originally a learned tradition, the iconography of the topos was widely diffused in popular culture, appearing in the decorative programs of medieval churches and noble houses, and in print by the end of the fifteenth century.[2] Descriptions of the life cycle are usually intended to confer a degree of self-knowledge on individuals, giving them markers by which to measure themselves; stages of life establish a set of common expectations for human beings as they negotiate the challenges of growing into adulthood, and then old age. The life stages in "Ages of Man" literature were not, however, necessarily reflections of social reality but vehicles for exegetical, allegorical, cosmological, and moralizing purposes.[3]

A life cycle describes a series of watershed moments, often ritualized in religious or social practices. Thus the skeptical Jacques, whose speech characterizes the process of moving through these watersheds as mainly negative (the schoolboy whines, the lover sighs, the soldier is quarrelsome, the justice is puffed up with his own importance, and so on), nevertheless offers a clear idea of what each stage of life might mean and how men of differing ages might perceive one another. In general, most life cycle illustrations, often found superimposed over archways, or presented in the form of the Wheel of Life (a depiction of the changes in life, with descent and ascent signifying the vagaries of fortune, balanced by hope of an eventual rise), did offer a graphic illustration of the life course as a process of maturation and decline. A new scheme appeared in the sixteenth century with Jorg Breu's *Nine Ages of Man*, shown in Figure 1.1, which depicts human life as an ascent to sagacity, followed by the descent into decrepitude and a waiting coffin.[4] The skeletal presence of Death presiding above the steps and a Last Judgment scene portrayed below the steps served as reminders of the traditional Christian view that human life was a preparation for the afterlife.

FIGURE 1.1: Jorg Breu, *The Nine Ages of Man*, c. 1540. Courtesy of the Bridgeman Library.

Although the illustration and discussion of a life cycle were common in Renaissance culture, its application to women is a bit more difficult to pinpoint. Jacques's speech, like most versions of the life cycle, focuses mainly on the experiences of elite males and their expected activities. Representations of the "Ages of Woman" were rare. In contrast to the many activities for males, accounting for the variety of expected qualities and capacities as scholars, hunters, warriors, and responsible public figures, women's life cycles offer less to distinguish one stage from another in the middle phases of women's lives. For women, one might conclude, life consisted of fewer changes, options, and roles.

Yet there are some illustrations and representations of the "Ages of Woman" that do reveal how gender factored into the trajectory of life. Some refer to the assumed foundational relationship of women to their sexual disposal in marriage by referencing the tripartite division of women into maidens, wives, and widows. When the duke in Shakespeare's *Measure for Measure* tries to locate a descriptive title for Mariana, who has been violated by the man she desires to marry, but is not yet married to him, he exclaims: "Why you are nothing then, neither maid, widow, nor wife!"[5] Very young children might not be differentiated by gender in Renaissance society, but once a girl came to sexual maturity, her life would be shaped by her role in marriage. In the English translation of the *Orbis Sensualium Pictus*, by the Czech educator John Amos Comenius, male and female stages of life are depicted as matched pairs and described in relatively neutral terms: boy/girl, youth/damsel, young man/maid, man/woman, elderly man/elderly woman, decrepit old man/decrepit old woman.[6] The seeming parity between male and female life stages in this image, however, probably offered support for the cultural image of woman as helpmeet to man.

Hans Baldung Grien's *Three Ages of Woman and Death*, shown in Figure 1.2, portrays a simple three-stage cycle, where the figure of the maiden occupies the foreground, sidelining the figures of infancy and old age. Unlike men, who were often considered to be in their prime during their fourth decade—that is, while they were in their thirties—women more quickly lost the quality that most completely defined them: beauty. Late medieval views of the "perfect age" for women also placed it in their second decade, from fourteen years and before marriage, rather than centering on thirty, or the fourth decade, as for men.[7] Grien's illustration, however, positions the young woman not as a figure to be celebrated, but one that serves a didactic purpose, warning the viewer against putting too much faith in things of the flesh. Death hovers behind the maiden's shoulder as she gazes into a mirror, raising an hourglass

FIGURE 1.2: Hans Baldung Grien, *The Three Ages of Woman and Death*, 1510. Kunsthistorisches Museum, Vienna. Wikimedia Commons: http://en.wikipedia.org/wiki/File:Baldung_Woman.jpg.

to indicate the brevity of female beauty and the shortness and vanity of human life in general.

In his 1585 version of the *Book of Huswiferie*, Thomas Tusser also viewed women as being in their prime through the years of their maidenhood and early marriage: women were at the epitome of their beauty ("in the world they do shine") in the second age, between fourteen to twenty-eight years. However, Tusser did not assign a mere three ages to women; instead he presented women's life course as six stages of fourteen years, which he labels a "prentis-ship." The two "first seven yeeres" has the young girl "whin[ing] for a rod," after which she enters maidenhood, a phase of life when she is "a pearle in the world." Thereafter, woman enters a decline ("trim beautie beginneth to swerue"), serving as matron or drudge before entering the stages of physical decrepitude and finally death.[8] Grien also confers more nuance in the cycle in his 1544 painting *The Seven Ages of Woman*. Here, the thickening and rounding of the women's bodies, the development and sagging of breasts, and alterations to the arrangements of hair portray female life stages as a progression from asexual infancy and girlhood to the physically developing maiden and nubile bride, concluding with the modest matron, veiled widow, and aged matriarch, whose body is obscured. The painting also reflects on the theme of fertility. The first four ages are placed in a meadow and framed by the foliage and fruit of a vine; the widow stands squarely on bare ground with the matriarch behind her, while the matron is poised in the space in between lush growth and barren rock. The stormy sky and black drapery, enveloping widow and matron, perhaps signal the onset of decay but there is little overt moralizing or evidence of aging beyond suggestions of wrinkling necks and faces. The visible flesh of the women is supple and their postures upright; the bodies of the matron and the veiled widow mask that of the oldest woman. By concealing her body the painting creates a link between a woman's extreme age and infancy; in the other life stages, female bodies are displayed to the viewer's gaze. In this portrayal of the female life cycle, the presence or absence of female fertility dominates the image.

Clothing was one common and obvious marker of a woman's life stage. Children's clothing helped constitute stages of development, social status, and gender. After being swaddled as newborn infants, babies and small children from propertied families appear to have worn a variety of items of clothing, including gowns, aprons and petticoats, or "coats," from as early as three months.[9] By the seventeenth century, wearing breeches was associated with entry into the next phase of childhood for boys from wealthier families.[10] Anecdotal evidence about the clothing of elite girls, however, suggests that parents dressed them like little women at much younger ages. Honor Basset, the granddaughter of Lady Honor Lisle, shed swaddling clothes for a kirtle and fur bonnet at the age of five months. Lady Anne Clifford recorded that her daughter Margaret wore her first whalebone bodice three days before cutting the leading strings off the child's coats "so she had 2 or 3 falls at first but no hurt with them."[11] Margaret was about two years and nine months old at this time, to modern eyes a late age for independent walking, but very young to wear the constricting clothes of adulthood. Did such clothing mean

FIGURE 1.3: Hans Baldung Grien, *The Seven Ages of Woman*, 1544. Courtesy of Art Resource, ART3106606.

that adults viewed little girls primarily as future women, or express a desire that female children would survive to reach adult maturity? Evidence from popular medieval tales suggests that, in the absence of depictions of female children, girls were encouraged to see themselves in terms of sinful or virtuous womanhood.[12]

Maidens were allowed to wear more revealing clothing than were women of any other status, displaying to prospective mates their attributes. Bodices could be low-cut, and hair might be uncovered, both conventions that were exploited by England's perpetually virginal Elizabeth I well into her middle age: the "Rainbow" portrait (c. 1600–1602) portrays the queen in an extremely low-cut dress, with her hair loose about her face, although she was in her sixties when it was painted. However, the social pressure for unmarried women to put themselves on display caused significant anxiety over the likelihood that they would become covetous of beautiful things at the cost of their chastity. Thomas Becon's 1564 *Catechism* warns that "maids desire nothing so greatly as gallant apparel and sumptuous raiment," and "whatever woman delight in gorgeous garments, she setteth forth herself to sale and declareth evidently her incontinency."[13] Because women's clothing was most often not their own, but bestowed upon them by a man (whether father, suitor or husband), it could be the site of intense emotion or the site of a power struggle. In Boccaccio's *Decameron*, the peasant Griselda is stripped and re-clothed by her aristocratic husband, an act that not only re-creates her as a suitable wife but also marks her as his possession, clothed in his "livery." Shakespeare's Kate and Petruchio in *The Taming of the Shrew* enact a tug-of-war when Petruchio first presents Kate with a cap and an elaborate gown, but then dismisses the haberdasher and tailor who made them, denying his wife new clothes until she submits to him in all things (4.3). T. E., an English compiler of laws pertaining to women, notes that "a Wife how gallant soever she be, glittereth but in the riches of her husband."[14] The wife in Samuel Rowlands's *'Tis Merry When Gossips Meet* recalls the many gifts she received while being wooed: "I had twenty pair of gloves/When I was a maid…Garters, knives, purses, store of rings."[15] She implicitly laments the limitations of marriage, in which a wife must sue for her clothing from a less generous mate. Given this subtext of property and propriety, the clothing of a wife was mainly expected to display her spouse's status and wealth by following the fashions of time and place, while remaining sufficiently modest to reflect well on his honor.

Dress in old age was still commensurate with class and wealth, but largely designed to conceal the ravages of age by translating beauty and adornment into sobriety. Thomas Becon admonished, "The duety of old women is…to wear no lyte apparel, but such rayment as become their age and profession."[16] Hester Archer, in her forties in the late seventeenth century, acted out the stresses of her mental illness by dressing herself up in the garb of an ancient crone: one evening in bed with her husband she "putt on an old woman's high crown'd hatt, and talked and discoursed like a distracted [senile] woman."[17] Poverty was often associated with old age in women, and so Archer also sometimes donned rags to signify her advancing years. The Italian painter Giorgione depicts in his famous portrait *La Vecchia* (*The Old Woman*, c. 1500–1510) a disheveled and poorly dressed woman with a bulbous nose, hunched posture, and lank hair escaping from her cap, as she clutches a scrap of paper on which is written *col tempo* (with time). Gray hair is rarely shown in formal and identified portraits of older women—artist and subject likely agreed on forms of disguise, whether through age-appropriate head gear or painterly invention (restoring the original hair color). However, old age for some women could be a period of comfort and success, reflected in their clothing choices. Elizabeth Talbot, Countess of Shrewsbury, chose to have herself painted by Rowland Lockley when she was in her seventies; although she wears a sober costume of black velvet, a cap, and a large ruff, the portrait also features hair still vibrantly red, and an enormously long strings of pearls upon which her hand rests. These pearls were her own investment over her lifetime, acquired one at a time until they formed a sign of her vast wealth during her final widowhood. As such, they remind the portrait's audience that age does have its rewards.[18]

The Renaissance may be characterized by social, economic, cultural, and political change, but the natural rhythm of the cycle of life seems to trump these changes when we are dealing with illustrations and disseminations of the "Ages of Woman" topos. In the remainder of this chapter, we will examine cultural evidence and representations of the major stages of women's life cycles—infancy and childhood, marriage and motherhood, and old age. In addition to the historical record, however, we have women's writings about their own life experience, particularly in the latter half of the sixteenth and throughout the seventeenth centuries. In these writings, we often find that while women understood, even embraced, the rubric of the life cycle, they did not always act out its prescriptive messages.

Gendered expectations and practices may have had less impact during birth and infancy than at other stages of the female life cycle. Pediatric advice often treated newborn infants as genderless beings, recommending only that they be bathed, anointed with oils, swaddled, and allowed plenty of sleep away from bright light.[19] In Jorg Breu's depiction, the infant is inivisible within the cradle, its gender—indeed its appearance—irrelevant; likewise, in the Comenius image of the "Seven Ages," a single, swaddled infant in a cradle represents infancy for both male and female.[20] Legal and administrative sources also referred to very young children in gender-neutral terms, as if their sex was of no significance. Sixteenth-century household listings, for instance, distinguish the sex of infants irregularly, if at all. According to the 1570 Norwich census of the poor, John Coker deserted his wife, Alice Reade, leaving her with her daughter from a previous marriage and two sons of their own as well as a "sukyng child" of no specific sex.[21] An unusually well-documented case concerning the maintenance of an illegitimate child, from Yorkshire in 1571, provides a detailed account of nursing arrangements made by the father and the disputed circumstances in which the child came to be returned to its mother, yet the child's sex was never mentioned.[22] Even bereaved parents did not always record the sex of infants that died at birth. Nicholas Assheton wrote that, after a violent delivery, God spared his wife but "took the child to his mercy."[23]

Generally, then, on the one hand, the terminology of early childhood tended not to be sex-specific.[24] On the other hand, there is evidence that the sex of a child was a matter of significance, even before birth. Obstetric texts advised on signs to tell the sex of the child: in keeping with traditional views of feminine inferiority, some medical writers believed that female infants grew in the left side of the womb and took longer to develop than male infants, who grew on the right.[25] The greater value attributed to maleness may also have led parents to hope for boys rather than girls. Thomas Bentley's 1582 publication, *The Monument of Matrons*, included prayers of supplication and thanksgiving for sons, not daughters.[26] For the social elite, with property and family name to pass on to the next generation, sons were the desired heirs. The arrival of a girl could be viewed with mixed feelings of disappointment, relief, and hope. As Lady Anne D'Ewes wrote to her husband, Sir Simonds, in 1641, "though we have failed in part of our hope by the birth of a daughter, yet we are likewise freed from much care and fear a son would have brought. Let us wait patiently on God; he will in his good time vouchsafe us issue male if he sees it good for us."[27] John Husee expressed similar sentiments in his congratulations to John and Frances Basset at the birth of a daughter, writing that "by God's grace at the next shot she [Frances] shall hit the mark."[28] The birth of a daughter confirmed the fertility of new parents and allowed them to hope for a son next time. It is more difficult to discern whether middling and working families had specific preferences, while very poor parents may have wondered how they would support a child regardless of sex. Birth order also influenced whether female infants were welcomed. After producing sons, parents might wish for a daughter and, in larger families, hope to keep a balance between daughters and sons.[29]

One way to assess whether girls were welcomed and valued would be to compare their rates of mortality, infanticide, or abandonment to those of boys. Unfortunately, statistical evidence tends to be patchy and problematic until well after 1650, both in England and in Europe. The registration of baptisms, marriages, and burials became mandatory for English parishes in 1538, but many records have not survived and there are also problems associated with under-registration. Studies of this material have not suggested widespread neglect of female infants and children. Demographers believe that the natural ratio of male to female births was 105:100, but that the imbalance between the sexes had disappeared by early childhood due to higher mortality among infant boys.[30] Many factors contributed to childhood mortality, including children's ages, the social status and wealth of their families, and whether they lived in urban or rural environments. Mortality rates were lower in rural communities than in towns, and among the wealthy compared to the poor. Infants in the first year of life were most vulnerable, with perhaps one-fifth dying before age one.[31] If the assumptions of demographers are correct, then the sex of female infants did not adversely affect their chances of survival.

Other scholars have argued that birth ratios skewed in favor of males may indicate selective infanticide or neglect of female infants.[32] The evidence is highly equivocal. Goldberg, for instance, highlights regional variations in medieval English coroners' reports, but raises the possibility that the larger numbers of accidental deaths recorded for female infants represent "a disguised form of infanticide."[33] Studies of fifteenth-century Florentine evidence have produced some of the plainest signs of differential care of female infants and children. Herlihy and Klapisch-Zuber found sex ratios of 128:1 in favor of male infants and 119:4 in favor of boys up to fifteen years of age in the Florentine Catasto, a tax assessment in 1427. They suggest that under-reporting of girls was significant. Fathers forgot to register daughters because they were more often absent from paternal households, being more likely to be sent out for wet-nursing as infants, to be sent into service to accrue a dowry as young children, or, if from a wealthy family, sent to be educated in a convent.[34] Children under fifteen did not contribute to the tax burden of the family, so the propensity of fathers to forget little girls suggests that adult men did not value their daughters. In the two decades between 1445 and 1466, Florence's Ospedale degli Innocenti took more girls than boys into care and received fewer requests from families for the return of girls from the hospital. Gavitt proposed that poverty and the prospect of having to supply a dowry for daughters accounted for the greater willingness of parents to relinquish female children to the institution permanently.[35] The hospital also recorded higher average rates of mortality for female than male infants during these two decades, although the reasons for the difference are difficult to pinpoint. However, it is difficult to ignore Gavitt's finding that in most years between 1445 and 1466, a greater proportion of female infants admitted to the hospital died within their first year of life than male infants admitted to the hospital, even if it is not possible to reconstruct the circumstances leading to their deaths.[36]

Looking at English evidence, the clearest indications of differential care come from analysis of medieval miracle stories in which sick or injured children were healed after adults sought the assistance of saints. Finucane found three times as many recorded miracles for boys than for girls, suggesting that parents and caregivers were more likely to seek supernatural assistance when boys were ill or injured. Reports of miraculous healing also indicate that boys recovered more swiftly than girls from illness, suggesting greater attention to boys' well-being.[37] The actions of medieval adults on behalf of boys in the miracle stories bear witness to the expectation, noted by Lady Anne D'Ewes, that sons elicited greater concern and anxiety. Such evidence suggests that even if Renaissance parents loved their children and did their best by them, girls do not seem to have been able to lay claim to the same degree of adult investment as boys.

Yet when Louis Haas challenged the "Ariès thesis," which claimed that the Renaissance had no concept of "childhood" and that parents were less attached to their children than modern parents due to the high rate of infant mortality (based on the important work of the social historian Philippe Ariès), he used a letter from the Italian author Giovanni Boccaccio that expressed profound sorrow on the occasion of his daughter's death.[38] After meeting Petrarch's granddaughter, Eletta, in 1366, Boccaccio recalled "being overcome with joy: I took her in my arms eagerly imagining that I was holding my own little girl... Ah, how often holding your child in my arms and listening to her prattle, the memory of my own lost little girl has brought to my eyes tears that I conceal from all."[39] Clearly Boccaccio's daughter was a beloved child. Other daughters were prized and doted on: Amelia Lanyer named her daughter, who died in infancy after many miscarriages, Odyllia, a name that seems designed to echo her mother's own; Anne Clifford hired babysitters for her three-year-old daughter when she had to be away from home, and liked the little girl to sleep with her. For her daughter's fifth birthday, her husband ordered the child's health be drunk by the household.[40] These examples indicate that there were strong deviations from the prevailing trend of paying less attention to, and investing less in, girl children.

Pediatric and pedagogical theory prescribed that infants and small children would be in the care of women. The mingling of little girls and boys under the care of women did not mean, however, that girls and boys were treated the same in the early years of childhood. In practice, expectations about gender pervaded the lives of small children, from their very first public appearance. The ceremony of baptism announced the sex of an infant and provided gendered support networks for children. In England, medieval baptismal rites required the priest to meet the baby, midwife, and godparents at the church door and to ask the sex of the child. Male infants were placed to his right, female infants to his left, echoing the association between femaleness, weakness, and imperfection found in the medical literature. Different prayers were said for boys and girls.[41] The sex ratio of godparents present at the church depended on the sex of the child, each child having two sponsors of the same sex and one of the opposite.[42] In the religious reforms of the sixteenth century, changes to the ceremony diminished sex distinctions by using a single prayer for girls and boys.[43] However, the practice of choosing two sponsors according to the sex of the child remained the same. Sponsors were required to supervise the physical welfare of godchildren until the age of seven, to ensure their basic religious education and to monitor their moral conduct into adulthood.[44] The customs of baptism helped ensure that children would have at least one adult of the same sex to monitor their welfare and guide them to adulthood.

Quotidian practices served to differentiate the rearing of girls and boys as much as life cycle rituals. The French physician Laurent Joubert implied that only in strictness of discipline were girls and boys to share a common experience of childhood, adducing proverbial wisdom that "the boy ought to be well fed, well beaten and poorly dressed; and the girl, well dressed, well beaten and poorly fed."[45] Social status, religious prescription, environmental factors, and children's physical development contributed to how children were nourished, but gender ideology also played a role in determining diet. While theorists debated the optimal length of infant nursing, popular beliefs may have contributed to the earlier weaning of girls. Joubert, for instance, attacked the idea, which he attributed to "our women" of Montpellier, that female infants should be weaned at eight to ten months of age, but male infants should suckle for two years. He argued that early weaning would cause the naturally moist female constitution to dry out, leading to early signs of aging in adulthood, so they should suckle for at least eighteen months.[46] Joubert's advice prescribed similar nutrition for male and female infants, despite assumptions about their different humoral constitution. Protecting girls from bad influences was a concern for Juan Luis Vives, who advised parents to take greater care when choosing wet nurses for daughters than for their sons.[47] As girls reached puberty, authors advised moderation in their diet in order to reduce the passions of puberty.[48] Some parents regarded a restricted diet as beneficial for little girls. Writing to thank his brother- and sister-in-law for taking his four-year-old daughter, Charity, into their household, the Calais Staple merchant John Johnson urged them to "let her be kept in awe, and not suffered to eat much flesh meats."[49] The main reason for limiting meat in Charity's diet was to counter her disposition to warts, but it was also consistent with the letter's affectionate warning not to indulge Charity or she would suffer more under maternal discipline on her return home. Practices like dietary differentiation are difficult to discern in historical sources, but such anecdotal evidence suggests the pervasive ways in which the experiences of girls were influenced by their gender as they were growing up.

According to theorists, the age of seven years or thereabouts was a significant age of development because children began to develop the faculty of reason. Writers generally did not refer explicitly to girls in discussions of the stages of childhood, but this developmental milestone seems to have applied as well to girls. Under canon law, for instance, at the age of seven both girls and boys were capable of making a promise to marry in the future, although such promises were to be confirmed at adolescence, defined as twelve years for girls and fourteen for boys.[50] Fathers were advised to take more control over rearing sons by the age of seven, and historians have identified signs of gender differentiation in children's activities from four or five years of age, suggesting that boys were spending more time in male company.[51] Although not exact about children's ages, *Advice for Housholders*, printed by Richard Grafton in London in 1542, reveals the gendering of education in the household. This work instructed merchants on how to educate children in virtue, through the inculcation of prayer and civility, from the time children were able to speak and understand. Fathers were to keep sons with them when at home, to model good behavior and manners, although the text also allowed for the hire of virtuous tutors or attendance at school. The author made mothers responsible for teaching daughters but advised fathers to ensure that girls were raised in "all feare and drede wt litle fauoure shewed them vntyll they bee of a perfyte age and vnderstanding," in contrast to his warning against "great chastising and ouer much feare in teaching" of young boys.[52] The education of boys was also to include instruction on how to earn a living, while the emphasis on teaching girls submission implies that the goal of female education was marriage.

Marriage itself could occur at various ages. The ideal marriage involved a young girl mature enough to bear children (that is, past menarche) and a man older than she, who would cultivate proper obedience and respect in her, while providing an income to support the household that she would administer; correspondingly, in contradiction to some legal versions of the age of consent that considered women underage far longer than men, the canonical age of consent for marriage was twelve for women, fourteen for men. In Cheshire, Katherine Busshell was contracted to marry in 1543 based on witnesses' understanding that her age was fourteen, something they identified by her size.[53] Menarche itself was contingent on body weight and diet; it might range from twelve to fifteen years with outlying cases at either extreme based on physiological conditions.[54] However, as Crawford and Mendelson point out, women did not mark their life stages by menarche, pregnancy, and menopause, but rather by marriage.[55] Although it was legally possible, marriage at a very young age was understood to carry risks: as Old Capulet remarks about his fourteen-year-old daughter in *Romeo and Juliet*, "too soon marred are those so early made [to marry]."[56] Among the middling and lower classes, women might marry much later because the pressure to immediately bear children was less intense in families with limited resources, but noble and gentle families contracted marriages between very young children to secure future dynastic returns.[57] In some cases, consummation of the marriage might be delayed to protect the young woman from harm: Anne D'Ewes lived chastely with her husband for the first eight months of their marriage, possibly because she had not yet reached menarche. Elizabeth Anderson was married to Edmund Morley in 1543 when both were minors, but their contract specified they would not consummate the marriage until Elizabeth was fifteen. When she died at age thirteen, her family tried to recoup the money spent on the contract; however, Morley's grandfather alleged the two had indeed had intercourse without the knowledge of Elizabeth's father, and so claimed the marriage was not void.[58] The English writer Elizabeth Cary was contracted to marry her husband, Henry Cary, at the age of seventeen, but lived apart from her spouse for more than a year; "He at the time they had been married, had been for the most part at the court or his father's house," and so did not yet know his bride at all.[59]

The ideological description of marriage in a patriarchal society was often at odds with its social importance and capacity to transform a woman's life. On the one hand, legally "marriage turned a woman into a non-person, her husband's dependant with no real will of her own."[60] Conduct literature emphasized the male head of household as the sole absolute power in the family, and encouraged women to submit cheerfully and without reservation to his law. On the other hand, marriage meant a woman gained control over her own household, and was recognized as an adult with certain rights and privileges. When William Gouge tried to admonish his parishoners that a wife's subjection to her husband required that she never dispose of the family's goods without his consent, his audience objected strongly, something he remarks on wryly in his 1634 *Of Domestical Duties*. Presumably, the main objection came from wives in the audience who, although they may have recognized that they did not legally own the family's goods, were accustomed to running their own households as they saw fit, and considered the finances part of their purview.[61]

Marriage was not an end in itself, although it might confer a degree of adult authority on a woman: its purpose was to legitimize sex, and create the next generation. Every woman was assumed to want children, as many as she could safely bear in a lifetime. As Nicholas Culpeper writes in 1651, "It is most certain that men and women desire children, partly because they are blessings of God…Or else, because they are pretty things to play withal."[62] Of course, Culpeper glosses over the main reason women were valued for their reproductive contribution in higher ranking marriages, namely the perpetuation of lineages. There was pressure on women not only to conceive but to conceive sons, especially if they were members of the aristocracy. The author of *The Fruitful Wanderer: or, a strange relation from Kingston on Thames* (1674) writes that "Sterility or Barrenness hath in all Ages and Countries been esteemed a Reproach."[63] Infertility could be read as a sign of sin, and remedies for it were a major component in nearly all medical texts, but also in handbooks for household recipes, and informal discussion amongst both men and women.[64] Jane Sharp, the author of a seventeenth-century book of midwifery, assures her readers that "to conceive with child is the earnest desire if not of all yet of most women."[65] Yet childbearing was a principal cause of mortality among women, so Sharp's hedged remark ("if not of all yet of most") may hint at some women's relief at the failure of conception. And women of the period may have had some basic knowledge of contraception: Anne Laurence found that although intervals between children increased for married women in their thirties, in certain cases women who married after thirty had children at shorter intervals, while Robert Jutte cites demographic studies showing markedly differential rates of birth among Protestants and Catholics as evidence for some knowledge of contraception.[66] Nearly every book on midwifery, including Jane Sharp's and Nicholas Culpeper's *A Directory for Midwives*, contains numerous examinations of what might hinder conception (along with remedies for infertility) or induce abortion. A discerning reader might have translated some "causes" into prevention or deliberate termination: Culpeper, for instance, lists "falls, blows, anger, fear, sorrow, running, leapings, liftings, immoderate exercise" as external causes of miscarriage.[67] Cookery books, herbals, and folklore could provide information to women about controlling fertility, although the efficacy of their recommendations is suspect.

For women who never married and never bore children, what did the life cycle mean? For religious women, that is, those in Catholic convents, clearly the commonplaces about maidenhood, marriage, and motherhood did not apply. But for single women outside of religious orders who never married, whether by choice or by necessity, the presumed lack of a cycle in their own lives probably did not eliminate a sense of life's passage, marked by the missed moments of transition through marriage and motherhood. The proportion of single women increased during the seventeenth century; some were servants or women for whom economic options made marriage less essential (as evidenced by the larger number of single women in towns where there was more available employment).[68] Amy Froide notes that single women comprised between 10 and 20 percent of the total population in England between 1550 and 1750, so they were a significant minority.[69] Most never-married women lived with parents or relatives for most of their lives, but a very few had independent means, and so more independent lives. What is more, as these women aged, they gained, rather than lost autonomy: Froide cites figures for Lichfield, Stoke-on-Trent, and Corfe Castle that indicate women under the age of forty-five headed their households in only 4.5 and 5.9 percent of cases, while those over forty-five did so at the rate of 36.4 to 40 percent (and this despite intense social and legal pressure to prevent single women running their own households).[70] If they lived to inherit family money, or to take over a family business, single women of the middling classes might find themselves enjoying an independent and secure old age.

Early modern conceptions of old age were influenced by both consistent physical and changing cultural attitudes. Bodies decayed, faculties decreased, and death approached at a fairly consistent rate, one that was, by our standards, accelerated for early moderns of all classes by the difficult conditions of life. But specific ideas about the significance of menopause, suspicion of old women's contaminating and dangerous tendency to subversive behaviors, and a cult of youth and beauty had more unpredictable effects for women.

As Aki Beam notes in the case of Hester Archer, the madwoman who donned an old woman's cap and acted out a form of senile dementia, her performance of various ages suggests that when she was in her mid-forties and so transitioning from one life stage to another, Archer "acted out her confusion about what her role really was."[71] There was no absolute dividing line that signified old age, leaving individual women to interpret the stage for themselves. Thomas Tusser's assignment of seven years to each portion of a cycle in life matches the early modern notion of a "climacteric," a period at the conclusion of which a person faced great danger; thus, Beam cites the "Great Climacteric," the age of sixty-three (nine times seven years), as the point at which many men and women believed they were truly old.[72] Certainly by that age, the physiological processes that produce the more obvious signs and sensations of decline are pronounced: Giorgione's *La Vecchia* displays the dowager's hump that results from osteoporosis; toothlessness (Jacques's "sans teeth") would have been a common complaint especially among women who had borne children, since pregnancy greatly decreases available calcium in the body, leading to the proverb "a child, a tooth." White hair, coarser features, wrinkled skin—these are all outward signs of the body's deterioration. The social and cultural significance, however, is partly an ideological by-product of the cult of youth and beauty fostered in the Renaissance. Erin Campbell posits that "gendered theories of beauty" guided early modern artists and writers: male beauty was timeless and enduring, generated out of character and virtue, while female beauty was transient, physical.[73] Paintings of old women like Giorgione's summarize all that is repulsive and fear-inducing about old age.

In Louise Gray's study of German pauper petitions, references to the physical decay of both body and mind figure repeatedly.[74] These documents reflect a division between the pleas of younger paupers, who more frequently blame divine agency for their afflictions, and older paupers, who associate their illnesses and loss of faculties with the ageing process. In her last years of life, Anne Clifford wrote nearly every day in her diary, "I went not out of the house, nor out of my Chamber today," and noted frequent bouts of "wind."[75] Since Clifford had spent most of her adult life fighting ceaselessly to regain estates alienated from her through entailment on male heirs, and had then traveled constantly between estates, houses, and building projects once she inherited, being too frail to leave her room must have been a severe trial.

Menopause itself was not a primary marker of the transition to old age, but the end of women's fertility signified, paradoxically, both her social uselessness and a degree of social empowerment that threatened male authority and control. Monthly bleeding (and to some extent, nursing an infant) was considered to maintain the delicate humoral balance in a menstruating woman's body; when bleeding no longer occurred, "bad" humors and excess blood had no outlet—they curdled, infected the body, poisoned it.[76] The consequences of menopause could be varied: women might become crabbed and malevolent, or, especially if they were widows and hence sexually experienced, they might become sexually rapacious. While she has plenty to be angry about, "old" Queen Margaret in Shakespeare's *Richard III* is also called "well skilled in curses," and is invited to pass along that skill to the widowed (and ageing) Queen Elizabeth; Richard, however, brands her a "hateful withered hag."[77] In Thomas Deloney's *Jack of Newbury* (1597), the protagonist is tricked into marrying his master's widow, Alice; she is of indeterminate age, but clearly infatuated with the much younger Jack. After many escapades and a long adjustment period, the two form a successful marriage, and Jack becomes one of the wealthiest clothmakers in England, one example of a positive outcome of lusty widowhood. However, when Theseus in *A Midsummer Night's Dream* wants an image to convey his frustration with the passage of time before he can marry Hippolyta, he berates the "old moon…[who] lingers my desires,/Like to a stepdame or a dowager/ Long withering out a young man's revenue," tapping into cultural assumptions about old women's drain on the resources of vigorous young people.[78]

From the image of the "merry widow" to early modern identification of old women with witches, increasing age and the release from childbearing could translate in popular imagination into the potential for disruptive behavior. Old women were said to wither physically, but they were also figured as a withering drain on others. At the bottom of the social scale, widowhood translated into poverty; widows were thus more often reliant on systems of poor relief, but also more likely to engage in petty crime—or at least to be suspected of doing so—again arousing fears about their dangerous influence.[79] But even at the very top of the social ladder, old women were resented: Queen Elizabeth could not die soon enough for some in her kingdom, who resented her weakness, which they feared translated into national vulnerability. A portrait of her painted after her death depicts her as an old woman (something she would

FIGURE 1.4: Allegorical portrait of Elizabeth I, c. 1610, attributed to Marcus Gheerarts. Wikimedia Commons: http://en.wikipedia.org/wiki/File:Elizabeth-I-Allegorical-Po.jpg.

never have allowed while alive), slumped in a chair, with Death looking over her shoulder and Old Father Time at her right. Though the portrait is part of a revival of her popularity during the troubled reign of James I, it evokes the deterioration of both body and spirit in this aged queen, who is "at the mercy of forces she cannot control."[80]

Emotionally, widowhood was more often a life-transforming experience for early modern women than was menopause, since the loss of familial authority and status women enjoyed during their husbands' lives, not to mention the loss of companionship, could be devastating. Crawford and Mendelson recount some wrenching examples of recorded loss: Lady Russell mourned having her husband to "walk with, to eat and sleep with," while of his patient Margaret Lancton, the physician Richard Napier wrote that she was "full of melancholy and ill thought and cannot rest day nor night…Tempted to drown herself."[81] However, for some widows, especially those of the upper classes with wealth, widowhood could be liberating and empowering. Anne Clifford remarks of her second husband, Philip Herbert, Earl of Pembroke, that he was "extremely chollerick by nature," a tiny reference in her otherwise positive account of his life to their unhappy marriage, during which they often quarreled and lived apart. Less than a month later, Clifford began to "enjo[y] herself in building" on her estates.[82] Elizabeth Talbot, Countess of Shrewsbury, had Hardwick Hall built for herself when she was in her seventies, and widowed for the fourth time (she had married George Talbot, Sixth Earl of Shrewsbury, when she was already forty-seven; he died in 1590). The fact that the great house was known by her maiden name, and that she emblazoned it with her initials—EH, for Elizabeth Hardwick—suggests that in her years as a widow and old woman she established a secure, individuated identity that bypassed that conferred on her by any of her marriages, even the happy ones.

Women's life cycles were thus dominated by their association with men, through the emphasis on preparing for marriage and motherhood, and the relative lack of differentiation in the arc of their adult years. The cultural devaluation of girl children, while not absolute in all cases, continued to influence women's portrayal at all of life's stages, since their only purpose was to serve men in marriage, serve family interests through childbearing, and then preferably disappear into obscurity. For most women, achievement of the usual milestones of life like getting married and bearing children did confer certain privileges, as well as a degree of authority and cultural recognition. But, despite the assumption that these milestones were universally desired, some women found it prudent to defer marriage and children, while others eschewed both altogether—and there is little evidence that these women were substantially less contented than their more traditional peers. Whether they ended up married or not, women mainly did count the years according to the life cycle rubric, even if it was in some areas (like the pinpointing of old age) too vague to help them classify themselves fully. Yet some also modified, ignored, or subverted the more misogynistic aspects of the life cycle apparatus, occasionally turning it on its head and enjoying a varied, rewarding existence beyond its simplified schema.

CHAPTER TWO

Bodies and Sexuality

MARA I. AMSTER

Woman was, from classical times onward, characterized by her corporeality; she was associated with her physical body while man was allied with his soul. As Aristotle noted in his *De Generationae Animalium*, "The male provides the 'form' and the 'principle of movement,' the female provides the body, in other words, the material."[1] Such a distinction made it nearly impossible to consider woman apart from her body since the former was defined fully by the latter; woman becomes synonymous with body and, as it happens, with a body that was almost always sexualized. Relatively little had changed by the sixteenth century. For the early moderns, the female body was weaker than the male body; it was colder than the male body; it was moister than the male body. These undisputable facts were taken as undeniable truths, as an official narrative in which one's particular place in society was determined by one's body. Heat is what made "men stout of courage, fierce…industrious, [and] politic," whereas woman's relative coldness—along with her "fatness, softness and laxity"—explained "her proneness to anger and venery [and her] imbecility of mind." As a "weak creature," one homily claimed, she was "more prone to all weak affections and dispositions of mind more than men be, and lighter they be and more vain in their fantasies and opinions." Women were morally inferior because of bodies that were "more wanton and petulant than males."[2] As a result, women—considered to be less trustworthy and less predictable, more prone to lustful imaginings, voracious appetites, and uncontrolled sexual

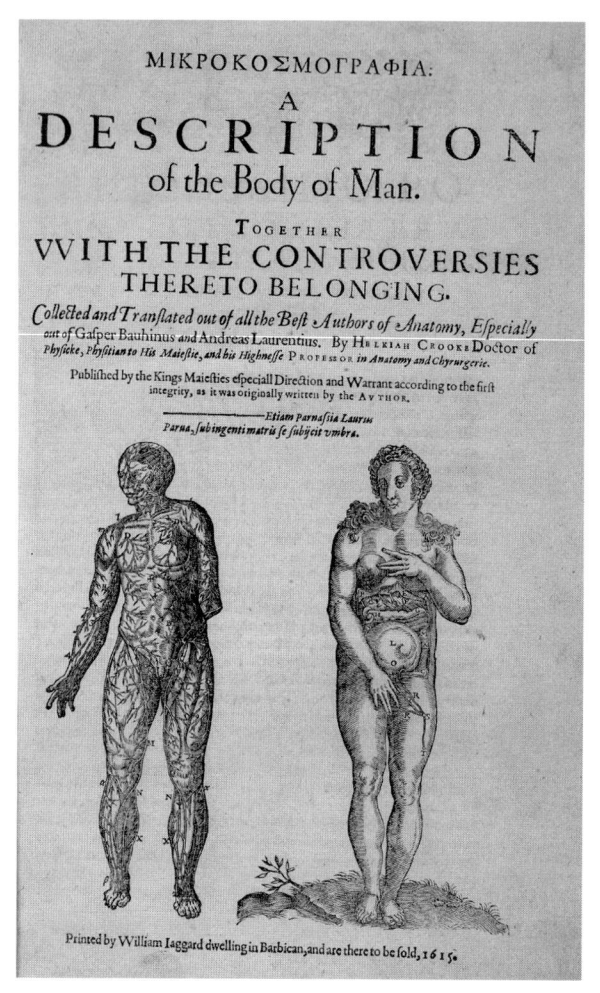

FIGURE 2.1: Title page, Helkiah Crooke, *Microcosmographia: A Description of the Body of Man* (1615). Courtesy of the Huntington Library, San Marino, California.

urges—were less suited for civic, political, and public action. Or, as Katherine Eisaman Maus summarizes succinctly, what makes early modern women women—specifically their moist, cold, troublesome wombs—also "makes them stupid."[3] It was, one might claim after assessing these facts, simple to make sense of the early modern female body.

This particular narrative of simplicity does get more complicated when one factors in the complex bodily functions of menstruation, lactation, and procreation; none of these functions were fully understood and all were vaguely threatening. Indeed, that so many gynecological tracts bore the phrase "secrets of women" in their titles—starting with the late thirteenth-century *De Secretis Mulierum*—tells us that the female body was not as self-evidently straightforward as some might claim; not only did it contain its own secrets but women, not learned medical men, had access to this information. Disruptions to the established binary—men as hot and dry, women as cold and moist—were treated as monstrous aberrations rather than ideological ruptures. When Othello, for instance, notes that Desdemona's hand is "hot, hot and moist," he reads it as a sign of her too "liberal heart" and another proof of her infidelity, not as a challenge to humoral theory.[4] Competing Aristotelian and Galenic theories of reproduction—did women produce seed as men did? did women need to achieve orgasm in order to generate or ejaculate that seed? what, beside for living space, did women contribute to the development of the fetus?—vied with one another for dominance. Even the Galenic one-sex model that argued for the complementarity of male and female bodies—illustrated in visual accounts of the reproductive systems in Andreas Vesalius's *De Humanis Corporis Fabrica* (1534)—was not as universally accepted as contemporary medical writers and modern critics might have us believe.[5] Nevertheless, one could continue to ignore these additional "facts"—perhaps ignore the female body itself—in order to maintain and sustain the desired coherent and smooth narrative and many, indeed, did just this. Yet, almost ironically, this maintenance relied, in great part, on an extreme focus on the body itself.

Why was understanding the female body so vital to the early moderns? In Mary Douglas's argument, the "body's boundaries can represent any boundaries which are threatened and precarious." For the early moderns, precariousness develops when masculine identity becomes defined, at least partially, by female behavior. To understand himself, therefore, "the male exhibits a compulsive desire to unlock the inaccessible sexual truth harbored by the [woman's] body." Unlocking this truth required more than surveying and policing the female body's boundaries, though that was an important part of the process. It also required the written construction of a body whose unpredictable sexual impulses and desires could be codified and categorized, a body that could be captured and rendered stationary in text, a body that could be read by those who perused it. For if female bodies provoked excitement and wonder with regard to their generative abilities, those very same bodies created anxiety and concern apropos of their sexual capabilities.[6] In order to manage the apprehension, a legible sexual female body needed to be written; what was chaotic needed to be controlled, what was fluid needed to be fixed. That textualized body, as we have noted, was described and detailed in anatomy books that sought to render those very "secrets" open to an educated male audience.[7] While both male and female bodies were opened up in these texts, the language used to express the unfolding of the latter is, as Patricia Parker has argued, marked by a certain voyeuristic fascination. The impulse to look, though, was matched by a fear of what one might see. John Banister, in his *Historie of Man* (1578), reverts to this fearfulness when he explains why he is not including a description of female parts in his anatomy text: "Because I am from the beginning persuaded, that, by lifting up *the vayle of Natures secrets in womens Shapes*, I shall commit more indecencie against the office of Decorum than yeld needefull instruction to the profite of the common sort."[8] There was something indecent, indecorous about "womens Shapes." No similar reticence accompanies the descriptions or performs a rationale for the absence of male bodies. Despite this ambivalence—to both see and avoid seeing, a state that is not unique to Banister—the project of making static in order to make simple continued.

Indeed, not only did it persist but throughout the early modern period it flourished; even as it became more and more difficult to make static and simple, the attempts to do so expanded from their place in the "official" theological, physiological, and legal texts to the realm of the "unofficial." Found in fictional and non-fictional writings, conversations about and examinations of the female body proliferated. No less provocative or pedagogical because of their position as popular English writings, these poems, plays, and conduct manuals similarly attempt to craft a legible female body. What is especially intriguing about these forums is that the explorations are marked by complexities and contradictions, echoing in many ways those paradoxes found in the medical and anatomical writings; within the texts we find the kinds of statements regarding the proper behavior of the female body that we might locate in sermons and medical tracts interspersed with examples of how that particular prescription is ignored, flouted, or compromised. We see, specifically, the body's ability to both adhere to and deviate from its expectations, sometimes just moments apart. It is not that the prevalent ideologies are overturned but, rather, that this multiplicity of voices serves as a challenge to the notion that there is a single coherent and comprehensive narrative or representation at play. Indeed, by looking at the ways these texts simultaneously construct and deconstruct the idealized sexualized female body—ordered and unruly, suitably fashioned and mis-dressed, legible and incoherent—we see just how contested that narrative was.

* * *

Shakespeare's "Rape of Lucrece" (1594) relates the oft-told story of Lucretia, the chaste Roman matron who is raped by her houseguest Tarquin and whose subsequent suicide leads her family to drive Tarquin into exile and, as a result, end the Roman monarchy and establish the Republic. Lucrece's body performs, we are told in numerous ways, as a text; it is disseminated by "Collatine the publisher" (33), makes public the result of her rape ("The light will show, character'd in my brow,/The story of sweet chastity's decay" [807–8]), and, finally, becomes a rallying cry for revenge ("How Tarquin must be us'd, read it in me" [1195]). Lucrece's story is not unique to Shakespeare—her tale is told in Bocaccio's *De Claris Mulieribus* (1374), Chaucer's *Legend of Good Women* (c. 1386), and Christine de Pizan's *Book of the City of Ladies* (1405) and portrayed in Botticelli's *Tragedy of Lucretia* (1505), Titian's *Rape of Lucretia* (1568–71), and Artemisia Gentileschi's *Lucretia* (1621), among others—but his repeated references to her body as a text to be read and interpreted is worth considering. It is, of course, because Lucrece is displayed that she becomes an object of lustful desire for Tarquin; it is when she presents her body publicly to her male family members that it becomes a visible representation of virtuous chastity. As both an image of provocation and symbol of purity, Lucrece's body, unchanged but from a living state to a lifeless one, contains contradictory meanings. That her body can be read in such seemingly opposed ways should make us question how stable either one of those readings is as well as how open the female body is to various interpretations.

Of course, the idea of reading a woman's body like a text is not unique to Shakespeare either; the metaphors of legibility abound in early modern writing. We find them in Francis Beaumont and John Fletcher's *The Maid's Tragedy* (1610–11) when Melantius, berating his sister for her adulterous affair, vows that "the world may read/Thy black shame" on her flesh, in John Taylor's "A common whore" (1625) when he notes that his subject's "faults are printed unto all mens sight,/Unpartially declar'd in blacke and white," and in Philip Massinger's *The Renegado* (1630) when Donusa asks her waiting woman Manto if "thy friends [could]/Reade in thy face thy maidenhead gone, that thou/Hadst parted with it?"[9] While it is true that the bodies being textualized are not always female—King John, for example, refers to himself as "a scribbled form, drawn with a pen/Upon a parchment" (Shakespeare, *King John*, 5.7.32–33)—there is a pronounced difference depending on the sex of the individual being depicted. Eve Rachele Sanders summarizes these differences: when a man is the subject, it is his soul that is textualized; when it is a woman, it is her sexual transgressions that surface as alphabetical characters.[10] Woman, body, and sexuality are, again, tied together tightly in order to form a clear narrative. Presenting a woman as a fixed image—that adheres to a certain formula whereby a specific sexual status manifests itself with a particular marking or message—is intended to demystify the uncertainty that her sexuality presents and to confirm that what readers of her body see accurately reflects what she is.

That so many of the early modern texts focus on deciphering a woman's sexual identity through a reading of her body should not surprise us given the period's almost obsessive concern with female virginity and chastity. The connection between a chaste body and a pure mind—and what that association means to her husband's honor and her family's reputation—underscores Lucrece's interior monologue as she debates what to do after Tarquin flees. That she refers to Collatine as the "[d]ear lord of that dear jewel I have lost" (1191) situates her chastity as his prized possession. If we consider that a woman was "understood either married or to be married," as T. E. noted in his treatise on women's legal rights, then it is not surprising that such a high priority was placed on the confirmation of a woman's chastity.[11] Every woman was subject to her father's or future husband's scrutiny; every woman needed to be identified satisfactorily. The frustration of failing at this activity is captured by Shakespeare's Duke in *Measure for Measure* (1604) when his attempts to situate Mariana in her proper place are thwarted: "Why you are nothing then: neither maid, widow, nor wife?" (5.1.177–78). Substantiating a woman's sexual status, assuring her chastity, was a way of verifying who, and what, she was.

This type of verification could not, of course, come from the mouths of the women themselves; they were, after all, graced with "imaginations...which have not repugnancy or contradiction of reason to restrain them."[12] Rather, the proof needed to be objective, unimpeachable; it needed to come from learned men who could decipher the body's appearance and its ability to narrate truthfully the woman's sexual experience or innocence. The anatomical texts sought to locate the proof of female virginity within the body; debates over the importance and significance of the hymen found in, among others, Helkiah Crooke's *Microcosmographia* (1615), Ambroise Pare's *Works of the Famous Chirugeon* (1634), Nicholas Culpeper's *A directory for midwives* (1656), and Jane Sharp's *The Midwives Book* (1671) tell us that the project was not completely successful.[13] The conduct manual discourses, conversely, attempted to situate that same proof on the body's exterior. And, just as the anatomical texts complicate the very equation they seek to establish with their simultaneous claims that the presence of the hymen "is a certain note of Virginity" and may not be, so too do the conduct manuals—and the fictions that make use of their pronouncements—prove equally contradictory, undermining the very claims of legibility they champion.[14]

The most easily identifiable aspect of a virgin's appearance is her blush; the rush of blood to her cheeks acts "as modest evidence/To witness simple virtue" (Shakespeare, *Much Ado about Nothing*, 4.1.37–38). The Petrarchan red cheeks and white skin—roses and lilies, rubies and ivory—of the beautiful beloved is something of a shorthand cliché for early modern writers; Lucrece, the chaste wife, blushes even while she sleeps: "Her lily hand her rosy cheek lies under" (386). To conduct writers as disparate as early sixteenth-century Spaniard Juan Luis Vives and Italian Baldessar Castiglione and early seventeenth-century Englishman Barnabe Rich, a woman's ability to blush signified the same thing: sexual naivete. Vives notes that "she can nat be chaste that is nat ashamed: for that is as a cover and a vaylle of her face." This cover, Rich agrees, acts as a sign of her modesty: "the blush of a womans face, is an approbation of a chast and honorable minde, and a manifest signe" of her disapproval of "any other lascivious" acts. "The light blush of shame," Castiglione says, should be present whenever "immodest or unbridled familiarity" comes near the woman. Without exception, Rich definitively states, the bad woman "can not blush."[15] The reddened cheeks—the outward sign of inner modesty—act as a natural indicator of a woman's innocence; the blush manifests itself at all moments when her sexual integrity is threatened. We need only think of Hamlet's characterization of Gertrude's re-marriage, sexual activity, and potential knowledge of her first husband's murder as "such an act/That blurs the grace and blush of modesty" (Shakespeare, *Hamlet*, 3.4.40–41) to understand how fully he has condemned her.

Claudio, in *Much Ado about Nothing* (1598–99), calls attention to this sign when he denounces his betrothed Hero at their wedding. "Behold how like a maid she blushes here" (4.1.34), he cries, disturbed by the fact that she can blush as if she were innocent when he is convinced she is not. He calls attention to her "exterior shows" (4.1.40) as a marker of her maidenhood even as he denounces her for her infidelity; she is, he declares, "but the sign and semblance of her honor" (4.1.33). Even in this moment of heightened anger as he fulminates against the failures of an ideological system that promises clarity and certainty, Claudio maintains his belief in that very same system. Claudio trusts in what he sees even when he maintains that appearances can be deceiving. The Friar, moments after Hero is spurned and left for dead, returns to this theme of appearance and the power of the blush to speak sexual truth. He tells her father, "I have mark'd/A thousand blushing apparitions/To start into her face" (4.1.158–60). The Friar uses these same signs as proof positive that

Hero's virginity is intact and, as the play shows us, the Friar is correct. Hero's ability to blush—quite often, it seems, since it is one of her most marked and remarked upon characteristics—serves as her body's signal that it is pure and confirms belief that bodily readings offered by the Friar, Vives, Rich, and Castiglione can be trusted.

Yet it becomes more complex when the authors gesture toward potential pitfalls in their own arguments. When Richard Brathwaite claims that the virginal maid has "never learned...to staine her spotlesse honour with

FIGURE 2.2: Title page, Richard Brathwaite, *The English Gentlewoman* (1631). Courtesy of the Huntington Library, San Marino, California.

a *painted blush*," his praise of her innocence alerts us to the possibility that other maids may have learned to stain and paint in order to mask their spotted status. This issue of learned innocence is raised, as well, by Thomas Salter, who believes that a maiden "shall bee readie but not to[o] bolde" to demonstrate her virtue "by a sodaine blushing, whiche immediately will overspread her lillie cheeks with roseate read." Though Brathwaite does not specify how the "painted blush" is achieved and Salter does not describe how this state of readiness is maintained, both men imply that blushing may have less to do with sexual status than with cosmetic skills. It is Thomas Tuke, in his diatribe against face-painting females and with a nod to the metaphor of legibility, who states outright what the other writers merely allude to: "Her own sweet face is the booke she most lookes upon…& as her eie…teaches her, sometimes she blots out pale, & writes *red*." That act of blotting and writing is made concrete in Alexander Oldys's *The London Jilt* (1683) when his prostitute Cornelia explains how it is done: "I took some *Spanish* Wool, which I macerated some hours in Brandy, by the force whereof, the Tincture of the *Spanish* Wool began to lose it self" to transform into "a colour, which seem'd to be altogether natural." If blushing is not something that occurs spontaneously, might this mean that it is female artifice rather than female naivete—the "naturalness" that *seems* rather than *is*—that the body is presenting? Or is it, as Claudio initially and wrongfully claims of Hero, "guiltiness, not modesty" (4.1.42) that is being announced by her reddened cheeks? Philip Stubbes, always suspicious of artificiality of any kind, wonders what purpose a woman would have for falsifying her blush: "If thou beest faire, why paintest thou thy selfe to seeme fairer? and if thou bee not faire, why dost thou hypocritically desire to seeme faire, and are nothing lesse?"[16] To follow Stubbes's unspoken train of thought, if the female body is able to create the appearance of innocence despite what may be a different bodily truth, what else might it be capable of? And what might it want to hide?

If the discourse of conduct and courtesy contains within it the idea that a woman's sexual status can both be read upon her face and manipulated by her to achieve a particular purpose, bodily certainty becomes anything but certain. What might it mean, for instance, if a blush could be simultaneously "a token of modesty, and yet an amorous sign," a means of proclaiming chastity and announcing sexual yearning? It is this heightened concern that woman may be able to control her body's appearance and, thus, hide its truth that seems to haunt so many of the early modern writings. "The [male] longing to 'know' women, to employ their flesh to answer questions about their being, their past, and their future" creates, Tassie Gwilliam claims, "considerable discursive energy."[17] That particular fraught energy is brought to life by John Webster in *The White Devil* (1612). If, as was the case with Shakespeare's Hero, we get hints that a woman's body may obscure its sexual truth, we also find that, in the end, the outward signs of her chastity accurately represent her inner state. Webster, though, shows us the dark possibilities of what happens when that body defies the desired narrative.

It is during Vittoria's arraignment to determine the role she played in the murder of her husband that the language of bodily discernment takes center stage. Legal proof, for prosecutor Cardinal Monticelso, is nonexistent—it is readily acknowledged that there is "no sound proof"—and so he turns to what might be called "ocular proof": Vittoria's face and physical appearance will prove her guilt much in the same way that *Much Ado*'s Friar claimed that the same attributes would free Hero from suspicion.[18] Monticelso swears that he will "paint out/[Vittoria's] follies in more natural red and white/Than that upon [her] cheek" (3.2.51–53). His reference to her complexion reminds us that her blushing and blanching should be the artless and innocent response to the indictments he is offering.[19] Yet, the Cardinal claims that his plain language, an ironic invocation of the colors most often associated with romantic rhetoric and Petrarchan poetry, is the antithesis of Vittoria's adorned and unnatural cheeks. Her painted face, he argues, is a sign of her inauthenticity and her sexual duplicity.

Consistent in his request that Vittoria be considered a spectacle open for interpretation—"Observe this creature," "And look upon this creature," "see, my lords," "[N]ow to your picture" (3.2.56, 119, 129, 243)—Monticelso advocates that there is truth to be found in reading her appearance. As such, he critiques not only her "red and white" cheeks but also the fact that she "comes not like a widow; she comes armed/With scorn and impudence" (3.2.120–21). Vittoria's lack of mourning clothes and her anger at being called to trial are interpreted as tokens of her marital faults, both legal and sexual; such outward signs provide, Monticelso argues, proof of her guilt. Yet, at the same time that he champions such an interpretation, Monticelso soundly rejects this simplistic conclusion that equates her appearance of impropriety with her actual sins:

> You see, my lords, what goodly fruit she seems,
> Yet, like those apples travellers report
> To grow where Sodom and Gomorrah stood,
> I will but touch her and you straight shall see
> She'll fall to soot and ashes. (3.2.63–67)

Here Monticelso envisions an apple composed of "soot and ashes," an object which "seems" pristine on the outside but whose facade serves to hide its inner rottenness. What appears placid—even edenic—conceals passion and poison. While claiming that Vittoria's cosmetically altered facade and improperly clad body alert us to her propensity for sexual immorality, Monticelso is simultaneously asserting that her exterior provides no guide to her inner reality, that the real danger posed by a woman such as Vittoria is that she cannot be adequately or accurately read. Yet, despite his acknowledgement of this paradox, it is this same outward facade, rather than any concrete legal proof, that he chooses to place on trial. If Hero was condemned and redeemed on the basis of her appearance, Vittoria is only condemned.

In addition to her problematic visage, Monticelso also points to Vittoria's clothing—the absence of her widow weeds—as a sign that she is falsely mourning the death of her husband; this evidence, along with the conclusion offered that an ill-clad widow must be an adulterous, murderous one, seems shoddy but proves persuasive. Both the body's actual exterior as well as the covers that were used to fashion it were intended to provide legibility. In a time in which medieval sumptuary laws still remained on the books, and much new legislation was being ratified by Queen Elizabeth in her 1562 clothing proclamations, the belief that what one wore should reflect who one was—socially, economically, sexually—was taken seriously. We might argue that even though women's clothing was exempt from legislation from 1510 through 1574—the emphasis was on establishing one's presence in the male social hierarchy—the interest in and concern with what women wore was still palpable.[20] The difficulty seemed to lie in the fact that many women did not adhere to the rules, those officially mandated or socially assumed, or, even more problematic for those reading them, that their bodies did not.

The "Homily Against Excesse of Apparel," published in *The Second Book of Homilies* (1562), speaks very clearly about such un-fashioned women: "For the proud and haughty stomachs of the daughters of England are so maintained with divers disguised sorts of costly apparel that, as Tertullian an ancient father saith, there is no difference betweene an honest matron and a common strumpet."[21] While the homily concerns itself primarily with effeminate men who are over-spending on their wardrobes, the distinction that it draws—or, more precisely, the lack of distinction on which it focuses—between "honest" and "common" women is important. This division, noted as well by both Claudio and Monticelso, is repeated throughout the early modern fictions. John Marston's *The Dutch Courtesan* (1605) proclaims in its front matter that "The difference betwixt the love of a courtesan, & a wife is the

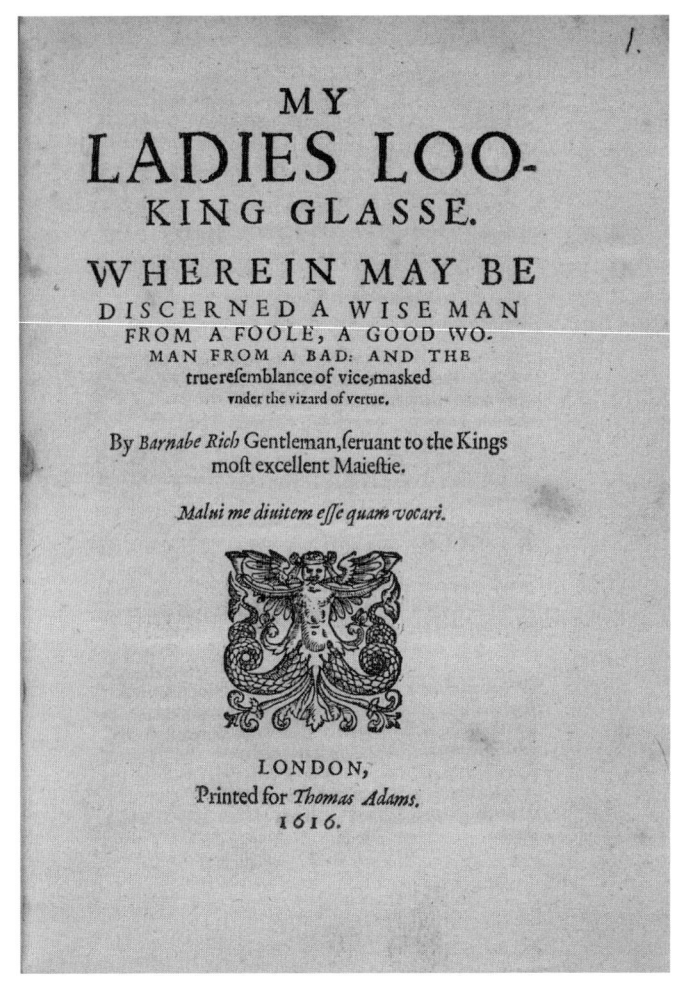

FIGURE 2.3: Title page, Barnabe Rich, *My Ladies Looking Glasse* (1616). Courtesy of the Huntington Library, San Marino, California.

full scope of the play," Barnabe Rich questions "how we might distinguish betweene a good woman and a bad," and the "Epistle Dedicatory" from William Wycherley's *The Plain Dealer* (1677) laments that "you can no more know a kept Wench from a Woman of Honour by her looks than by her Dress." While historical records indicate that there was little evidence that the London streets were full of mis-dressed men and women, such facts should not cause us to overlook the tensions that are manifest in the fictional and non-fictional writings.[22] These writers call attention to the lack of obvious differentiation: how can a man tell, upon first looking at a woman, into which category she should fall? And what risks—both minor and severe—may accrue to him (and her) if he judges incorrectly?

It would seem as if the danger presented by a mistaken identification would fall more heavily on the woman. Early modern city comedies, for instance, abound with situations where the wives who work in their husbands' shops are mistaken for prostitutes selling a different set of goods. The constant shopkeeper refrain of "What is't you lack, gentleman? What is't you buy?"—found in Thomas Middleton and Thomas Dekker's *The Honest Whore* (1616), Middleton's *A Chaste Maid in Cheapside* (1613), Ben Jonson, George Chapman, and John Marston's *Eastward Ho* (1605), and Jonson's *Bartholomew Fair* (1614), among others—shows us how easy it was to draw attention to the double entendre. That many of these women are out of place, both geographically and sartorially—"dressed more like a Lady or Person of Quality than a good Housewife, who minds the affairs of her household," as John Dunton wrote[23]—only heightens the potential for inadequate differentiation.

To be accosted as if one were a common whore was bad enough and contained numerous embarrassing possibilities; to have embarrassment turn into something violent was a likelihood that was always present. In Aphra Behn's *The Rover* (1677), disguise and masking are all-important to the plot's twists and turns. Twice Florinda, a high-spirited yet chaste young woman, is mistaken for a prostitute both because of her presence in public and her wardrobe choices; stage directions tell us that she dresses like a gypsy in 1.2, "in an undress" in 3.5, and masked in 4.2 and 5.1. It is in that state of "undress" at night in the garden that she is first taken for an "arrant harlot."[24] Interestingly her attacker's assumption is challenged for a call to bodily legibility: "couldst not see something about her face and person, to strike awful reverence into thy soul?" (3.6.24–25), another man asks. Florinda's social and sexual status—high-born and virginal—should, her defender claims, be legible even if she is disguised. What should be self-apparent, though, is not, and when Florinda is once again mistaken for a whore, the situation turns ugly. Blunt, already fooled by a woman whom he misread, rails and threatens Florinda:

> [I] will be revenged on one whore for the sins of another. I will smile and deceive thee, flatter thee, and beat thee, kiss and swear, and lie to thee, embrace thee and rob thee…and strip thee stark naked, then hang thee out at my window by the heels, with a paper of scurvy verses fastened to thy breast. (4.5.50–55)

It seems important to note that, even in his fit of anger, Blunt himself makes use of the tropes of legibility, wanting to uncover the woman's secrets and then write her character for others to see. As might be expected in a romantic comedy, Florinda's chastity remains intact and she is granted a happy ending; the interlude with Blunt is, like many other similar mis-dressed moments, ultimately harmless. While Florinda's character endures hardships, there is no real risk offered to an "honest" woman from the men who misread her since eventually one who reads her correctly comes to the rescue.

The same, though, cannot be said for the misreading men; our fictions show us that the threat posed by "disorder in the dress," to quote poet Robert Herrick, "kindles" far more than sweetness and "wantonness"; it very well may create the kind of "bewitch[ing]" he does not anticipate.[25] There are, we might argue, two types of disordered dressing, both of which lead to a difficulty in distinguishing sexual legibility. The first, cross-dressing, is a problem more commonly associated with male actors and the theater; the second, which we might call cross-bodying, is caused when the body beneath the clothing is not just the unexpected sex but something far more suspect. In this second case, it is not just the clothing that allows for a potentially dangerous confusion on the part of the male reader but the body itself.

Anti-theatricalists were obsessively concerned with the fact that the theater allowed for a world where an individual's exterior did not match his interior: boys played girls, players acted the roles of monarchs. At its simplest, cross-dressing on stage violated the edict in Deuteronomy 22:5: "The woman shall not wear that which pertaineth unto a man, neither shall a man put on a woman's garment: for all that do so are abominations unto the Lord thy God." At its more complicated, the theater, with its use of cross-dressing, was a world that encouraged not only sodomy and effeminacy, according to its critics, but it misled its audience to embrace a type of counterfeiting that damaged the ability to distinguish and discriminate. Philip Stubbes summarizes this stance: "Our apparel was given us as a signe distinctive, to discerne betwixt sexe and sexe, and therefore one to weare the apparel of another sexe, is to participate with the same, and to adulterate the veritie of his owne kinde." Stephen Gosson takes this charge one step further: "Every man must shew himself outwardly to be such as in deed he is...to declare ourselves...to be otherwise than we are, is an act executed where it ought not, therefore a lie."[26] When what is intended to differentiate—"our apparel"—becomes an illegible sign, a deliberate counterfeit, or a lie, any effort to forge that much-desired narrative of simple bodily legibility begins to unravel. While Stubbes, Gosson, and their fellow critics were focused primarily on male actors, it is possible to apply their argument to female characters that cross-dress or wear clothing that does not succeed in properly identifying themselves.

We tend to consider theatrical cross-dressing characters, like Shakespeare's comic and romantic heroines, as resourceful women who temporarily don male attire in order to achieve a specific goal (for *The Merchant of Venice*'s Portia, it is to rescue her husband's best friend from Shylock's bond) or to gain a sense of safety (as is the case for *As You Like It*'s Rosalind, *Twelfth Night*'s Viola, and *Cymbeline*'s Imogen). That these "women" return to their proper clothing at the play's end—with the strange exception of Viola who is still in her Cesario clothing when Orsino proposes to her—assures the audience that, within the world of the play, outer and inner do, eventually, match. Equally important is the fact that these cross-dressed women never deny their heterosexual desires even as they remain faithful and chaste; indeed, often it is their cross-dressing that allows them to satisfy that very desire.

Early modern drama, though, does contain examples that complicate this easy acceptance of female-to-male dressing, underscoring the anxieties present in the words of Stubbes and Gosson but doing so in unexpected ways. One of the most notable instances is found in Thomas Middleton and Thomas Dekker's *The Roaring Girl* (1611) with the dramatic representation of real-life cross-dressing Moll Frith. The fictional Moll—"mad Moll, or merry Moll, a creature/So strange in quality"[27]—is known for her wearing of male apparel and, because of this, defies easy categorization: "'tis woman more than man,/Man more than woman" (1.2.130–31). Her dress is taken as a sign of her sexual and moral promiscuity; sumptuary offenses are seen as leading the way to greater social transgressions. Sir Alexander believes she can be trapped into theft, Mistress Openwork decides her husband and Moll are having an affair, and Laxton thinks that she will be willing to prostitute herself ("I'll lay hard siege to her, money is that aqua fortis that eats into many a maidenhead" [2.1.179–81]). Moll's becomes the body upon which social fears—the inability to identify correctly the women who populate the markets and streets or understand female sexual desire—are written and read.

While hints are dropped that Moll may be a hermaphrodite—Sir Alexander, serving as voyeur during a scene at the tailor's, refers to her as a "monster with two trinkets" (2.2.76–77) and Moll herself claims that she is "man enough for a woman" (2.2.43)—the play never seriously engages with this idea. Philip Stubbes, however, would not hesitate to categorize Moll in this manner; in writing about women who wear male apparel, he notes, "Wherefore these women may not improperly bee called *Hermaphroditi*, that is Monsters of both kindes, halfe women, half men. Who if they were naturall

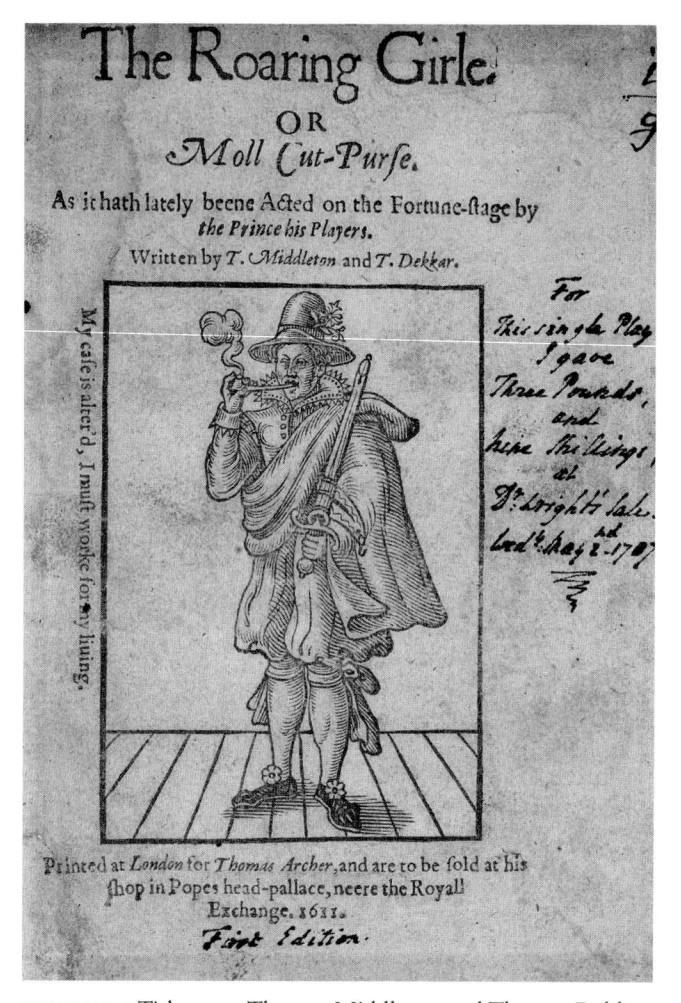

FIGURE 2.4: Title page, Thomas Middleton and Thomas Dekker, *The Roaring Girl* (1611). Courtesy of the Huntington Library, San Marino, California.

women, and honest Matrones, woulde blush to go in such wanton & leud attire." For Stubbes, the fashion dictates the body underneath it rather than vice versa. Stubbes's rhetoric and his return to the importance of the blush aside, there does remain the difficulty of determining just what Moll is. While early modern anatomical and biological theories staunchly denied that men could degenerate into women, Galenic notions of heat did allow for the reverse: a woman could become more perfect, could become a man. As Ambroise Pare writes, "Certainly women have so many and like parts lying in their wombe, as men have hanging forth: onely a strong and lively heat seemes to be wanting, which may drive forth that which lyes hid within."[28] *The Roaring Girl* does not seem to be presenting the possibility that Moll's genitals may be "drive[n] forth" even if she does seem to be possessed by a "lively heat," but it does gesture toward the none too secure divide that separates male and female bodies as Moll moves back and forth across this narrowing abyss.

This constant movement seems to offer Moll a freedom that the shopkeeper wives are denied, but it also opens up the possibility that misidentification can become more than simply comic. If we recall Laxton's words about "lay[ing] hard siege" to Moll's "maidenhood," we recognize an aggressive tinge to his language that seems excessive to his character. Yet it is not Moll who is in danger here; rather, it is Laxton himself who is physically and linguistically bested by her. He is punished, we might argue, because he consistently misreads the individual in front of him, seeing a whore where there is none. Laura Levine, in her study of theatrical cross-dressing, argues that the inability to differentiate men from women can cause "the cultivation of doubt" and the production of "violent rage." Indeed, in their study of hermaphroditic discourses, Ann Rosalind Jones and Peter Stallybrass note the establishment of a consistent pattern: when a Renaissance man attacks female manliness, he is attempting to shore up his own masculine identity.[29] Once again, we see how the need for bodily boundaries is established. As the play demonstrates, it is never Moll's chastity that is under siege—we never doubt her ability to defend herself against Laxton or deal with the various other threats with which she is challenged—but, rather, it is the precarious masculine prerogatives of the men in the play that are being called into question.

That Moll never subverts the accepted heterosexual social system—she aids Sebastian and Mary in marrying, and remains chaste throughout—and that *The Roaring Girl* is a comedy work to lessen any real threat posed by the cross-dressed woman in this particular play. Much as in *The Rover*, generic conventions allow the specter of the sartorially illegible woman to be presented in a relatively safe space, albeit one that provides more potential difficulties than those of Shakespeare's comic worlds. What both plays, though, highlight is the fear that a man will not be able to recognize and properly identify the woman he sees; for while both the gallants in *The Rover* and the rogues and shopkeepers in *The Roaring Girl*, Florinda and Moll, respectively, look like prostitutes, neither of the women are and it is in those moments of misidentification that both comedy and potential tragedy develop. It is in Edmund Spenser's non-dramatic, non-comic allegorical poem *The Faerie Queene* (1590) that we can see what it would look like if the anxieties raised by the anti-theatricalists and the conduct book writers were to be fully realized.

Much of Book One of the poem is concerned with teaching the hero, Redcrosse Knight, how to read correctly, how to extricate himself from Errour's Den and locate the House of Holiness, and how to differentiate between the lascivious allure of the Catholic Church and the chaste beauty of Protestantism. Reading bodies, specifically that of Duessa, the allegorical Whore of Babylon, is very much part of those lessons and speaks in conversation with the concerns of early modern writers regarding the secrets that lie hidden upon and within the female body. Twice in the poem Spenser allows Duessa to be seen naked; the first time Redcrosse hears about Fradubio's experience seeing her in the water, the second time he is part of the group that strips and exiles her. Duessa's monstrousness is highlighted in both of these moments, but more interesting is how we are allowed to both see and not see simultaneously. Jenny C. Mann, in comparing the medical and literary discourses surrounding hermaphrodites, notes that while the former sought to describe the subject under examination with "a clearly articulated genital composition," the latter "seems not to want to look after all."[30] We might argue that John Banister's fears of "lifting up *the vayle of Natures secrets in womens Shapes*" places him with Spenser and the poets, not the anatomists. It is almost as if the possibility of what might be seen could never match the horror or hope of what is there to see.

The first time that we hear about Duessa's body is from Fradubio, who recalls how he was able to catch a glimpse of her "in her proper hew"; unlike the beautiful woman he thought she was when she outshone his previous beloved, he now sees a "filthy foule old woman."[31] However, the language that Fradubio uses to describe just what it is that he sees when she is bathing is full of equivocation:

Her neather partes misshapen, monstruous,
Were hidd in water, that I could not see,
But they did seeme more foule and hideous,
Then womans shape man would believe to bee. (1.2.41)

Fradubio sees nothing—he "could not see"—but claims that these parts "seeme" worse than anything man could imagine. As Melinda Gough notes, his confused and confusing language suggests that we are presented not just with Duessa's "hideous" body but with Fradubio's failings as a reliable reader.[32] The inability to put into words what he sees, or thinks he sees, speaks, we may argue, to the very difficulties inherent in a project of static legibility; Duessa's body, whatever it looks like, fails to conform to any of the available or established early modern narratives. It is beyond representation. The "secrets of women" that the anatomists were so committed to discover remain, even when the body is laid bare, inaccessible to the male viewer.

Greater accessibility to Duessa's "neather parts" is granted when she is stripped for the second time; this time the voyeuristic horror of Fradubio turns into a form of group sadism as Redcrosse, Arthur, and Una "strip her naked all" (1.8.46). The description of the naked Duessa works as an anti-blazon, categorizing her "craftie head," "her rotten gummes," her "dried dugs," and her "wrizled skin" (1.8.47). Yet after an entire stanza that details with growing specificity her horrific body parts, once again the narrator turns away from description: "Her neather parts, the shame of all her kind,/My chaster Muse for shame doth blush to write" (1.8.48). Spenser's "chaster Muse," like Banister and the poets of the hermaphroditic writings, looks away. There is something about this stripping of Duessa that is reminiscent of anti-theatricalist Anthony Munday's railing against the nature of theatrical disguise. Munday writes, "It were il painting the Divel like an Angel, he must be portrayed forth as he is, that he maie the better be knowne. Sinne hath always a faire cloake to cover his filthie bodie. And therefore he is to be turned out of his case into his naked skin, that his nastie filthie bodie, and stinking corruption being perceived, he might come into the hatred and horror of men."[33] Sin, in *The Faerie Queene*, comes in numerous forms but here it is gendered female and it, like Munday's devil, has hidden her filthiness in the guise of beauty and that "faire cloake" must be removed. The problem here is not the same as we have seen with Florinda or Moll; here it is not a simple matter of disordered dress, as much more is at stake with the misreading of Duessa.

While Moll, who ends the play in the same cross-dressed clothing as she began, does not allow us to solve the puzzles posed by her body, Duessa's body is supposed to be fully recognizable because it is revealed. It is after her "filthy feature [is] open showne" that she can be allowed to "wander wayes unknowne" (1.8.49). She has, the group believes, had her "face of falsehood" (1.8.49) fully removed. However, the poem itself disallows for that possibility; Duessa does return, proving that the danger her sexualized body poses is not mitigated through the stripping away of her clothing.[34] If the concern is that wearing the clothing of the opposite sex or the social category obscures the truth of the female body, the fact that the naked Duessa poses as much of a threat as the clad one demonstrates that undressing does not provide accurate legibility. Even though her ability to confuse even further Redcrosse's shaky moral framework is dismissed, the fact that Spenser has constructed a character whose beautiful facade can hide such a monstrous interior is anything but reassuring. Duessa may be unmasked, uncovered, but her secrets remain present in both the equivocating descriptions and her eventual return.

The description of Duessa's body reminds us, in a way, of Claudio's vision of Hero as a "rotten orange" and Monticelso's of Vittoria as a sooty apple; for both of these men, the female body simultaneously spoke its inner truth and disguised it with a beautiful and false facade. Duessa's body is corrupt and decayed to an extent unseen in the two dramas. Her bald head is "overgrowne with scurfe," her breath "abhominably smeld," and her breasts are oozing "filthy matter" (1.8.47). Susanne Scholz writes that the representation of Duessa speaks not only to the fears that female beauty was deceptive but that the female body could, especially when belonging to a sexually active woman, house contagion. Indeed, it is hard not to notice that the description of Duessa's rotting body—with its scabs, baldness, smells, missing teeth, and general deformation—is reminiscent of those bodies afflicted with syphilis.[35] Her ability to deprive Redcrosse of his "manly forces" as he "pourd out [his wooing] in looseness" (1.7.6, 7) only heightens the sense that she poses not only a spiritual threat to his body but a sexual one as well.

Syphilis has, of course, a complicated history with each European country foisting its origins off on one another or, since it appears to be first diagnosed in the 1490s, on the New World's inhabitants. While there were numerous theories that attributed the disease to divine anger at ungodly behavior, by the seventeenth century medical specialists latched onto a theory of putrefaction whereby the disease, created in a woman's overly warm womb, was the result of too many different samples of male sperm mixing together. "The Pox is a contageous Distemper occasioned by contact and by means of a Venomous Salt, proceeding from the mixture and corruption of the seeds of divers persons received and contained in the wombs of publick women," explains French physician Nicholas de Blegny. This theory is curious for two reasons, both connected to the desire for female legibility and simple sexual narratives. First, it ascribes to women not the usual coldness but, rather, the traditionally accepted attributes of male heat generated in an action that has nothing to do with procreation and is, indeed, the opposite of reproductive activity. As such, it questions long-held ideological beliefs about humoral theory and woman's position according to it. Second, and perhaps more relevant, is that the theory clearly creates a sexually active female body that hides disease within it: "This thynge [the disease] as touchynge women resteth in theyr secrete places," wrote Ulrich von Hutten in his medical tract. Indeed, it is the woman's body that becomes the "locus of corruption."[36] The fears that the early modern writers espoused regarding the potential for a woman's body to contain a truth different from that which was visible becomes a reality in the writings about the syphilitic female body. Her sexual body is, despite all efforts, ultimately illegible and, quite possibly, deadly.

* * *

When Shakespeare's Cymbeline is told about his now-dead wife's hatred for him and her thwarted plan to murder his daughter, he asks, "Who is't can read a woman?" (*Cymbeline*, 5.5.48), admitting that he has been unable to decipher the Queen's motivations, desires, and murderous deceits. In trying to understand how he could have so severely misread her, he argues for his own otherwise infallible reading ability:

> Mine eyes
> Were not in fault, for she was beautiful;
> Mine ears, that [heard] her flattery, nor my heart,
> That thought her like her seeming. (5.5.62–65)

His initial question, in many ways, could provide a key with which to consider so many of the early modern writings, be they fictional or non-fictional, official or popular. Categorizing women as sexually voracious, as prone to dissembling, as "in her Loves more Passionate and more furious in her follies" because of her colder moister body made sense to the early moderns;[37] it was a way of organizing what could be seen as dangerous and uncontrollable. Yet, in the move to make the female body organized, codified, classified—that is to say, legible—the bodies themselves, or at least the way they were being written, seem to create their own contradictions and inconsistencies. The exterior accurately reflects the interior, except when it does not; the body's secrets can be made visible, except when they cannot; female sexual status can be read upon her face, on her body, or through her clothing, except when it cannot. Still, the desire to craft these clear, cogent sexual narratives continues throughout the period, speaking, perhaps, to an oddly optimistic belief in the very possibility of a narrative that could make women less mysterious. The project of legibility, we can claim, was unsuccessful, but the texts it produced—the portraits of sexualized female bodies—remain eminently readable.

CHAPTER THREE

Religion and Popular Beliefs

MEGAN L. HICKERSON

DUAL CLASSIFICATION

Renaissance Europeans perceived their world as harmoniously organized by a system of dual classification: all things have opposites, their differences from which depend on their core similarities.[1] In ancient Greek, medieval, and early modern thought the binary of male and female comprised the most obvious duality within this system. Thus men and women, rather than being two wholly separate sexes, are two versions of humanity so alike that their differences carry profound meaning: insofar as they differ, the qualities distinguishing them from each other are caused by virtues or assets associated with the former (strength, reason, potency, for example), but missing in the latter. In effect, woman's differences from man are privations.[2]

The Renaissance concept of dual classification, which owed its structure to Aristotle's thought, organized a system of correlative opposites in which one element is explicitly superior to the other. According to Aristotle, the binary male/female provides the basic rubric for all other opposed sets, with the male principle active, formative, and perfect, and the female passive, material, and deprived: other parallel binaries include form/matter, act/potency, perfection/imperfection, completion/incompletion, and possession/deprivation, as well as light/darkness, strength/weakness, spirit/matter, reason/unreason, and emotional control/lust.[3] In Aristotle's terms, the male of the species is nature's attempt at perfection: he is complete, active, potent, and hot, while the female is the opposite of these things, with all other of her imperfections stemming from her coldness and lack of physiological completion. Similarly, in medieval and Renaissance Christian terms, man is God's perfect creation, while woman, who is understood to be imperfect, provides the necessary physical apparatus and material allowing for procreation. Even Christ's dual nature was thought to reflect this dichotomy of male and female: as God (clearly male in Renaissance terms) gave Christ his divinity (spirit), so the human female, his mother, Mary, gave him his inferior human nature (matter).[4] In addition, the superior/inferior arrangement of the elements informing dual classification organizes a hierarchy of religious ideas associated with male and female, including God and the devil, heaven and hell, angels and demons, grace and nature, good and evil, the invisible and visible churches, "true" and "false" religion, and, ultimately, Christ and Antichrist. The female—in social relationships and in religion—is thus necessarily associated with physiologically and morally inferior concepts to those represented by the male, including flesh and fleshly concerns (such as lust and materialism), disorder, and even evil. While in social and ecclesiastical institutions such an alignment of the female with inferiority was thought to be mitigated through male control over women and their behavior, women who were outside male control provided potent and visible signs of the world turned upside down.

Along with conceptually organizing their world in dualist terms—with profound implications for the ordering of gender relationships—Renaissance Europeans frequently and festively performed deliberate inversions of conceptual opposites. Such performances required an understanding of the symbolic importance of rightly ordered opposing sets, as well as some recognition of the theoretical implications of their inversion, as essentially the breakdown of natural and social order. Concepts of dual classification and inversion were thus at the heart of ritualistic forms of social shaming like *charivari*; enactments of what Natalie Zemon Davis has described as the topos of the "woman on top"; Roman Catholic religious festivals such as Carnival or the "Feast of Fools" (characterized by deliberate, performed "misrule"); and ideas about "true" religion, "false" religion, and witchcraft. In deliberately performing inversion, as scholars such as Davis, Robert Darnton, and Peter Burke have argued, Renaissance and early modern men and women expressed frustration with existing, "natural," social hierarchies, while also reaffirming them.[5] As an essentially carnivalesque figure, for example, the *performed* "woman on top" (as Davis refers to her) subverts while also reaffirming gender norms.[6] Conversely, the "woman on top," who actually exists outside the safe boundaries of deliberate performance, threatens order and gender norms in a way that her performed counterpart does not.

The validation of social norms through the enactment of inversion is nowhere clearer than in the ritual of *charivari*, performed throughout the early modern period (c. 1350–1789) as a means of enforcing gender and other social norms.[7] In the *charivari* (called a skimmington in England), men dominated or socially embarrassed by their wives—or otherwise involved in gender relationships thought compromising to the stability of patriarchal order—were shamed through loud, public mockery. In a common form of this ritual, a male householder accompanied by a noisy crowd would be forced to ride an ass or a horse backwards as a reflection of the backwards nature of his household; illustrations of such ritual punishment often depict men being dominated by women, as in Figure 3.1. In other forms, processions of men led by "lords" ("kings" or "abbots") of misrule were either beaten with domestic items associated with women's domain (such as cutlery, pots and pans, trenchers, or household keys), or assaulted in ways suggestive of symbolic emasculation (beards pulled or genitalia kicked).[8] In both forms of *charivari*, men's neighbors mocked them in ways signifying the topsy-turvy and thus *dangerous* nature of their gendered relationships, relationships that they should have been—but

FIGURE 3.1: A skimmington. *Roxburgh Ballads,* vol. 1, p. 451.

were not—capable of managing in a manner *both* supportive of *and* symbolizing patriarchal order.

One common context for the performance of *charivari* during the early modern period was the religious festival of Carnival. In Carnival, Renaissance Europeans indulged in deliberate, organized excess, which included engaging in performances of inversion that mocked "natural" order as it existed in both public and private spheres, in preparation for the deprivation of Lent. While a number of scholars have argued that Carnival (as an example of institutionalized disorder) served to provide a release for the pent up frustration of "the people," it and other festivals like the Feast of Fools also provided a stage for performed inversion which served, in fact, to reinforce existing order. Such performance involved the appointment of lords of misrule who would direct games, races, processions, and masques such as *charivari* and various "mockings" of sieges, sermons, trials, weddings (in which the bride was a man), and even farm work (with a woman laboring to push a plow, for example). This literally was the world upside down, a festival of food and sex, but also of licensed subversion and aggression and the enactment of conflict between opposites within dichotomous sets.[9] So, for example, Carnival itself—"excess"

FIGURE 3.2: Detail, Pieter Breugel the Elder, *The Battle Between Carnival and Lent*, 1559. Kunsthistorisches Museum, Vienna. Wikimedia Commons: http://en.wikipedia.org/wiki/File:Pieter_Bruegel_d._%C3%84._066.jpg.

played by a fat, jolly man—and Lent—"deprivation" played by a thin, old woman—did battle in a context in which the topsy-turvy world of Carnival (misrule by inversion) sought to supplant the everyday. Here, social hierarchy saw reversal, with servants portrayed mastering their masters, and women mastering their husbands and stepping outside their appointed roles in various ways. Indeed, as Burke argues, "Carnival was, in short, a time of institutionalized disorder, a set of rituals of reversal…in which Folly was king."[10] And yet, disorder institutionalized is order reaffirmed—Carnival ultimately gives way to Lent. Inversion in the context of Carnival provided enactment of the absurd as *recognizably* absurd. This world in which women could be seen to dominate their menfolk (or servants their masters) was understood as a world comprising an inversion of natural order. The subversion or inversion of patriarchal order as performed *in* Carnival was reaffirmed as unnatural.

EVE AND MARY

Popular ideas about the gendering of social order—represented and affirmed by its symbolic inversion—found parallels in and were informed by religious beliefs about gender and the "problem" of women (often expressed in the genre called the *querelle des femmes*), who were theoretically both the same as and vastly different from men, being both human and yet inferior and of a substantially different nature. In the Middle Ages and Renaissance, women were believed to have been eternally disgraced through the role of the first woman, Eve, in delivering sin to the world. Christian beliefs about Eve's culpability for the Fall, and thus for all sin, were buttressed by classical ideas regarding women's essential nature, ideas that surfaced and were popular during the High Middle Ages (c. 1100–1300). For example, Galenic humoral theory suggested that unlike hot and dry men, women's imbalance of humors, which made them cold and moist, caused their insufficient development; their lack of completion was evident, for instance, in their reproductive organs, which remained internal as inversions of "perfect" externalized male organs. Women were thus misbegotten, failed, underdeveloped, and incomplete.[11] As Anthony Fletcher argues, the institutions of early modern patriarchy rested on two mutually reinforcing foundations: "the subordination required of women as punishment for Eve's sin, which was fundamental to biblical teaching, and…women's natural physical inferiority."[12] According to such thinking, certainly by implication—as Stuart Clark notes—Eve's physiological condition informed her collapse in the face of the devil's temptation: her reason was undeveloped, making her inherently contrary, lustful, emotional, and easy to tempt into sin.[13]

As the Roman Catholic Church reached the height of its institutional power in Latin Christendom, religious ideas and constructs both rationalizing and facilitating women's subordinate status grew increasingly rigid. Scholastic theologians like Thomas Aquinas (1225–74), working out of the new universities, applied Aristotelian deductive reasoning (in the context of Aristotle's own ideas about woman's imperfect nature) to the question of Eve's nature as one of an unerring God's perfect—and yet clearly imperfect—creations. As Aquinas concludes in *Summa Theologica* (1265–74):

> It seems that woman ought not to have been produced in the original production of things. For Aristotle says that the female is an incomplete version of the male. But nothing incomplete or defective should have been produced in the first establishment of things; so woman ought not to have been produced then... Only as regards nature in the individual is woman something defective and *manqué* [misbegotten]. For the active power of the seed of the male tends to produce something like itself, perfect in masculinity; but the procreation of a female is the result either of the debility of the active power, or of some unsuitability of material, or of some change effected by external influences, like the south wind, for example, which is damp, as we are told in *De generatione animalium*. But with reference to the nature of the species as a whole, the female is not something *manqué*, but is according to the plan of nature... and is directed to the work of procreation.[14]

Women, argues Aquinas, are imperfect individuals. However, they are perfect in their individual imperfection for the purpose of procreation: God did not err in his creation of Eve despite her imperfection. Thus, while explaining God's creation of the first imperfect woman—who then brought sin into the world—Aquinas affirms Aristotle's views of both her passive role in reproduction and her essential inferiority to man.

Of perhaps more importance than simply woman's difference from man—and, more particularly, Eve's difference from Adam—is the related idea of women's contrariness to men. As an opposite to (perfect) man, woman is not just different from but exactly contrary to him, and in her contrariety lies subversion not just of man, but of the principle of humanity's general good. As Joseph Swetnam described her in 1615, woman is "nothing else but a contrary unto man... because in all things there is a contrary which sheweth the difference betwixt the good and the bad."[15] And yet, even the element "Woman" carries opposites within itself—contrary "types" of women. While woman's contrary and threatening nature is universal to her sex, as individuals, women's relationships with men—principally marital and/or sexual status—provide means for categorizing them according to a positive/negative set *within* the female principle. Helpfully, the Bible provides archetypes of female "types" in the personalities (as interpreted by early Christian theologians) of first, the temptress, whose disobedience brought sin into the world, and second, the Virgin, whose obedience made her a vessel carrying man's salvation.

When it comes to the Christian legacy for ideas about women, an important implication of the story of the Fall and Adam and Eve's subsequent expulsion from Paradise is clear in rhetoric emerging from the "primitive" Christian church. For example, in an extraordinary work of misogynist rhetoric, the Christian apologist Tertullian (d. c. 220 C.E.) describes women as eternally shamed by the sin of the first woman, Eve:

> And do you not know that you are (each) an Eve? The sentence of God on this sex of yours lives in this age: the guilt must of necessity live too. *You* are the devil's gateway: *you* are the unsealer of that (forbidden) tree: *you* are the first deserter of the divine law: *you* are she who persuaded him whom the devil was not valiant enough to attack. *You* destroyed so easily God's image, man. On account of *your* desert—that is, death—even the Son of God had to die.[16]

Woman lives Eve's legacy and by it should be shamed. Woman-as-Eve was thus viewed within the Christian paradigm, with ambivalence and fear, as lascivious, garrulous, and disobedient. The solution to the problem of woman, however, inherent to this discourse, lies in women's acceptance of Eve's punishment for her transgression in Eden: pain and sorrow in childbirth, desire for her husband, and subjection to his will (Genesis 3:16). Woman's responsibility, according to the paradigm centralizing Eve as the prototype for all women, is to submit in her shame to male authority, living the image of ideal Renaissance womanhood, described by Ruth Kelso as "chaste, silent, and obedient."[17]

Ideas about Eve articulated in the second century survived into the Middle Ages, the Renaissance, and the Reformation. Even apart from increasingly available vernacular versions of the Genesis story, medieval and contemporary Genesis-based literature in Latin and vernacular languages circulated widely during the sixteenth century throughout both Catholic and Protestant countries, influenced by early Christian poetry and polemic casting Eve as the agent of human sin and as an impious wife to the exceptional Adam (despite occasional nuanced expressions of her beauty or feelings of guilt).[18]

Sixteenth- and seventeenth-century iconography often went so far as to depict a number of "monstrous" creatures as female, including the serpent in the Garden of Eden, sometimes clearly paired with Eve in ways suggesting homoeroticism. As Samantha Riches suggests, "Eve is thus damned on all counts, as a weak woman who fell, as a temptress who beguiled an innocent man, and as a sexualized creature in pursuit of inappropriate, hedonistic pleasure."[19]

There is, however, an available counterpart to Eve: the saint by whose emulation individual women could partially mitigate woman's salacious nature.[20] This is the Virgin Mary, the biblical woman most explicitly conforming to the ideological bent of Eve's punishment involving obedience to men and redemption through childbirth. Mary, a clearly contrary figure to Eve, is Christianity's archetype of female sanctity. And yet, her image also serves, like Eve's, to reflect Christian ambivalence towards women and particularly towards women's sexuality. Mary's sameness *to* Eve—as woman and thus as the embodiment of fleshly sin—necessarily informs the significance of her difference *from* Eve, that difference located in her singular separation from the taint of human sexuality. As Marina Warner has argued, the idea of Mary's virginity was so important to the fathers of the early church that it overrode even scripture (which does not cast Christ's mother as a perpetual virgin).[21] The Virgin's image and cult, actively promoted by the Catholic Church during the late Middle Ages and Renaissance, provided women with both a model for "holy" celibacy as a life choice and a focus for comfort in the painful and dangerous experience of childbirth. However, it also foregrounded Mary, not just as a virgin and not just as a mother but as both: as a *virgin* mother, impossible for real women to emulate, whose distance from sexuality is so important that she is ultimately cast as immaculately conceived herself. Thus despite acting as an intercessor and/or idealized model for women in Catholic Christendom, Mary was nevertheless quite far from providing a *realistic* model for female behavior or penitence, or even an alternative to women's sinful nature as represented by Eve. Instead, while becoming the mirror image of and model for the celibate nun, the Virgin represents an ideal according to which the natural female condition is inherently flawed, and female sexuality, including natural motherhood, represents sinful concupiscence: even within marriage, according to this paradigm, women cannot be pure unless they reject their sexuality altogether.[22]

Contemporaneously with the cult of the Virgin during the late Middle Ages and Renaissance, the figure of Mary Magdalene also grew significantly in popularity.[23] And yet, while no biblical text suggests that any of the figures from whom the character Mary Magdalene was constructed (Mary of Bethany, Mary of Magdala, and a female sinner) were prostitutes or former prostitutes,

FIGURE 3.3: Michelangelo Buonarotti, *Adam and Eve*. Sistine Chapel, Vatican. Courtesy of Art Resource, ART 214644.

FIGURE 3.4: Lucas Cranach the Elder, *Adam and Eve*. Private collection.

as a cult figure Mary Magdalene is most significant as the latter and thus as a fallen female penitent.[24] Providing an alternative both to Eve (the occasion of original sin) and to the Virgin (who helps redeem the world through an act no human female can emulate), the Magdalene exists in church tradition not only a woman specially favored by Christ but also as a woman both fallen, like Eve, through the lust so characteristic of her sex, and redeemed—in a manner analogous to an idea of Mary's redemption of all Eve's daughters—through rejection of her sexuality.

The rejection of female sexuality centralized in both Marys—virgin mother and penitent whore—is related to a broader idealization of the rejection of the flesh characterizing primitive Christianity, which is influenced by both Neoplatonic understanding of bodily desire as impeding knowledge of God, and classical traditions identifying flesh with the female principle and spirit with the male.[25] The imperative to virginity as both sacrifice and route to female redemption for female sin, in tandem with the explicit example of Christ's chaste and obedient mother, also informs most of the *vitae sanctarum* (written lives of female saints) of holy women popular during the late Middle Ages and Renaissance, many of which were gathered in the thirteenth century in Jacobus Voragine's *Legendum Aurea* (*The Golden Legend*, written in Latin and translated into various vernacular languages). The stories (and the cults inspired by them) are principally of virgin martyrs (only five of Voragine's forty-one female martyrs—not including St Ursula's 11,000 virgins—were ever married), whose devotion to Christ (whom they marry in death as chaste brides—*sponsa Christi*) was, according to their *vitae*, proven in their vows of lifelong virginity. Indeed, the primary mark identifying these women as Christians is virginity, not confession.[26] In a typical *vita*, the female martyr's persecution begins due to her refusal to marry, with specifics of her faith—which she rarely expresses beyond identifying herself as a Christian—secondary to her commitment to virginity. Even those female martyrs who are not virgins have, by their deaths, almost always become celibate. To the horror of later Protestant polemicists, they reject their spouses, and thus their sexual lives, for Christ.[27]

THE PROTESTANT REFORMATION

Popular female saints of the late Middle Ages and Renaissance, as models of female sexuality rejected, typify, like Mary, the ideal Christian woman: they are "chaste, silent, and obedient." It is important, however, to see in these models of female sanctity distinct contrariety to the "other" woman—Eve—as part of a paradigm of femaleness which grew increasingly rigid as western Europe experienced growing religious division, as well as demographic, economic, and political strain. Following from the Protestant and Catholic Reformations, fears associated with imagined, autonomous female power, emerging against a backdrop of social and political instability, contributed to the creation of a context in which women were increasingly seen either as (good) wives—including, in Catholic areas, as "brides of Christ"—or as (bad) whores. The "good" was thought to shore up a patriarchal order in crisis, while the "bad" typified dangerous disorder, representing—as inversions of virtuous womanhood—the "world turned upside down."

The impact of the Protestant and then Catholic Reformations on women has been a matter of some vigorous debate since the 1980s.[28] Popular views of the Protestant Reformation as essentially progressive have necessarily also involved considering it as having had a positive impact on women and their autonomy, as, for example, according to Steven Ozment's analysis of German Protestantism as liberation from late medieval, Catholic, "antifeminism."[29] Nevertheless, much significant recent scholarship describes an increased limitation on European women's autonomy and freedom of movement during the sixteenth and seventeenth centuries in Protestant *and* Catholic Europe; according to such analysis, both Protestant and Catholic Reformations were domesticated according to remarkably similar misogynist theologies of gender.

While an assessment of the Protestant Reformation's practical impact on women is inevitably complicated by issues such as specific confession, social status, occupation, age, and region, it is nevertheless clear that interpretations suggesting that Protestantism served to weaken or mitigate traditional Christian misogyny are flawed. For example, in *The Holy Household: Women and Morals in Reformation Augsburg* (1989), perhaps the most influential book-length study addressing the impact on women of the magisterial Reformation, Lyndal Roper successfully demonstrates that Protestants (in this case in Augsburg) domesticated reform through a "reinscribing of women within the 'family,'" where the Protestant family was modeled on the household-based craft workshop.[30] Such family structure—both domestic and occupational—operated both within the framework of the patriarchal marriage and under the absolute authority of the patriarch. Following the Reformation, this was the model for the operation of all society: thus, those who fell outside the confines of patriarchal marriage were likely to be considered threatening to social and spiritual order. According to Roper, marriage was thought both to reflect and to provide stability to broader social order: "[l]ike other sanctified relations of authority and submission," she argues, "marriage was conceived in bilateral terms: the governance of the husband was counterpoised to the subordination of the wife, who ought to 'obey him as her head.'" As she concludes, "This paradigm of the relations between the sexes so saturated Reformation thinking that the discourse of wifehood began to displace that of womanhood altogether."[31]

Because the politics of marriage was central to the institutionalization of the magisterial Reformation—to its transformation from disorderly subversion to the religion of society—the perceived threat of sexual disorder increased, with women bearing the brunt of that shift. In response to interpretations like Ozment's, Roper, Susan Karant-Nunn, and others have argued that the fact that Protestant reformers tended to view marriage in positive terms does not equate to a weakening among Protestants of misogynist ideas about women. Indeed, the Reformation's extreme emphasis on patriarchal marriage seems to have contributed to a straightening of categories of identity available to women such that unmarried women were now seen as agents and symbols of disorder, necessarily deviant.[32] One result of this was the closing of many cities' brothels, previously regulated and tolerated as contributing *to* social order.[33] Crucially, now prostitutes, rather than operating as a separate category of dishonorable but non-criminal women, came to symbolize women who were outside the male-headed family, and so, by extension, also disorder and lust. In effect, with the institutionalization of Protestantism, the whore—symbolically opposed not just to the "good" woman but to the entire patriarchal ethic—became a "moral category" rather than a social entity.[34] Since Protestantism fundamentally distrusted women who operated outside marriage, whether living alone or within female communities like convents or béguinages (religiously focused communities of laywomen), all such women came to be viewed through the Protestant lens as whores, leading to a popular and institutional status quo according to which women were categorized in dualist terms, *either* as wives *or* as whores: opposites to each other and yet, because they were all women, also the same as each other.[35] And yet, differences between these two types of women were enhanced by the types' very likeness, for any early modern woman could easily be tarnished with the accusation of whoredom: as the English Protestant polemicist John Bale put it, "a whore at first blush seemeth only a woman."[36]

The importance of female domesticity to magisterial Protestantism detected by scholars like Roper and Karant-Nunn, as well as by Merry Wiesner, myself, and others, reflects both early modern commitment to the idea of a binary cosmos divided into male and female properties and specific ideas about women's nature characterizing the thought of reformers like Martin Luther.[37] Wiesner notes:

> The word Luther uses again and again in his descriptions of this ideal woman is *natural*... What is "natural" for Luther comes both from what

he views basic human nature to be, and from the order he feels God imposed on the world. Women's subjection to men is inherent in their very being and was present from creation—in this Luther essentially agrees with Aristotle and the classical tradition...This subjection was made more brutal and harsh, however, because of Eve's responsibility for the Fall—in this Luther agrees with the patristic tradition...Obedience had replaced chastity as women's prime virtue...Marriage and motherhood, instead of virginity, was now a woman's highest calling...Men choosing to remain celibate were going against their natural sexual drive, but Luther does allow that the ability to remain truly celibate, though rare, could be a gift from God. Women choosing to remain celibate, however, were not only fighting their natural sex drive, which Luther and everyone else in the sixteenth century felt to be much stronger than men's, but also the divinely imposed order which made woman subject to man. For Luther it was inconceivable that a woman would choose not to marry.[38]

Similarly, John Calvin stressed what scholars call the "double subjection" of women following from Eve's sin. Created, according to Calvin, to be subject in the first instance to male authority, Eve was then punished for her responsibility for the Fall by having her natural subjugation to Adam, and thus all women's subjugation to men, made more severe.[39] The emphasis on the example of Eve present in such magisterial Protestant thought is critical: along with demoting celibacy from a superior state to marriage (and posing celibacy and marriage as diametrically opposed to each other in terms of their moral value), Luther and many other reformers tended against emphasizing the Virgin Mary and other, usually virgin, female saints as important indicators of women's natural potential (or indeed, as models for female emulation).[40] While Mary was an ambiguous model for Catholic women, she nevertheless served as the "best" in a "best/worst woman" dichotomy permeating Catholic Christian thought. Thus, while her *obedience* still elicited some praise from Protestant polemicists, her demotion from the extraordinary status she enjoyed in Catholic Christendom left emphasis on Eve as the principal archetypical Protestant woman: she is the root of all sin, without a comparably important positive female biblical figure to serve as counterweight. Post-lapsarian Eve became a contrary figure only to the innocent Adam; as Wiesner remarks, "Luther's de-emphasis of the role of Mary...thus stressed the negative side of all women's 'nature.'"[41]

The magisterial Protestant construction of women and their relationships with men, according to which women were systematically both reinscribed in households under male authority and measured according to a rigid and limiting dichotomy, informs interpretations of the century following the Reformation (c. 1540–1650) as witnessing what some historians have called a "crisis in gender relations." This is a term Roper uses to describe the impact of Protestant thought on female and (as important) male identity, linked to the Protestant rejection of an ideal of lifelong celibacy for either men or women. Indeed, with the Reformation came intellectual associations in Protestant thought between the institution of clerical celibacy and what was deemed by reformers to be rampant Roman Catholic whoredom (with avowed clerical celibacy instituted as a cover for sexual deviance), but also between Catholic clergy and men feminized as disorderly women, including in their supposed engagement with "unnatural" sexual behavior.[42] Thus, in Protestantism, the emphasis on the sanctity of marriage, along with the ethic of orderly, patriarchal marriage, served to buttress an idea of masculinity as proven through the imposition of male sexual and social authority over women—all women. Women outside male control were thought of not only as individually disorderly but also as sexually aggressive, transgressive symbols of emasculation, and therefore as subversive of a form of authority associated with "true" religion.

And yet, some recent scholarship has also argued for a broad "crisis of patriarchy" across both Protestant and Catholic Europe (c. 1550–1650), stemming from a number of destabilizing and mutually reinforcing phenomena: new religious division, the priorities of centralizing monarchies, demographic change, climate change, scarcity of resources, and early forms of capitalism. Thus, while the idea of a gender crisis (and/or crisis of patriarchy) necessarily interacts in Protestant areas with the issue of the Reformation's impact on women and female autonomy, as a phenomenon it was neither Protestant nor Catholic, to either's exclusion of the other.[43] Indeed, while a number of scholars have applied themselves to considering the impact of Protestantism on women and ideas about them, others have constructed a model according to which both Protestant and Catholic parts of Europe during the period of the Reformation saw increasingly rigid restriction of women's movement and autonomy. Significantly, it was during the Catholic Counter-Reformation, for example, that the mandatory cloistering called for in a papal bull issued by Boniface VIII, *Periculoso* (1298), found reassertion and widespread (if still incomplete) enforcement. Not only convents but tertiary and other communities of laywomen acting in service to the public or as missionaries were theoretically to be either dissolved or enclosed, according to the late decree (XXV) of the Council of Trent (1545–1563), which met partly in response to the Protestant challenge; such enclosure was subsequently reaffirmed in the bull *Circa*

Pastoralis (1566) by Pope Pius V. The purpose of this was to protect the chastity of women linked to the Church, especially in light of the Protestant claim that clerical celibacy served as a cloak for whoredom. In this, Tridentine enclosure served a propagandistic purpose that had been absent when Boniface VIII first issued *Periculoso;* and yet, as Francesca Medioli notes, behind the decision at Trent to reaffirm and enforce Boniface's earlier call for enclosure also lay an "underlying philosophy" revealed in a proverb circulating during the Renaissance, *aut virum, aut murum* (either a man or a wall).[44]

In the parts of Europe that remained Roman Catholic during the period of the Renaissance and Reformation, not just female *religieuse* but also laywomen experienced a constriction of their life options outside marriage, finding themselves facing stricter enclosure than they had before the mid-sixteenth century. In Seville, for example, Mary Elizabeth Perry argues, the city's response to various factors exemplifying "patriarchy in crisis," including increasing attempts by the Counter-Reformation Catholic Church to impose orthodoxy, was to enhance the authority of the local political system (closed to women), increase the number of guild regulations (excluding women or restricting their activities), and importantly, to enclose them: "for officials of this period," Perry asserts, "restoration of the social order required the sword of authority repaired and the wandering woman restrained."[45] This involved a re-categorization as especially threatening of women living "outside respectability." Here, as in many parts of western Europe, the "order-restoration function of gender" became "especially visible," with "evil" women—those operating contrary to the natural God-Man-Woman hierarchy—cast as carrying the potential to destroy the social order. As in reformed Protestant areas, Catholic reform applied a "theology of purity" to the social sphere, according to which the "good" and "true" were equated with "conformity to gender expectations," especially by women: in an echo of *Periculoso*, Perry concludes, the women of Counter-Reformation Seville thus "required special enclosure...for they had to be protected from their own weakness, and society had to be protected from their propensity for disorder." As in Augsburg, so in Seville: women—good and bad—were hidden behind the walls of homes, convents, and brothels.[46] "If any Reformation was successful in the sixteenth century," concludes Merry Wiesner, "it was that 'of the women' in the first sense, a restriction of women's sphere in independent actions and an increase in the power of male heads of households, both temporal and spiritual."[47]

The argument over the impact of the Reformation on women seems, therefore, no longer to hinge on the question of which confession, Roman Catholic or Protestant, was more initially restrictive; instead, some consensus now exists that both Reformations had a deleterious effect on women's autonomy. In Counter-Reformation Catholic Christendom, concerns over internal unity, sociopolitical stability, and the institutional legitimacy of the church contributed to an effort to ensure stability and moral purity by enclosing religious and laywomen. In the case of Protestantism, the rejection of clerical celibacy, while in Lutheran terms freeing women and men from an unnatural, imposed, and sin-facilitating "virginity," seems also to have accompanied an enhanced emphasis on patriarchal authority within the household. It certainly does not reflect a decline among Protestant reformers of misogynist attitudes towards women's corrupt, lustful nature, as some scholars have previously suggested. Perhaps more significantly, the rejection of an ideal of lifelong virginity for women (and men) in Protestant Europe operated hand in glove with the promotion of marriage as a woman's (and a man's) only natural destiny. Thus women functioning outside patriarchal marriage—including those inhabiting convents—were categorized in terms previously reserved for prostitutes.

ECCLESIA AND THE WHORE OF BABYLON

The Protestant re-categorization of women finds its way into literature that poses not just two types of women against each other, but also two types of men and—signified as two types of women—two types of churches. As the ethic of Protestant marriage enhanced the authority of the male head of family, Reformation polemic also sets him against the Protestant *image of* the Roman Catholic priest, who is, in turn, portrayed as an essentially feminized figure, rejecting the responsibility and power associated with masculinity in order to debauch other men's wives and daughters, and even other men. As such, male Catholic clergy join Catholic nuns in Protestant rhetoric as something akin to disorderly women: not only are they opposed, as non-men, to Protestant men *qua* men, they are also opposed, as actual whores within the category *woman*, to good, virtuous women. And just as the Catholic clergy is feminized as the wrong female type, so is the church itself: both Catholic clergy and the false "holy mother church" are depicted as whores, female and unmarried despite pretentions to *sponsa Christi*, opposed to the "true" church of magisterial Protestantism which is the chaste bride of Christ, submissive the way a good wife should be to her divine, firm but loving husband.[48] John Bale and John Foxe, for example, two important Tudor English Protestant polemicists, produced histories of the "true church" according to which she (as *Ecclesia*) appears as a chaste bride of Christ, standing against the "false" church embodied as the whore of Babylon, or *Pornopolis* (city of whores), as Foxe calls her in his play *Christus Triumphans* (1556). Along with other images of female monsters representing either the papacy or the Roman Catholic Church, images of the papacy as the Whore of Babylon abound in exegeses of Revelation (like Bale's), in martyrology, and in Protestant bibles produced in vernacular languages. Such images inscribe upon renderings of the Whore of Babylon as a woman seated on the seven-headed beast trappings associating her with the Roman Catholic Church, and even more clearly with the papacy. While even the woodcut of the Whore of Babylon produced by Albrecht Durer for his (pre-Reformation) 1498 Apocalypse has been interpreted as anti-papal, later Protestant images explicitly portray an association between the Whore and the papacy. For example, like Whores proliferating in other forms of Protestant literature, Lucas Cranach's Whore, as she appears in Martin Luther's German bibles of 1522 and 1534, wears a papal tiara. In addition, king's kneel before her; thus she embodies not just Protestant fears of the papal antichrist, but also mirrors, in her inappropriate ascendency over men, the pope's antichristian dominance over secular authority.

Such characterization of the Catholic Church by Protestant polemicists took place in a context in which both Catholics and Protestants feared the destruction of "true" Christian religion, while also often anticipating the "end of days" described in the New Testament book of Revelation. Protestant historians chronicling the history of the "true" church saw persecution of "true" Christians, within an increasingly persecuting society, as indicative of an approaching apocalypse in line with Revelation 6. They sought to identify Antichrist and found him inhabiting the Catholic Church, embodied as the Whore of Babylon.[49] In fact, the Roman Catholic Church as the Whore of Babylon is both partnered with (as in Foxe's *Christus Triumphans*) and conflated with Antichrist: as a female figure symbolizing the inversion of the natural order, she—the ultimate "woman on top"—serves the end, like all inversion, of destroying (specifically) Christian civilization. As the whore represents the opposite of virtuous womanhood, and thus right social order reversed, so the Whore of Babylon as Antichrist represents an opposite to Christ, or true religion reversed. Contributing to the potency of this construct is, again, the Protestant view of clerical celibacy as both a veil for whoredom and a sign of Antichrist's invasion of the church: individual Catholic whores serve the great whore, Antichrist, who is both the Whore of Babylon and the Roman Catholic Church. Thus, for women, convent life—the only real alternative to marriage prior to the Reformation—is not only rejected in a model of Protestant domesticity but is also explicitly cast as whoredom and service to Antichrist, contrary both to virtuous womanhood and to Christian religion. Symbolically,

FIGURE 3.5: Albrecht Dürer, woodcut, *Whore of Babylon*, 1497–98. Staatliche Kunsthalle, Karlsruhe. Wikimedia Commons: http://commons.wikimedia.org/wiki/File:Woman_of_Babylon_by_Durer.jpg.

this is true of all life choices for women outside chaste marriage and ultimately motherhood. The wrong type of woman—like the wrong type of clergyman—represents not just social disorder, but outright service to Satan and the destruction of Christendom.

If one sign of the Roman Catholic Church's whoredom, and thus service to Antichrist, lies in the institution of clerical celibacy, the other principal sign of Antichrist's presence in the Church, according to Protestant polemic, is its usurpation of secular authority. So the Whore of Babylon not only stars as the papal church in Reformation polemic but she is also shown towering over kneeling kings eager to sip at her "cup of fornication" and submit themselves and their realms to her authority. While the church's claims to authority over princes was a long-standing political issue in Catholic Christendom, images such as the ones found in Bale's *Image* or Luther's New Testament enhance, through the gendering of the figures in question, what they see as the inverted nature of a church-state relationship with the church ascendant: not only is the church *as* church wielding misappropriated power, but in such portrayal, a woman also presides, quite unnaturally, over men kneeling before her. She has achieved her ascendency through seduction—the exercise of sexual power, symbolized by her "cup of fornication," as is depicted in Foxe's *Christus Triumphans*.[50] In England, for example, where royal power dramatically posed itself in opposition to papal usurpation, contributing to the construction of much-discussed English anti-popery, the distinctly female Whore of Babylon became a symbol, as Frances Dolan has effectively argued, not just of papal usurpation but also of foreign, and yet also frighteningly domestic, danger.[51]

So potent became the linked constructs of male authority (as a mirror of royal authority and thus social order) and royal authority over the church (mirroring the orderly household and thus, again, social order) that during the years immediately preceding the Glorious Revolution in England (1688–89), popular literature produced in the context of severe conflict between the new "Tory" and "Whig" political parties deployed explicitly gendered imagery to describe the proper ordering of church and state. And yet, even despite intra-Protestant wrangling and dramatic mutual antipathy between parties, British Protestants, whether Whig or Tory, Anglican or dissenting, cast the state/church hierarchy in terms modeling the patriarchal household. In the broadside *Babel and Bethel*, for example, published in 1679 during the period of popular, English Protestant anxiety known as the "Popish Plot," the king, Charles II (1660–85), sits enthroned next to "Rome's Scarlet Whore" (as she is described in the text accompanying the image). The Whore wears a papal tiara and holds a large set of keys, both of which symbolize the pope's presumed power to loose and bind souls on earth and in heaven and thus the basis of his (mis-)assigned secular/temporal authority. She (for this pope is a she) reclines in a languid pose, as two princes kneel with their heads bowed before her. She holds two swords along with her keys, symbolizing her claim to spiritual authority, but also her usurpation of temporal power over the princes who submit to her authority. Adding to the eroticism of the image of the provocatively posed female pope, the only visible tool of royal authority is a scepter shared by and held between the two kings, placed suggestively between the Whore's legs and yet clearly set at a lower, subordinate level both to her and to the signifiers of her power: she is dominant, both magisterially and sexually.

Meanwhile, on the "Bethel" side of the image, the English king points his own phallic scepter at a kneeling woman wearing a church on her head, much like a hat. She is in a submissive posture, hands raised as if in supplication to the king; indeed, she is, as the accompanying text reads, "like Esther" before the Persian king Ahasuerus (Xerxes) in tendering "Her Supplications to the Faiths Defender [sic]." For what does she plead? In this case for the execution of papist traitors and thus the defense of the Protestant faith, which she represents as an opposite to the woman seated at a direct diagonal from herself. As the enthroned woman, identified as "Rome's Scarlet whore" and adorned as the pope, represents the papal church, so the kneeling woman, identified as Esther and literally wearing the church, represents true religion: she is *Ecclesia*, the true church.

Significantly, the respective status of these two female churches—as either "true" or "false"—is explicitly linked to their postures relative to the royal men paired with them as representing either "Babel" or "Bethel." While the

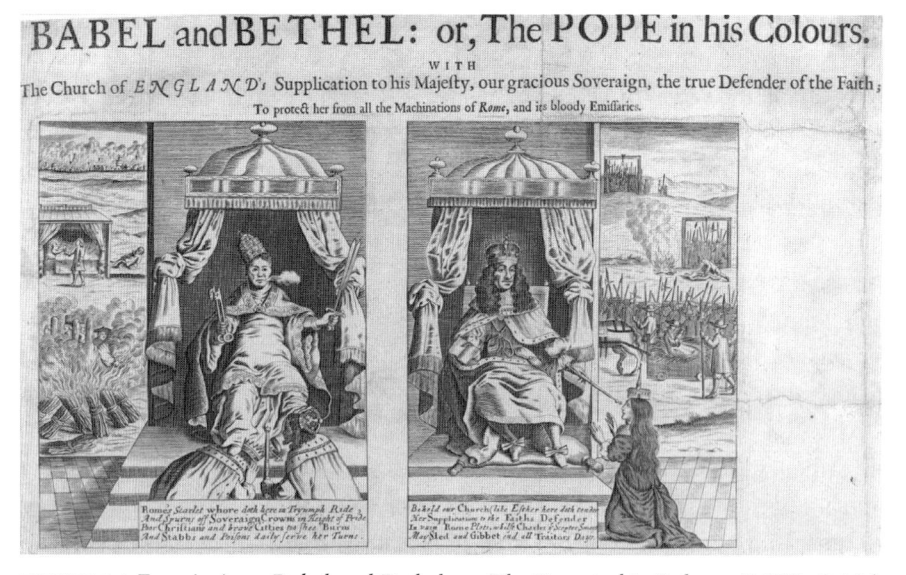

FIGURE 3.6: Frontispiece, *Babel and Bethel: or, The Pope in his Colours* (1679). British Museum, London.

subject of this broadside is on one level simply expressive of the long-debated question in Latin Europe regarding the right relationship between spiritual and temporal authority (certainly nothing new to the early modern period), it is nevertheless notable that in expressing anxiety over this relationship, early modern religious and political polemicists routinely enhanced their descriptions of the right order of royal and ecclesiastical authority by deploying gendered imagery and metaphor: if an ascendant pope troubles, an ascendant female pope troubles even more. Charles, meanwhile, resplendent in his royal estate, embodies appropriate, patriarchal manhood in his dominion—magisterial, but also discernible as both social and sexual. Notably, his phallic scepter points down towards its owner's kneeling, female subject and, as Esther, even his bride (Esther was married to Xerxes). In this, Charles sits as an inversion of the kings positioned at a direct diagonal from him, whose shared scepter serves symbolically to enhance their subordinate status. They are weak, submissive, and emasculated, while he is strong, ascendant, and virile. There are thus three sets of pairs contained within this broadside: those of Bethel and Babel, with the latter element representing the world turned upside down and, indeed, the destruction of Christendom; those of Charles II and the kings of Babel, with the latter representing the world turned upside down and, indeed, the destruction of Christendom; and those of the two female churches, "our Church" (as it is described in the text) and the papal Whore, with the latter representing the world turned upside down and, indeed, the destruction of Christendom.

WITCHES

It seems an inescapable conclusion that relationships existed between new European religious division, the "crisis of patriarchy" and fears of an upturned world associated with the century between about 1550 and 1650, and the European "witch craze" occurring during the same period.[52] The breakdown of "universal" Latin "Christendom" provides the necessary context for a century of religious war, which, in turn, contributed to the emergence of what historians call confessionalization: a status quo according to which religious conformity to state churches under state control, within developing sovereign nation-states, was required of subjects as a show of loyalty. In addition, demographic change, endemic warfare, and economic instability all contributed to concerns over the stability of the patriarchal order, the foundation of which was male control over women: again, the belief that orderly women under male control both represent and contribute to social order hinged on the related idea that disorderly women represent social disorder.[53] In this context, witches served as particular threats, not just as diabolical enemies to Christian civilization but as powerful women operating outside of and above male control.

Witches *qua* witches were armed by the devil to fight Christian civilization; in nation-states whose stability rested on the twin and mutually reinforcing pillars of centralization and confessionalization, this meant they also threatened the political order. In addition, as inappropriately powerful women, they threatened the social order, which in the context of a "crisis of patriarchy" also meant they threatened the political order. As both witches and disorderly women, therefore, witches had to be dealt with by godly magistrates; as Stuart Clark has argued, not only was witch belief inseparable from broader early modern conceptions and fears of disorder, witchcraft prosecution was seen as a critical test of political legitimacy. This was particularly so in a context in which authority was seen as divinely appointed (and maintained). Indeed, the danger of this particular threat to order rested exactly in the equivalence (as contrary figures) of witches to godly magistrates, the former serving the devil and the latter serving God. As Clark notes, "demons and witches became the perfect antagonists of those who claimed power by divine right, since their defeat could only result from supernatural, not physical superiority ... symmetry [between servants of God and the servants of the devil] was as important as their opposition."[54]

However, witch belief should also be seen as a dramatic example of the implications of ideas about women and their nature associated with the paradigmatic concept of dual classification. Early modern witch belief hinged on the notion that to invert natural order was to destabilize, and that those who sought such inversion were in league to destroy order and ultimately, therefore, Christian civilization. In a context in which religious division and then religious war caused severe anxiety about "true" Christianity under siege, those who represented the antithesis of order easily came under suspicion. Anxiety over a series of imagined inversions of right order (threatening, among other things, patriarchal order) thus led to a specific form of prosecuting of women believed to have agreed to a pact with Satan. Importantly, this aid to him in his conflict with Christianity provided women (as an exchange) with exactly the kind of power that made them particularly dangerous: the power to act according to their natural impulses.

While the Protestant and Catholic Reformations did not create either witch belief or the belief in witchcraft, Catholic perception that being a witch was a crime in itself (rather than requiring a crime of action in the form of *maleficium*, or harmful magic) emerged during the late fifteenth century, when Catholic Christendom was affected by increasingly widespread heresy and noisy anticlericalism. While some scholars have warned against exaggerating the significance of the notorious *Malleus Maleficarum* (written by the Dominican inquisitors Heinrich Kramer and Jacob Sprenger [1486]) in forming early modern thought about witches, nevertheless this text certainly reflects the ease with which movement between anxiety about witches and the identification of women as witches took place. The *Malleus*, which came two years after Pope Innocent VIII re-categorized all witches as heretics—enemies to Christianity and the church, whose magical power must come from the devil since it does not come from the church—employs topoi according to which women's essential natures, as inheritors of Eve, make them easy targets for the devil's snare. Women, in their related lusts for sex, autonomy, and revenge, turn to Satan for access to all these things, fornicating with him and serving his anti-Christian purpose in exchange for inappropriate power:

> As for the first question, why a greater number of witches is founding the fragile feminine sex than among men…the first [reason] is that they are more credulous; and since the chief aim of the devil is to corrupt faith, therefore he rather attacks them…The second reason is, that women are naturally more impressionable, and more ready to receive the influence of a disembodied spirit…The third reason is that they have slippery tongues, and are unable to conceal from their fellow-women those things which by evil arts they know…But the natural reason is that she is more carnal than a man, as is clear from her many carnal abominations. And it should be noted that there was a defect in the formation of the first woman, since she was formed from a bent rib, that is, a rib of the breast, which is bent as it were in a contrary direction to a man. And since through this defect she is an imperfect animal, she always deceives…And as to her other mental quality, that is, her natural will; when she hates someone whom she formerly loved, then she seethes with anger and impatience in her whole soul, just as the tides of the sea are always heaving and boiling…No might of the flames or of the swollen winds, no deadly weapon, is so much to be feared as the lust and hatred of a woman who has been divorced from the marriage bed…And indeed, just as through the first defect in their intelligence they are more prone to abjure the faith; so through their second defect of inordinate affections and passions they search for, brood over, and inflict various vengeances, either by witchcraft, or by some other means. Wherefore it is no wonder that so great a number of witches exist in this sex…To conclude. All witchcraft comes from carnal lust, which is in women insatiable.[55]

Woman, defective from her first creation, is imperfect and thus naturally deceptive, vengeful, garrulous, prone to hate, and, most of all, sexually insatiable. Thus, like Eve herself, she provides an easier target for the devil than the man Adam. In drawing women in this way—and particularly their relationship with witchcraft—Kramer and Sprenger echoed popular ideas about women, and their work also foreshadows descriptions of women as witches that followed over the next two centuries not just in Catholic but also in Protestant Europe. As these Dominican inquisitors described the woman witch in 1486, so the Protestant Englishman Alexander Roberts described her in 1608:

> This sex, when it conceiveth wrath or hatred...is unplacable, possessed with unsatiable desire of revenge, and transported with appetite to right (as they thinke) the wrongs offered unto them: and when their power herein answereth not their will, and are meditating with themselves how to effect their mischievous projects and designes, the Divell taketh the occasion, who knoweth in what manner to content exulcerated mindes, windeth himselfe into their hearts, offereth to teach them the meanes by which they may bring to pass that rancor which was nourished in their breasts, and offereth his helpe and furtherance herein.[56]

Witchcraft, as understood by early modern men and women, is an inversion of Christianity, most frequently participated in by inversions of human and Christian perfection:[57] for the witch, Satan replaces God, evil replaces virtue, the witches' *sabat* replaces the mass, demons' actions replace angels' actions, witches' actions replace the virtuous behavior and ministration of godly men, and so on. In this context of Christianity inverted—of witchcraft as anti-religion—witches operated both as inversions of "good" women—even going so far as to kill babies rather than fulfill their natural purpose as mothers—and as inversions of the male clergy who dominated Protestant and Catholic institutions.

Witches were therefore clearly inversions of what women should be, but this does not express the full extent of early modern anxiety regarding the operation of gender in witch belief. Since women (according to the concept of dual classification) are contraries to men, with the effect that even deviant men can be cast as bad women (as we have seen in Protestant discourse regarding the Catholic clergy), in the world upside down the opposite also applies: women who defy their natural roles can appear as men, or rather as "other" than women. The iconography and literature exhibiting this in the case of witches, for example, tends to invert the meaning of symbols associated with female domesticity and "natural" womanhood on the one hand, and male power on the other, often through parody. For example, in Hans Baldung Grien's woodcut, *The Bewitched Groom* (1544), the torch-wielding witch triumphs over not just the groom but also the tool and symbol of his masculine occupation and male identity, his pitchfork. Rendered impotent, it lies under its equally impotent, unconscious master, while the horse's backward glance confirms the topsy-turvy nature of the scene (the very presence of the horse, as a symbol of masculinity, serves to enhance this meaning): here is an inversion of right order caused by the witch's inappropriate seizure of power.

Witches' seemingly relentless determination to subvert natural order abounds in text and image, in parodic depiction of their relationships with men, with other women, with their own bodies, and with children. The "witch's teat," for example, by which witches were believed to nurse their demonic familiars, parodies the natural function of lactation, by which women feed their children; their power to render men impotent and their tendency to kill babies, both described in great detail in the *Malleus*, parody women's reproductive purpose; and in iconography, the frequent presence of brooms—positioned either in erotically suggestive ways or in ways either reflecting or enhancing a witch's power—parodies the idea of brooms as symbolic of female domesticity, of women's role both *in* the household and *inside* the home. In addition, while the broom in its right use is a tool of a "natural" woman's trade conducted indoors, it either frees unnatural women—as witches—from what should be their proper, enclosed sphere, or otherwise conquers masculinity (and thus patriarchal order), just as does the witch's power to interfere with male potency.

In addition to parodying, and thus inverting the meaning of symbols traditionally associated with appropriate women's roles, early modern images of witches often explicitly masculinize their bodies, essentially portraying *female* witches as men. For example, in Albrecht Dürer's *The Witch* (c. 1500), the eponymous subject has long flowing hair and breasts and holds a broom, all these things serving to identify her as a woman. And yet, many elements also serve to undermine the impression of the witch as *legitimately* a woman. First, she sits astride a ram (a symbol of both male sexuality and the devil), but backwards in a manner reminiscent of *charivari*, the ritualistic punishment of men who allow upsetting of the proper gender order in their households: thus, her pose—like *charivari*—both suggests and critiques inversion, and specifically inversion of the gender order. To add to this effect, as the witch sits she holds a broom that should symbolize her feminine domesticity, but is instead provocatively placed in a manner intended to evoke the phallic as it protrudes in front of her from between her legs; the eroticism of this positioning is also enhanced

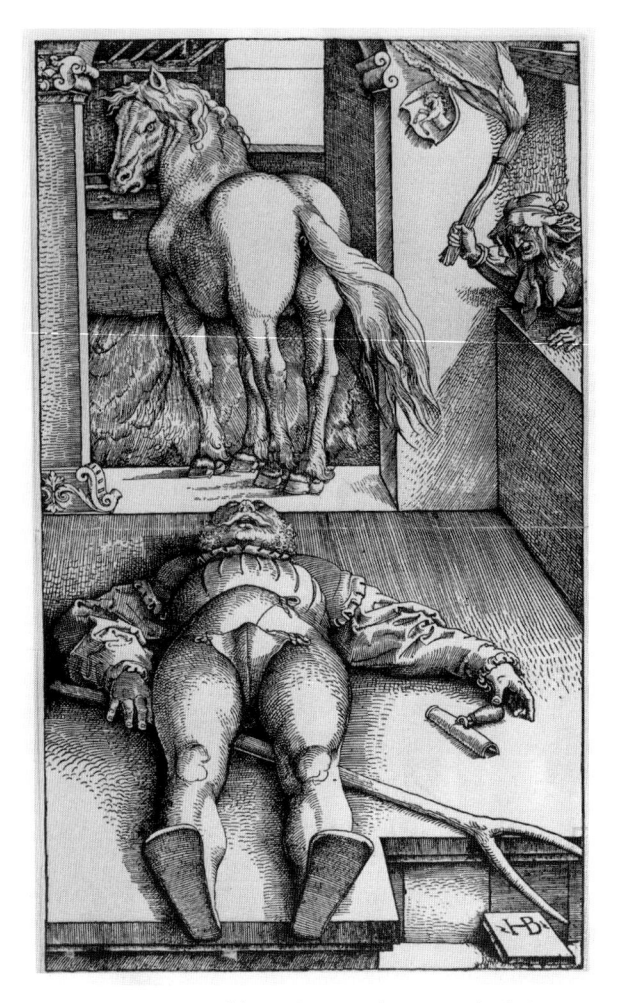

FIGURE 3.7: Hans Baldung Grien, *The Bewitched Groom*, 1544–45. British Museum, London.

by the presence of the ram between those same legs. The woman is, in addition, clearly post-menopausal; she is weathered in appearance with sagging breasts, the latter strongly indicating her status as a woman who can no longer fulfill what was believed to be women's purpose.[58]

Despite her withered breasts and ancient countenance, however, this elderly, female witch created by Dürer has the frame and musculature of a man in his prime: broad shoulders, defined abdominal muscles, and powerful arms and legs. In taking power inappropriate for a woman and rejecting what should be her female role—misusing her broom and her sexuality, for example—this woman seems to have adopted a third, ambiguous gender. Having indulged in

FIGURE 3.8: Hans Baldung Grien, *Three Witches*, 1514. Foto Marburg/Art Resource.

her misbegotten female nature, in the process rejecting her social identity as a woman, this witch remains a woman of the worst sort, but is neither wholly female nor wholly male. Whereas Dürer shows his mannish and yet female witch in isolation—alone in her inappropriate power and sexual ambiguity—Baldung also masculinizes one of the witches featured in a series of prints describing the activities of a coven. In *Three Witches* the mannish, aged witch, as leader of her coven, directs her young charges in an erotic dance, as one of them—reminiscent of the horse in the same artist's *Bewitched Groom*—views the world through her legs, literally turned upside down. The erotic positioning of the nubile witches, along with their subordination to their older companion, contributes to the idea that these young women are participating not just in sorcery but in sexual deviancy.

Other prints in the Baldung series depict witches in similar topsy-turviness, which foregrounds the dominance of the post-menopausal witch, the eroticism of the (always nude) witches in their relationships to one another, and the dangers the coven poses to men, to male potency, and to patriarchal order. In particular, Baldung's mannish, elderly witch presides in *Witches' Sabbath* (c. 1510); here she conducts a black mass, defying the natural elements, while one of her young charges—in an echo of Dürer's *The Witch*—rides backwards on a ram, holding the pitchfork she has taken from a man whom we see imprisoned in the clouds. Meanwhile, other pitchforks litter the ground—suggesting multiple conquests of male power and, presumably, multiple imprisoned men—where they are sat upon by the members of the coven. In all things these witches live lives of subversion, symbolized by the topsy-turvy gaze so prominently featured in *Three Witches*.

Dürer's and Baldung's witches reflect deployment of the topos of inversion, so important to early modern men and women in their expressions of anxiety about both social order and the role of gender in ensuring its stability. While the "woman on top" as a parodic figure served symbolically to shore up patriarchal order during the period, the *real* woman with misappropriated power—such as the witch—so embodied the topsy-turvy that she could lose her clear identification as physiologically female. Indeed, the most terrifying figure imaginable, Antichrist, embodied in the false church, was best expressed as a "woman on top"—a whore, holding aloft her "cup of fornication," having seduced the princes who should dominate her into submission to her inappropriate authority. Against this context, real women were thought either to preserve order through their safe placement behind walls or to threaten it. If safely contained, whether in the marital home (as symbolized by the authority of a husband), in the convent, or even in the brothel, woman-as-Eve was protected; or rather, society was protected from her. When loose, beyond patriarchal control, she was—also as Eve—a dangerous figure, the only alternative to safe, married, domesticity, both symbol and cause of the world turned upside down.

CHAPTER FOUR

Medicine and Disease

MARGARET HEALY

Even though the female body was taken from the male, it cannot be compared to it. It is true that in shape it is similar to the male body, for woman too is formed as a human being, and like man she carries God's image in her. But in everything else, in its essence, properties, nature, and peculiarities, it is completely different from the male body. Man suffers as man, woman suffers as woman; but both suffer as creatures beloved by God.[1]

In sixteenth-century Europe the traditional Galenic medical paradigm of the sexed body underwent a radical challenge. The Swiss-German physician Theophrastus Bombastus von Hohenheim (1493–1551), or Paracelsus as he was commonly known, determined on the basis of his own experience as a practitioner that women's bodies were "completely different from the male" and that they therefore required a completely new medical approach and treatments. In his view, humoral medicine had simply got it wrong: his Galenic colleagues' failure to recognize "microcosma," as he renamed woman's body, and their "lumping it together with the 'small world' of man" evidenced the injustice and blindness of the learned, university-trained physician who "has a skin before his eyes."[2] Woman must be gazed at anew with clearer vision. But what was her new appearance, and what had she looked like before?

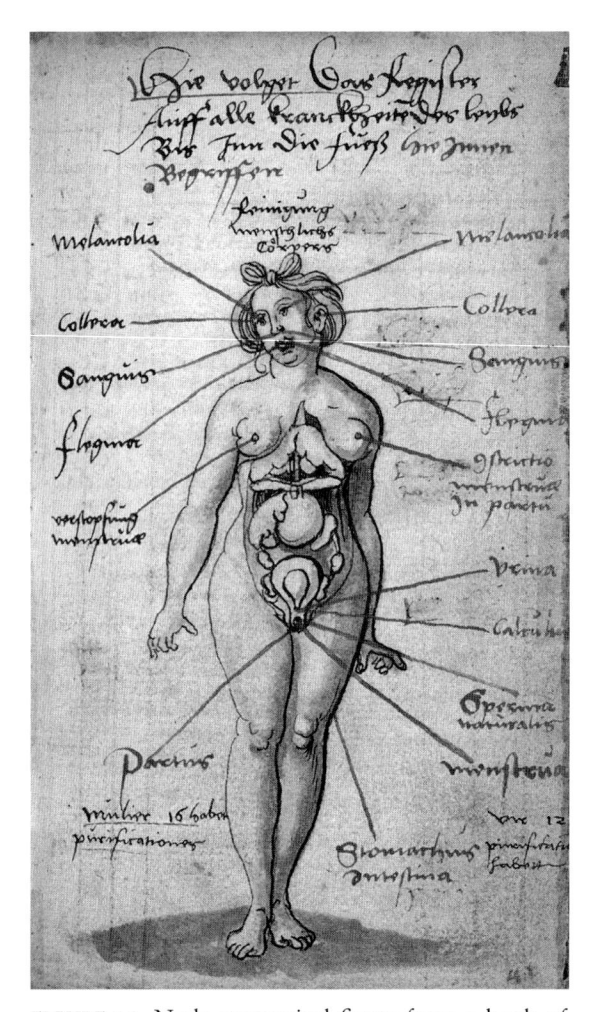

FIGURE 4.1: Nude anatomical figure from a book of medical receipts, sixteenth century. Wellcome Collection, L0023522.

Until Paracelsus's intervention, the authority of ancient Greek, Roman, and Hebrew influences was unrivalled in interpreting and constructing the body in European culture. The understanding of "woman" in the Renaissance was embedded in two ideologies: the Hebraic-Christian tradition of equating Eve with the Fall, and the Aristotelian-Galenic account of her nature and physiology.[3] According to the first, woman's suffering in her menses (her "curse"), as in childbirth, was God given and a consequence of her fatal transgression. In the second, philosophical tradition, "woman" fared no better: here she was an unfinished or imperfect man. This is how Helkiah Crooke described in 1618 the common conception of the formation of the sexes at birth:

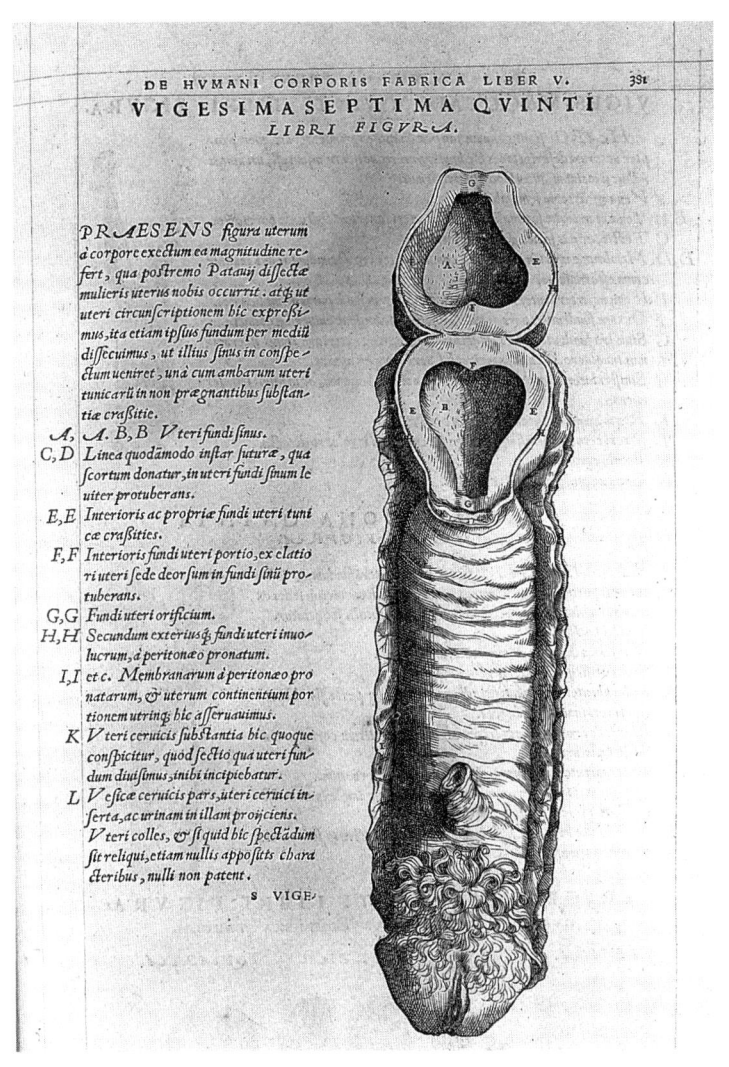

FIGURE 4.2: Andreas Vesalius, *De Humani Corpore Fabrica*, illustration of a uterus resembling a penis, 1543. Wellcome Collection, L0015865.

[I]n males the parts of generation are without the body, in females they lie within because of the weakness of the heat which is not able to thrust them forth... the neck of the womb is nothing else but the virile member turned inward and the bottom of the womb nothing but the scrotum or cod inverted.[4]

Lacking sufficient heat at conception, the woman's sexual parts remain inside her body; humorally, she is colder and moister than the male and therein resides the problem of menstrual blood and the diseases associated with it. Whilst men burn off any excesses of the blood humor, women retain it; it is their "natural disease" that must be purged monthly. Crooke was, however, notably skeptical of the female-as-aberrant-male bodily model he was describing: "this opinion we cannot approve...it is unworthily said that she is an error or a monster in nature."[5]

However, this traditional paradigm had an ancient heritage and was underpinned by the scholastic medicine taught in the universities; it proved extremely tenacious even in the face of Paracelsus's assault. Thus in 1671 the feisty practicing midwife Jane Sharp reproduced her still authoritative account of woman as deficient man, adding:

> So a woman is not so perfect as a Man, because her heat is weaker, but the Man can do nothing without the woman to beget Children, though some idle Coxcombs will needs undertake to shew how children may be had without use of the woman.[6]

Less perfect women might be, but it was precisely this lack, Sharp countered, that enabled humans to procreate.

Male inscriptions from this period about women's "flowers" and fertility are indicative of the intense anxiety generated by the social contradiction of which menstrual blood was the marker—that is, the undeniable potency and creativity of the (culturally constructed) weaker sex.[7] In early modern England, menstrual blood was enmeshed in a deeply ambivalent and florid web of potent myths and rules; as this exerpt from a popular text makes clear, it symbolized both creation and corruption, nurture and venom:

> If the hair of a menstruating woman be taken, and placed under a dungheap or clod of earth, or where the dung was made during winter or summer, by the virtue of the sun there will be engendered a long and powerful snake.[8]

Menstruation was, in fact, fundamental to sex, gender, and disease constructs and it was surrounded by taboos, as this wedding sermon published in 1617 reveals. William Whately instructed the newly wedded that:

> Their nuptial meetings must be seasonable, and at lawful times. There is a season when God and Nature sejoins [separates] man and wife in this respect. The woman is made to be fruitful; and therefore also moist and cold of constitution. Hence it is that their natural heat serves not to turn all their sustenance into their own nourishment; but a quantity

redounding is set apart in a convenient place to cherish and nourish the conception, when they shall conceive. Now this redundant humour (called their flowers or terms) hath (if no conception be) its monthly issue or evacuation...[which] always after childbirth...is larger and longer...Now in all these...occasions, it is simply unlawful for a man to company with his own wife. The Lord tells us so. Leviticus 15 vers 19–25; also ch. 18 ver.19; also ch. 20 ver.18. Of which places it is needful that married persons should take note: to which I send them...Where God threatens death to the offender, can the minister be faithful if he do not plainly declare the offence? This fault is by GOD condemned to the punishment of death, Leviticus 20: 18.[9]

As we might expect in Protestant England, the biblical word features prominently in accounts of the prohibitions surrounding menstruation. Leviticus instructed the Hebrew faithful that a woman with an issue should be "put apart" for seven days and that a man and woman who contravened this law would be "even both cut off from among their people" (20:18).[10] Interestingly, this prohibition was not restricted to Jews but seems to have been widely observed by ancient and medieval gentile cultures. What is striking, though, is how the marginalia in the sixteenth-century Geneva Bible (the text deposited in all English churches in the sixteenth century) inserted even more dire warnings than the Jewish original: the Geneva Bible urged, in the manner of Whately's sermon, that any man who touched the bed or "companied with" a menstruating woman "should die."[11]

Menstrual blood was considered so toxic that it could excoriate the penis and cause diseases; it was commonly argued that the new Renaissance disease syphilis—the Pox—was initially engendered by the unnatural copulation of a menstruating prostitute with a leper.[12] Measles and smallpox, meanwhile, were contracted in the womb and showed themselves in childhood when—as Simon Kellwaye put it—the "filthy menstruall matter" separated from the "naturall blood" in a purifying process. When the menstrual matter was "hoate and slimy" it produced smallpox, if "dry and subtill,...the measels."[13] Additionally, menstrual blood proved that women's bodies were inefficient, less perfect than men's, and potentially hazardous. Lacking sufficient natural heat they simply could not burn up humoral surpluses or purify their blood. *Aristotle's Master-Piece* cites this as evidence that women were not so strong, wise, prudent, or reasonable as men: *her* "faculties" were hindered in operation because of this lack.[14] Her inferior nature was thus the legacy of her unfinished bodily model and this understanding justified male dominance and female subjugation. In a fascinating aside in *The Sicke Woman's Private Looking-Glasse*,

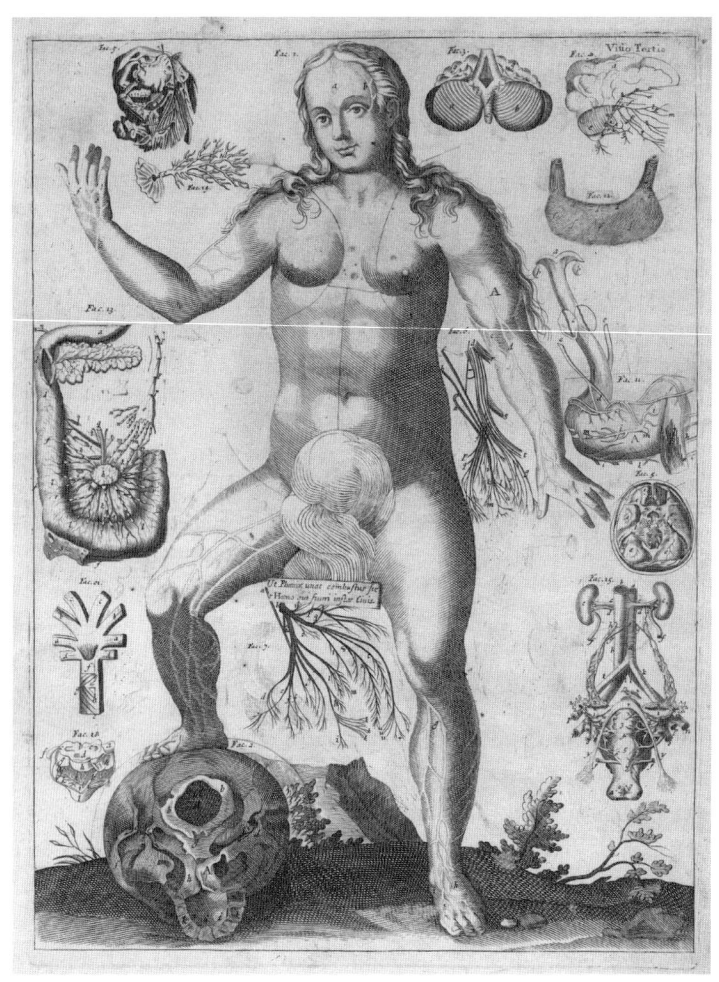

FIGURE 4.3: Female anatomical figure, London, 1702. Wellcome Collection, L0041290.

John Sadler makes exception of one type of woman: "the Amozonites, who being active, and always in motion, had ther fluxions very little, or not at all."[15] In most women, however, the excess, impure matter had to be shed regularly. But as *Aristotle's Book of Problems* warns: "when the Flowers do run from a Woman, then a most venemous Air is dissolved in them which doth ascend into the woman's head." The evil vapors multiply when they reach the eyes and seek passage through "insensible holes" or pores. This is how a menstruating woman's glance tarnishes a mirror. In the way that she transmits "evil," she resembles that "venemous and infected" beast, the Basilisk.[16]

This situation did not improve in periods of amenorrhoea or post-menopause: then, the poisonous matter simply accumulated as "black and dark Smoke" in the brain.[17] Women who suffered "stoppages" of their "terms" became subject to a range of illnesses: "frenzy of the womb" and melancholy, madness, hysterical fits, and breaking out in sores.[18] Or worse—they were imagined to become murderous, as Lady Macbeth's spine-chilling invocation of the powers of darkness reveals:

> Come, you spirits
> That tend on mortal thoughts, unsex me here,
> And fill me from the crown to the toe, top-full
> Of direst cruelty. Make thick my blood,
> Stop up th'access and passage to remorse,
> That no compunctious visitings of nature
> Shake my fell purpose, nor keep peace between
> Th'effect and it. Come to my woman's breasts,
> And take my milk for gall, you murd'ring ministers,
> Wherever in your sightless substances
> You wait on nature's mischief. (Shakespeare, *Macbeth*, I.v.39–49)[19]

"Visitings of nature" was an early modern euphemism for menstruation. In Lady Macbeth's belief system (one possibly shared by many in the original audiences) "stoppages" led to moral fog, mystical mischief, and dire bloody acts—a perverse inversion of maternal nurturing behavior.

Paradoxically, health required women to undergo their natural "disease" at regular intervals—if not, finances permitting, they had to be artificially bled by a surgeon. Post-menopausal women—their brains bulging with toxic smoke—were imagined to be particularly venomous: the glance of an old lady, or the vapors emitted from her mouth, could dry up a nursing mother's milk, cause animals and children to sicken, and even kill a baby in its cradle. It is not difficult to see how it was most commonly "old beldames" who were implicated in witchcraft. Indeed, as Stuart Clark describes in *Thinking with Demons*, one famous commentator, Pierre Crespet, argued "for a general affinity between the hideousness of old women and the repulsiveness of the demonic," suggesting that bewitching was the direct result of the "predomination" of menstrual blood as evil fumes in the head.[20]

Yet, this is not the whole of the story and, as the anthropologists Thomas Buckley and Alma Gottlieb caution in their seminal study, *Blood Magic*, it is overly reductionist to attribute one meaning to menstrual blood in any culture. As even Pliny acknowledged, menstrual blood was linked to a range of positive as well as negative effects: it encouraged the fertility of wheat fields and it was used to treat gout, goiter, hemorrhages, puerperal fever, worms, headache, and hydrophobia.[21] It was an ambivalent signifier, then. But in ancient Rome, as in early modern England, it was certainly construed as powerful. Far from being a signifier of shame, blood from the womb might have been associated with pride because it symbolized fertility and potency: in fact it was a sign of something that men could not achieve and might even envy.

At least one northern European physician, Cornelius Agrippa, writing in Latin in 1529, argued that women were superior to men because they could produce milk that nourishes human life, and only they had a natural process to rid the body of poisons.[22] Others, like the physician Thomas Raynold, lambasted the shameful lies and slander told about menstrual blood:

> Is it to be thought that nature wold feade the tender and delicate infant in the mothers womb, with the refuse of the blud, or not rather with the purist of it...Yet much more are to be detested and abhorred the shamefull lyes and slaunders that Plynie, Albertus Magnus de secretes Mulierum and dyvers othermore have wrytten, of the venemous and daungorous infectyve nature of the womans flowers or termes: The which al be but dreames and playne dotage; to reherse...here were but losse of ynke and paper.[23]

Raynold's book was extremely popular, undergoing thirteen editions between 1540 and 1634. In actual fact we probably learn most about such troubling myths in treatises that sought to undermine them. For example, in Reginald Scot's famous treatise *The discoverie of witchcraft*, the author ridiculed the assertion that "old...bowed women" were often found to be witches because of their evil humors and "venomous exhalations" causing them to "belch up a certaine breath, wherewith they bewitch whomsoever they list."[24]

The most common type of outpouring on the matter is perhaps that which simply articulates the contradictions in the medical and popular understanding of this natural phenomenon and tries to account for them. The physician John Sadler argues, for example, that the "monthly flux of excrementous and profitable bloud" must be "pure and incorrupt, like unto the bloud in the veins" because it is for

> the propagation and conservation of mankinde...the child whilst it is in the matrice is nourished with this bloud...being out of the womb, it is still nourished with the same; for the milke is nothing but the menstruous bloud made white in the breasts; and I am sure woman's milke is not thought to be venomous, but of a nutritive quality...It may be objected, if the bloud bee not of a hurtfull quality, how can it cause such venomous effects, as if the same fall upon trees and herbs it maketh the one barren, and mortifies the other. And Averroes writes, that if a man

accompany with a menstruous woman, if she conceive, she shall bring forth a Lepar. I answer, this malignity is contracted in the wombe; for the woman wanting native heat to digest this superfluity, sends it to the matrice, where seating it selfe untill the mouth of the wombe be dilated, it becomes corrupt and venomous, which may easily be, considering the heat and moisture of the place. This bloud therefore being out of his vessels, offends in quality.[25]

So, menstrual blood is matter out of place: excrementous, corrupt, and venomous, leaving disease and disaster in its wake; yet it is also pure, profitable, and nourishing. Sadler manages to accommodate these binaries and paradoxes in his perplexing constructions of female physiology.

The confused and contradictory nature of such descriptions was undoubtedly influenced by the increasing impact throughout the seventeenth century of the Paracelsian medical paradigm that reached the height of its appeal in England from 1570 to 1670. Books of Paracelsian and Helmontian alchemical medicine in both Latin and the European vernaculars poured from the presses in these years. As we have seen, this did not, however, result in an immediate and wholesale paradigmatic shift: rather, a multiplicity of often hybrid medical models of the body competed for attention, and because Paracelsian understanding absorbed traditional lay and folkloric modes of healing, including the herbal and mineral recipes of wisewomen, it was itself eclectic. It shared with these latter traditions a profound imbrication in the natural world and this reveals itself in Paracelsus's frequent recourse to vocabulary and images from nature and horticulture.

In Paracelsus's writings, woman "is the field and garden mould in which the child is sown and planted."[26] She is the tree while the male is the fruit: "Man is to her what the pear is to the tree. The pear falls, but the tree remains standing" and "by that much woman is also superior to man."[27] Further, in contradistinction to Aristotelian, Galenic medicine, both men and women produce "seeds" and contribute to the form of offspring:

When the seed is received in the womb, nature combines the seed of the man and the seed of the woman. Of the two seeds the better and stronger will form the other according to its nature…The seed from the man's brain and that from the woman's brain make together only one brain; but the child's brain is formed according to the one which is the stronger of the two, and it becomes like this seed, but never completely like it. For the second seed breaks the force of the first, and this always results in a change of nature.[28]

FIGURE 4.4: A seated woman giving birth, 1583. Wellcome Collection, V0014910.

Paracelsian medicine relied not on book learning but on experience and the careful and continuous observation and recording of the natural world. This is very apparent in his medical writings:

> God wills to make man out of two, and not out of one; he wills man composed of two and not of one alone... In all trees, the same comes from the same; similarly all walnut trees bear the same nuts, without any difference. The same is true of man. If he had been born only of one individual, he would be like his father, and this father would be his father and mother in one. Then there would be only people of one kind, and each would look like the other, and all would have the same nature. But the mixing of the seeds of man and woman results in so much change that no individual can be like the other... Each individual's seed breaks the unity of the other, and that is why no man is like another.[29]

Here, the observation of walnut trees underpins Paracelsus's theories about reproduction. Woman appears to be equal to man in her ability to contribute seeds and shape the next generation; and, in Paracelsus's constructions, she seems to lose much of her menstrual toxicity. She is the sea, she is mother, she is fertile:

> What causes the sea to rise? Just as the sea expels things and falls, one may understand woman as a mother of children...Because woman is a mother, she produces such rivers in herself, which rise up and flow out every four weeks...Thus the menstrual blood is an excrement of things flowing into the matrix, which die there and are expelled...As long as pregnancy lasts, there is no excrement...then all things in her are like summer...only pleasure and delight.[30]

But even for Paracelsus, at the end of the day woman collapses into womb in a strikingly reductive and disappointing manner:

> He who contemplates woman should see in her the maternal womb of man...How can one be an enemy of woman—whatever she may be? The world is peopled with her fruits, and that is why God lets her live so long, however loathsome she may be.[31]

In a variety of sometimes surprising and paradoxical ways, then, early modern medical accounts of woman—whether as failed man or radically "other"—managed to inscribe her inferiority. Indeed, medical authority usually functioned to bolster the fragile assertions and justifications of patriarchal hegemony.

"A GREAT RABBLE" OF "PRESUMPTUOUS" WOMEN: FEMALE HEALERS

In this situation, how could "she"—at her best the personification of robust and fertile nature—be a healer, let alone a physician? Curiously, given ancient humoral constructions of woman's intellectual deficiency, the history of female medical practitioners extends back at least as far as the fifth century B.C.E. in Greece.[32] Holt Parker provides the example of one Phanostrate from Attica (c. 350 B.C.E.) whose gravestone bears the inscription "midwife and doctor."[33] He maintains that woman practitioners must have been a "part of daily life" in the Roman Empire as well as in ancient Greece, evidencing the writings of Galen and others that cite the "opinions and recipes of male and female doctors indiscriminately."[34] In keeping with this, Tacitus, too, describes women functioning as surgeons and treating the wounds of men whilst not flinching when counting the gashes.[35] In the ancient world, Parker observes, female practitioners seem to have shared a similar education to male doctors and to have been readily accepted in their communities.[36]

In the "dark" European Middle Ages there is evidence that women legally practiced medicine in Salerno and Paris in the twelfth century.[37] In Naples in 1321 Francesca de Romana was licensed to practice medicine generally.[38] In German-speaking towns, city chronicles and tax registers offer numerous references to female physicians, particularly Jewish women. They were probably trained by medical masters in a type of apprenticeship.[39] Indeed, women seem to have been involved in all aspects of the healing arts in the Middle Ages: they set bones, cured eye diseases, treated pain from gout, removed bladder stones, and treated gynecological disorders as well as practicing obstetrics.[40]

As among the best educated in society, religious men and women were practitioners, transcribers, and disseminators of medical knowledge, and the first hospitals were religious institutions. The German nun Hildegard von Bingen (1098–1179) was renowned for her medical acumen and authored two scientific works (1151–58): one of simple medicine (*Physica* on natural philosophy) and one of composite medicine (*Causae et Curae*). She probably had a Latin education and studied Greco-Roman medicine and that of the school of Salerno, through manuscripts housed at her mixed monastery for men and women in Disibodenberg.[41] She undoubtedly also drew on oral folk traditions and the skills she learned from fellow practitioners, herbalists, and gardeners in her healing community. Knowledge of plant physiology especially informed Hildegard's understanding of the body, and Victoria Sweet has illustrated how deeply she drew on the understanding of *viriditas*, or greening power, in the thoroughgoing agricultural society she inhabited.[42]

Her medical treatments include bloodletting, herbal remedies, poultices, incantations (healing by the power of the spoken word), and the use of magic stones as well as miraculous healing (involving making the sign of the cross over diseased parts of the body) and the sanctified word.[43] Acts performed by holy women involved a special relationship between the woman and God and were thus often construed as "white magic."[44] This recipe of Hildegard's in *Physica* is particularly indicative of why this was the case:

> For a fever you take a ripe beech nut, mix it in spring water and say "through the holy girdle of the holy incarnation by which god became

FIGURE 4.5: Depiction of Trotula of Salerno from a manuscript of the late twelfth or early thirteenth century. Wikimedia Commons: http://commons.wikimedia.org/wiki/File:Trotula_of_Salerno.jpg.

man, grow weak, you fever and you feverish conditions, and weaken your cold ness and heat in this person." Then give the person the water to drink.[45]

But the key authoritative roles of monastic men and women in healing the sick were shortly to change: after 1163 they were forbidden to leave the monastery to study medicine; and in 1215 the Fourth Lateran Council put an end to the religious undertaking of surgery involving "burning or cutting." The Benedictine order, nevertheless, seems to have maintained a tradition of medical study.[46]

In the lay world things were changing too. In 1422 in Naples, Costanza Calenda became the first woman to receive a doctorate in medicine from a university;[47] however, she was probably a rare case, and the founding of universities and the licensing of physicians undoubtedly functioned to bar most women from practicing professionally in the early modern period. The pharmacy guilds excluded women and traditional wisewomen who prepared medications, and they were often declared to be quacks, or worse, witches.[48] The infamous text *Malleus maleficarum* (1487) linked women to magical practice because of their "gender-specific weaknesses: woman's lack of steadfast faith and her intrinsically superstitious nature, both of which automatically render her susceptible to temptation by the devil." Thus "a predilection for demonic magic became a biological...trait."[49]

It was certainly becoming increasingly dangerous to be the embodiment of mysterious and ambivalent female nature. As Sigrid Maria Brauner describes:

> During this period, since she is identified with the ambiguous powers of nature, woman, as nature's representative, becomes a field of projection for all problematic areas emerging in the process of civilization and capitalization...For the new sciences in particular, woman and the female body represent chaotic nature's resistance to scientific enquiry and technical domination.[50]

In the sixteenth century the female body becomes "both a site of anxiety and a screen for the projection of these anxieties."[51] As a largely solitary autonomous figure, unregulated, with no institutional affiliations, the female healer was construed by the patriarchal hegemony as particularly troublesome. As we have seen, the medicine that dominated the universities was based on ancient book knowledge; by contrast the medicine of laywomen was empirical, based on firsthand experience of using plants and herbs in curative regimes.[52] As Nancy Nenno argues convincingly:

> At a time when nascent medical institutions were attempting to establish an independent realm of authority, when Church authorities were attempting to eliminate...pre-Christian traditions, and states began to regulate medical practices, the woman healer became a target for anxieties about autonomous medical practice, pagan traditions and demonic magic.[53]

Also in the sixteenth century, female healers were dangerously aligned with "sorcerors" and witches: "vile people...traffic...in physicke...Midwives...Witches,

Conjurers."[54] Undoubtedly such constructions suited the College of Physicians' vigorous attempts to eject female practitioners from the lucrative medical marketplace.

Nevertheless, women remained crucial to health and healing in the early modern period. As Mary Elizabeth Fissell argues, by putting women at the center of the picture rather than the margins, and considering more general care of the body rather than simply the practices of learned physicians, we arrive at a less hierarchical and more accurate reflection of how people were cared for at times of acute and chronic sickness and in childbirth.[55] Deborah Harkness describes how in 1566, surveying the medical marketplace available to consumers, the physician John Securis lamented the vast array of "unlearned surgeons, meddling empirics and 'presumptuous' women [who] offended his sense of proper medical order": Securis seems to have been offended by the wealth of unlicensed competition.[56] Likewise, John Hall, an eminent surgeon, complained about the "great rabble of women" who intruded into his medical domain in the 1560s.[57] It seems that women practitioners were certainly out there in abundance, although they were marginalized and demonized by such prejudicial accounts. In recent decades midwives particularly have been "recuperated as competent practitioners with their own unwritten knowledge and practices transmitted orally from teacher to student."[58] Meanwhile, the instrument-wielding man-midwife has emerged as the villain of the piece rather than the hero and savior of women in childbirth.[59]

In these revisionist histories (which are quite different from those of traditional medical history), women are very much at the center of a spectrum of caring and healing activities that may well have been far more efficacious and comforting to suffering bodies than the traumatic, invasive, and painful "cure" regimes associated with early modern "professional" medicine practiced by an elite flotilla of learned (and expensive to consult) physicians. There is, after all, little evidence that learned medicine was helpful beyond its placebo effects. As Fissell suggests, "hardly anyone was 'cured' of an ailment in the early modern period: they endured."[60] This might help to explain why traditional healers like the famous Margaret Kennix were protected from the onslaughts of the College of Physicians by the queen herself—Elizabeth I.[61] Traditional folk healing practiced by skilled women might well have been a safer choice than consulting a learned physician. It is significant in this regard that early modern drama often foregrounds the woman healer as socially marginalized yet possessing an oracular nature and heightened spiritual and curative powers. As William Kerwin describes, the female empiric on stage frequently refutes the attacks on women practitioners—she is not malevolent and she is usually highly skilful.[62] Thus Helena in Shakespeare's *All's Well That Ends Well* works by inspired merit; where both Galenic and Paracelsian physicians had failed, Helena is successful in curing the king's chronic ailment.

In fact London had only thirty university-trained physicians serving 200,000 people in 1600.[63] Analyses of municipal records suggest there were sixty female practitioners in London in 1600, not counting midwives.[64] Elizabethan poor laws often led to the employment of women healers by parish officials.[65] "Man-midwives" were moving into the obstetric marketplace and this probably accounts for why midwives tried to professionalize and "incorporate" their status in order to protect their rights but were never granted a charter.[66] It is likely that the College of Physicians did not want the competition: their records from the seventeenth century show an increasing effort to marginalize midwives and female healers. For example, the college warned Susan Fletcher "to desist from her practice," which consisted of "treating sore breasts with a lotion comprising milk, white bread and herbs."[67]

Importantly, through researching sources other than those connected with learned physicians, surgeons, and their professional bodies, Harkness has enabled us to glimpse the vast array of women doing medical work in

FIGURE 4.6: A hospital ward in the Hotel Dieu. Wellcome Collection, M004486.

London—the great "presumptuous" "rabble" detested by Securis and Hall. Sources such as parish records, probate records, lists of immigrants to London, hospital records, and manuscripts help us to "catch them working alongside their husbands in surgical shops and public markets, follow them as they work in London's hospitals, and go door-to-door as they visit houses suspected of containing plague or other infectious diseases at the request of the city's parishes."[68] But they are firmly installed as healers in private houses, too, and, indeed, in their own homes. As Margaret Pelling has argued, at times of illness the first place people turned to was the household where women's presence, knowledge, and skills were focused.[69] Thus Lady Grace Mildmay received instruction at home in "phisicke and surgerie"; she particularly studied William Turner's *Herbal*. Her journal between 1570 and 1617 suggests she carried out a wide range of medical activities—these were integral to her religious, charitable duty.[70] As part of their traditional caring and nurturing role in the household, women were expected to make medicines and many of the ingredients needed to make them could be found in the kitchen: olive oil and lanolin (as emollients and carriers); wine and vinegar and honey; and animal parts such as thyroid, pancreas, liver, testicles, gallbladder, and uteri. The kitchen garden provided stones and bones and domestic plants including cannabis, opium, solanum and hyoscyamus, and mandragora.[71] That amounts were measured in domestic terms such as a handful, pinch, fistful, an eggshell's worth, points to the centrality of the domestic kitchen in medicine production.[72]

As Francis McKee has described, Paracelsian medicine encouraged the practice of writing cookery and recipe books.[73] This can partly be attributed to the centrality of the stomach in chemical medicine as the site of the most important "archeus," or essential force, in the body. The latter distinguished between toxic and nutritive substances entering the body; furthermore, digestion, which involved chemical transformation, was closely connected to chemical philosophy.[74] Because women were traditionally associated with the household practices of brewing and cooking, they were construed as having greater insight into these areas than men. Paracelsus had even declared:

> A Physitian ought not to rest only in that bare knowledge which their Schools teach but to learn of old Women, Egyptians, and such like persons; for they have greater experience in such things than all the Academicians.[75]

Watching household chores led the alchemical adept to decipher "signatures" of the celestial.[76] As Paracelsian medicine gained support and currency in England, so did the receipt book. In the 1650s, printed recipe books like that of Elizabeth Grey, Countess of Kent, entitled *A Choice Manual of Rare and Select Secrets,* were extremely popular—the latter went through at least twenty editions.[77] As Sir Hugh Plat's works reveal (notably *The Jewell House of Art and Nature*, 1594), cures and medical receipts or simple pharmacy were very closely aligned with cookery in the early modern period.[78]

Lady Margaret Clifford was particularly noted for her alchemical "receipts": a manuscript volume that once belonged to her is entitled *Receipts of Lady Margaret Wife of George, 3rd Earl of Cumberland for Elixirs, Tinctures, Electuaries, Cordials, Waters etc.*[79] Lady Margaret seems to have been famous for "chymical extractions" from minerals, herbs, and flowers—her medicines.[80] Thus Anne Clifford says of her mother in the "Great Book of Records of the Cliffords":

> She [Margaret Clifford] was a lover of the study and practice of alchemy...by which she found out excellent medicines...she delighted in distilling of waters and other chemical extractions, for she had...knowledge in most kind of minerals, herbs, flowers, and plants...the infusion she had from above...both divine and human...caused her to have...sweet peace.[81]

Penny Bayer notes that the Appleby Great Picture Triptych (1646) features a particular volume above Margaret Clifford's Head: "a written hand Booke of Alkumiste Abstracions of Distillation & Excellent Medicines."[82]

Other well-to-do housewives loosely or more thoroughly involved in healing activities include Elizabeth Grey, Lady Margaret Hoby, Lady Anne Halkett, Mary Trye, Elizabeth Cellier, and Elizabeth Clinton.[83] Lady Margaret Hoby recorded in her diary that she frequently offered "salve[s]" to poor women in her community.[84] During the Restoration the kitchen became particularly notable with the publication of a work purported to contain the manuscript recipes of Queen Henrietta Maria (*The Queen's Closet Opened*, 1655). It went through five editions before 1680 and inspired other women, notably Hannah Woolley, the first English woman to publish a cookery book—*The Ladies Directory*. McKee foregrounds this revealing new insertion in the second edition to *The Queen's Closet Opened* (1661), which closely aligned cookery with chemistry:

> In regard of the Benefit which so many have received from these, which we shall now rather call Experiments than Receipts contained therin...neither have we known of any that have bought it, who have not testified

their high esteem therof. And indeed, how should it otherwise be, knowing out of what Elaboratories it was produced?[85]

The dividing lines between experimental chemistry and cookery, the kitchen and the laboratory, were very blurred indeed.

A fascinating study of the papers of Elizabeth Freke (1641–1714) confirms that, in common with many of her female contemporaries, this elderly widow's pronounced interest in the production of medicines in and for her household meant that she frequently engaged with commercial medical advice and actively sought out new recipes for her collection from among her friends, relatives, and acquaintances.[86] She kept an impressively extensive range of "common cure-alls" and ready-made medicines for particular ailments in her cupboards and chests.[87] There were herbal and spice remedies for everything from "weakened stomach," "coughs and general weaknesses of the lungs" to "fevers" and "weakness of the heart, head and brain."[88] Elaine Leong has estimated that at least 10 percent of recipes for remedies required the use of a "still" for distillation purposes; this indicates how the production of medicines in the household was closely associated with fashionable alchemy in the seventeenth century.[89] Intriguingly, the traditional healing and medicine-making roles of women had become tightly aligned with chemistry and thus, with the new science. Wise-women had cunningly swapped their spells for "stills" and they remained at the epicenter of caring, healing culture, working from their kitchens as well as in the shops, markets, and hospitals of London.

CHAPTER FIVE

Public and Private

DANIELLE CLARKE

She was so farre from the gadding disposition of other talking, walking women, that she was for the most part as a Snail, *Domi-porta*, within her own shell and family.[1]

William Gouge's funeral sermon on Mrs. Margaret Ducke, printed in 1646, mobilizes a familiar *topos*, as he stresses the triangulated relationship between virtue, piety, and the household, and uses a familiar source from scripture to demonstrate Mrs. Ducke's exemplification of the virtuous wife—Proverbs 31:29. The image of the snail, carrying his shell (or house) on his back, works in two ways here: first, in providing a metaphor for the boundary that marks woman's proper place concerning her own private life ("her own shell"), and second, in suggesting that her restriction to that sphere persists even as she moves about in the world. As the snail carries his shell with him wherever he goes, so the virtuous woman brings her modest confinement to the domestic sphere irrespective of the company or circumstances in which she finds herself. Thus, the ideology that attempted to drive a wedge between private and public and to align such a division neatly with gender reveals the contradiction at its core: privacy (and the nexus of associated meanings that go with it) is not exclusively or even primarily *spatial*; rather, it is *cultural*, to be discerned by the interpretation of signs (gesture, apparel, manners) and, most important of all, through speech—a topic I will return to later in this discussion. Questions of privacy and morality as they relate to women are questions of *ethos* rather than of location, although early modern England does maintain a series of social rules about where, and with whom, a woman might appear in public.

Gouge's formulation of the ideal woman as one who avoided unnecessary public exposure (which was reprinted in one of the most influential collections of exemplary lives, Samuel Clarke's *Ten Eminent Divines* [1662]) was relatively common over the course of the sixteenth and early seventeenth centuries, as a range of commentators struggled to bring inherited gender ideologies, reformed thinking on the role of the wife and her place within the household, and the tradition of exemplary women inherited from classical and scriptural texts into some kind of coherent alignment. It turns up, for example, in Lancelot Andrewes's posthumously printed *Pattern of Catechistical Doctrine* (1650, first published in 1630) in a section devoted to conduct. He states:

> [T]o the same purpose doth the Apostle advise women, and in the midst of his lessons to them, as a special means to observe the rest, he bids them to be as snails...*domi porta, keepers at home.* In this point, following the example of *Sarah*, of whome we read, that she was for the most part, either in the *tent*, or at the *tent door*.[2]

The scriptural texts referenced in the margin are Paul's Letter to Titus 2:3, 4 and to Genesis 18:6, 9, and 10. Much as Gouge marshals Proverbs 31 in support of his highly restrictive vision of a woman's role, despite its clear acknowledgment that the woman's contribution to the household is moral, spiritual, and economic, as well as nurturing, so, too, do Andrewes's sources have a somewhat tangential relationship to his commentary. Chapter 2 of the Epistle to Titus, for example, outlines principles of good conduct for both sexes, balancing young and old, male and female in a repeated pattern of antithesis. The verses that Andrewes cites actually say nothing about women and the household (numbering is the same in the Geneva Bible and the King James Version):

> The aged women likewise, that *they be* in behaviour as becometh holiness, not false accusers, not given to much wine, teachers of good things; That they may teach the young women to be sober, to love their husbands, to love their children. (Titus 2:3, 4)

The combination of restraint in public conduct with domestic duty echoes down the centuries, but like other key verses in the Bible, the division between public and private is not quite as stark as Renaissance commentators often suggest. The text that Andrewes is thinking of, when he reaches for the snail image, is verse 5 ("*To be* discreet, chaste, keepers at home" [*domus curam habentes*]).³ This slippage, together with the buried allusion to Cicero, is entirely typical of Renaissance writing practices, but it should alert us to the complex set of intersecting belief systems that constitute prescriptivism on questions of gender and, in turn, constitute early modern thinking about the relative status of the private and public spheres

To return to the repeated invocation of the book of Proverbs, chapter 31 in particular, in support of a circumscribed domestic role for women, here too we find that early modern commentary repeatedly interprets the text in terms of a much more solid boundary between public and private than the biblical text strictly warrants.⁴ This suggests a particular investment on the part of Renaissance writers in the delineation and demarcation of the fluid boundary between public and private, as well as reflecting the increasing tendency for economic production to move outside the home. Domestic economy covered a far broader range of activity than modern housewifery suggests, but by and large concerned the preparation and preservation of goods purchased or produced outside the household itself. This is in contrast to the vision of the household presented in the Bible, and to the late medieval household, which often was the site of production of goods to be sold outside the home as well as being consumed within it.⁵ This early transition to the separation of production and consumption marks the nascent capitalism that is so often identified as one of the key drivers of the "rise of the individual," and it is important to note in passing that this may well be—in part—at the expense of one key aspect of female agency. It is the contention of some critics, and of this piece, that this agency is replaced by a set of anxious contestations about the other kinds of functions that take place in the ideal household, nurture in particular (and what is nurture but the way in which an individual is made social?). As Wendy Wall's highly pertinent question would have it:

> Rather than restricting domesticity to the "first school" in which political, sexual, and social subjection was inculcated, then, might we see the household as implicated in various modes of subjection and identification?⁶

The household, then, is far from sequestered from the public gaze; on the contrary, what happens within it comes to signify social order (or lack of it), and questions of regulation are routinely focused on female conduct and male authority—in other words, the household becomes a kind of simulacrum for other issues of political import, which is perhaps why the early modern period is so concerned with articulating prescriptive ideologies for it.

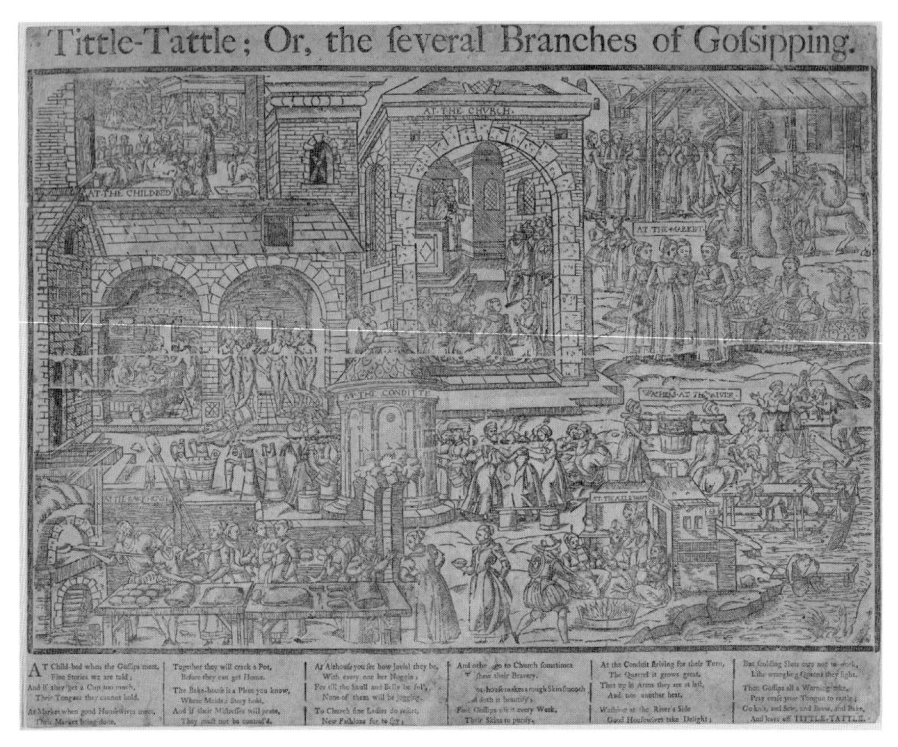

FIGURE 5.1: *Tittle-Tattle: Or, the Several Branches of Gossipping*, c. 1640. Courtesy of the British Museum, London.

HUSBANDS, WIVES, AND THE ORDERLY HOUSEHOLD

The transition to a more restricted notion of economic productivity, and an expanded conceptualization of the ideological function of the household can clearly be seen in the kinds of reinterpretations that Protestant thinkers make of key biblical texts. John Dod and William Hinde's *Bathshebaes Instructions* (1614), for example, transforms the encomium to a good wife in Proverbs 31, articulated in terms of her economic productivity both within *and beyond* the household ("she considereth a field, and buyeth it: with the fruit of her hands she planteth a vineyard," v. 16), into a moral manifesto on proper wifely conduct in the public sphere:

> [F]or you may see many women, which although sometimes they be farre from the crime of adultery, not onely in act, but also in consent; notwithstanding by reason of their gesture and behaviour, they are not free from all markes and notes of immodestie.[7]

This hardening of the edges of a division between public and private, and its mapping onto gender ideologies, is a notable feature of prescriptive texts from the Renaissance period, and receives perhaps its highest and most aesthetic expression in Milton's account of the "separate but equal" model in *Paradise Lost*. Yet Milton's articulation of a seemingly restrictive ideal is more nuanced and more ambiguous than many commentators allow. One of the most frequently quoted passages used to support the view that Milton's view of gender relations is limited and misogynist is that voiced by Adam at the beginning of Book IX, in response to Eve's announcement, "Let us divide our labours, thou where choice/Leads thee or where most leads."[8] That Eve speaks first here marks an immediate disturbance to Milton's ideas of right order, homologous to temporal sequence and hierarchy, but drawn ultimately from the Pauline injunction for women to obey their husbands and to keep silent (I Corinthians 14:34–35). It is also this scriptural authority that Milton has in mind when he describes Eve as "retired in sight/With lowliness majestic" (VIII. 41–42), and as rejoining the theological discussions and "thoughts abstruse" (40) that take place between Adam and Raphael, preferring instead to receive her instruction directly from her husband. Milton's careful demarcation of capacity from decorum echoes a contradiction that runs all the way through humanist thought on the topic of women's education:

> Yet went she not as not with such discourse
> Delighted or not capable her ear
> Of what was high. Such pleasure she reserved,
> Adam relating, she sole auditress:
> Her husband the relater she preferred
> Before the angel and of him to ask
> Chose rather. (VIII. 48–54)

The passage from I Corinthians, and Milton's adumbration of it at numerous pressure points throughout *Paradise Lost*, attempts to drive a wedge between public and private conduct. Yet in *Paradise Lost*, Eve's apparently willing dependence upon Adam's authority in preference to God's proves to be her undoing, as the following lines, in their sensuality, suggest:

> He, she knew, would intermix
> Grateful digressions and solve high dispute
> With conjugal caresses (from his lip
> Not words alone pleased her). (VIII. 55–58)

Passion and reason are problematically entwined in this primal scene of conjugal instruction.

The problem in *Paradise Lost*, as elsewhere, is that the woman's centrality to social reproduction means that attempted confinement to domestic tasks and spaces cannot be divorced from her symbolic importance. Eve is the figure who reveals the limits to Adam's exercise of authority; equally, as the above passage suggests, she tests the boundaries of his own self-governance, too. The first couple, privately ensconced in the Garden of Eden, stand in for a whole series of ideas and ideologies about obedience, hierarchy, and government, as many critics have noted. So when Adam seeks to contain Eve's autonomy (expressed, as so often in *Paradise Lost*, by means of spatial metaphors), his appeal is to the division of roles:

> Well hast thou motioned, well thy thoughts employed
> How we might best fulfil the work which here
> God hath assigned us, nor of me shalt pass
> Unpraised, for nothing lovelier can be found
> In woman than to study household good
> And good works in her husband to promote. (IX. 229–34)

This passage brings us back to the book of Proverbs, alluded to glancingly in lines 232–34 ("she looketh well to the ways of her household, and eateth not the bread of idleness," 31:27), yet the problem here is that as yet, Eve has no "household" as such—no coming together of generations and hierarchies to be ordered, fed, and instructed—so the role that Adam attempts to assign to her can be theoretical only (she is "*to study* household good," 233, emphasis added). The private sphere to which she properly belongs in what *Paradise Lost* asserts as a divine order is a distinctly postlapsarian phenomenon, and Milton implicitly acknowledges that the private sphere of the household is a matter of public interest and import by refracting the story of the creation and fall through the lens of Renaissance thinking about the household and *oeconomia*:

> [I]t was only through the definition of conjugal femininity as the symbolic boundary of "good husbandry" (the displaced marker of the husband's accountability as head of the household) that good husbandry could come to claim as its sphere nothing less than "out of bounds-ness" itself—the time/space of opportunity, both for negotiation and for the production of rhetorically persuasive fictions.[9]

As Lorna Hutson argues, the space of the household is posited as private, yet proves to be anything but; equally, over the course of the Renaissance, the gendering of the private sphere becomes more fragmented and complex, whilst retaining its enormous symbolic power. And ethical conduct and the exercise of civility are tested most rigorously within the open confines of the domestic space; thus questions of governance are inextricably tied up with questions of female virtue and character, so that the figure of the good wife confers both grace and authority on the husband. Eve's fall is Adam's, even before he actually eats the apple: "And me with thee hath ruined, for with thee/Certain my resolution is to die!" (IX. 906–7). The threat of conjugal loss prompts a transition in Adam's feelings towards Eve from condescending appreciation to true affective love—a loss of autonomy that is in itself a kind of fall:

> How can I live without thee, how forgo
> Thy sweet converse and love so dearly joined
> To live again in these wild woods folorn?
> Should God create another Eve and I
> Another rib afford, yet loss of thee
> Would never from my heart. No! No! I feel
> The link of nature draw me, flesh of flesh,
> Bone of my bone thou art and from thy state
> Mine never shall be parted, bliss or woe. (IX. 908–16)

Adam's words here consciously echo both the book of Genesis (2:23) and the Book of Common Prayer (derived from the same source), which interpret the verse analogically; as the congregation of the church is subject to Christ, "so lykewyse let the wyves also be in subjeccion unto their owne husbandes in all thynges" (BCP, 1559, sig. O8v). The state of matrimony is far from a private matter—though it closely concerns private conduct—but symbolizes the relationship of God to the church: "instituted of God in Paradise in the time of mannes innocencie: signifying unto us the misticall union, that is betwixt Christ and his churche" (sig. O5r-v).

* * *

Many of the reformist thinkers of the Renaissance period are concerned with more clearly demarcating the boundaries of the household and aligning them more neatly with paradigms of gender (often textually based). Dod and Cleaver's *A godlie forme of householde government* (reprinted eight times between 1598 and 1630) represents this dynamic very clearly and is worth quoting at length:

> This is also a dutie not to bee forgotten, namely, that husbands be diligent and carefull to make provision for their houses, to clothe their wives

> decently, to bring up their children virtuously, and to pay their servants dulie...The dutie of the husband is to get goods: and of the wife to gather them together, and save them. The dutie of the husband is, to travel abroad to seeke living: and the wives dutie is to keep the house. The dutie of the husband is, to get monie and provision: and to the wives, not vainly to spend it. The dutie of the husband is, to deale with many men; and of the wives, to talk with few. The dutie of the husband is, to be entermedling: and of the wife, to be solitarie and withdrawne. The dutie of the man is to bee skilfull in talke: and of the wife, to boast of silence. The dutie of the husband is, to be a giver: and of the wife, to bee a saver...The dutie of the husband is, to be lord of all; and of the wife, to give account of all. The dutie of the husband is, to dispatch all things without doore: and of the wife, to oversee and give order for all things within the house.[10]

Arguably, this passage is more in thrall with its own rhetorical process than it is in any sense an accurate descriptive account, but nevertheless it articulates an apparently immoveable line between the world of "abroad" (the sphere of public discourse, economic activity, and the exercise of power) and the territory of the "house" (the space of retreat, conservation of wealth, and limited verbal exchange). These arenas are, in turn, neatly mapped onto the differentiated roles of husband and wife; yet, as Hutson has observed:

> [T]here is, for all its predictability, a puzzle about the very symmetry of this formulation of conjugal interdependence. It is, simply, too symmetrical to be anything other than a fiction.[11]

As Hutson goes on to point out, the division of (gendered) labor that in its use of antithesis seems so logically compelling is in fact based not on a division but on usurpation, as the traditional sphere of the household, troped in scriptural and other texts as the stronghold of female power and influence, is brought under male surveillance. Rather than being an agent in her own right in the household, the woman in this formulation (and the many others like it) is a symbol of male power: "The woman, as good wife, is merely the example of his ability to govern."[12] In other words, the separate spheres model is more complex than it immediately appears, less a descriptive account of idealized behavior than a powerfully symbolic site for the inscription of power and ideology, of which gender is one highly significant expression.

FIGURE 5.2: Dancers in a square. Frontispiece, *Roxburgh Ballads*, vol. 7, pt. 21.

Together with the renewed emphasis on a restricted and restrictive role for women in a re-formulated household, there was an increasing recognition and perception of the household as the site of ideological and subject formation. If, as Hutson suggests, the conduct of the wife is used as an index of the male subject's moral capacity, then it follows that her behavior, as much as his, will be subject to public scrutiny. Thus, at the very moment of their inauguration, the terms "public" and "private" prove not to be oppositional at all. This paradox allows for a good deal of instability, such that the household can be used as a form of restriction, but equally, its public orientation and permeability also enable female agency to escape its confines. Many examples of the scrutiny and surveillance of women's conduct (particularly, although not exclusively, wifely conduct) can be found in early modern texts, including drama. A particularly incisive and revealing dramatization at what is at stake in the politics of the household, and the degree to which such politics overspill the boundaries of the "domestic," can be found in Elizabeth Cary's 1613 play, *The Tragedy of Mariam, The Fair Queen of Jewry*. This play is perhaps doubly ironic in its complex approach to these issues, as despite its interest in the impact of wifely conduct on the public sphere, it was never performed in the public theater, because to do so would have been to call its author's sexual reputation into question by making her words accessible to the paying public. Yet the case is more complex: Elizabeth Cary is not identified by name on the title page, but her initials are prominently displayed, and the dedicatory verses clearly identify her as female. She is described on the title page as "that learned, virtuous, and truly noble Ladie, E.C."; but subsequently as "Mistris Elizabeth Carye" (sig. Ar). The particular form Cary chose for her drama also reveals a good deal about the multiple anxieties that attended the circulation of a woman's words; she chooses to write in the form of the closet drama, strongly influenced by the English dramatic interest in Seneca, and enthusiastically embraced by the circle of writers connected to Mary Sidney Herbert, Countess of Pembroke (Samuel Daniel, Fulke Greville, and Mary Sidney herself), primarily because it was seen as an elevated dramatic form with which to counter the potentially tainting and immoral effects of the public theater. Conveniently for a woman writer, however, the form enabled—indeed, encouraged—connections between the personal and the political, taking as its most frequent subject the complexities of the relationship between private actions and public reputation. Unsurprisingly, perhaps, a favored topic for such dramas—designed to be spoken, probably in a domestic or private setting—was the story of Antony and Cleopatra, a narrative that specifically invited dramatists to examine the relationship between emotion and action.

Cary's play uses different material, focusing on the figure of Herod and his wife, Mariam, and setting her play in Palestine. However, the events in the play are contextualized at several points by the ripple effect of the relationship between Antony and Cleopatra across the Roman Empire: the heroine, Mariam, is held up implicitly as the virtuous counterpart to Cleopatra's enticing and destructive beauty. In other words, she is presented as the private ligature for a public, and dynastic, alliance; Herod is a usurper, and it is Mariam's heritage that secures whatever legitimacy his position carries. In turn, this means that matters of rule and state turn on the private conduct of a marital relationship, and it is the private duties of marriage that Mariam refuses to carry out, thus, within the metaphorical and symbolic logic of early modern thinking, destabilizing not only the marital unit, but the state itself. The logic of this position, however, is that female subjectivity as exercised within the apparently self-contained domain of *oikos* might, by analogy, have a direct correlative in the *polis*. In the case of *Mariam*, this provides a useful lever to displace an illegitimate ruler; yet by the same token, that very illegitimacy was veiled or masked by the institution of marriage.[13]

The place of female subjectivity within marriage is understood in contradictory, even volatile, ways in early modern texts. On the one hand, the woman becomes, through the institution of marriage, "one flesh" with her husband. Legally, she has no personhood beyond her husband. On the other, she is acknowledged to play a key role in shaping the household (and its members and dependents), as well as in ensuring the conformity of her husband to social norms; and thus the figure of the wife is crucial to social and ideological reproduction. *The Tragedy of Mariam* is, amongst many other things, an examination of the place of female subjectivity in the process of social reproduction, one that draws attention to the power that might be exercised in the interstices between private and public. At the end of the play, after Mariam's death (and interestingly, the obliteration of the female body appears to be the price exacted for the exercise of subjectivity), Herod laments his disregard for his wife:

> I had but one inestimable Jewell,
> Yet one I had no monarch had the like,
> And therefore may I curse my selfe as cruell:
> Twas broken by a blowe my selfe did strike.
> I gaz'd thereon and never thought me blest,
> But when on it my dazzled eye might rest:
> A pretious Mirror made by wondrous art,
> I prizd it ten times dearer then my Crowne,
> And laide it up fast foulded in my heart:
> Yet I in suddaine choler cast it downe.
> And pasht it all to peeces: twas no foe,
> That robd me of it.[14]

Several aspects of Herod's speech are pertinent. The analogy of Mariam with a "Jewell" suggests the way in which women are valued as commodities, embodying symbolically the economic value that they transfer from father to husband (and thence to sons), and that they are agents of exchange. Women, through this multiply nuanced metaphor, are also ornamental, supplementary. Finally, the term "jewell" is a frequently used euphemism for female genitalia, and thereby, chastity, which is the foundation upon which female power is based within a logic that dictates the transfer of actual and social capital along bloodlines in a culture that cannot guarantee (or verify) paternity. Yet Herod's metaphor also gestures towards the dynastic power that is vested in Mariam as the daughter of a legitimate king. Herod makes the point that he "prizd it ten times dearer then my Crowne" without fully acknowledging that this "jewell" is what makes his crown in the first place. Herod's use of the image of the mirror in this speech again points us towards the ways in which marriage, and conduct within marriage, is cathected.

The mirror image is widespread in early modern culture, used both as a metaphor for political critique (*The Mirror for Magistrates*, most famously) and as a figure for self-examination and self-scrutiny. All sorts of things might function as metaphorical mirrors: souls, texts, bodies, wives.[15] In conduct books, for example, the image of the mirror signifies the affective aspect of marriage, namely the wife's role in assuring and confirming her husband's identity, and, in responding to his emotional and spiritual needs, she should be "a glasse that reflecteth and returneth upon a man his owne image…an other selfe, him selfe before himselfe."[16] However, rather than reflecting her husband's mood, Mariam in the play repeatedly resists it, contravening the idea that a wife is the image or shadow of her husband, "whose face must be hir daylie looking glasse, wherein she ought to be always prying, to see when he is merie, when said, when content, and when discontent, wherto she must always frame hir owne countenance."[17] Mariam refuses to fit her mood to that of her husband, "My Lord, I suit my garment to my minde,/And there no cheerfull colours can I finde" (4.3.5–6). This formulation subtly counterposes a "minde" that is Mariam's own, that lies outside of the marital structure and provides a space from which domestic resistance might originate: as she refuses to conform to Herod's image of her, she undoes the economy of power that underlies marriage and, by extension, the state. The image that Mariam returns to Herod is one that marks his tyranny and fragmentation on the surface of her body, and renders him incapable of rule (because he cannot govern his wife), thereby inverting the mirror image: "There is *a Looking Glasse* for thee…to see thy selfe in, and to shew thee what thou art."[18]

* * *

The Renaissance period had a powerful, if unstable, understanding of the relationship between public actions and private life. Yet for all the critical emphasis in recent years on the continuities between the early modern and modern periods, the evidence from textual and visual sources suggests that ideas of character, privacy, and the public sphere differed from the contemporary in subtle but far-reaching ways. Modernity both overstates the public-private divide (a disjunction predicated on the alienation of workers from the products they made, and thus implicit within advanced capitalism) and underplays the degree to which these nascent spheres (*polis*, marketplace) reinforce key binaries that underlie the Western tradition (male/female, reason/passion, public/private) even as these are problematized and reconfigured.[19] Rather than the new energies brought to the social world by trade, individualism, and the turn to the vernacular, thus opening up a liberatory space for gender roles, the evidence suggests a remarkable degree of continuity and the powerful persistence of ideas about how men and women should behave. To a large extent, this is registered more powerfully at the level of discourse than at the level of practice, although gender ideologies do undergo limited but incremental change. To a large extent, these changes appear in the expansion and augmentation of existing roles and conceptions. In turn, the emergent notions of the individual that have animated debate on the Renaissance since Burkhardt, notions that presuppose an individual who is somehow *continuous* across spheres that are otherwise distinct, turn out themselves to be powerfully gendered. As Joan Kelly pointed out in her seminal article "Did Women Have a Renaissance?" in 1977, various developments in the Renaissance period actually contributed to a sharper demarcation of gender roles along the public/private axis:

> The bourgeois writings on education, domestic life, and society constitute the extreme in this denial of women's independence. Suffice it to say that they sharply distinguish an inferior domestic realm of women from the superior public realm of men, achieving a veritable "renaissance" of the outlooks and practicalities of classical Athens, with its domestic imprisonment of citizen wives.[20]

As Kelly notes, however, such distinctions were also strongly inflected by other factors, notably social class and economic status. As David Cressy has argued, the further down the social scale you go, the more poverty conspires to produce an equal division of labor, although not necessarily of power or status.[21] Yet marriage and the household in the sixteenth and seventeenth centuries were not in any sense exclusively private institutions, as Cressy notes:

> A married couple could hire servants, raise children, and exercise the powers of patriarchy. Their authority proceeded from their condition.

> A husband was expected to govern his wife and household, and the wife was supposed to command those beneath her through a mediated extension of patriarchal power. Each gained status that could be exercised in the public arena as well as the private domain.[22]

Indeed, as Cressy's careful formulation suggests, marriage and the household are the ligatures between public and private and are therefore imbricated in their definition.

Mostly, the Renaissance understood the private and the public to be related aspects of an individual's life, but did not assume that one mapped unproblematically onto the other: thus the unorthodox behavior of some eminent males did little to scupper highly successful careers, although such antics did damage the perception of their *ethos*.[23] But the key point here is the way in which *ethos* itself is profoundly inflected by gender; for a woman, *ethos* could only be properly said to matter if certain keystones of conduct were incontrovertibly in place: chastity, obedience, although not, generally, silence.[24] Incursions into spheres defined as "public" (matters of law, politics, religion, trade, writing) were not de facto prohibited for women, but did necessitate her moral (and often marital) status being above reproach. It is interesting, however, that many women who pushed at the boundaries of cultural prescriptions for women were those who had already fallen foul of social norms in some way (Elizabeth Cary, Mary Wroth, Mary Queen of Scots). In other words, if their reputations as women and worthy wives were already in doubt, some women clearly felt that something might be salvaged by asserting their integrity. Other women who wished to involve themselves in the cultural mainstream had to devise subtle and often complex strategies to enable them to combine public action with a reputation for virtue. All authority was ultimately mediated through the male term, and women proved to be remarkably adept at negotiating and appropriating what power was granted to them in a strongly patriarchal system. Thus women frequently utilize the master discourse of religion (which, it should be remembered, traverses the public-private divide in interesting and unstable ways in this period, as well as being virtually identical with politics) as an authorizing stance. Questions of conscience, for example, required the devout woman, in some circumstances, to make public profession, even defying her husband in order to obey divine law. The power of the spirit to move a woman to speak, confess, prophesy, or proselytize could be invoked in circumstances where this was more a question of recall than of the present: many women's writings of this period claim that their authority derives not from the fallen and sinful body of the woman who writes them, but from the divine imperative that animates them. This may seem limited and contingent to us, but nevertheless provided a platform from which conformists and non-conformists alike might use words and print to assert agency in the world. Readers of such texts as Ann Askew's *Examinations* (1563), or Elinor Channel's *Message from God* (1653–44) were likely to see inherent female weakness as an indelible sign of God's power working in the individual for the benefit of the community at large. Equally, many women chose to write in forms or genres that—at least on the surface—did not necessitate the personal. It should be said that Renaissance literary culture more generally valorized the conventional, the stylistic, the programmatic, and was less interested than modern readers in notions of authenticity or individualized emotion. Thus, forms like translation or imitation often enabled women to add gendered perspectives in the interstices of long-established texts and traditions. Mary Sidney Herbert, for example, dealt with a powerfully mainstream text as she paraphrased the Psalter (a project started by, and thus authorized by, her brother, Philip), yet often revealed her consciousness of gender issues as she worked on multiple versions, and shaped her phrasing accordingly. In Psalm 50, for example, the version prepared for the copy intended for presentation to Elizabeth I in 1599 reads:

Naie ev'n thy brother thie rebukes disgrace,
and thou in spight diffam'st thie mothers sonne:
And for I wink a while, thie thoughts imbrace:
god is like mee, and doth as I have done.[25]

This more "public" text echoes the text of the Psalter reasonably closely ("thou slanderest thine own mother's son," 50:20), but the alternative version focuses more precisely on the obligations of the bond between mother and child:

Thy tongue a stamp that coines but fraud and lyes
Ev'n to disgrace of him; whom to thee tyes
The sweet strait band of calling one your mother. (B text, ll. 53–55)

The key point here is that in terms of speech, articulation, and writing—those very modes that create a ligature between internally lived experience and the public world where they might have effects and consequences—women are constantly negotiating the boundary of what might be said and utilizing socially sanctioned modes and forms in order to assert their agency. Sometimes, as in the case of Lady Mary Wroth, the effort backfires spectacularly, revealing in the process, however, exactly where the boundary was *perceived* to lie.

In many ways, women often turn their exclusion from more formal rhetorical modes of articulation to their advantage: either, as in the case of Mary Sidney or Katherine Philips (to name but two), learning such techniques outside of institutional sites and through their reading, or elevating the embrace of plain speech to an ethical and moral principle by claiming that the words as written come directly from the heart—or sometimes, from God. When Anne Wheathill, for example, presents her collection of prayers to a female readership in 1584, she consistently mobilizes this idea in her prefatory epistle:

> [A] small handful of grose hearbs; which I have presumed to gather out of the garden of Gods most holie word. Not that there is anie unpurenes therein, but that...my rudeness may be found to have plucked them up unreverentlie, and without zeale.
> Whereupon of the learned I may be judged grose and unwise; in presuming, without the counsell or helpe of anie, to take such an enterprise in hand: nevetheles, as GOD dooth know, I have done it with a good zeale, according to the weaknes of my knowledge and capacitie.[26]

Wheathill's subjection of herself to a higher authority is signaled subtly, but consistently ("presumed," "rudeness," "unreverentlie"), and she positions herself specifically in *opposition* to "the learned," having undertaken her word "without the counsell or helpe of anie." Her "weaknes" is, at one level, the source of her authority, as "zeale" (often understood as a code word for Puritan sympathies) takes the place of preoccupations that might stand between author and subject. As Elaine Beilin has argued, Wheathill "writes plainly, in the style long established as appropriate for godly instruction."[27]

For all the posturing represented by the so-called humility *topos*, and the necessarily circumspect nature of much writing by women, it is nevertheless the case that even the printed text can provide some examples of how women negotiated the contradictions that were contingent upon conducting life in public spaces. The historical and textual record is full of examples of women going about their daily business, transacting business (printing and brewing, for example), taking lawsuits, presenting petitions at court, inspecting lands and properties, attending church, copying down sermons, buying and selling goods at market, and frequenting the shared spaces of village, town, and city. London as a teeming, growing metropolis is a particularly interesting site to examine the relationship between private and public as it relates to women.[28] London's social structures were necessarily more fluid and more mobile than other towns and cities; the city depended heavily on the inward migration of workers from London's hinterland (and beyond), particularly to provide domestic service. The imperatives of nascent capitalism often meant that profitable businesses were sustained by women when men were absent (or dead). As Helen Smith and others have argued, London contained a significant number of female printers, for example, and brewing was often the province of women, too. Thus London was home (however temporary) to a good number of single, young women, often separated from their families. Estimates suggest, for example, that levels of literacy were higher amongst London women—either because reading was taught more often within households, or because women passed this skill on to one another informally. Equally, it may be that girls sent to London to seek work were more likely to be literate, as their prospects would be seen to be better. The economic and social reality of large numbers of young women who were effectively outside the usual forms of control may account for the focus in popular texts upon the negative stereotype of transgressive femininity—the gadder, the gossip, the whore. It is notable that images of these stock figures (whether textual or visual) tend to represent them as occupying specific spaces (often public, but secluded—the shop, the tavern) but that these are sex-segregated, and therefore all-female, entities. This is the inevitable consequence of ideologies of gender that insist on segregation and demarcation, namely that the sequestered space potentially becomes one of misrule and subversion—at least in the imaginations of those who are excluded, even if such exclusion is the consequence of their own privileged logic. Gossips in particular are generally depicted as passing their time bewailing the inadequacies of their menfolk—undoing the male term upon which they are supposed to depend. As Richard Baxter wearily noted in the 1680s, the *"abundance of loquacious women"*

> will sit a whole hour together with you, yea many hours, to tell you first how the affairs go between them and their husbands or children and servants; and then talk of their cattle, house, or land; and then tell you of new, and enter into a long discourse of other mean matters…they then tell you what this body said to them, and what the other body said, and then they tell a story of the old times.[29]

However negatively such speech is troped, and its concerns represented as trivial, it nevertheless symbolizes a form of female power and agency that lies outside of male regulation—it marks the point at which the household (or other space) no longer neatly symbolizes the exercise of male authority. Male fear of what goes on in female spaces is of alternative alliances and forms of power,

"Thus lerne the younger, of the elders guiding/Day by day, kepying such scoles/ The simplymen, the[y] make as foles":[30]

> [T]he characterization of gossip as female reflected an uneasy awareness that women exchanged news among themselves which they might conceal from their husbands. Men worried about the subversive implications, fearing such behavior would undermine the respect and authority they claimed as husbands and fathers.[31]

Yet forms of exchange presented through the framework of "gossip," might, as Bernard Capp and others have suggested, in fact represent interventions in community affairs and public life—ensuring, for example, that certain norms of behavior were observed, or that individuals were held to their promises.[32] Certainly women, and women's speech, played a key role in determining and maintaining an individual's reputation or *ethos*. And contrary to male anxiety on this matter, women's speech, as the work of Laura Gowing has demonstrated, was largely a socially conservative force that tended to maintain the status quo rather than to disrupt it.[33]

Despite the fact that *public* speech in the form of publication was generally thought to be off-limits for women, various forms of textual exchange were used to develop networks and to establish good character. Writing, for women, was not necessarily or automatically transgressive, and could serve as a means

FIGURE 5.3: Tavern scene. *Roxburgh Ballads*, vol. 2, p. 31.

by which political ideals or action might be circulated and supported. Evidence has been uncovered by feminist scholars of the ways in which women writers might intervene in key religious controversies; for example, the figure of Anne Cooke Bacon, who, sanctioned by the Archbishop of Canterbury, translated John Jewel's *Apologia ecclesiae anglicanae*.[34] Women utilized forms such as letters as ways of creating textual communities of like-minded thinkers, allied by blood, political allegiance, or religious conviction.[35] Whilst prescriptive texts certainly counseled against women's involvement in public life, a range of other materials suggested that women were as bound by questions of faith, conscience, and duty as other individuals, and that in certain circumstances they were bound to profess and bear witness publicly. Many of the key figures in John Foxe's *Book of Martyrs*, for example, are women who, sanctioned by the higher calling of their faith (duty to God being more important than obedience to an apostate husband), defy their husband's authority in order to speak and write publicly of their Protestant convictions. Even if, as would seem to be the case, these women's voices are being used to serve and authorize a particular agenda, it is still true that women's words were not simply confined to the realm of the private.

One fascinating text that brings together many of these issues is Isabella Whitney's *WYLL and Testament*, printed in her collection of adages and verse epistles, *A Sweet Nosgay*, published in London in 1573. Her text is perhaps best described as a miscellany, bringing together versifications of sayings from another author, Hugh Plat, which attempt to function as moral prophylactics against the epidemiological contagion of the plague (and other urban diseases), but also to protect morality from the moral and social dislocations that are seen to be endemic to London life.[36] What is remarkable about the collection, however, is the way in which Whitney stages the dynamics of textual exchange within her volume, in order to create a community of readers for her texts, readers who will view her writing as enhancing her credit, rather than as damaging her reputation. Whitney reveals and exploits the instabilities of textual production, and its potential for the forging of provisional identities (gesturing towards a private individual who is only made known—invented—by the fact of public circulation), as well as locating the fluidity of identities in the interaction between text and reader; a reader who necessarily constructs an "author" as a point of origin for meaning. Thus, the gendered dynamics of textuality and publication are here turned on their heads—Whitney's logic being that surely writing might be used just as well to the end of establishing female *virtue*. In this way, then, the private person is juxtaposed with the public world, yet both are insistently implicated in each other. More specifically, the public institutions that embody civic virtue and pride (the courts, the markets, St. Paul's) are appropriated specifically to Whitney's private vision. London's public spaces and institutions are rendered from a unique perspective, namely that of the private citizen—but her gender makes her reclamation of the position of citizen a powerfully assertive stance. One of the key texts in her miscellany is the formally inventive and generically ludic mock-testament, which inverts Whitney's relation to the city of London (where it is assumed that she was in service) and imaginatively asserts that its wealth is in fact hers to bequeath. The poem traverses the topography of London not simply in spatial terms, but also in cultural and socioeconomic ones; the speaker is thus both marginal to the city and its wealth, and a central part of its shifting social fabric. The idea of "service" is consistently ironic, and a careful wedge is driven between the idea of credit as monetary and the notion that "credit" speaks to the moral capacity of the speaker or agent to fulfill promises made. The whole point, of course, is that the city of London fails in its duty of reciprocity.

For women of royal blood (even, or especially, if this was at dispute), there was a direct ideological contradiction at work; on the one hand, the monarch's body politic was seen to be divinely sanctioned and to pass seamlessly from one ruler to another. On the other, the monarch's body natural was deemed to embody ideals of nation, unity, and order, and indeed, well into the early modern period, to have sacred and healing powers, as the continuation of the Maundy Day ceremonies implicitly acknowledged. It was assumed to be a male body, as underlined by the aggressively masculine iconography of the latter part of the reign of Henry VIII. Equally, there was an irresolvable opposition at work in the relationship of male courtiers with a female monarch; superior in terms of status, but inferior in terms of the natural laws that governed the pervasive gender hierarchies of early modern culture.[37] Questions of authority and legitimacy were wont to dog female monarchs, as commentators feared the subjugation of the body politic to the body natural through the means of matrimony at the same time as they required the appearance of social conformity that marriage embodied. These issues are thrown into sharp relief by the various exchanges, diplomatic and otherwise, that took place around the failed negotiations for Elizabeth I to marry François, Duc d'Anjou (previously Alençon), in the late 1570s and early 1580s (following from similar discussions in relation to his elder brother, Henri, at the start of that decade). Perhaps due to the fact that Elizabeth was self-evidently past secure childbearing age at this point, the issues raised by the potential match were even more acute, one court official calling it "but treason." Rival political factions were divided on the issue—whether the outside chance of a secure succession (albeit involving a Catholic marriage), which would short-circuit the claims of Mary Queen of Scots, outweighed the very real dangers imposed by the implied submission of the body politic through marital means. The responses to this perceived crisis are well known—John Stubbes's *The Discoverie of Gaping Gulf* (1579), and Sir Philip Sidney's letter opposing the match—but less well known are Elizabeth's own letters regarding the situation. Whilst these are inevitably couched in diplomatic language (and were undoubtedly the work of more than one hand), nevertheless the evasion of the language of selfhood and privacy is notable. In response to the communication of Alençon's emissary that one of his patron's key demands was that "the said duke might jointly have authority with us to dispose of all things donative within this our realm and other our dominions," Elizabeth writes:

> [T]he inconveniences were laid before him by our said Council, who declared unto him that it was a matter than greatly touched our regality, in so much as Monsieur might have thereby *vocem negativam*. And also that in the marriage between the king of Spain and our late sister, the contents of that demand was by especial article prohibited in the treaty between them...yet was he not without great difficulty drawn to desist from urging us to yield our consent therein, notwithstanding he was plainly given to understand that our consenting thereto could not but breed dangerous alienation of our subjects' goodwill from us.[38]

The key term here is "consent," which doubles both for the agreement to marriage and for the articles of the treaty—body politic and body natural are thus inextricable in this circumstance; equally the "us" has a double referent, ostensibly to the person of the monarch, but also implicitly to the "us" of the putative couple. In her letters directly to Alençon, Elizabeth appears to write in her own person, using "I." Yet, this stance is deceptive, as it simply uses the language of proximity to drive home the same essential message:

> My dearest, I give you now a fair mirror to see there very clearly the foolishness of my understanding, which I once found so suited to hoping for a good conclusion, weighing the place where you reside with the company that is there. We poor inhabitants of the barbarous isle must be careful in appearing for judgment where such ingenious judges of our knowledge hold their seat in so high a place in your favor. But in making my appeal to Monsieur alone and undivided, I will not let my suit drop. And if you would have me given over to the rack, I will not put a gloss

on this text, assuring myself that you understand it only too well...I can only be she who has lodged you in the first rank of what is dearest to me, as God can best witness.[39]

Elizabeth re-applies the conventional humility *topos* to the nation that she embodies ("the barbarous isle"). The pronoun instability in this passage is indicative of the complexity of the queen's identity, writing to Alençon in her own person, yet reasserting in this guise her authority as monarch. Elsewhere, of course, Elizabeth—for her own rhetorical advantage—makes a certain amount of mileage out of the *idea* of herself as a private person. Her speech at the closing of Parliament in 1576 can be seen as a key document in relation to Elizabeth's complex negotiation of her gender (and incidentally, an interesting commentary on whether femininity is necessarily aligned with the private, rather than the public, sphere). She begins by carefully distancing herself from the masculinist discourse of rhetoric, subordinating her skill (although not her authority) to Parliament itself: "If any look for eloquence, I shall deceive their hope; if some think I can match their gift which spake before, they hold an open heresy."[40] As she reflects on the "restless care" of her reign, Elizabeth astutely attributes her success not to herself, but to divine Providence: "My sex permits it not." Constancy, a virtue frequently required of women, is here elevated into a political principle:

> [W]hereas variety and love of change is ever so rife in servants to their masters, in children to their parents, and in private friends one to another (as that though for one year or perhaps for two they can content themselves to hold their course upright, yet after, by mistrust or doubt of worse, they are dissevered and in time wax weary of their wonted liking), yet still I find that assured zeal amongst my faithful subjects.[41]

The language of friendship and privacy is here consistently mobilized in order to assert Elizabeth's aloofness from such mutable and transitory concerns: "all those means of leagues, alliances and foreign strengths I quite forsook and gave myself to seek for truth without respect, reposing my assured stay in God's most might grace with full assurance. Thus I began, thus I proceed, and thus I hope to end."[42] The buried issue that she alludes to here, of course, is the question of matrimony, as subsequently becomes clear, at least by inference:

> [I]t shall not be needful, though I must confess mine own mislike so much to strive against the matter as, if I were a milkmaid with a pail on mine

arm, whereby my private person might be little set by, I would not forsake that single state to match myself with the greatest monarch. Not that I condemn the double knot or judge amiss of such as, forced by necessity, cannot dispose themselves to another life, but wish that none were driven to change such as cannot keep honest limits.[43]

This complex statement provides a revealing instance of the contested nature of privacy and its intersections with gender; whilst Elizabeth claims that class offsets the demands of public life (if, indeed, "little set by" means "of little account"), she also undermines this reading by her grandiose claim that *even if* her private decisions had no public impact, nonetheless she would not trade her "private person," or her "single state" for even the most advantageous of matches. This is a powerful assertion of the integrity of the private self, all the more so for being articulated in an institution that embodied masculine power; yet it very cleverly uses the conditional and the theoretical to make an assertion that runs contrary to accepted ideals of womanhood. It suggests, in short, that gender, and femininity in particular, often sharpened and complicated accepted ideas about the relationship between private and public.

Renaissance society was powerfully conformist in many things, and deeply rhetorical, using a plethora of stock phrases and adages alongside an array of easily recognizable conventions for expressing every aspect of human experience. The point at which words fail to convey experience (surely a key pressure point on the public-private divide) was itself a convention, a heightening device, a means of marking an individual's mastery of a foundational discourse. Traditional social values received repeated and heavy emphasis, and many of these were both self-consciously ideological (and reinforced through Althusserian means) and inherited from the medieval period. Ideas of female inferiority and identification with the domestic world of the household and childbearing proved surprisingly durable in the face of not one, but many epistemological revolutions: traditional divisions between the sexes are diversified and adapted to new circumstances, but they endure, at least at the level of prescription. But what is intriguing about the early modern period is the development of new discourses of virtue that promote female agency in certain spheres and contexts, albeit in carefully circumscribed ways.

Just as classical texts bequeathed the Renaissance a set of easily recognizable types of virtue and vice, biblical texts were mined for examples of conduct, morality, and behavior. In the case of female examples, these were mostly neatly arrayed on either side of a binary split between morality and immorality, and were deployed in a spirit of familiar exchange of example and counterexample. Figures such as Deborah, Judith, Esther, Susannah, and Jael were used to provide precedents for female courage, leadership, constancy, and capacity to rule. Of equal importance for the consideration of the influence of textual traditions and models on early modern conceptualizations of women's language are the nonspecific textual cruxes of the Bible—the Pauline epistles in particular—where moral issues relating to the place of women's speech are played out, with arguably real effects in real households and communities.[44] Questions surrounding scriptural exemplarity are, in principle, similar to those arising from the classical tradition—certainly, many of the key hermeneutic methods of selection, commentary, and application are analogous—but there are also significant differences. In the first instance, the authority of the text is not in dispute, but its interpretation often is—and the grounds of the debate are often concerned not so much with textual authority but with issues relating to historical or cultural context; the points at issue are concerned with the *application* of the text. Second, modes of transmission, with their explicit emphasis on the relationship of the individual to the word, often overtly include women as part of the target audience, whether through her reading a commentary or sermon, hearing them read, or via the husband's role as moral and spiritual head of the household. Third, the tradition of scriptural commentary, based around exemplary figures and key textual passages, hybridizes with a range of other textual forms to produce a generically diverse body of material that has as its end the translation of scriptural example into moral action in the world, even where this "action" might properly be defined as inaction in the face of apparent temptation or provocation. Unsurprisingly, such examples focus on the woman's role in the family and in the household, and stress the importance of proper conduct and the correct use of language and speech.

It would be an error to assume any degree of uniformity in terms of the relationship of women to the public sphere—England was widely seen as a paradise for women, at least compared to the dynastic restrictions of French Salic law, and, as we have seen, many women circumvented the limitations placed on their public participation in inventive and intelligent ways. It is certainly true that English women were relatively visible in the public sphere (not least as monarchs), and political and cultural discourses developed complex and subtle ways of dealing with the potential contradictions that this entailed. Women, as Barbara Harris has convincingly argued, played key roles in the creation and maintenance of networks based on kin, politics, and religion, many of which had significance beyond the familial.[45] A good example of this would be Mary Sidney Herbert, Countess of Pembroke, who tirelessly capitalized on her fraternal legacy (as the sister of Sir Philip Sidney) and her status as the living heir of the great Protestant earls to advance a particular form of poetic and cultural Protestantism that undoubtedly carried a powerful political charge, as her poem addressed to Queen Elizabeth in 1599 reveals.[46]

Commentators varied widely in their attitudes to key questions, such as women's education, female regiment, and the capacity of women to understand and comment on complex theological questions. Yet despite this variability, a number of social taboos were consistently upheld: the innate inferiority of women to men; the need for women to defer to male authority in all key matters; the proscription of women entering public spaces or discourses without male authorization of some form. These cultural norms had clear and unambiguous counterparts in law, too, notably the notion of *coverture* whereby upon marriage a woman (and everything she owned) became the legal property of her husband. The private, in this context, often means the loss of autonomy rather than the assertion of independence. Legally, again, a wife's lack of personhood under the law sometimes enabled a degree of nonconformity that was more problematic for men—not only was the intrusion of the state into matters of the household resented and resisted (the household being troped, in effect, as an autonomous state in and of itself), but usually it was the head of the household (father/husband) who was legally responsible for ensuring observance. Despite their institutional marginality, evidence of various kinds suggests that women were very important in ensuring the continuity of Catholicism, and in promoting Counter-Reformation thought and practice.[47] The concern of the authorities to remove children from recusant households attests, too, to the central importance of the maternal figure in the moral and spiritual education of children—this was a key tenet of Protestant re-formulations of the role of women.

The "separate spheres" model of understanding gender roles and relationships in the Renaissance had a powerful hold as feminist literary critics and historians turned their attention to the 1500–1700 period. As such, it was heavily dependent on conceptual models formulated in relation to the nineteenth century, and sometimes conflated prescriptive writings with lived reality. As the work of numerous scholars has demonstrated, women's participation quite frequently extended to activities that might subsequently have been defined as belonging to the public sphere (economic activity, engagement with the law, local politics, religion and spirituality), but were often viewed as a key part of the work of the household, understood not as a private place of familial retirement but as a microcosm of the world at large, whose thresholds were permeable and often fluid.

Emergent technologies (including writing as well as print, which are, primarily, technologies of the word) also played key roles in reconfiguring some aspects of the public-private divide. A largely pre-literate society, to take but one example, will develop very different notions of public and private to those of the Internet age, because such technologies function within a framework that sees face-to-face and collective forms of social interaction as the norm against which other more disembodied encounters are measured and through which they are understood. Equally, the increasing availability of print to some extent eroded a classical distinction between *polis* and *oikos* precisely because of the transmission of ideas and debates across the boundary of the household. The point being, of course, that "public" and "private" are relative terms, locked into a binary definition in ways analogous to the pastoral's interest in *otium* and *negotium*: it is more than serendipitous that the latter term *contains* the former, and that the exploration of one might well be a means of alluding to the other. It is perhaps hard for us to imagine what the public sphere might be in the Renaissance, lacking (amongst other things) a representative or accountable political system, mass media, etc., but texts and other evidence suggest that it was a world of masculine endeavor, of action, intellect and decision, of honor, chivalry, and politics, often defined against less manly pursuits, and against home and family.

Many concepts fundamental to the functioning of early modern English society have been replaced or overturned by the liberal consensus: obedience, honor, chastity, and continence. These qualities were judged by a person's actions, which were understood to have been primarily forged in the crucible of the household. In profound and far-reaching ways, family was destiny. In turn, a person's qualities were judged in relation to a complex nexus of discourses and ideologies, but specifically in terms of how far that person fulfilled (or deviated from) his or her socially allotted role. Paradoxically, public and private were both articulated as rhetorical oppositions, as well as being experienced as a continuum. At the level of discourse, one was constantly expressed in terms of the other, with commentators, acquaintances, and gossips fine-tuned to root out inconsistencies. Yet this opposition is not quite identical with the public-private divide as theorized by Habermas and others in the context of the rise of the late eighteenth-century and early nineteenth-century bourgeoisie, and as this essay suggests, these terms are in play in the period, but are flexible and friable. Other—more strictly historical—terms will enable us to track the nexus of connections between space, place, and social status in a period where the household is understood variously, and as a construct that constantly mediates the relationship between private and public.

Much has been written on the emergent concept of privacy in the early modern period—much of it predicated on a rather one-dimensional idea of the medieval period—in the case of England, seeing this as an ongoing process culminating in the arrival of a fully fledged concept of private life at the Restoration. This idea of privacy is broadly coincident with an idea of interior life, again broadly speaking, one seen as emerging with the habits of self-examination fostered by Reformation focus on the unmediated relationship with God. It is perhaps unsurprising that such ideas of privacy are often identified within newer, looser, more informal types of writing such as the diary.[48] It is certainly true that over the course of the early modern period, generic diversification is a significant feature, with a clear transition away from the classically inflected, highly formal stylistic models of the earlier Renaissance towards looser, more hybrid forms often based on different kinds of literate practice, usually undertaken initially in the household. These are large generalizations, but the highly rhetorical character of sixteenth- and early seventeenth-century writings—masculine, orientated towards the public world, based around the cementing of homosociality as expressed through a stylistic code—gradually gave way to more open-ended types of writing, often autodidact in character that drew heavily on the kinds of writing that might be done without the benefit of formal education. It is often noted that the output of writings by women (as one, admittedly flawed, measure, perhaps, of their participation in public discourse) increases exponentially after the Restoration, a fact often attributed to the re-ordering of gender hierarchies (or their subordination to other kinds of alliances) during the English Civil War. However, it seems possible that the mode of discourse changes (as Hobbes, amongst others, notes) and that the emergent notions of privacy and intimacy as traced by Francis Barker in Pepys's diary in fact start to favor the kinds of generic forms and written styles that women were using all along.

It is hard to draw definitive conclusions about the relationship of public and private in any period, but the early modern is perhaps particularly resistant to schematic analysis, not least because it is in this period that such notions are in the process of formation and re-formation—the latter most particularly, as the return *ad fontes* prompted both by the assimilation of humanism and the Reformation paradoxically drew attention to the ways in which parallels and analogues from classical and scriptural texts decidedly did *not* apply to the rapidly emerging social and economic conditions that shaped sixteenth- and seventeenth-century England. However, it is clear that the concepts of public and private were under scrutiny, and that gender was a key axis around which such ideas were articulated; there was a considerable gap between ideology and practice, slippage that proved felicitous for women who sought to redefine the parameters of the private sphere and to make the point that the home and the household were something more than private. Having said that, of course, this argument (that the private is ultimately anything but) leads to a certain circularity, and it is significant that it is not until the Civil War and its aftermath that this ultimately classical ideal of the household is finally broken down. Notions of privacy are also definitively undermined by the reality of living conditions for most people, and by the fact that the female body was in some sense held to be legitimately subject to public scrutiny and surveillance.

CHAPTER SIX

Education and Work

MEG LOTA BROWN AND KARI BOYD MCBRIDE

Though few people of the early modern era were literate, all were educated to assume their proper place in society; often that education was quite programmed and intentional, despite the fact that very few children, girls or boys, went to school and neither girls nor boys, men nor women among the peasantry were likely to be able to read or write at this time.[1] Parents were responsible for training their children (or sending them to others to be trained) to assume roles appropriate to their status, whether as agricultural laborers, household servants, skilled artificers, merchants, clergy, courtiers, or monarchs. And every girl, regardless of her social situation, was educated in domestic skills, something that set girls apart from boys. Any person of the era who wrote about education stressed that girls were to be instructed very differently from boys. All women learned sewing and needlework, which were often lauded as the mark of feminine virtue—something for which there was no equivalent for boys, whose training tended to depend very much on their class. Even when girls' education was not elaborately theorized (as, for instance, in the case of girls of low social status), they were still taught a very different set of skills from boys. More than anything else, education was meant to fit a child for a particular social role, which is perhaps why some moralists thought that too much education was a danger for women and for all people of lower social status.

In addition, girls' education was always designed to protect and preserve their chastity and virtue, so some educators recommended limiting even elite girls to reading the Bible and religious works and discouraged their learning of Latin and Greek, which might expose them to obscene or frivolous literature. (Few educators encouraged boys to read such works, either, but it was assumed that elite boys needed to learn Latin to read philosophy and other ancient literature.) Similarly, girls from most Jewish families were not encouraged to learn Hebrew, which was, like Latin and Greek, the language of scholarship and—even more important for both Christianity and Judaism—the language of Holy Scripture. Both Christian and Jewish scholars typically argued that girls who studied holy works in the ancient languages would become sexually promiscuous. The Mishnah (the collection of Jewish law and commentary) quoted the revered Rabbi Eliezer as saying, "Everyone who teaches his daughter Torah, it is as if he taught her lechery."[2] Too much learning was also thought to make girls masculine; one rabbi writing about learned women used masculine pronouns and suffixes to describe them. And Leon Modena (1571–1648), an Italian rabbi of Venice, though he taught both girls and boys as part of his official duties, did not educate his own daughters, who could neither read nor write. Indeed, even after their marriages, they could maintain contact with their father, renowned as "one of the greatest masters of Hebrew letter writing in Italy, if not all of Jewish history," only by having their husbands write letters for them.[3]

For some Christian as well as Jewish moralists, too much learning or the wrong kind of learning would, at the very least, distract women from their duties as wives and mothers. At the worst, it would corrupt their chastity and virtue and perhaps turn them into mannish, lascivious monsters. Nonetheless, sources show that some "Jewish women in Italy taught children the Hebrew letters and the correct reading of scripture in Hebrew, though translation and commentary were reserved for male teachers."[4] Indeed, girls' education in general became more common in the Renaissance. Despite the widespread objections from many religious writers and cultural commentators, it is nonetheless a fact that many middle-class and aristocratic girls *were* educated, some of them as extensively as boys. In this case, as in many others, too much credence cannot be given to the writings of conservative moralists, whose diatribes against certain activities are often the best proof that those activities were common.

Works on pedagogy were written by the hundreds during this period, and almost everyone who wrote on education felt obliged to include some mention of women's proper education. Authors would often append to the tract a list of learned women throughout the ages as a justification for their own educational theories. While many moralists were leery of overeducating women, a fair number of authors, both male and female, wrote enthusiastically in support of women's education and published elaborate programs of study for women. Most elite children continued to be schooled at home by private tutors at this time. Such a practice had always guaranteed that many—perhaps most—girls from aristocratic families would have access to education up to a point (though they could not, of course, go to a university, which elite boys typically attended from about the age of fourteen). Indeed, one recent scholar has suggested that education was quite widely available to girls: "[i]t is modern scholarship, rather than early modern, which has caused the woman scholars of the sixteenth and seventeenth centuries to vanish."[5] Even middle-class girls began to enjoy greater and greater education during the Renaissance as schools proliferated in many parts of Europe. Children in these schools learned reading, writing, and mathematics; some were introduced to other languages, even Latin, which remained the mark of a true education throughout the era. Girls' schools of this sort were also noted for teaching dance and music, as these skills were thought to be particularly appropriate to women.

In some cases, girls' musical education might be quite advanced, as their teachers were among the finest musicians of the age. For instance, Antonio Vivaldi (1678–1741), one of the most admired musicians of the Baroque era, was for many years the *maestro di violino* (string instrument master or teacher) and later *the maestro de' concerti* (orchestra master) at the Ospedale della Pietà, a girls' orphanage in Venice. He wrote some of his finest compositions, including instrumental works and sacred vocal works, for the all-girl orchestra there. Similarly, when the disruptions of the Civil War in England (1639–49) broke up the royal and aristocratic courts, musicians who were formerly employed writing court music and producing concerts and masques had to make a living outside those circles. Henry Lawes (1596–1662) had been Gentleman of the Chapel Royal and a member of the King's Musick, but after the breakup of the royal court, he took a job teaching at Mrs. Salmon's School in Hackney. There he taught, among other young women, Mary Harvey, Lady Dering (1629–1704), the first English woman to publish music under her own name. Elaborate musical and dramatic productions were quite common in both girls' and boys' schools. The composer Henry Purcell's (1659–95) opera *Dido and Aeneas*, for instance, was first performed in 1689 by the "Young Gentlewomen" of "Mr. Josias Priest's Boarding School at Chesley" near London, according to the title page of the libretto published that same year. Convent girls' schools in northern Europe regularly staged plays, both ancient and modern; by the eighteenth century, girls in those schools were learning and performing the works of the French neoclassical dramatist Jean Racine (1639–99) and others.[6] And many Continental convent schools were known for the high quality of their music and music instruction. The celebration for Margaret Clement's fifty-year jubilee (the fiftieth anniversary of her profession as a nun) at Louvain was marked by an entire week of musical performance, with choirs and viol consorts from all the local convents. The High Mass culminating the week of festivities featured her own nuns singing a piece specially composed for the event, with viols accompanying the entire service. Even the musicians from the court of Archduke Albert of Austria (1559–1621) joined in the musical celebration.[7]

Literacy in one's own language—one's "mother tongue"—was generally on the rise in this period. Indeed, Protestants insisted on literacy, as they held that salvation was predicated *sola scriptura*, that is, on scripture alone, rather than on sacraments, penitential acts, or good works. This belief led to the translation of the Bible into the vernacular not only by Protestants but also by Catholics, who wished to counter the overtly Protestant perspective of some translations with their own version. There developed, then, a literate population who believed that salvation was based on their ability to "read, mark, learn, and inwardly digest" the "holy Word" of God, as one collect of the Church of England put it.[8] In addition, the fact that the Catholic Church continued to hold the Vulgate in particular esteem during this period and continued to celebrate liturgies in Latin meant that Catholic children who were educated at all tended to learn at least some basic Latin, and sometimes they became quite fluent in the language. Despite the misgivings of conservative rabbis, many elite Jewish girls were also educated, sometimes learning Hebrew as well as Greek (for the study of philosophy) and Latin (for the study of poetry and rhetoric); as in the case of Christian girls, however, they were often kept from reading anything remotely corrupting or salacious, including the works of poets like Dante (1265–1321) and Petrarch (1304–74), both of whom wrote in Italian.[9] The sixteenth-century woman Fioretta of Modena, Italy, was "very learned in Torah, Mishnah, Talmud, Midrash, Jewish law, especially Maimonides, and Kabbalistic literature." She raised her grandson, who became the scholar and author Rabbi Aaron Berechiah of Modena (d. 1639), and supervised his education. He in turn credited her with his scholarly gifts. Jewish women like Fioretta who were notably learned might be known by the title *rabit* or *rabanit*, a woman who participates in rabbinic discussions.[10] So the Renaissance was for some women a time of expanded opportunities in terms of what is usually thought of as education, that is, learning based on reading and writing. Furthermore, the Renaissance revival of learning—the recovery of ancient

Greek and Roman philosophy, literature, and rhetoric—meant that the body of knowledge that one might study was exponentially expanded in this period. And the flowering of humanism—a philosophy that emphasized the accomplishments of human endeavor and arts rather than seeing human beings only in terms of life after death and the judgment of God—meant that academic and artistic accomplishment came to be seen as compatible with piety and as something to be desired rather than feared.

FIGURE 6.1: Title page, *The Accomplished Ladies Rich Closet* (1675), by Hannah Woolley. Wellcome Collection, L0043956. Woolley's books of household recipes and tips were typical of the kind of practical education for women in the seventeenth century.

Some proponents of humanism, both Jewish and Christian, departed from the long tradition of resistance to girls' education and argued that elite girls as well as boys should be given a liberal education. Such learning included training in the *trivium* (grammar, rhetoric, and logic) and the *quadrivium* (arithmetic, geometry, music, and astronomy). Even girls who did not enjoy an extensive education benefited nonetheless from the humanist outlook and from the growing demands of urban culture and economy, which required a labor force of women and men with literacy and numeracy skills. Glückel of Hameln (1647–1727) is a good example of a woman who was fully competent in both writing and keeping accounts. She was able to take over her husband's business at his death in 1690; Glückel was merely one of thousands of Renaissance widows who managed businesses. Italian humanists saw it as the mother's particular duty to teach her children the alphabet and basic reading skills; children often learned first to read a vernacular Psalter (the 150 Psalms of the Bible), and many of them would memorize all the Psalms in this manner. Boys would then be sent away to schools where they would receive extensive training in literature as well as instruction in Latin, which was essential for anyone pursuing a public or academic career. In Italy as elsewhere, girls' education was concentrated on sewing, reading, and learning the virtues (*le virtú*). With some notable exceptions, girls were less likely than boys to be sent out to school; rather, they would continue their training at home in domestic arts and, among families of means who could afford special tutors, in music, dancing, and art. But, contrary to this norm, post-Reformation English Catholic families often sent their children to convent schools on the Continent for an education so as to avoid the explicit Protestantism of English schools.

There were also day schools for local girls in Italy early in this period, usually at a convent where they were taught by nuns; such establishments often became boarding schools by the late fifteenth century, where girls lived and learned until they reached marriageable age or made their vows as nuns.[11] For instance, Laura Cereta (1469–99) of Brescia was sent to a convent school at seven years of age to learn reading, writing, needlework, and basic Latin. (By this time, Brescia had ten monasteries for women housing eight hundred nuns, many of whom were involved in the work of educating young girls.) Though Cereta was back and forth between convent and home for the next few years, she was sent at the age of nine to the same "erudite woman" to be instructed in the Latin canon of literature. She was married at fifteen, but her husband died less than two years later; she spent the rest of her short life as a scholar, meeting regularly with other intellectuals of the region, giving public readings of her essays, and keeping up close friendships with many of the scholar-nuns of the area. Indeed, the scholarly life was thought inappropriate for a married woman, who would be distracted from her studies by her duties to her children and to overseeing the management of her household. Consequently, Italian women scholars of the fifteenth century tended to be either widows like Cereta, or unmarried women, or nuns, and all lived cloistered, whether at home or in a monastery or convent. (Men, of course, could both marry and pursue the scholarly life, as they would have a wife to see to all the "distractions" of family life and personal care.) Cereta was particularly interested in women's education and argued that "[a]ll human beings, women included, are born with the right to an education":

> For some women are concerned with parting their hair correctly, adorning themselves with lovely dresses, or decorating their fingers with pearls and other gems. Others delight in mouthing carefully composed phrases, indulging in dancing, or managing spoiled puppies. Still others wish to gaze at lavish banquet tables, to rest in sleep, or, standing at mirrors, to smear their lovely faces. But those in whom a deeper integrity yearns for virtue, restrain from the start their youthful souls, reflect on higher things, harden the body with sobriety and trials, and curb their tongues, open their ears, compose their thoughts in wakeful hours, their minds in contemplation, to letters bonded to righteousness. For knowledge is not given as a gift, but [is gained] with diligence. The free mind, not shirking effort, always soars zealously toward the good, and the desire to know grows ever more wide and deep.[12]

Note that Cereta was careful to align her learning with chastity and virtue, a theme that occupied all writers on education, even women themselves.

Even before Cereta's time, there were Italian women well known as humanists, perhaps the most famous of whom was Isotta Nogarola (1418–c. 1466). Although she was very well educated by her parents and lived out her entire life in their home engaging in continuing study, she was unable to enter the ranks of learned men, most of whom had no interest in a woman scholar. Nogarola engaged in a lengthy and spirited correspondence with the Venetian humanist Ludovico Foscarini wherein they argued about the guilt of Adam and Eve and, by implication, the relative virtue and wisdom of women and men. Nogarola argued that Eve was less to be blamed for sin than Adam because she was less capable and weaker—not the defense one would make today, but a skillful and creative handling of the scriptural materials and arguments that were available to her.[13]

FIGURE 6.2: *The Lesson*, drawing by Jacob Toorenvliet, 1650–1719. Courtesy of the British Museum, London.

Nogarola had been preceded in Italy by Baptista di Montefeltro (1383–1450), a learned woman who corresponded at some length with the Lord of Pesaro, a noted humanist. Upon marrying his son, she found herself in a miserable marriage to a man who was despised by all and who was ultimately exiled. She returned to her family's home and lived there until taking vows in the Franciscan Order of Santa Chiara. When the Holy Roman Emperor Sigismund of Luxembourg (1387–1437) visited Urbino in 1433, he was greeted by a Latin oration that Montefeltro had composed. Leonardo Bruni (1369–1444), a celebrated Italian humanist and the Apostolic Secretary to three popes, addressed his treatise on women's education to her. He wrote, "I am led to address this

Tractate to you, Illustrious Lady, by the high repute which attaches to your name in the field of learning; and I offer it, partly as an expression of my homage to distinction already attained, partly as an encouragement to further effort." Like all humanists, he was devoted to the study of correct Latin, and he recommended this even for women:

> This leads me to press home this truth—though in your case it is unnecessary—that the foundations of all true learning must be laid in the sound and thorough knowledge of Latin: which implies study marked by a broad spirit, accurate scholarship, and careful attention to details. Unless this solid basis be secured, it is useless to attempt to rear an enduring edifice. Without it the great monuments of literature are unintelligible and the art of composition impossible. To attain this essential knowledge we must never relax our careful attention to the grammar of the language but perpetually confirm and extend our acquaintance with it until it is thoroughly our own.

He recommended reading Christian writers, of course, but also the ancient Greek philosophers Plato (427–347 B.C.E.) and Aristotle (384–322 B.C.E.), as well as the Roman authors Virgil (70–19 B.C.E.), Cicero (106–43 B.C.E.), Sallust (86–34 B.C.E.), Livy (c. 60 B.C.E.–17 C.E.), Seneca (3 B.C.E.–65 C.E.), and Statius (45–96 C.E.).

However, Bruni argued that some studies are not appropriate to women:

> Thus there are certain subjects in which, whilst a modest proficiency is on all accounts to be desired, a minute knowledge and excessive devotion seem to be a vain display. For instance, subtleties of Arithmetic and Geometry are not worthy to absorb a cultivated mind, and the same must be said of Astrology. You will be surprised to find me suggesting (though with much more hesitation) that the great and complex art of Rhetoric should be placed in the same category. My chief reason is the obvious one, that I have in view the cultivation most fitting to a woman. To her neither the intricacies of debate nor the oratorical artifices of action and delivery are of the least practical use, if indeed they are not positively unbecoming. Rhetoric in all its forms—public discussion, forensic argument, logical fence, and the like—lies absolutely outside the province of woman.

The prospect of a woman trained in argumentation seemed to horrify even the most progressive pedagogue. Bruni argues that women should study history and poetry, "a subject with which every educated lady must shew herself thoroughly familiar, for we cannot point to any great mind of the past for whom the Poets had not a powerful attraction," and she must study the Virtues. Though Bruni's pedagogical program for women is constrained compared to what men were to learn, it nonetheless represents for its time a remarkably liberal view of women's abilities and potential.[14]

Montefeltro was a particularly apt recipient for Bruni's educational tract, as she was known for her poetry as well as her Latin prose works. She in turn educated her granddaughter, Costanza Varano (1428–47), a woman who "had a visible public role as a learned woman from as early as her teens" and who left "an extensive oeuvre": "four Latin orations, nine Latin letters, and eight poems, of which one oration, three letters, and one poem are addressed to other women." Costanza died in childbirth, leaving the deathbed poem "Constantia Sforza ad circumstantes demum ad virum in extremo vitae" (Costanza Sforza to the bystanders and to her husband, from her deathbed). Her husband had their daughter, Battista Sforza, educated as extensively as her mother had been, and the girl gave her "first (miniature) public oration in Latin at the almost unprecedentedly tender age of four." Even after her marriage, she "continued studying Greek": "[b]y the time she was fifteen, she was mandated full powers by her husband to rule his vicariates during his frequent absences...Thus, her education was not an elegant accomplishment, but an aspect of her fitness for rule."[15] One can thus track four generations of learned women in one noble family, and this kind of inheritance of learning was fairly common. It suggests that the education of but a single woman within a family might have an ongoing and growing influence on girls' learning, as women tended to pass along that tradition of education to their daughters and granddaughters.

Fra Sabba Castiglione (1480–1554), founder of a school in Faenza for poor children, also wrote about the ideal education for elite girls. Contrary to those who suggested that education made women unfit to be wives and mothers, he argued that the young woman who could not read the great Italian writers and poets—Dante, Petrarch, and Boccacio—would be seen as a "rustic" and as having been "poorly brought up." He counseled against too much reading of frivolous literature or focusing all girls' education on singing, music, and dancing. Rather, the bulk of young women's education should be based on reading the Bible, saints' lives, and other religious and spiritual works. Similarly, Silvio Antoniano (1540–1603) advocated teaching elite girls arithmetic (so as to enable them to keep accounts and run a household), reading, and writing; he even argued that poor girls and those of lower social status should be able to read their prayers. But he thought learning languages, especially Latin and Greek, as well as the study of poetry and rhetoric to be a waste of girls' time—much better that they concentrate on sewing and cooking.[16]

Among the most influential early modern works on pedagogy was Desiderius Erasmus's *The Education of a Christian Prince* (1516). Erasmus, chief among the humanist thinkers and writers of northern Europe, is also known for his praise of one of the most accomplished and well-educated women of the early sixteenth century, Margaret More Roper (1505–44). The daughter of Sir Thomas More (1478–1535), she was one of the first girls to benefit from the expansion of girls' education in England. Indeed, More and Erasmus seem to have used Margaret as the exemplar for a "humanist political project" that they hoped would revolutionize the courts of Europe. They wished to foster virtue and scholarship among the rulers of Europe in place of the hunting, dancing, fancy dressing, and other mindless pursuits, which they saw as frivolous and unworthy. More and Erasmus reasoned that if elite girls were well educated, they would attract and foster the development of virtuous noblemen rather than the greedy and self-serving fops that populated the courts of Europe.[17] Though this particular humanist plan did not bring about the kind of complete social revolution More and Erasmus had hoped for, Margaret's accomplishments exceeded all their ambitions: she was known for her learning among the literati of Europe. She was absolutely fluent in both Greek and Latin (as well as all modern European languages), so much so that she was able to translate a treatise by the church father Eusebius (c. 260–c. 341) from Greek into Latin and to translate Erasmus's own Latin treatise on the Lord's Prayer into English.

The German church reformer Martin Luther (1483–1546) advocated that lower-class girls as well as boys be better educated, particularly in religion. The Protestant reformers Jean Calvin (1509–64) and John Knox (1505–72), however, were not particularly interested in girls' education; Knox did not even discuss the question, and Calvin advocated only elementary education for girls, though always separate from boys, a common theme of the day. But Luther wrote, "Above all, in schools of all kinds the chief and most common lesson should be the Scriptures... And would to God each town also had a girls' school, in which girls might be taught the Gospel for an hour daily, either in German or in Latin." He argued that "even a girl has enough time that she can go to school for an hour a day and still perform her household tasks." Though this statement seems dismissive of girls' academic potential, he called for the same amount of study for boys, who would spend the rest of their days working as apprentices to learn a trade. For children of higher social rank, he called for the study of languages, history, music, and "the whole course of mathematics."[18]

Though many educational reformers maintained that girls should be taught by women, there were not nearly enough educated women for this purpose (a problem that, for obvious reasons, tended to replicate itself). Furthermore, many teachers of the day were itinerant or lived independently, something that was deemed unacceptable for women. Partly in response to this ongoing problem, the German educator Wolfgang Ratke (1571–1635) called for the establishment of a normal school to train teachers, one that would prepare an equal number of women and men for teaching. Ratke's ideas, as propounded in *The New Method* (1617), included the insistence that children not be taught by rote learning (the primary pedagogical method of the time) but rather that they understand the principles behind any study. He also thought that learning should proceed from experience. Ratke's theories inspired the great Czech-born educational theorist Johann (or Jan) Amos Comenius (1592–1670), a Moravian minister who published his theories in the *Great Didactic* (1632). He insisted that all children should be educated, "boys and girls, both noble and ignoble, rich and poor, in all cities and towns, villages and hamlets."[19] He argued that, since all human beings are rational creatures, and there is no way to know God's plan for them, girls as well as boys should learn in both the vernacular and Latin. Comenius carried his ideas to all parts of Europe, including Poland, Sweden, Germany, Hungary, and England, but most considered his theories too radical, and he saw little of his program implemented in his lifetime.

One of the most famous Renaissance educational programs for women was laid out in *De Institutione Feminae Christianae* or *The Instruction (or Education) of a Christian Woman* (1523) by Juan Luis Vives (1492–1540). Vives was a humanist and, like many scholars of the day, he was at home in a number of countries and cities, including his native Valencia as well as Paris, Bruges, and London. He was a friend and correspondent of Erasmus's and of other literati all over Europe. Vives dedicated his treatise to Catherine of Aragon (1485–1536), wife of Henry VIII (1491–1547) and queen of England—something that made Vives *persona non grata* at the English court when Henry divorced Catherine in 1533 in order to marry Anne Boleyn (c. 1500–36). But Vives's educational program had a significant impact on elite Englishwomen, including Henry's daughters Elizabeth I (1533–1603) and Mary I (or Mary Tudor, 1516–58), both of whom were educated according to its principles and were remarkably learned and eloquent in many languages. Both women translated works from Latin into English when they were still quite young.

Mary was a patron and promoter of learning during her short reign (1553–58), and Elizabeth was able to lecture her Parliament in fluent Latin throughout her life. Though Vives was as concerned as any writer of the day with preserving young women's chastity and virtue, he stood apart from most cultural arbiters in his recommendation that elite girls be taught Latin (though this idea may have originated with Catherine of Aragon herself, who wished to see her children educated according to the most progressive humanist scholarship). Vives's educational program begins in infancy; like many writers of the era, he recommends that girls be suckled by their own mothers rather than a wet nurse so as to avoid ingesting anything evil or vile:

> The maid [girl child], whom we would have especially good, requireth all intendance [attention] both of Father and Mother, lest any spot of vice or uncleanliness should stick on her. Let her take no such [evil] things, neither by her bodily senses and wits, nor by her nourishing and bringing up. She shall first hear her Nurse, first see her, and whatsoever she learneth in rude and ignorant age, that will she ever labor to counterfeit and follow...
>
> After that she is once weaned and beginneth to speak and go, let all her play and pastime be with maids of her own age, and within the presence either of her mother or her nurse or some other honest woman of sad [solemn, sober] age, that may rule and measure the plays and pastimes of her mind, and set them to honesty and virtue. Avoid all mankind away from her; nor let her not learn to delight among men.[20]

When the girl is ready to learn—sometime between four and seven, depending on the child—Vives would have her learn to read, but, to keep her from idleness, she should learn at the same time to spin (something that would never have been recommended for boys): "Therefore let her both learn her book, and beside that to handle wool and flax, which are 2 crafts yet left of that old innocent world, both profitable and keepers of temperance, which thing specially Women ought to have in price [to prize]." She is also to learn cooking so as to be able to please her parents, husband, and children with delicacies. Vives defended his claim that girls should be taught, offering many examples of learned women who were chaste and who modeled their lives on the ideal woman "who clearly despised all pleasure of the body, and lived perpetually a maid."[21]

Like most moralists of the period, Vives seemed to contradict himself when it came to discussion of who should teach young girls, for the dominant opinion was that women should rarely speak and should not teach. So, like Bruni,

Vives wrote that girls need not be taught eloquence: "As for eloquence, I have no great care, nor a woman needeth it not, but she needeth goodness and wisdom," which Vives suggested she can get only through study. So he compromised, naming a few women of the ancient world who were eloquent, and allowed, "If there may be found any holy and well learned woman, I had leaver [rather] have her to teach [girls]. If there be none, let us choose some man well aged, or else very good and virtuous, which hath a wife, and that right safe enough, whom he loveth well, and so shall he not desire other."[22] Note here how it is not the potentially adulterous man's responsibility to be virtuous, but all depends on the desirability of his wife and the adequate protection of the young pupil. Given this thinking about men's lack of responsibility for their actions, it is not surprising that parents and educators were concerned with protecting girls' chastity.

Vives provided an extensive list of those works a young woman should *not* read, and then recommended that she read Holy Scripture and religious works by the Church fathers Ambrose (333–397); Jerome (c. 342–420), who is today infamous among feminist scholars for his misogyny; Augustine of Hippo (354–430); and Gregory the Great (590–604); as well as the ancient authors Plato, Cicero, and Seneca.[23] Vives also laid out the appropriate diet for a young woman: no hot meat and no wine, but rather mild, cool foods that will keep her chaste. Likewise, she should have no "hot" exercise (especially dancing) or things that "fill the mind with filthy and lecherous heat."[24] And he argued at great length about her dress; she should wear only the most modest clothing and jewels.

Anna Maria van Schurman (1607–78), a remarkably well-educated Dutch woman who read Hebrew, Chaldean, Syriac, and Arabic as well as Latin and all the vernacular languages of Europe, also proposed a curriculum for girls. She wrote a treatise on education that was first published in Latin in 1638 and later translated into French and then English as *The Learned Maid or whether a Maid may be called a Scholar* (1659).[25] The book is in the form of letters to a man who had lent the author some books but who objected to women's learning. Van Schurman argued that women's confinement to learning needlework was merely the result of custom and that "it is impossible that generous souls, which are capable of everything, should be contained with the strict limits which common error has prescribed for them."[26]

Van Schurman's book inspired Bathsua Reginald Makin (c. 1608–c. 1674), a learned woman and governess to the English royal family, to write an *Essay to Revive the Antient Education of Gentlewomen in Religion, Manners, Arts and Tongues* (1673). To support her argument, Makin provided an extensive

FIGURE 6.3: Bathsua Makin (née Reginald), etching by William Marshall, after unknown artist, 1640s. Courtesy of the National Portrait Gallery, London.

list of learned and virtuous women of the past as well as those of her own time, including the daughters of Lord Burghley (chief minister to Elizabeth I); Queen Christina of Sweden; the Cooke sisters; Princess Elizabeth (daughter of King James VI and I); Lady Grace Sherrington Mildmay; Lady Arbella Stuart; and Margaret, Duchess of Newcastle. She also included the poets Mary, Countess of Pembroke; Katharine Philips; and Anna Maria van Schurman herself, among others. Such a list suggests that the learned women of Europe were aware of one another and of their "membership" in a community of female scholars. Makin corresponded with van Schurman, and she may well have done so with others she named. In her book, she argues that God must surely approve of women's education: "Had God intended Women only as a finer sort of Cattle, he would not have made them reasonable. Bruits, a few degrees higher than Drills [Baboons] or Monkeys, (which the Indians use to do many Offices) might have better fitted some men's Lust, Pride, and Pleasure; especially those that desire to keep [women] ignorant to be tyrannized over."[27] She laid out a detailed program for teaching grammar and language to children and advertised her own school "for gentlewomen" where, beginning at age eight or nine, girls could be educated in needlework, dancing, music, singing, writing, keeping household accounts, English grammar, Latin, and French. Those girls who wished to expand their knowledge might also have taken up Greek, Hebrew, Italian, and Spanish. Makin had already published a book entitled *Musa Virginea Greco-Latino-Gallica, Bathsvae R. (filiae Henrici Reginaldi Gymnasiarchae et Philogotti apud Londonenses) Anno Aetatis Suae Decimo Sexto edita* [The Virgin Muse in Greek-Latin-French, by Bathsua R. (daughter of Henry Reginald, schoolmaster and linguist of London), published in her sixteenth year]. The small book consisted of poems to members of the royal family in Greek, Latin, and French. However, when Makin was later introduced to King James as a prodigy, scholar, linguist, and the author of the book, he asked, "Yes, but can she spin?"[28]

Most significant for the development of learned women in France was the tradition of the salon, literary gatherings in the houses of aristocratic women where the erudite exchanged ideas and read from their works and others'. The earliest salon was hosted by Catherine de Vivonne, the Marquise de Rambouillet (1588–1665), beginning after her retirement from court life in 1608 and running continually until midcentury. Moreover, Rambouillet's salon was imitated by many other women. The literati of France attended regularly, among them Marie de Rabutin-Chantal, the Marquise of Sévigné (1626–96). The Marquise de Sévigné was a remarkably learned woman who had been raised by her grandfather and then, on his death, sent to be educated under the direction of her uncles. She was widowed young and never remarried, occupying herself instead with the education of her daughter and later her granddaughter. At her death, she left a collection of 1,500 letters addressed principally to her daughter (to whom she wrote daily), which were so highly esteemed for their wit and erudition that they were copied and circulated among the learned aristocracy of France. They were eventually collected into eight volumes and published in 1727. In the letters, she discusses an education program designed for her granddaughter that would focus on history, geography, and literature.

One of the most ambitious educational projects of the period was the mission of the religious women of the Institute of the Blessed Virgin Mary, founded by the English Catholic Mary Ward (1585–1645). Ward saw herself as called to lead a "mixed life," that is, to take vows and to live celibate under a religious rule but not to be cloistered. She believed her mission was to found an order dedicated to the education of young women. She inspired many followers, whom she called her Companions (as Ignatius of Loyola had termed his seminarian colleagues), to work toward the same ends. Ward and her Companions founded many schools for girls, especially on the Continent, where girls were given an extensive education. Ward thought that training in Latin in particular was essential for girls' preparation for the spiritual life and second only to prayer in their formation. She wrote in 1627 to Winifred Bedingfeld (1606–66), Ward's Companion and founding member of the house in Munich, regarding two of Bedingfeld's pupils who were learning Latin:

> *Pax Christi!* These [greetings] are indeed chiefly to congratulate the unexpected progress of your Latin schools. You cannot easily believe the content I took in the themes of those two towardly girls [whose writing Bedingfeld had sent to Ward]. You will work much to your own happiness by advancing them apace in that learning, and God will concur with you because his honour and service so require. All such as are capable invite them to it, and for such as desire to be one of us, no talent is so much to be regarded in them as the Latin tongue.[29]

Ward reiterated these sentiments in a letter to her close Companion Winifred Wigmore (1585–1657), then the novice mistress at the house in Naples, regarding the education of girls in her care. In this letter, Ward also responded to those who thought education would make girls less virtuous:

> I would have Cecilia and Catherina begin out of hand to learn the rudiments of Latin; fear not their loss of virtue by that means, for this must and will be so common to all as there will be no cause for complacency. I would not have their other work be hindered, but what time can otherwise be found besides their prayer, let it be bestowed upon their Latin.[30]

In addition to Latin, Ward thought girls should learn

> a sense of duty, Christian doctrine, good morals, how to serve God, reading the common and Latin languages, writing, household management,

liberal arts [grammar, rhetoric, logic, music, arithmetic, geometry, and astronomy], singing, painting, sewing, spinning, curtain-making, in a word, all those liberal exercises which are more suitable for every state of life.[31]

Ward's curriculum represents a perhaps unique melding of girls' traditional education in domesticity and piety along with all the subjects that marked boys' education in the period. Ward's institute was a remarkable success even in her lifetime. She had gathered sixty sisters before she died, many of whom headed the schools in operation for girls; there were more than a hundred in Germany alone by the next century. But the political situation in England—the hostility to Catholics and the prohibition against teaching Catholic doctrine—meant that Ward's educational program was not able to prosper there until after her death. The two schools that did open, one in Hammersmith near London in 1669 and another at the Bar Convent in York in 1686, operated in secret in the seventeenth and eighteenth centuries.[32]

Even children of lower social status who did not benefit from humanist learning and educational programs like Ward's were educated in the skills they would need as adults. For girls, this meant that they would learn domestic skills, whether manual labor or, in the case of middle-class and aristocratic women, how to manage a household. Either way, the work demanded a range of skills that girls learned first from their mothers and any older sisters and then, beginning around seven years of age, from other women, often in another household. In England in particular the practice of fostering—of sending one's children to live with others and taking others' children into one's household—was nearly universal. Boys who were sent out in this manner to learn a trade were often formally apprenticed to a master, but girls were more likely to work as domestic servants or as ladies in waiting, depending on their status. Some elite girls might even get a formal education in literature, languages, music, and art in this way, but it was considered most important for them to learn social skills and manners and to mix in society.

In addition to interest in pedagogy and women's education in this period, moralists were concerned with the behavior of women in all aspects of life, and there was a florescence of conduct manuals and books. These works laid out the appropriate behavior, dress, and activities for women as well as for men of the middle and upper classes. Such treatises served as a kind of ongoing education for people through their adulthood. Probably the most famous was Baldassare Castiglione's (1478–1529) *Il Libro del Cortegiano* (1528), translated into many languages, including Latin, Spanish, German, and English, notably by Sir Thomas Hoby as *The Book of the Courtier* (1561). At the heart of Castiglione's program is the idea of *sprezzatura*, the ability to display one's accomplishments artlessly and easily. While Castiglione claimed, "Everything that men can understand can also be understood by women," the bulk of his advice is for elite men. And, indeed, women play a very limited role in the dialogue about courtiership that he invented in *The Courtier*: two of the women named do not contribute at all to the conversation. Above all for Castiglione, women were to cultivate virtue, particularly chastity, and "[t]o have a sweetness in language and a good utterance to entertain all kind of men with communication worth the hearing, honest, applied to time and place and to the degree and disposition of the person which is her principal profession."[33]

Among the most popular conduct books in England during the seventeenth century were Richard Brathwaite's (c. 1588–1673) *The English Gentleman* (1630) and *The English Gentlewoman* (1631). What sets Brathwaite's work on women apart from his discussion of men is a focus on women's appearance: though women were frequently excoriated for their reputed obsession with clothes and makeup and counseled to care more about their inner virtues, here it is Brathwaite who seems obsessed with women's exterior and what it communicates about their virtue. Even his subtitle demonstrates this focus: *The English Gentlewoman Drawn Out to the Full Body: Expressing What Habiliments [Clothes] Do Best Attire Her, What Ornaments Do Best Adorne Her, What Complements Do Best Accomplish Her.* (Compare his companion title: *The English Gentleman: Containing Sundry Rules, or Exquisite Observations, Tending to Direction of Every Gentleman, of Selecter Ranke and Quality; How to Demeane or Accommodate Himselfe in the Manage of Publick or Private Affaires.*)[34] Every chapter of Brathwaite's book for gentlewomen comments on their dress and appearance. In addition to conduct manuals, the treatises of the Woman Controversy, the early seventeenth-century English pamphlet debate on the nature of womanhood, always included a discussion of women's proper behavior and particular virtues and vices. Even literature on religious and romantic topics often had a didactic side; it functioned as a tool of continuing education for women and served to police their behavior and activity.

Education for early modern women was a disputed and contentious topic, but the very fact that it was being widely discussed implies that their education had come to seem less radical than in earlier centuries. The Renaissance is the first time in history that so many girls were educated, and some of them to the full extent of learning available. Many moralists continued to resist educating girls and, even more, having women teach, often referring to the biblical passage in 1 Timothy 2:11–14:

> Let the woman learn in silence with all subjection: But I suffer not a woman to teach, nor to usurp authority over the man, but to be in silence. For Adam was first formed, then Eve: And Adam was not deceived, but the woman being deceived was in the transgression.

But, as many women of the time pointed out, even in this very restrictive and misogynist passage, there seems to be an assumption that women will indeed learn, if only in silence. Defenders of women's access to learning used this loophole to frame their arguments, making the best of the conservative material that was at hand and continuing to struggle to make women's education the norm rather than a dangerous exception.

CHAPTER SEVEN

Power

HOLLY HURLBURT

How might we understand "power" in terms of Renaissance woman? Then as now, power might best be comprehended politically, or as access or proximity to rulership or governance. The sheer number of female rulers in Renaissance Europe (c. 1400–1600) is remarkable, given the widespread acceptance that although women were important as the progenitors of future monarchs, as the second sex, they were regarded as physically, morally, and intellectually unfit to rule. In France, this belief became legally enshrined via a clause added in the fifteenth century to Salic law that forbade female property inheritance. Elsewhere, well-established traditions of misogyny discouraged female rule, since patriarchal discourse associated femininity in its various forms with weakness whereas power was thought to be masculine. But despite these and other beliefs that fostered pronounced hostility to females in politics, Giovanna II of Naples (r. 1414–35), Isabel of Castile (r. 1474–1504), Mary of Burgundy (r. 1477–83), Mary Queen of Scots (r. 1542–67), Mary Tudor (r. 1553–58), Jeanne d'Albret, Queen of Navarre (r. 1555–72), and Elizabeth Tudor (r. 1558–1603) all came to power through direct inheritance rather than marriage, and ruled either alone or jointly with their spouses. At least two of these reigns, those of Isabel (who for the most part retained independent rule over Castile even after her marriage to Ferdinand of Aragon) and Elizabeth (famously the only unmarried female ruler of the time period), lasted decades and were periods of relative internal stability, military victory, expansion in Europe and abroad, Atlantic colonization, economic growth, and cultural flowering.

Despite their different marital status, Isabel and Elizabeth (and their propagandists) engaged in a myriad of similar strategies to counter or overcome objections to female rule. Each made explicit reference to their ties to their fathers, powerful male predecessors. While distancing herself from her inept half brother Enrique, Isabel associated herself with her father, Juan II. Likewise, Elizabeth frequently reminded her subjects that she descended from Henry VIII, whose portrait by Hans Holbein the Younger hung prominently in her Privy Chamber at the palace at Whitehall. Further, both queens probed the flexible boundaries of their gender and sexuality. Each associated herself with the Virgin Mary. While Elizabeth and her courtiers increasingly embraced the chastity of the Virgin in the 1570s, Isabel encouraged comparisons with the Virgin as a mother whose male offspring would redeem the world. Using sexuality to mediate their femininity, conversely each woman would situate herself as a "virago"—a woman with unnatural, masculine strength and military acumen. Although neither woman rode into battle, Isabel began her reign with a military reference. A ceremony to announce her succession to Castile's throne in 1474 set a martial tone, when a nobleman led her procession carrying a sword rather than the usual scepter. Subsequently, during the long war for the reconquest of Muslim Granada, Isabel appeared before the troops and rode with them at the start of campaigns. In addition, her militarism was suggested by her use of the heraldic symbol of a bundle of arrows. Similarly, Elizabeth famously rallied her troops garbed in armor before the 1588 Spanish invasion, allegedly saying: "I know I have the body of a weak and feeble woman, but I have the heart and stomach of a king, and a King of England too."[1] Witnesses to this speech stressed the queen's androgyny—that in dress, appearance, and behavior she seemed both man *and* woman, a strategy to which she appealed multiple times during her reign. Mary of Burgundy used this tactic as well. For example, her seal depicted her at the hunt—a pastime often associated with men and militarism, but sidesaddle rather than astride her horse. In playing with the malleability of gender norms, these and other ruling women drew inspiration not only from French warrior martyr Joan of Arc but also from the literary trope of warrior queen, which included such figures as the legendary female warrior Amazons, the huntress Diana, and the knightly Risamante in the chivalric romance *Floridoro* (1581), authored by female writer Moderata Fonte. These figures, like the queens they came to represent, constantly confronted gendered expectations, embracing their femininity when necessary but also evoking a royal, militant masculinity. As Caterina Sforza, regent of the Italian city of Forlì allegedly declared, "If I have to lose, although I am a woman, I want to lose in a manly way."[2]

Sforza was one of the dozens of Renaissance women (referred to hereafter as "ruling women") who came to and exercised political power beyond simple inheritance. Because the European system of monarchical rule relied on succession, in many places it was possible or indeed necessary for women, and especially mothers of young heirs, to act as regents for extended periods of time. This expectation fell not only on queens but on duchesses and other wives of regional rulers, and was especially pronounced in Northern Italy, where a number of small- to medium-sized principalities including Mantua and Ferrara coexisted with the larger republics and principalities Milan, Florence, and Venice. Thus on behalf of her sons Sforza oversaw the Italian cities of Imola and Forlì from the time of the murder of her spouse, Girolamo Riario, in 1484 until and after her remarriage in 1498. Caterina Corner, Venetian-born wife of King Jacques II of Cyprus, was pregnant when her husband died. She gave birth and acted as regent for Jacques III until his death, and then continued to rule Cyprus, at least in name, for nearly fifteen years, until she was forced to abdicate by Venice, which annexed the island to its maritime empire. Catherine de Medici, the widow of Henri II of France, acted as regent for her sons Charles IX (three years) and Henri III (one year), and continued to influence their rules well after they came to the throne.

Wives also could temporarily steer the ship of state in the absence of warrior husbands. In fifteenth-century Aragon, this type of regency was institutionalized, with queens such as María of Castile, wife of Alfonso V, taking the title of lieutenant (from *locum tenens*, literally "in the place of"). Her husband's frequent long absences in the Kingdom of Naples meant that María served as lieutenant for two periods during her life, in 1421–23 and again for a much longer period from 1432 to 1453, during which she oversaw all the king's Spanish territories. Each time, the document that legitimated her rule guaranteed her powers "equivalent to his own as king, and that she had the authority to rule independently. María had full sovereign power over all civil and criminal jurisdictions...including the army and military orders. Her authority superseded all other officials."[3] Likewise, her successor as Queen of Aragon, Juana, took the office of lieutenant and acted as negotiator during civil war in Navarre. Even where regency did not come with official titles and privileges, as it did in fifteenth-century Aragon, it had the explicit sanction of male rulers. In his frequent absences, Duke Ercole d'Este left Ferrara in the capable hands of his pious and popular wife Eleonora d'Aragona, while her daughter Isabella d'Este maintained the city of Mantua in the absence of her husband, Francesco, captain-general of the Venetian army. Fathers (and mothers) of princesses anticipated that such provisional assumptions of power might be necessary: generally they provided their daughters with education in preparation, which was supplemented by male advice, as in the case of Eleonora, to whom the treatise *Del modo di regere e di regnare* (*On Ways of Governing and Ruling*) by Antonio Cornazzano was dedicated, or Isabel of Castile, who received *Jardín des nobles doncellas* (*Garden of Noble Maidens*) from Martín de Córdoba in 1469, five years before her reign began. Acting as temporary regent occasionally involved intervening during crisis situations: for example, Cornazzano praised Eleonora's defense of her husband's city in his absence. Day-to-day regency duties might involve frequent consultation with a spouse's governing councils or advisors, convening courts and representative bodies, filling vacant posts, as well as receiving and granting petitions.

Rulers relied on other female family members as well. Anne of France, herself the daughter of King Louis XII, acted as regent on behalf of her brother, Charles VIII, both in his youth and in his adulthood, during the 1494–95 invasion of Italy. Louise of Savoy, mother of Francis I, not only acted as regent of France three times during his Italian wars, but in 1525–26 she herself traveled to Spain to negotiate his release when he was captured. Given the size of the Holy Roman Empire, a territory comprising Spain, Germanic territories, and portions of Italy and the Netherlands in the sixteenth century, it is no wonder that its ruler, Charles V, relied on Isabella of Portugal, Margaret of Austria, Mary of Hungary, and Margaret of Parma, his wife, aunt, sister, and illegitimate daughter, respectively, all of whom served as regents in Spain and the Netherlands, while he contended with threats from France, Turks, and Protestants in Germany. It seems evident from these and other examples that ruling, whether by men or women, was a collective endeavor.

Still more ruling women never actively reigned, but nonetheless used their prominent status to exercise influence upon their spouses. Although her husband, Ludovico Gonzaga, seems not to have named her regent during his absences, Barbara of Brandenburg nonetheless acted on his behalf. She frequently carried news between the Marquis of Mantua and his councilors, read and forwarded his letters, and provided newsworthy gossip to his ears. Alfonsina Orsini, mother of Lorenzo de' Medici, Duke of Urbino, was also not officially named regent, but assumed the office while her son was at war from 1515 to 1519, meeting with and advising various Florentine committees, as is indicated by marginalia in the records of a finance committee, noting that a given policy was established "by the commission of the most Illustrious Lady Alfonsina."[4] As physical embodiments of alliances between states, ruling women were natural diplomats and worked not only to solidify ties but also to act on behalf of their families and homes. Thus Ippolita Sforza, daughter of Duke

Francesco Sforza of Milan, was betrothed to Alfonso, heir to the Kingdom of Naples at age nine in 1455, to confirm an alliance between those two states established the previous year at the Peace of Lodi. Nonetheless, during over twenty years as a princess at the Neapolitan court, Sforza assisted in the negotiation of a treaty between Naples and Florence while also providing valuable information for her brother, now Duke of Milan. Even after they removed her from power, former queen Caterina Corner continued to advise the Venetian Council of Ten via letters and petitions, advocating for family members and former staff in Cyprus: her counsel was frequently accepted and followed, making hers a rare instance in which a female was able to directly influence a republican system of government.

By counseling their spouses, women such as Brandenburg and Sforza tacitly followed the guidance of fifteenth-century author Christine de Pisan, whose work *The Treasure of the City of Ladies* begins with a section addressing powerful women. The text offers, in addition to the usual advice to women about dress, modesty, and comportment, instruction to ruling women on mediation and negotiation: "the proper duty of the wise queen and princess [is] to be the means of peace and concord, to work for the avoidance of war because of the trouble that can come from it."[5] In a letter of 1405, approximately the same time that Pisan wrote *Treasure*, she urged Isabeau of Bavaria, Queen of France, to heed this same advice. Pisan implored the queen to intervene in squabbles between the Dukes of Burgundy and Orléans, acting as "the medicine and sovereign remedy to cure this realm."[6] Female negotiating, peacemaking, or mediating seems to have been a common activity for ruling women, especially when kinship was involved. Margaret Tudor proposed to her husband James IV of Scotland that she and Catherine of Aragon, her sister-in-law, be allowed to meet in order to avert war between Scotland and England in 1513. In 1529 former sisters-in-law Margaret of Austria, aunt of Holy Roman Emperor Charles V, and Louise of Savoy, mother of King Francis I, with her daughter Margaret (later Queen of Navarre), negotiated the "ladies' peace" at Cambrai, ending years of strife between those two rulers. Margaret of Austria justified the diplomacy of women, writing that unlike men, who could not sacrifice "what they held most precious, their honor...ladies might well come forward in a measure for submitting the gratification of private hatred and revenge to the far nobler principle of the welfare of nations."[7] Although ruling women actively reigned as regents only occasionally, their position and gender gave them access to many indirect avenues of power.

Pisan firmly believed in women's wisdom and governing capabilities, as she indicated in an earlier work, *The Book of the City of Ladies*. As part of a larger defense of women against the misogyny of the time, the author presented examples of successful female rulers from mythology (the Amazon Penthesilea), ancient history (Artemisia, wife of Mausolus of Caria), and recent French history (Queen Jeanne d'Evreux), lest "anyone says that women do not have a natural sense for politics and government."[8] The ability of women to rule, and rule well, formed a sizable plank in the larger debate over the nature of women, the so-called *querrelle des femmes*, which continued to rage across Europe during the Renaissance. The title alone of John Knox's 1558 pamphlet *The First Blast of the Trumpet against the Monstrous Regiment of Women* aimed a diatribe against all female rulers, but especially Catholic monarchs Mary Tudor, Mary Queen of Scots, and her mother and regent, Marie of Guise, and identifies his work as the most vituperative. In it, Knox rehearsed the standard Aristotelian rhetoric against women—that biology left them "weak, frail, impatient, feeble and foolish, and experience hath declared them to be unconstant, variable, cruel, and lacking the spirit of counsel and government."[9] Further, Knox claimed that female rule threatened the natural order, and most alarming, subverted the divine law of God as demonstrated in the gendered order of creation, and in the writings of church fathers from Paul to Augustine. Similar works proliferated across Europe especially in the sixteenth century, no doubt responding to what their authors regarded as the disquieting expansion of female authority. For example, *The Marvelous Discourse on the Life, Actions and Misconduct of Catherine de Médicis, the Queen Mother* (1574) attacked the powerful French queen mother for her Italian birth, her alleged affection for the ideas of her countryman Niccolò Machiavelli, her associations with witchcraft, and the corruption of her children, which by association meant all of France.[10] In many such cases, the powers ascribed to women as "daughters of Eve" were malevolent—powerful women were caricatured as sexual temptresses, or worse, in league with the devil.

But the disciples, male and female, of Christine de Pisan fought back. Because the courts of Northern Italy featured so many rulers' wives who offered patronage opportunities to humanist authors, a genre of writing flourished that mirrored and expanded upon Giovanni Boccaccio's fourteenth-century compendium *On Famous Women* and Pisan's fifteenth-century *Book of the City of Ladies*. Many of these texts illustrated the capabilities of ruling women. In addition to Cornazzano's treatise on ruling dedicated to Eleonora d'Aragona, Sabadino degli Arienti catalogued the deeds of more recent historical women, including Ippolita Sforza and her mother, Bianca Maria Visconti, in his *Gynevera, de le clare donne*, a work dedicated to and celebrating the virtues of yet another ruling woman, Ginevra Sforza Bentivoglio of Bologna. Other Italian works from the period challenge, implicitly or explicitly, the Aristotelian notion that women are innately inferior, saying instead that custom and lack of education and opportunity made them so. Citing Plato, among others, sixteenth-century Venetian scholar Lucrezia Marinelli expanded upon Pisan's notion of women as peacemakers, proclaiming, "Oh, how many women there are, who with their greater prudence, justice and experience of life, would govern empires better than men!"[11]

Meanwhile, John Aylmer, tutor to Lady Jane Gray; David Chambers, who dedicated his work to Catherine de Medici; and Henry Howard responded directly to Knox, citing successful female rulers, noting not only that Adam and Eve were created equal but also invoking the metaphor of nation as family, which proved that women, as wives and mothers, are already equipped to rule. This debate likely reached its largest audience in book three of Baldessare Castiglione's *Book of the Courtier* (1528), widely read and translated in the sixteenth century. Castiglione imagines a group of courtiers who engage in a series of debates for intellectual stimulation and amusement. Elisabetta Gonzaga, wife of Guidobaldo da Montefeltro, Duke of Urbino, directs the proceedings, but the debate itself is shaped entirely by the contributions of male courtiers. Although he repeatedly notes that he is shaping the ideal court woman, and not a queen, the character Magnifico Giuliano nonetheless praises female ruling ability, observing, like Marinelli, "Do you not know that Plato, who was certainly no great friend of women, put them in charge of the city and gave all the military duties to men? Don't you think that we might find many women just as capable of governing cities and armies as men?"[12] Citing examples from Italy and France, Magnifico gives a detailed account of the deeds of Isabel of Castile, leaving the group to debate whether her deeds were her own, whether she "was praised for many acts for which King Ferdinand was responsible," or whether her greatness derived from female ability to inspire men to heroism in battle.[13] The courtiers, and indeed Europe in general, did not reach a consensus about ruling women: were they innately capable, unfit usurpers, or, in the words of theologian John Calvin, speaking of Elizabeth I, deviations "from the original and proper order of nature" so that only occasionally was there a woman "so endowed that the singular good qualities which shone forth in them, made it evident that they were raised up by divine authority?" This notion of female exceptionalism was perhaps the most common explanation for female rule: as Filippo Strozzi observed about his mother-in-law, Alfonsina Orsini, she did what would be "impossible for another woman, and easy only for a few men."[14]

Ruling women themselves fought against a slew of negative stereotypes or general ambivalence, engaging in certain strategies to fashion themselves as effective, deserving, and oftentimes exceptional rulers. Motherhood was perhaps the most important vehicle whereby women, whether regal, elite, or bourgeoise, asserted direct or indirect political power, as children (and especially boys) were regarded as essential for the maintenance of family history and honor. Despite proscriptive literature that advocated the separation of boys from their mothers at a young age, many maintained close ties throughout adulthood. Henry VII of England frequently kept his mother, Margaret Beaufort, at court, included her in royal rituals, such as the coronation of his wife, and named her his executor on his deathbed. For widows of rulers, motherhood granted them a legitimate right to oversee their young sons. Catherine de Medici, mother of twelve children, including three successive kings of France and the queen of Navarre, overtly used her maternity and her recognized status as a mourning widow (always dressed in black) and good mother to secure her position as regent for Charles IX from 1560 to 1563. She enhanced this dual image of widow/mother by equating herself with Artemisia, widow of Mausolus, whose image in works of art demonstrated her overseeing her husband's tomb, and her son's education and training. For widows with young children, like Catherine, motherhood was a defining characteristic. When separated from her children during the siege of Forlì in 1488, Caterina Sforza threatened their captors, saying that "she is carrying one [child] in her body." In Machiavelli's account, Sforza went so far as to "uncover to them her genital members, saying that she still had means for producing more children."[15] Even with her spouse dead, and his heirs captured, Sforza suggested she might be pregnant with another son to avenge his parent and reestablish rule. Although labeled a "bad mother" as a result of this legend, Sforza (or Machiavelli) understood that the power of female procreation was significant.

But motherhood was a far more involved duty than the ability to bear a healthy heir. Florentine noblewoman Alessandra Strozzi was not only widowed; she was also charged with restoring her family's honor. Her husband had been exiled prior to his death; her sons came of age working for the family bank in Naples, while she remained in Florence where she sought to arrange advantageous marriages for her sons and daughters as part of a larger strategy to return them to respectability. Indeed, many mothers played active roles in seeking out and negotiating marital ties for their adolescent offspring, male or female. Catherine de Medici pursued an alliance with Elizabeth I for several of her sons. Margaret, the widowed Countess of Bath, arranged marriages for seven of her twelve children before her death, and engaged in several strategies to ensure improved social status. Mothers had tremendous authority over their sons and daughters, often overseeing their training and education, instilling their values, arranging their futures, and acting as guardians of their family names and honor.

In the Ottoman Empire, where the mothers of several sixteenth-century sultans were politically active—educating and guaranteeing the succession of their sons against other contenders, acting as advisors once their sons achieved the throne—women constantly pursued their own political and diplomatic agendas. Venetian-born Nurbanu Sultan, mother of Sultan Murad III, who was the first to hold the title of *valide sultan* (royal mother), worked to maintain diplomatic ties between her home state of Venice and that ruled by her son, going so far as to intervene with an admiral in order to prevent war between the two states. Likewise, the success of English negotiations with the Ottomans in the 1590s was achieved "by meanes chefelie of the Turks mother['s] favoure," in this case Safiye Sultan, the mother of Murad's successor, Memhed III.[16] Safiye, like ruling mothers Lucrezia Tornabuoni, wife and mother of Piero and Lorenzo de' Medici, respectively, and Margaret Beaufort, mother of Henry VII, were the frequent recipients of petitions whose authors hoped these women would intercede with their sons. A Pisan nun wrote to Tornabuoni in 1467, addressing her as "most illustrious mother," imploring her to ask Piero to prevent Florentine soldiers from stealing convent stores.[17] She received similar requests even after the death of her husband and during the ascendancy of her son, despite the nominally republican system in place in Florence. Royal wives and mothers both received and sent petitions, while petitioning was one of the few means that non-royal women possessed to interact with or influence political machinery. Thus the above-referenced nun, among others, appealed to Lucrezia Tornabuoni, and Katherine Blount petitioned Chancellor Thomas Cromwell in 1536 in an attempt to secure a position for her son, while Elizabeth, Countess of Worcester, and Lady Elizabeth Musgrave wrote to him lobbying for the interests of their husbands. What we might call women's informal politicking was often effective and certainly occurred more frequently than documents might suggest.

In addition to lending their support to petitions of all kinds, ruling and elite women created and facilitated patronage networks through their courts. Courts grew larger and their rituals more ostentatious during the Renaissance as princes consolidated their power and became ever more eager to flaunt it. In many places, ruling women had their own courts with their own budgets. A 1476 inventory identified some fifty persons who served Eleonora, the Duchess of Ferrara, not including her ladies in waiting. Queen Elizabeth of York, wife of Henry VII, had eighteen women who attended her. Perhaps the largest women's court of the era belonged to Catherine de Medici, whose retinue grew as she took on greater responsibility monitoring her sons' reigns: from 316 persons in 1569, her court employed 666 persons in the years immediately before her death. Filling these offices gave ruling women the opportunity to construct elaborate social and political networks. Conversely, service as a lady in waiting (usually reserved for noblewomen), nurse, or other female servant to a ruling or elite woman meant opportunities to establish patronage networks, to receive valuable assistance in arranging marriages for themselves or their family members, and to accrue financial gain in the form of salary, gifts, or even offices. Successive queens of England Katherine Howard and Katherine Parr gave their ladies jewelry, velvet gowns, and other gifts. Bona of Savoy, wife of Duke Galeazzo Maria Sforza of Milan, gave the son of her midwife, Caterina da Corte, a lucrative post monitoring grain prices, which later devolved to his mother. She did not occupy the office; rather she rented it out to a man, securing a significant income. Marguerite de Selve was lady in waiting to Marguerite de Navarre and subsequently to her daughter, Jeanne d'Albret. Jeanne arranged de Selve's marriage and provided her a substantial wedding gift and employment for her spouse. At her death, Jeanne gave Marguerite jewelry, and Jeanne's son, Henri de Navarre, later King of France, gave her a grant of land. Further, Marguerite was able to use her position to gain positions for her brother and three children. Courts were thus both expressions of a ruling woman's power in their sheer size and the loyalty they demanded, and a means for ruling women and others to indirectly influence politics.

Many noble and merchant wives likewise managed significant households. Venetian humanist Francesco Barbaro wrote that wives "ought to attend, therefore, to governing their households just as Pericles daily attended to the affairs of Athens."[18] Given the size and holdings of some aristocratic and merchant households, management itself must have been a full-time job, especially given the frequency with which male heads of household were away from home. Although their authority frequently went unrecognized, non-ruling women also served as "regents" for their absent husbands, who might be away from home for long periods of time engaged in trade, politics, work, or war—thus the number of households controlled by women surely rose in the tumultuous sixteenth century with Atlantic exploration and religious warfare. For French noblewoman Anne Baillet, management in her husband's absence included overseeing wine production, inspecting construction work, visiting estate managers, preventing poaching, and writing an inventory. While her husband attended the court of Henry VIII, Anne Lestrange took in rents and fees from her husband's tenants, profits from sales of wood and malt, and other moneys. She used these to pay household staff and buy provisions for her children, and to pay off clients in the family's service. Although Barbaro surely did not mean to suggest this, his equation of household management with governing was employed by other thinkers, male and female, including Henry Howard, author of the defense of Queen Elizabeth referenced above, to justify female rule.

As indicated by the accounts of Anne Lestrange, managing the household in a spouse's absence also meant control of the significant power of the purse. Some women did this as stand-ins for their spouses, as in the cases noted above, but others owned property and controlled goods outright, despite judicial attempts to prevent wealth, and especially land, from falling into women's hands to thwart the division or alienation of family holdings. Laws dictating female property rights varied from place to place; everywhere structures existed that limited but did not eliminate a woman's right to inherit. For example, in many places a woman's wealth, property, and even her dowry were controlled by her spouse during marriage, but, in England and France at least, a wife could retain property if stipulated in a marriage contract. Not surprisingly, the Renaissance women with the most economic power were clearly wealthy widows. Widowhood was fairly common for women of all social ranks, who if they survived the perils of multiple childbirths, led more sheltered lives than their spouses and were thus more likely to survive them. The much-bemoaned problem of Renaissance dowry inflation nonetheless meant that some widows inherited considerable sums, and as executor for their husband's estate or their children's inheritance, managed and oversaw massive fortunes. Further, many husbands left their wives inheritances over and above the dowry, including property, cash, jewelry, and household goods. As many women had spent their lives managing their spouse's property, they were well-equipped to do so, and to do so capably, after their husband's death. Widows, acting on their own or through agents, purchased land, loaned money to family and friends, invested in business or state-run ventures such as tax farming, and left sizable bequests to family and friends, thus acting as significant agents in early modern economies. The very wealthy Alfonsina Orsini, widow of Piero de' Medici, inherited property from her natal family, and presumably using the proceeds from it, her dowry, and other wealth, purchased one palace and constructed another in Rome.

In addition, wealthy widows possessed "unprecedented control over their own persons," that is to say, they had sufficient personal and financial freedom to choose to remarry or not.[19] Women could rarely refuse their family's choice for their first marriage: Cecilia Gonzaga is a famous exception, choosing the convent over her father's choice of spouse. It was much easier for widows to refuse offers of remarriage: after the death of her husband Thomas, Lord Berkeley, his widow refused a marriage arranged by Thomas Cromwell, writing, "my stomach cannot lean there, or yet to any marriage."[20] She did not remarry. Wisely, Christina of Denmark, widow of the last Sforza Duke of Milan, declined to become the fourth wife of Henry VIII in 1538, marrying instead the Duke of Lorraine three years later. Many husbands left their wives financial and emotional incentives not to remarry: Venetian nobleman Nicolo Mudazzo promised his wife "an additional 50 ducats a year, two beds, and all her clothing" if she remained a widow and with their children.[21] Despite these sorts of incentives, many widows, especially younger women, did remarry, and found that they, like Christina of Denmark, could be choosy and improve their social standing. Englishwoman Margaret Donnington married three times, and ascended the social scale from wife of a mercer, to wife of a courtier, and, finally, to the peerage when she secured an earl as her third spouse.

Wealth and inheritance allowed ruling and elite women to extend their patronage to the arts. In the same way that they employed and dispensed favors to members of their households, court women retained artists, musicians, and writers. Cultural patronage provided them both with the ability to associate themselves with the powerful men in their lives, and also to make visible statements of their virtues, intellect, and individual authority. Many women were named as their spouse's executors, and were thus directly involved in or responsible for elaborate tomb projects or other forms of commemoration for him or other relatives. As we have seen, Catherine de Medici associated herself with Artemisia of Caria, and like her role model, Catherine planned a mausoleum for Henri II—the Valois chapel in the abbey church of St. Denis, intended to serve also as a tomb for herself and their children. Often women constructed memorials according to testamentary instruction, but with their own interpretations. Venetian noblewoman Agnesina Badoer reinterpreted her father's testamentary wish that she complete his funerary chapel, commissioning a space in the church of San Francesco della Vigna that commemorated her natal family and her husband, Girolamo Giustinian. Such monuments, which often included brief references to these women as patrons, recalled their service as good wives and mothers, and reflected their need to balance natal and marital family interests, but also situated them as powerful financial and cultural arbiters, as well as guardians of natal and marital family fame. Service to kin and clan may also have been a main motivating factor for those elite women who were patrons of urban palaces or villas. We might expect ruling women to be patrons of architecture due to their sizable courts, but this practice was also not unheard of for noble widows as well. As noted above, Alfonsina Orsini built a palace in Rome, and finished a villa begun by her father-in-law, Lorenzo de' Medici. Widowed Caterina Piccolomini constructed the Palazzo delle Papesse in Siena beginning in 1460 with funds provided by her brother, Pope Pius II. Palace construction was significant for the sheer size and expense of the undertaking, but also because palaces were associated with particular lineages—palace patronage by women allowed them to contribute to the fame, magnificence, and continuity of natal or marital clans in ways usually reserved for men. By commissioning and constructing palaces, like Ippolita Pallavicina-Sanserverina did in sixteenth-century Piacenza, women took charge of the physicality of the households over which they reigned.

In addition to acting as patrons to individual works of art, a handful of Renaissance women collected art, antiquities, gems, and other artifacts. Two women known for their collecting zeal were Isabella d'Este, Marchesa of Mantua, and Margaret of Austria, regent of the Netherlands. Upon her arrival in Mantua, Isabella designed and filled spaces specially designated for her with antique Roman statuary, gems, and mythological paintings that celebrated female learning and virtue. Her brother, husband, and son sought her advice for their own studios and collections. Likewise, Margaret's Palace of Savoy in Mechelen featured her collections of books, maps, religious paintings, statues, ivory, 170 items from the New World (including items given by conquistador Hernán de Cortés to her nephew Charles V), and portraits of European rulers, many of whom were family. Her collections demonstrated power through association: her kinships with the ruling houses of Europe, and her immediate family's conquest of the recently "discovered" New World. More than just hobbies, the accumulation and display of these goods were strategies on these women's parts, meant to project a particular vision of them as erudite.

As noted above, ruling women were more likely than most women to receive an education, and many were eager to pursue erudition into adulthood. Isabella d'Este has often been called the "ideal" Renaissance woman in the modern sense of that term—and indeed she cultivated a wide array of pursuits to demonstrate her well-roundedness. She was the patron of several poets (and thus the object of several poetic celebrations of her virtue) and retained a tutor to aid in her study of classical languages. Other elite and ruling women found that a demonstrated education, deployed judiciously, enhanced their reputations. Marguerite of Navarre benefited from the rigorous education provided her and her brother Francis I (at the order of their mother, Louise of Savoy), pursued a lifetime of scholarship, supported scholars including humanist Cornelius Agrippa, and authored devotional poetry, secular and religious plays, and a collection of tales called the *Heptameron*. A select few female authors sought court patronage as well. Christine de Pisan was the first European female "career" writer, who as a widow wrote poetry in addition to the above prose works in order to attract court patronage, including that of the queen of France, whom she also sought to advise, as seen in Figure 7.1, an illumination from Pisan's collected works, copied by the author expressly for the queen, depicting the author presenting her works to the queen. Venetian Cassandra Fedele wrote laudatory epistles to Isabella d'Este, her mother, Eleonora, and her aunt, Beatrice, Queen of Hungary, as well as Isabel of Castile. Fedele preached what she practiced: she was invited to speak before the Venetian doge and Senate on the topic of education for women. Other learned women used their erudition to petition powerful men: Costanza Varano wrote to Pope Eugenius IV and King of Naples Alfonso of Aragon, and delivered an oration to Francesco and Bianca Maria Visconti Sforza of Milan, calling on each to assist in the restoration of family lands. These and other Italian elite and ruling women,

FIGURE 7.1: *Christine de Pisan Presents Her Book to Isabella of Bavaria*, c. 1400. British Library, London. Courtesy of Art Resource, ART194412.

followed by women elsewhere in Europe, benefited from the vogue of humanism, using it as a means to exercise a voice in the affairs of their gender, their families, and their states.

It should not surprise us then, that when Leonardo da Vinci drew Isabella d'Este in preparation for a never-completed portrait, he depicted her with a book (no longer visible from cropping of the drawing), as many powerful women cultivated the image of learning. Among the things collected by Isabella and Margaret of Austria, among other ruling women, were images of themselves. Their portraits functioned quite differently than those of marriage-age women, whose depictions were often distributed to prospective grooms. Isabella commissioned portraits from Leonardo, Mantegna, and Titian, among others, which she distributed to family, friends, and other contacts. Likewise, Margaret commissioned many copies of the same portrait to be sent to ruling houses of Europe (one was found in the collection of Henry VIII) and given as gifts to courtiers, a common practice with male rulers. These and other ruling women worried over the appropriate face to present in such a public medium. A draft proclamation of 1563 indicated that newly crowned Elizabeth I sought to stop the production of unofficial and shoddy images of her royal self. Like Margaret and Isabella, only more so, the demand for the queen's image was overwhelming: the 1563 proclamation declared that "all sorts of subiectes and people both noble and meane" desired the image.[22] The queen's image was equally coveted outside of England—both as enticement to marry her, and as a reflection of her power and beauty. Travelers reported finding her portrait as far afield as Florence, and in Constantinople, where the sultana received a miniature or cameo portrait of Elizabeth set with rubies and diamonds. The queen appeared not only on official portraits but in miniatures, medals, illuminations, woodcuts, and engravings featured in books including the Bible and a popular sixteenth-century atlas, indicating that her image found its way into many homes. There is tremendous variety in the images of the queen, but certain common features stand out, especially concern with elaborate clothes and beauty. Likewise, Isabella's vast correspondence, preserved in the state archives in Mantua, shows that she was quite concerned with her depiction, insisting that it should project beauty, which in the Renaissance was understood to indicate virtue. No wonder both Isabella and Elizabeth did not allow their official image to age—in portraits of each from the last decades of their lives, there is a concerted effort to preserve youth, beauty, and with it feminine influence.

A variation on the female ruling portrait emerged in the sixteenth-century court of Cosimo I de' Medici: the mother/son portrait. The essential nature and

FIGURE 7.2: Miniature portrait of Elizabeth I, Nicholas Hillyard. Ham House, London. Courtesy of Art Resource, ART394821.

power of motherhood, as discussed above, is captured in an image by Agnolo Bronzino that depicts Eleonora of Toledo, wife of Cosimo I, Duke of Florence, with her son Giovanni. Her daughter, Isabella Orsini, likewise is depicted in a portrait with her son Virgilio. In each image, the mother, garbed in costume meant to suggest wealth and power of her family, has a protective hand on her male offspring, while confronting the viewer with her gaze. Both children emphasize the significance of their mothers: Giovanni grasps the stuff of her gown, while Virgilio outright gestures to his progenitrix. The creation of this genre in sixteenth-century Florence, and its transmission to France and Europe in the seventeenth century, suggests a growing awareness by ruling women of the need to engage multiple media in order to project the identity of good mother.

Another source of feminine influence in Renaissance Europe was piety. Biblical figures such as Deborah or the Virgin Mary were among the few positive role models for women, and especially ruling women. Not surprisingly, ruling mothers were often associated with the Virgin, as we saw above with Isabel of Castile, and with queen mother Louise of Savoy, whose close relationship with her son Francis I elicited the parallel during her stints as regent. For Pisan, the identity of a ruling woman began with her love of God, which would guide her away from the vices so commonly attributed to her sex. Piety was an integral part of many women's lives: elite, mercantile, and even lower-class women manifested their spiritual devotion as patrons of religious works and institutions. Such patronage might include bequests to religious institutions or gifts of religious paraphernalia—at the church of Sant'Agostino in Padua, Marietta Dandolo Bragadin paid to restore the crucifix, commissioned a tabernacle, and donated altar cloths and a chalice. Lower-class women might make more modest religious bequests, through membership in confraternities, or on their own, such as Lucia, wife of the mason Vito, who donated five ducats towards a new altarpiece in Santa Maria Formosa, Venice. Other women commissioned works designed for their personal devotion: the series of devotional diptych portraits commissioned by Margaret of Austria, depicting her image facing a scene of the Crucifixion or Virgin and Child is an example. Such works, common in northern Europe, illustrated the patron in the act of prayer—in Margaret's case the interaction between her and the holy family may have been intended to suggest divine sanction of her political position. Similar portraits appeared in books of hours—devotional texts commonly owned by Renaissance women, such as that of Catherine of Cleves, commissioned to commemorate her wedding.

Catholic Renaissance women—ruling women, elites, merchants' wives—were especially generous to convents and other charitable institutions, often those specifically dedicated to women's causes, providing sizable gifts or endowing whole institutions outright. Famed Venetian courtesan Veronica Franco left instructions in her will of 1564 that after the death of her kin, a portion of her investments should be allocated to a charity that provided dowries for poor women; some years later she petitioned the Venetian government, asking that they found a home for impoverished women with children, called the Casa del Soccorso. María de Zuñiga founded the community of Santa Cruz in Spain for wives and widows of members of the Military Order of Santiago, whereas Paola Malatesta Gonzaga, wife of the Marquis of Mantua, founded the monastery of Corpus Christi where she and her daughter Cecilia later retired. In Valladolid, Spain, women were responsible for the foundation of more than 60 percent of convents. Widows were both common patrons and frequent beneficiaries of convents, which provided an alternative to remarriage: the Spanish humanist Juan Luis Vives wrote that "when she no longer has a husband, she should turn to the holy spouse of all women, Jesus Christ."[23]

In addition to being frequent recipients of female patronage, convents themselves were microcosms of female authority. Although increasingly overseen by male church officials, nuns nonetheless practiced limited self-governance, voting on their members and electing their leaders (a practice most alarming to Protestants, who pointed out that women had "neither the reason nor understanding to govern").[24] Such complaints nonwithstanding, recent scholarship has shown that like wives who managed homes, many convent communities were adept at managing their ever-expanding convent properties and the wealth derived from them. Convents, like monasteries, were important sites for charitable contribution, and over centuries some institutions accrued not only significant wealth but also political power. For example, the convent of Sant Pere de les Puelles in Barcelona operated a mill and market on one of its estates, and had the right of appointment in the local church. In a way similar to wives who contributed to the family economy with their baking, brewing, and other activities, convents also rounded out their budgets with their own labor, earning and contributing to local and regional economies in areas such as weaving, baking, sericulture, lace-making, and embroidery. Nuns used their corporate earnings as well as individual wealth to maintain, but also enhance, decorate, and to a degree, personalize, their compounds. When Elena Foscari, the sister of Venetian Doge Francesco Foscari, became abbess at the ancient convent of San Zaccaria in the mid-fifteenth century, she donated eighty ducats for a new organ, and orchestrated a renovation of the church's chancel. She and Marina Donato, the prioress, paid for the central two-sided altarpiece, while two other altarpieces were financed by nuns Margarita Donato and Agnesina Giustinian.

Individual nuns were often influential beyond the confines of convent walls, despite the best attempts by church officials to enforce claustration. Many nuns came from the most elite families, and kinship ties gave them influence with local and regional governments. Scholastica Rondinelli, the abbess of Le Murate in Florence, petitioned the government for subventions for her convent, and wrote to members of the Medici family, requesting (and usually receiving) favors such as permission for family members to return from exile. Medici patronage was crucial in the rebuilding of the convent after a 1470 fire, a project that allowed Rondinelli to expand convent space to include a scriptorium. Pious suasion and mystical visions even inspired a few Catholic religious women to adopt an overtly political stance: stigmatics María de la

Visitacíon and Lucia da Narni advised Spain's Philip II and Ercole I of Ferrara, respectively, while Lucrecia de León experienced (or fabricated) elaborate dreams in which she upbraided Philip II for his maltreatment of the poor, and predicted his assassination. Other nuns used their reputations for extreme piety to further reform agendas: Magdalena de San Jerónimo founded a rigorous house for the reform of prostitutes, Santa Maria Magdalena in Valladolid in the early seventeenth century, while St. Teresa of Avila founded no fewer than sixteen convents.

Although women were not overtly powerful in Protestant movements that swept through sixteenth-century Europe, their voices contributed to criticisms of Catholicism, and some ruling women were nonetheless quiet facilitators of reform movements. Marguerite de Navarre (author of *Mirror of the Sinful Soul*, a poem later translated by twelve-year-old Elizabeth Tudor) sponsored reformist theologian Guillaume Briçonnet, corresponded with John Calvin, and mediated on religious reform with her brother, the king of France. The court of Marguerite's contemporary kinswoman, Renee of France, Duchess of Ferrara, was likewise a center of Protestant ideology that attracted the likes Calvin himself.

Patronage, piety, management, motherhood—these were some vehicles to enhanced authority in the Renaissance for *some* women, especially elites. The question of the state, status, and standing of Renaissance women has long been debated in academia. Nineteenth-century historian Jacob Burckhardt, citing examples such as Isabella d'Este, optimistically claimed that women "stood on a footing of perfect equality with men."[25] More recently, in the 1970s, Joan Kelly countered with the question, "Did women have a Renaissance," which she answered in the negative, by arguing that modernizing forces, such as state building and capitalism at work in Renaissance Italy, meant women "experienced a contraction of social and personal options that men of their classes did not." Looking mostly to literary evidence, Kelly found that in comparison to the era that preceded it, the Renaissance left woman as "an aesthetic object: decorous, chaste, and doubly dependent—on her husband as well as the prince."[26] Burckhardt's and Kelly's claims for the triumph or tribulation of Renaissance women have been equally challenged by scholars in the past forty years, who have demonstrated in a wealth of monographs and articles the ample and complex middle ground between these two extremes. Although emergent merchant capitalism meant women's work possibilities declined in some areas, their investment capability rose in others. Although some humanist authors echoed the classical age's dictums on female inferiority, some women used their humanist education to challenge these ideas. Although social norms dictated that woman's place was in the home, some homes were centers of tremendous wealth and influence. Although laws existed to limit female inheritance of property or rule, women nonetheless inherited both, all of which suggests a considerable chasm between the ideals of patriarchy and the practical considerations of day-to-day life. Women were not without power in the period, nor were they anywhere near an "equal footing with men"—even a figure as powerful as Queen Elizabeth battled the forces of misogyny that declared her biologically and intellectually incapable of rule, and was forced to carefully negotiate existing belief systems in order to legitimate and maintain her reign. "Negotiation" and "mediation" are common terms in recent scholarship on Renaissance women, which suggest that some women possessed both "agency," the ability to act on their own behalf, and the ability to develop strategies to operate within existing systems of patriarchy that defined them as secondary. The in-between, informal authority that many wives and widows exercised, whether within the narrow confines of the home or the wider polity, reflects what Sharon Kettering has insightfully called the "actual power of noblewomen…hidden behind institutional powerlessness."[27] Power (and for that matter the notion of "having a Renaissance") for women *and* men in the early modern period was relative, and most frequently a function of class, kinship, and status.

CHAPTER EIGHT

Artistic Representation

MARY ROGERS

What sort of a Renaissance did women have in relation to the visual arts? Answers have naturally been diverse. The existence and the careers of female artists have received attention in exhibitions, and their critical reception examined in the light of contemporary notions of women's capacities.[1] The influence of women on art as patrons, consumers, or spectators has been studied, both as individuals and as members of subgroups such as nuns or widows.[2] Meshing with a wider interest in the material culture of the Renaissance, rather than just what has been considered fine art, new consideration has been given to the artifacts in the domestic settings in which women spent most of their lives, which have formed the subject of several recent exhibitions.[3] All this has meant that there has been a certain shift away from general studies of the representation of women. Although this chapter will present a far from comprehensive overview of women as depicted in the portraiture of the Italian Renaissance, I will indicate how these images connect with the world of material culture, with social customs and ethics, and with cultural and aesthetic ideals involving women. No artistic genre connects more closely with the historical actualities of women's lives than does portraiture. Yet portraiture does not reflect passively what lay before the artist's eyes; rather, it articulates networks of relationships and ideal forms and identities in which the sitter and the commissioner (unlikely to be the same person with female portraits) and their associates might be involved. How can we see changes in the ways in which women are shown that are more than just changes in style, but are those that respond to, express, or shape novel social and cultural female types? Or, alternatively, do many portraits reinforce conservative roles and stereotypes? If one agrees with Margaret King that, though little changed in the political or legal position of women at the time, something happened in women's sense of self, how clearly does portraiture express this new consciousness?[4] To what extent can we see at least some portraits as containing elements of female identity-fashioning, whether concurring with or challenging current ideals?

That females were portrayed at all might seem an obvious indication of social change. From about the 1450s or 1460s, non-royal women in some number came to be thought worthy of commemoration, their images to be conserved by family, friends, and descendants.[5] In the past it has been easy to assume that the rise in portraiture was connected with some purely Italian, and classically Burckhardtian, rediscovery of the world and of the individual at the dawn of the Renaissance in the early fifteenth century.[6] However, this is contradicted by the priority of autonomous female portraits in the Netherlands, some of which certainly date from the 1430s if not earlier, and which show women who, judging by their costume, seem to be not of exalted social standing but, rather, young women from the burgher classes, as in Campin's *Portrait of a Woman* in the National Gallery in London.[7] Very few painted female portraits made in Italy have been preserved from a similar time, other than those of members of ruling houses, such as the c. 1435 *Portrait of a d'Este Princess* by Pisanello in the Louvre, or images of donatrixes in devotional art, as in Masaccio's *Trinity* (Sta. Maria Novella, Florence) from the 1420s. Even more striking is the difference in format and its psychological consequence: the Italian examples are seen in profile, with eyes averted, whereas the Netherlandish sitters, shown in three-quarter view, can engage the spectator with seeming frankness. Only at a considerably later date do the sitters in Italian portraits seem to project such a calm acceptance of their visibility. However, probably mainly from the 1450s, we find in Florence, but not in other cities, a few dozen paintings of young women seen in profile, many by unknown painters, but with the best examples attributable to major artists such as Antonio and/or Piero Pollaiuolo and Alesso Baldovinetti (*Portrait of a Lady*, National Gallery, London, c. 1465). These portraits have attracted attention as illuminating gender relationships and social ideals in fifteenth-century Florence and as challenging the view that the Renaissance involved a general awakening of interest in the individual character.[8] Their visual language does not facilitate exploration of individuality beyond the delineation of the particularities of forehead, nose, and chin, or of inner life, due to figures' apparent flatness, stasis, and averted gaze. Usually weighed down with heavy, extremely expensive brocades, jeweled necklaces, or hair ornaments, these girls appear primarily as objects for the display of wealth. It is assumed that these mostly unidentified young women were newly betrothed or married members of Florentine elite families, and that therefore their presentation connects with the upper-class culture of opulent display for reasons of status and family honor that flourished in the later fifteenth-century years of a Florence dominated by the Medici regime. This culture differed greatly from the more austere humanist ideals that have been thought to shape the innovative Florentine public art early in the century.

Evidence of the customs and attitudes surrounding marriage among wealthy Florentines of the fifteenth century is provided by many family *ricordi*, or letters, none more vivid than those of that formidable mother-in-law Alessandra Macinghi Strozzi as she considered possible wives for her sons.[9] Using information from associates as well as covert observations in church, her very practical comments favored girls of good, but not outstandingly distinguished, families who were sensible, cheerful, and capable as well as pleasant-looking and dignified in demeanor.[10] Such requirements accorded with the ideas of humanists who wrote early examples of the distinctively Renaissance genre of

FIGURE 8.1: Alesso Baldovinetti, *Portrait of a Lady*, c. 1465. National Gallery, London. Courtesy of the National Gallery.

treatises on marriage, the family, or the upbringing of children, treatises that were much indebted to ancient Greek texts.[11] The Venetian patrician Francesco Barbaro, writing in Latin on wifely duties around 1415, sketched an ideal wife as one who was worthy to continue the family line because she was chaste, virtuous, and of distinguished ancestry: fine though not extravagant costume and jewelry could appropriately signal her elevated status.[12] After her wedding, she would be a capable mistress of her household, maintaining an ideal of *ordine* through her restrained behavior and careful supervision of servants: learning, lively conversation, or cultural interests are not mentioned. The well-trained wife of the old merchant Giannozzo in Leon Battista Alberti's dialogue on the family in Italian, dating from the 1430s, was likewise reported as being a diligent and deferential conserver of the family goods, accepting that she must never enter her husband's study or meddle in his business affairs.[13] These verbal portraits imply, or sometimes state explicitly, notions of womankind rooted in the current theological and biological conceptions of female nature that the other contributors to this volume have outlined.[14] These ideals are echoed in later Florentine biographies, such as those by Vespasiano da Bisticci in the 1480s, and, more partially, in the family *ricordi* and *memoriale* of patrician males in other cities.[15] With certain modifications, they are perpetuated in many sixteenth-century treatises, such as the widely disseminated (and plagiarized) writings of Juan Luis Vives, or those by Lodovico Dolce, and most girls of affluent families are likely to have been trained towards some version of this conservative wifely ideal.[16]

Not only the Florentine profile examples, but many Italian portraits into the sixteenth century and beyond seem to show such a girl shortly before or after her marriage, sometimes alone, sometimes with her husband in a single panel (as with Lorenzo Lotto's *Messer Marsilio and his Wife* in the Prado) or in paired or pendant images (such as Raphael's *Agnolo* and *Maddalena Doni* in the Uffizi). These young women, though painted in very different styles, convey similar ideals of wifely virtue: modest, chaste, upright behavior communicated by control of the body and especially the eyes, and elevated family status, communicated through lavish dress and accessories. One useful example among many, probably made in Milan around 1525, is Bartolomeo Veneto's *Portrait of a Lady* in Ottawa, where the rich red dress and ribbons on the turban, the finely embroidered shirt, and the expensive gloves speak of the affluence of the sitter. Her averted eyes suggest not the coquettish allure of many of the artist's other painted women, but a demure wifely behavior that would have been learned and approved. X-rays reveal that elements in the costume were changed, seemingly by the original artist, perhaps showing the importance attributed by the owners to keeping dress up to date, or, probably more likely, marking a change in status of the woman from betrothed to bride that was thought deserving of commemoration.[17] Other instances of portraits of richly dressed yet modest young women from mid- to late sixteenth-century Bologna have been analyzed by Caroline Murphy as records of the conspicuous consumption surrounding upper-class marriages in that city, despite clerical disapproval.[18] These paintings by a female artist, Lavinia Fontana, perpetuate the idealized appearance of the girls at the time, serious and dignified in bearing, modest in their averted eyes, and wearing an extremely expensive costume to mark both the religious and social significance of this crucial rite of passage and the wealth and status of their own and their husbands' families.

FIGURE 8.2: Bartolomeo Veneto, *Portrait of a Lady*, c. 1525. National Gallery of Canada, Ottawa. Wikicommons: http://en.wikipedia.org/wiki/File:Veneto_0022.jpg _at_the_Easel_Painti.

Paintings like these form a large part of surviving Renaissance female portraits. One easy judgment has been that they present an essentially conservative and masculine view of women, as images of passive virtue unthreatening to the male observer.[19] It would matter little that the young brides, their female relatives, and, in the case of the works by Lavinia Fontana, the artist would have complied with such a role. However, the emphasis on opulent costume in all these images can be viewed more positively, for a deeper understanding of the significance of clothing in the urban centers where the images were produced illuminates not just costs but values. Not just material status but perceived family honor, taste, and experience in ornamenting a bride were involved, the whole process being circumscribed both by custom and by law. The practicalities of producing such images are not clear, but propriety might have excluded much in the way of sittings, making modern expectations that they convey "personality" unrealistic. Painters might have been asked to record in detail the customary presents of jewelry or expensive fabrics given by members of both families when marriage negotiations reached an advanced stage. These may well have cost one hundred times more than the handiwork of the painter, and perhaps would have been loaned to artists rather than observed on the girls.[20] (There would have been practical reasons for these pictorial records, in an era where disputes often arose over expensive possessions and undelivered dowry goods.) In the selection of such appropriate items, many parties might have been involved, some of whom, in the many Italian cities where luxury textiles were produced and imported, could be highly discriminating about quality and value. A range of skills might have been employed by female as well as by male family members, from seeking out specially valued fabrics, to concocting symbolic or heraldic devices to be incorporated into clothing or jewelry, to proficiency in needlework such as the delicate dark embroidery seen on exposed undershirts, conceivably the work of the bride or a relative.[21] Furthermore, the pleasure principle should not be excluded, including the vicarious pleasure of older family members. "As she is beautiful and the wife of Filippo Strozzi, she will need beautiful jewels. Just as you have honor in other things, she doesn't want to be lacking in this," wrote Alessandra Strozzi to her son about her future daughter-in-law. Earlier, she had claimed of another son: "He feels he can't do enough having things made, because she's beautiful and he wants her to look even more so."[22] Thus the paintings are the relics not just of an oppressive male ideology, but also of a female culture working in collaboration with men, where clothing was an indication of worth and taste as well as being a source of enjoyment.

These "marriage paintings" were not snapshots, recording one moment in time where the bride was dressed in all her costly finery, but, rather, they were synthesized stages in a long-drawn-out process taking place between betrothal and a short period after marriage. It was only within this timespan that the sort of lavish display found in so many portraits was deemed legitimate by sumptuary laws in several cities: the marriage portrait can be seen as illustrating a phase, not a moment, when a young woman was a legitimate object of visual pleasure, available to public viewing in processions and other festivities. It can surely be assumed that many young wives, in other respects largely passive participants in the whole process, would have found this attention highly enjoyable. Alessandra Strozzi remarked rather sourly in January 1466 that, despite current economic decline in the city, brides delighted in wearing their lavish dowries of silk and jewels when they went out.[23]

Furthermore, the claim that all examples of the betrothal or marriage portrait show a comprehensive repression of female individuality can be challenged. Some observers have detected a certain pert, jaunty, or self-confident air in many of the maidens. One might connect this sort of poise in the Baldovinetti with a social culture in Florence that, though limited by modern standards in its view of female capabilities, delighted in the graceful bearing of well-brought-up girls when they were visible in public, serving important foreign visitors at table, or participating in musical performances.[24] That the marital customs in Florence involved commemorating such girls in portrait form, rather than by other means, supports such sentiments, as does the fact that a distinctively Florentine artistic culture, by the 1450s and 1460s, frequently depicted lively, though carefully modulated, female elegance, as with Desiderio da Settignano or Filippo Lippi.

If we move to other regions and to later periods, we can also find several portraits of young ladies whose confident, less retiring demeanor suggests their knowledge of their attractiveness. This may have to do with the later and wider cultural celebration of physical allure that will be discussed below or, on a more material level, with economic factors. The inflation of dowries in the sixteenth century, especially in the Veneto, created numerous losers amongst middle-class girls (those forced to marry below their station, or reluctant entrants to convents), but also a minority of winners who were fully conscious of the attractiveness of their wealth as well as their beauty. The young lady portrayed by Veronese, now in Douai, might be one such portrait; she was evidently from a family well able to afford her luxurious velvet, lace-trimmed dress, and the heavy gold belt she rather complacently handles.[25]

Attention to documentary sources and theoretical writings, then, illuminates a large category of portraits of women, and similar methods can be used in for those presenting women at other stages in their lives. Images of clearly pregnant wives are few, although the unknown sitter presented in Raphael's c. 1506 *La Gravida* (Pitti Palace, Florence) is an early example. It was very common for pregnant women to make their wills before the hazardous process of childbirth, and one might expect portraits to have been made to preserve the image of a beloved wife. Perhaps it was thought that young wives were adequately commemorated by their wedding portraits; many other portraits may indeed represent pregnant women, although they are not recognized as such. It has recently been argued that Leonardo da Vinci's *Lady with an Ermine* (Czartoryski Museum, Kraków) depicts Cecilia Gallerani, the mistress of Lodovico Sforza (Il Moro), in late 1490 or early 1491, when she was pregnant with his son.[26] Though the animal has usually been understood both as a play on Cecilia's surname in Greek and as a symbol of chastity, other readings are possible in the light of this pregnancy theory. Cecilia's hand both caresses the ermine, perhaps also alluding to Lodovico, who had been recently invested in the Neapolitan Order of the Ermine, and rests against her stomach, allowing an initiated viewer to understand the bond between the lovers, while not rendering it explicit.

Paintings celebrating women in their roles as mothers are generally unusual before the middle of the sixteenth century unless dynastic considerations are involved, as in the well-known c. 1550 *Portrait of Eleonora da Toledo and Her Son* by Bronzino.[27] However, before this date there are several group family portraits produced in Venice, by artists like Lotto (the 1547 *Della Volta Family* in the National Gallery in London) or Licinio (the c. 1535–45 *Family Group* in the Royal Collections at Hampton Court), where the sitters, though evidently affluent, seem not to have come from the patrician class.[28] Even more rarely in Italian art, as opposed to the art of northern Europe, are wives portrayed with poses or accessories that suggest the virtuous domesticity that was, as all writers of conduct literature agreed, to industriously conserve and to order the goods of her husband's household.[29] Andrea del Sarto's c. 1515–25 *Woman with a Basket of Spindles* (in the Pitti in Florence) is one example where skill in weaving, traditionally associated with virtuous femininity, can be read to stand for a range of domestic virtues.[30]

The third phase of life for women remaining in the secular world was widowhood, a state experienced by a much larger proportion of women than is the case today, sometimes at a young age and only briefly, before remarriage, sometimes in maturity or old age. As is usually noted, widowhood was an

FIGURE 8.3: Leonardo da Vinci, *Lady with an Ermine* (Portrait of Cecilia Gallerani), c. 1490/1491. Czartoryski Museum, Kraków. Courtesy of Art Resource.

ambiguous, often problematic state for Renaissance societies.[31] However, while many widows were poor or vulnerable, fortunate ones might attain a degree of autonomy in financial and other terms. This could permit cultural endeavors including the patronage of art, as women now had the legal authority to order works of art without the intervention of a male intermediary. Especially during the later sixteenth century, the era of Catholic reform, widows endowed many altarpieces or chapels that included self-representations, though to deflect any accusations of vanity, these usually showed them in modest scale and costume, with gazes averted from the spectator, or with emphatically wrinkled and uncomely visages.[32] Widows are also portrayed within extended family groups and in autonomous widow portraits, where the subject, dressed simply, mainly in black, and with a sober or mournful expression, may be seen with accessories referring to her piety or to famous widows from history.[33] Clearly these can be related to the ideal role of the widow recommended by churchmen or secular writers of conduct literature throughout our period, involving an austere nun-like existence faithful to the memory of her deceased husband, eschewing vain pleasures and concentrating on unostentatious religious devotion.[34] It cannot be assumed, however, that such images amounted to a woman's own declaration of her new identity and way of life. Just as wills show husbands attempting to control their widows' destinies from beyond the grave, so, too, as Allison Levy has pointed out, there are indications that husbands or other relatives commissioned portraits of future widows prior to their spouses' deaths. Such images, then, might constitute declarations not of female self-awareness but of male intent, or even warnings, for their wives.[35] In contrast, there are also more ambivalent images, on the one hand incorporating references to piety or good works, on the other presenting the sitters with dress and demeanor that accentuate their physical charms, holding out the possibility of remarriage. Correggio's *Portrait of a Lady* (c. 1518–20) in St. Petersburg and Bugiardini's *La Monaca* (c. 1506–10) in the Uffizi in Florence are two such examples.[36]

So far we have been dealing with representations of women who were little known beyond their own family circle, portrayed in conformity with affluent middle- or upper-class social norms. What, though, of images of that smaller category of females who cultivated virtues broader than just modesty, piety, obedience, and diligent childrearing and household management? Mention of a "Renaissance man" usually evokes someone who had, as humanists recommended, a solid educational foundation of classical languages and literature, equipping him for participation in many practical and cultural pursuits. To some extent, there did come to be "Renaissance women" of this kind, although there were fewer of them and both their education and the practical uses to which they put it were circumscribed. During the period covered by this volume, education for the majority of women continued to focus on piety and domestic skills, yet for a small proportion education broadened, whether conducted in the convent, in select private schools, or in the family home. In the sixteenth century the dissemination of printed books aided those who wished to expand their horizons later in life.[37] By the middle of that century and later, a small but significant number of women had published their own writings and attained local or sometimes national fame, as had a select number of female artists, musicians, and performers. Such women were certainly conscious of their own novelty in their quest to justify their efforts, establish their fame, and broaden contemporary notions of female capabilities. To what extent do their images in the visual arts seem to exhibit a similar awareness, as part of their bid for fame? The development of this type of "new woman" and her representations can now be examined further.

In the early fifteenth century, humanist learning was mainly the preserve of aristocratic women who might be educated together with their brothers and a few of their associates at schools, such as Vittorino da Feltre's at Mantua or Guarino's at Verona, where the famous Nogarola sisters studied. Both the learning and the cultural contacts of some of these women and the difficulties they could experience in furthering them are documented.[38] A leading Florentine humanist like Leonardo Bruni, for example, could, in a letter of 1424 directed to Battista Malatesta Montefeltro, both encourage women in wide-ranging learning in Christian and classical authors, and steer them away from the study of mathematics or of the rhetoric that might be used in political or legal contexts.[39] Many writers followed this disapproval of women's public orations, based on the strictures of St. Paul, and set limitations on their pursuit of learning. Cecilia Gonzaga (1416–51) fought with her parents to be allowed to enter a convent, perhaps for educational as well as religious reasons, rather than to marry and continue a life at court; eventually she became, in 1445, a Clarissan nun. Two years later, a medal by Antonio Pisanello, perhaps made to compensate her family for her absence, celebrates the "virgin Cecilia," still shown on the obverse in secular dress. On the reverse, however, she is celebrated with a combination of medieval and classical imagery that was appropriate for a woman who was a devout Christian yet versed in the new learning. With traditional medieval symbolism, a shaggy unicorn rests his horn on the lap of a virgin who has tamed him. Yet the nudity of the maiden and the crescent moon also suggest the goddess Diana, with whom chaste Renaissance women were later happy to be identified. The abbess of the Benedictine convent of S. Paolo, Parma, for example, had an image of the goddess frescoed by Correggio over the fireplace in her reception room in the 1510s. The extent to which Cecilia herself might have encouraged this memorialization of her determined virginity, or even contributed to the imagery, is unknown but not inconceivable. The notion of the goddess Diana as dedicated to virginity and encouraging those wishing to reject worldly pleasure emerges very clearly in a work Cecilia is likely to have read, Boccaccio's *De mulieribus claris* ("Life of Camilla").[40] Certainly later in the century, aristocratic women showed interest in devising appropriate personal emblems to decorate their clothing, jewelry, or apartments, which might suggest their interior life and personal values, serving as kinds of intellectual self-portraits.[41]

FIGURE 8.4: Antonio Pisanello, medal of Cecilia Gonzaga (reverse), c. 1447. British Museum, London. Courtesy of Art Resource.

Later in the century, the cultural achievements of some aristocratic women seem to have produced less conflict with their life at court, and indeed became celebrated. One indication of this lies in a biographical genre that attained popularity in several languages beginning in the latter half of the fifteenth century, the collections of lives of "famous women" adapted from Boccaccio and, before him, from Plutarch.[42] These now came to include Renaissance women as well as heroines or villainesses from ancient history and myth, or from Jewish or Christian traditions. The rigid moralism of Boccaccio's *De mulieribus claris*, based on the chastity/lack of chastity dichotomy, was relaxed to favor more varied positive qualities, including learning and eloquence as well as an often freshly observed beauty. The pioneering work was the unfinished *De mulieribus admirandis* of Antonio Cornazzano, written c. 1466–68 and dedicated to Bianca Maria Visconti, Duchess of Milan; the collection of Giovanni Sabadino degli Arienti from the 1490s, named after Ginevra Bentivoglio of Bologna, was perhaps the most vivid.[43] The genre was perpetuated by the expanded and translated versions of Boccaccio's lives made by Giuseppe Betussi, published in 1547 and later.[44] Though these biographical compilations never became international best-sellers like Baldassare Castiglione's *Il Cortegiano*, where, as will be seen, a somewhat different court lady is sketched, they do celebrate new types of meritorious woman such as, in the case of Sabadino, a recent saint and devotional writer of Bologna, Caterina de' Vigri, or the Veronese humanist Isotta Nogarola. Both Sabadino and Cornazzano showed particular interest in the group of women brought up at the courts of Milan, Bianca Maria Visconti (1425–68), Ippolita (1445–88), and Battista Sforza (1446–72), or of Naples, Eleonora (1450–93), Beatrice (1457–1509), and Isabella (1470–1504) of Aragon. Several of their biographies sketch a new type of courtly lady, who as well as showing dignity, beauty, modesty, and piety possesses learning and eloquence, which might even be deployed in public settings. Ippolita had a fair knowledge of Latin and read aloud with a mellifluous voice; with an eloquence confirmed by other sources, she would speak not only on the morally improving potential of the reading of books, but on history, statecraft, and other topics often thought unsuitable for women, such as arms, riding, hunting, falconry, and agriculture.[45] According to Sabadino, her mother, Bianca Maria Visconti, also spoke fluently and forcefully and enjoyed the company of learned men, and Battista Sforza could give orations and talk intelligently on military matters, something that is plausible for consorts who would have had to take charge of the government of the state when their *condottieri* husbands were away on campaigns.[46] This stress on learning and eloquence was repeated in other *Famous Women* collections, and by the time of Betussi's editions of Boccaccio, concepts of such talented women, "virile" by virtue of their political roles or exceptional abilities, were taking shape.[47]

A group of much-admired portrait busts, some existing in more than one version, are identifiable with four of these aristocratic ladies. They clearly show the stylistic characteristics of the peripatetic sculptor Francesco Laurana, particularly his tendency to a geometrical idealization of form. Laurana mainly worked in the south of Italy and Provence and is known to have been in Naples c. 1473–75.[48] This is the likely dating of at least two of the busts; the sitters' identities are established by inscriptions carved into the bases: the *Battista Sforza*, Duchess of Urbino (Bargello, Florence) and the *Beatrice of Aragon* (Frick Collection, New York). The *Battista Sforza* may be a posthumous work, based on a death mask taken when the duchess died in 1472. The *Beatrice of Aragon* is likely to have been made when the sitter's betrothal to Matthias Corvinus, King of Hungary, which took place in 1474, was being negotiated. If another elaborately polychromed and gilded bust, in the Kunsthistorisches Museum in Vienna, shows Beatrice's sister, Eleonora, as is often accepted, this would have been made a year earlier, for her betrothal to Ercole I d'Este, Duke of Ferrara, in 1473. Though these sculptures differ greatly in physical condition and in the physiognomies they portray, they all project an aristocratic dignity and sense of thought. The latter two also display in their youthful features and downcast head and eyes the virginal modesty thought appropriate for aristocratic brides.[49]

Though the historical Beatrice and Eleonora both became important in the cultural lives of their respective domains, it is the busts by Laurana commemorating women at a later stage in their lives that more strongly, though in different ways, communicate the intellectual qualities associated with the new type of court lady. These busts are the already mentioned *Battista Sforza* and one other more problematical type, which originally existed in two versions: one in the Frick Collection and the other in the Staatliche Museen in Berlin. The busts have been widely accepted as depicting Ippolita Sforza, Battista's cousin and near coeval, on the basis of comparisons with Ippolita's authenticated portraits

FIGURE 8.5: Francesco Laurana, *Bust of Battista Sforza* (Duchess of Urbino), c. 1473. Museo del Bargello, Florence. Image courtesy of Art Resource.

shown in miniatures, and her presence in the south of Italy after her 1465 marriage to the Duke of Calabria. If done around the same time as the bust of Battista, both women would have been in their late twenties. Opinion has differed as to the relative quality of the two works, and assessments have been made more difficult by the extensive damage suffered in the Second World War by the Berlin version, which today is known in its complete state only through old photographs and casts (Victoria and Albert Museum, London).[50] However, if the Ippolita Sforza identification is accepted, correlations with her literary image can be found.

As is usual with Laurana, the idealized figure, shown at rest with downcast eyes, combines a dignified aristocratic poise with the suggestion of inner thought. The simple yet very delicately detailed style and dressing of the hair contributes to the calm and closed silhouette, set off by the *all'antica* reliefs on the horizontal base. The obscure classical subjects of the antique reliefs, which differ in the New York and Berlin versions, have never been

FIGURE 8.6: Nineteenth-century cast after Francesco Laurana, *Bust of a Lady* (Ippolita Sforza?). Victoria and Albert Museum, London. Courtesy of the Victoria and Albert Museum.

satisfactorily explained despite ingenious attempts, but they might in a general sense convey the sitter's learning, as did the imagery in the Cecilia Gonzaga medal. Sabadino's biography vividly evoked Ippolita's beauty and her bearing, which combined dignity with modesty, and her gestures, as when she would raise her eyes towards those to whom she was granting an audience, and modestly lower them again.[51] As was conventional, he noted the loveliness of her hands (omitted in the bust as was usual at this date) but enlivened his account by mentioning her idiosyncratic gesture of stroking her right glove against her gown as she pondered a problem. In keeping with her moral qualities, such as piety and compassion for the poor, Ippolita's clothing was said to be not luxurious but indicative of her taste, favoring dark-colored silks and modest veils.[52] The simpler dress in the Frick bust contrasts with the rich patterning of the brocade gown of the Berlin version, which seems to have been coarsely executed, possibly the work of an assistant at best.[53] Laurana's bust goes some way, then, towards suggesting Ippolita's modest thoughtfulness and her cultural interests, but his *Battista Sforza* accords even more with what we know of the duchess from Sabadino and other sources.[54] It is markedly more sober in the costume, in the styling of the hair, and in the simplification of form: Battista was not celebrated for her beauty but rather for her piety, learning, and just rule of Urbino when her duke was absent due to warfare, and in the bust we accordingly have a sense not of grace, but rather of austere dignity and vigorous authority. It certainly seems closer to the literary characterization of the learned duchess, competent in government, effective in oratory, and pious enough to have been rumored to wear a hair shirt under her clothes, than is the more famous likeness by Piero della Francesca (Uffizi, Florence), where she is garbed in cloth-of-gold brocade and laden with pearls. While it is true there is nothing to specifically suggest Battista's intellectual interests, the bust strikes a forceful, uningratiating note that is not found again until the 1550s, a time when female writers or painters are depicted in ways that unequivocally celebrate their talents. Bronzino's *Laura Battiferra* in the Palazzo Vecchio, Florence, from c. 1555, is a well-known example, where the dress is likewise sober, the line of forehead and nose strong rather than graceful.[55] Even if the poet holds a verse by Petrarch rather than one by herself, the intensity of her gaze excludes the possibility of her being thought only a genteel dilettante: the fervor of her apparent desire for study, poetic inspiration, or consequent fame is akin to that found in the self-presentations of writers like Laura Cereta or Isabella Andreini.[56] An earnest sobriety also characterizes many of the numerous self-portraits by Sofonisba Anguissola done in the 1550s, sent as gifts to important people to publicize her combination of painterly talents, virtue, and noble birth.⁵⁷ Some, like the one at Lancut, show her plainly dressed in the act of painting, not always the choice of Renaissance self-portraitists keen to stress the intellectual rather than manual nature of their profession.

The learned aristocratic lady, the female writer or painter, thus, seems to have been, if not absolutely new, then a distinctive type in Renaissance life, first celebrated in the biographies after about 1460–70, and gaining more widespread attention after c. 1540, when Veronica Gambara, Vittoria Colonna, and then Sofonisba Anguissola came to enjoy fame and status.⁵⁸ Yet the works discussed above are only a few where such women's commitment to learning and culture were celebrated, or even implied, in visual art. This, admittedly, must be a tentative statement, since many portraits of all types have been lost,

FIGURE 8.7: Sofonisba Anguissola, *Portrait of the Artist*, c. 1557. Museum, Lancut, Poland. Wikicommons: http://en.wikipedia.org/wiki/File: Self-porait_at_the_Easel_Painti.

and female writers of distinction or fame were, though significant, small in number. However, it seems noteworthy that, apart from classical figures from her *studiolo* paintings which may refer to her obliquely, there is only one surviving image of Isabella d'Este that suggests her intellectual or cultural endeavors as opposed to her delight in lavish, sometimes innovative, dress. This is the drawing by Leonardo da Vinci in the Louvre of c. 1500, where a small volume held by the lady can just be discerned: but even this might be a book of devotion rather than one related to new learning. For all that some Renaissance thinkers questioned the idea that nobility came from birth, rather than from talent and *virtù*, success at court tended to be esteemed more highly, and thus deemed more worthy of commemoration, than artistic talent. When she became a courtier in Madrid after 1560, Sofonisba Anguissola portrayed herself as a sumptuously dressed, bejeweled figure, seemingly without any attributes of painting or learning.[59] Moroni's *Portrait of a Lady in Red* (National Gallery, London, c. 1555–60) is thought to represent the Countess Lucia Avogadro, who published several verses within the poetic anthologies of the mid-sixteenth century, yet the picture incorporates no allusions to her literary talents, concentrating on her social distinction, as communicated by the formality of her full-length, seated pose and her shimmering satin gown. Even a father like Annibal Guasco, so proud of the talents that he had carefully nurtured in his daughter Lavinia, advised her when serving as a lady-in-waiting at court to maintain her skills in singing, in playing stringed instruments, and in calligraphy in private, thereby presenting a humble demeanor to avoid jealousy.[60]

Perhaps a challenge to the lady of talent and learning was the evolution of a different ideal, of a lady who is still cultured and accomplished, but in a less formidable way: her attraction came from her combination of beauty and social graces. This seems to emerge from a fusion and mutual reinforcement of poetic and artistic ideals, which would then feed into that best-seller of the sixteenth century, Castiglione's *Il Cortegiano*. As is well known, the Florentine culture of the 1470s and 1480s in the circle of Lorenzo de' Medici was much preoccupied with beauty in both the philosophical and literary senses.[61] Marsilio Ficino's interpretations of the philosophy of Plato attributed an elevating significance to the experience of visual or aural beauty; for Tuscan poets, notably Poliziano and even Lorenzo himself, who were steeped in the writing of Dante and also in Petrarchan poetry generally, this came to mean the beauty of a beloved lady who led the lover/poet upwards. Ritual jousts took place in honor of such literary *innamorate* as Simonetta Vespucci or Lucrezia Donati, and evoking the beauties of such women with compelling eloquence presented a challenge for poets, met most famously in the elaborate description in Poliziano's *Stanze per*

FIGURE 8.8: Leonardo da Vinci, *Portrait of Isabella d'Este* (Marchioness of Mantua), drawing, c. 1500. Louvre, Paris. Wikicommons: http://en.wikipedia.org/wiki/File: Isabella_d%27este.jpg.

la Giostra of the radiant, golden-haired Simonetta Vespucci.[62] Aware of such literary conventions but also building on preexistent studio traditions, Florentine artists such as Leonardo, Verrocchio, and Botticelli produced their own interpretations of comparable feminine grace. Both in technique and in imagery they followed divergent, probably competitively divergent, stylistic paths. In his c. 1475 *Ginevra de' Benci* (National Gallery, Washington, D.C.), Leonardo found a way of depicting golden hair and smooth, pale skin by manipulating contrasts of light against dark that was more naturalistic than Botticelli in his so-called *Bella Simonetta* (Städel Kunstinstitut, Frankfurt, c. 1480–85), where elaborately dressed, abundant hair, lit with gold pigment, tumbles "neglected with art." In Verrocchio's sculpted *Lady with the Flowers* (Bargello, Florence, c. 1478), often thought to be another portrait of Ginevra de' Benci, the artist adopted the conventional poetic motif of the lovely female gathering flowers into her graceful hands, found in verses written in honor of Ginevra but also found in Petrarchan poetry generally.[63] The Botticelli may not have suggested a particular woman at all, but rather an ideal of beauty: the figure's dress and accessories evoke both a fantasy antique world and the features of Petrarch's Laura.[64]

This interest in presenting portrait-like images of female beauties informed by poetry spread to other cultural centers like Milan, Venice, and the Rome of Leo X in subsequent decades, with literary figures like Pietro Bembo, the son of Ginevra de' Benci's platonic lover, Bernardo Bembo, and painters like Raphael, Palma Vecchio, and Titian being important protagonists. This ground has been well trodden in recent years: here space permits only a brief discussion of a number of facets of these artistic developments that had many repercussions for the representation of females.

The first of these relates to the stylistic changes effected first by Leonardo in Milan in the 1490s and then (independently or not) by Giorgione and subsequent Venetian painters. These artists showed the figures of their sitters with ampler forms, which were softened by their emergence from shadow, made more telling by the subordination of costume detail, and frequently shown in actual or potential motion. In these changes, the current quickening of interest in the artifacts of classical antiquity probably played a part. In the case of Leonardo, his writings provide evidence of his personal taste for the charm that chiaroscuro could lend to faces (something he probably observed from Netherlandish portraits seen in Florence and Milan), and his interest in finding poses and movements for female figures that were decorously graceful and flowing.[65] The latter can be seen as part of a concern, long-standing in Florentine art, to effect a reconciliation between the lively mobility of many Greco-Roman female figures, enhanced by their body-hugging drapery, and contemporary belief in the decorous control of women's bodies, usually draped in heavy fabrics.[66] While only full-length figure compositions enabled painters to address these problems fully (in works like Leonardo's *Madonna and Child with St. Anne* or Giorgione's Fondaco dei Tedeschi frescoes), some experimentation in portraiture could make for a new expressiveness, as faces emerge from shadow, turn, and respond to the spectator or to some other enigmatic and intriguing event. Leonardo's c. 1490 *Cecilia Gallerani* is a notable example, but many painters in Florence, Milan, Venice, and Rome, like Andrea del Sarto, Luini, Sebastiano del Piombo, or Raphael, explored these effects in their different ways. We can also see the movement and direction of gaze being calibrated according to the status of the figure or the subject matter. Cecilia Gallerani, in the Kraków portrait, is granted a lively responsiveness not felt appropriate for a high-status aristocratic consort such as the Isabella d'Este, Marchioness of Mantua, whom the artist would later portray. The painted Cecilia's liveliness may also connect with Leonardo's personal admiration for a lady who, in her cultivated conversation and literary interests, certainly counts as one of the new Renaissance women.

Partly, perhaps, in response to this and other engagingly mobile female images, writings on female beauty from around 1500 have more to say about the charms of women in motion. In his very popular love dialogue set at an idealized version of Caterina Cornaro's court at Asolo, *Gli Asolani* (1503), Pietro Bembo's enamored Gismondo evokes a courtly beloved, possessing not only the familiar standard features of beauty but a delightful mobility as she strolls over flowery meads or gracefully sings and dances.[67] In Castiglione's even more celebrated *Cortegiano* (c. 1513–24), a speaker, Giuliano de' Medici, outlines his feminine ideal: a court lady (*donna da palazzo*) who combines moderate beauty with elegant and well-tempered conduct; conversation that is neither ponderous nor licentious, but well suited to every occasion; and a graceful accomplishment in dancing and music making. The most notable quasi-philosophical treatise on feminine beauty, that by the Florentine Agnolo Firenzuola (c. 1540), set in the provincial milieu of Prato, delights in the varied facets of female loveliness that are decently on display, which are analyzed with much emphasis on Ciceronian notions of harmony and the golden mean and which often involve charming gestures and movements.[68]

This cross-fertilization of ideas from art and prose and poetic writing provides a context for the more enterprising ways of portraying women, found especially beginning in the 1510s and 1520s. Fine costume may continue to be a concern, but there is more striving for a generalized beauty, smoothing and regularizing forms and features and implying gentle mobility. The female sitters face towards the spectator, but not always in a consciously enticing way, and they may handle books, musical instruments, and other accessories (Bacchiacca, *Portrait of a Lady with Music Book*, Getty Museum, Los Angeles, 1530s). How far these paintings are meant to suggest serious female talent in studying, playing, or composing is debatable: Castiglione's court lady is temperate and modest, neither outshining her mistress nor challenging her courtiers with her talents or intellect. These portraits of "accomplished" rather than professional young women might be symptomatic, therefore, of the diffusion outwards of the ideal of the moderately cultivated *donna da palazzo* to professional and mercantile classes aspiring to commemorate broader virtues than just chastity or wealth among their female members. Certainly by midcentury some middle-class women were participating in the musical and literary lives of their cities, and praise for female beauty and accomplishments, whether well founded or merely gallant, was a common theme in urban culture. In one sense, then, these portraits of women with books or musical instruments register, and might even promote, a positive social change, the widening of cultural opportunities to those of moderate means and moderate beauty, a change that would be followed in urban societies elsewhere in Europe. In another, though, this unthreateningly accomplished feminine ideal, amounting to a taming and domestication of female cultural attainments, might have acted as a constraint in real life for the types of intellectual or creative women discussed earlier, who might be pressured to mask their professionalism in the interests of elegance or social acceptability.

In other respects, however, the widening of the range of portraiture offered attractive opportunities both for artists and for the self-fashioning of

FIGURE 8.9: Francesco Bacchiacca, *Portrait of a Lady with Music Book*, c. 1530s. Los Angeles, Getty Museum. Courtesy of the Getty Museum.

actual women. Among the female portraits from the 1480s and 1490s, some have figures that seem to move from an actual social setting into a fictional world, like the Botticelli *Simonetta*, with her pseudo-antique costume, or the bust-length nude by Piero di Cosimo, the *Cleopatra* in Chantilly. This type of portrait, which has been called the "fancy portrait" or "quasi-portrait," found success in many centers in Italy, especially after around 1500. The features seem more idealized than specific, and semi-contemporary, semi-historic costume and accessories identify the woman as a biblical, saintly, or mythological figure. Portraiture here becomes less about reinforcing a stable social identity through dress or physiognomic quirks, than producing a suggestive *invenzione*. To this the spectator, who might not know the identity of the sitter (if indeed there was a particular sitter as opposed to a hired model), would bring a range of associations, based on reading as well as experience. Christian lore, modern lyrical and pastoral poetry, and classical knowledge might all be involved. Palma Vecchio's *Blonde Woman*, for example (National Gallery, London, c. 1525), might represent either the Roman goddess Flora (as suggested by her semi-nudity and the flowers in her hand), a contemporary courtesan styling herself as Flora (as suggested by her contemporary *camicia*), or only the artist's imagined ideal. To the extent that such portraits become primarily demonstrations of the technical and imaginative skill of the artist in giving apparent flesh to his notion of beauty, rather than collaborative endeavors involving input from the sitter and her associates, they can well be said, in Elizabeth Cropper's words, to "belong to a distinct discourse from which the woman herself is necessarily absent."[69] Yet in other cases, where what is clearly a particular individual is given saintly or mythological attributes, the situation is rather different. Such paintings—Savoldo's c. 1530–40 *Portrait of a Lady with the Attributes of St Margaret* in the Capitoline in Rome would be a good example—might speak of the religious motivations of the sitter, or of her identification with the virtues and protection of a saintly namesake, in this case one providing protection in future childbirth. Where the sitter is shown as a nymph or an antique shepherdess (the work of Palma Vecchio provides several examples), we can see analogies with the disguised identities and the role-playing we find in poetic or other literary exchanges such as those in Laurentian Florence or, later, between Bronzino and Laura Battiferra, in which a portrait of her is mentioned.[70] More mundanely, we can see analogies between the "guised" portraits and the professional names and the stagecraft of actresses and courtesans in the years after 1500. Often the names they adopted were those of the Greco-Roman past, and it seems likely that some of the bizarre outfits with which they piqued the interest of their clients were similar to the fanciful pseudo-antique get-ups

FIGURE 8.10: Palma Vecchio, *Blonde Woman*, c. 1520. Courtesy of the National Gallery, London. Courtesy of the National Gallery.

we sometimes observe in the painted beauties of Venice, those of Paris Bordone in particular.[71] Such courtesans—another type of "new woman" flourishing in the years after 1500—might often wish to have their cultural achievements, or pretensions, memorialized in a range of ways, as they were in the encomia of the time.[72]

It is now time to return to the questions posed at the beginning of this chapter. If female portraiture does demonstrate the greater visibility of women, it was a visibility that came late, after around 1450, and was less due to changes in women's position than to general prosperity and the growth of a rich material culture delighting in display, a culture that could afford affluent women some opportunities for exercising their taste and discrimination. Only gradually did the Renaissance as an intellectual movement provide a small number of women with the opportunity to forge new identities for themselves, whether

FIGURE 8.11: Girolamo Savoldo, *Portrait of a Lady with the Attributes of St. Margaret*, c. 1530–40. Galleria Palatina, Capitoline Gallery, Rome. Courtesy of Art Resource.

based on learning or the emulation of the "famous women" of antiquity. Still fewer of these either encountered artists responsive to their talents, as Leonardo may have been for Cecilia Gallerani or Bronzino for Laura Battiferra, or were in a position to disseminate these identities in artistic images. Though some of Italy's women painters enjoyed successful international careers, they remained obscure in subsequent centuries, while it was the literary and pictorial allure of its Petrarchan beauties and courtly ladies that seduced other European countries and transformed their art.

NOTES

Introduction

1. While she trained with two respected artists, Bernardino Campi and Bernardino Gatti, Anguissola could not participate in the usual apprenticeship (not only because she was a woman but also because she was nobly born); while she learned to prepare her own paints and canvases, she could not enter a studio to study the nude form. See Ilya Sandra Perlingieri, *Sophonisba Anguissola: The First Great Woman Artist of the Renaissance* (New York: Rizzoli International Publications, 1992), pp. 35–75.
2. In her *Portrait of Amilcare, Minerva, and Asdrubale Anguissola* (c. 1557–58), by way of contrast, Anguissola depicts her father, Amilcare, and brother touching hand on hand, the boy looking up at his father while the patriarch gazes out of the frame at the viewer; Minerva stands to Amilcare's right, outside this physical and visual contact, looking on; only her dress touches her father's knee. This painting captures a more traditional version of family portraiture, in which patrilineal connections are singled out as more important than other forms of family relationships.
3. Perlingieri calls the moment of the image "vivid psychological drama" with tension between the playfulness of the children and the servant's anxiety (*Sophonisba Anguissola*, p. 88). This kind of portraiture precedes its corollary in the Dutch and Flemish works of the seventeenth century, and may well be considered one influence on those later artists who, like Van Dyck, clearly knew of and admired Anguissola.
4. Jacob Burckhardt, *The Civilisation of the Renaissance in Italy*, trans. S.G.C. Middlemore (New York: MacMillan and Co., 1904), p. 395.
5. Burckhardt, *Civilisation*, p. 399.
6. Juliet Dusinberre, *Shakespeare and the Nature of Women* (London: MacMillan, 1975) was reprinted in 1979, and second and third editions were issued in 1996 and 2003; Natalie Zemon Davis, *Society and Culture in Early Modern France* (Stanford, CA: Stanford University Press, 1975).

7. Joan Kelly, "Did Women Have a Renaissance?" in *Women, History and Theory: The Essays of Joan Kelly* (Chicago: University of Chicago Press, 1984), p. 47.
8. Linda Bamber, *Comic Women, Tragic Men: A Study of Gender and Genre in Shakespeare* (Stanford: Stanford Univiversity Press, 1982), pp. 1–2.
9. Christiane Klapisch-Zuber, *Women, Family and Ritual in Renaissance Italy* (Chicago: University of Chicago Press, 1985), p. 20.
10. Retha M. Warnicke, *Women of the English Renaissance and Reformation* (Westport, CT: Greenwood Press, 1983).
11. In *Chaste, Silent and Obedient, English Books for Women 1475–1640* (San Marino: Huntington Library Press, 1988), Suzanne Hull surveys the literature of conduct to find that the same ideological prescription informs most of the texts intended for women's reading.
12. Interestingly, some of those cases were celebrated examples of saints who could not be dissuaded from a divine vocation; famously, for instance, Saint Clare absconded from the marriage arranged for her to enter a life of poverty and worship alongside St. Francis of Assissi. For an account of two other saints who resisted marriage, see Carole Levin, "St. Frideswide and St. Uncumber: Changing Images of Female Saints in England," in *Women, Writing, and the Reproduction of Culture in Tudor and Stuart England*, ed. Mary Elizabeth Burke, Jane Donawerth, Linda L. Love, and Karen Nelson (Syracuse, NY: University of Syracuse Press, 2000), pp. 223–37.
13. *The Itinerary of Fynes Moryson*, vol. IV (Glasgow: Hames MacLehose and Sons, 1908), p. 169.
14. *Shakespeare's Europe: A Survey of the Conditions of Europe at the End of the Sixteenth Century Being unpublished chapters of Fynes Moryson's Itinerary (1617)*, intro. and ed. Charles Hughes (New York: Benjamin Bloom, 1903 and 1967), p. 168.
15. Depending on where one lived, syphilis was variously called French, Italian, or Spanish.
16. See Monica Chojnacka, "Women, Charity and Community in Early Modern Venice: The Casa delle Zitelle," *Renaissance Quarterly* 51, no. 1 (Spring 1998): 68–92.
17. Thomas Overbury, *His Wife, with additions of New Characters* (London: Laurence Lisle, 1622), H6.
18. T. E., *The Lawes Resolution of Womens Rights* (London, 1632), p. 6.
19. John Knox, *The first blast of the trumpet against the monstrous regiment of women* (1558), p. 9.
20. Baldassare Castiglione, *The Book of the Courtier*, trans. Sir Thomas Hoby (London: J. M. Dent, 1994), p. 212.
21. These aspects of *The Courtier*'s marginalization of women's power are main themes of Kelly's "Did Women Have a Renaissance?"
22. Robert Filmer's *Patriarcha, or the Natural Power of Kings* (London, 1680), p. 12, was written either shortly before or possibly during war, although not published until long after Filmer's death.
23. *The Political Works of James I*, ed. Charles McIlwain (Cambridge: Harvard University Press, 1918), p. 307.

24. William Gouge, *Of Domesticall Duties: Eight Treatises*, 3rd ed. (London, 1634), p. 17.
25. *A true copy of the peititon of the gentlewomen and tradesmen's wives…*(London, 1642), p. 1.
26. Qtd. in Susan D. Amussen, *An Ordered Society: Gender and Class in Early Modern England* (New York: Columbia University Press, 1988), p. 62.
27. Amussen, *Ordered Society*, pp. 62–63.
28. Duplessis-Mornay (1549–1623) and fellow Huguenot Hubert Languet are attributed with authorship of the *Vindiciae Contra Tyrannos* (*Defense Against Tyrants*, 1660), a response to the violent repression of Protestants in late sixteenth-century France.
29. Jacqueline Broad and Karen Green, *A History of Women's Political Thought in Europe, 1400–1700* (Cambridge: Cambridge University Press, 2009), p. 55.
30. *Elizabeth I: The Collected Works*, ed. Leah Marcus, Janel Mueller, and Mary Beth Rose (Chicago: University of Chicago Press, 2002), p. 59.
31. *Elizabeth I*, p. 326.
32. Warnicke, *Women of the English Renaissance*, p. 86.
33. Martin Marty notes, "As much as he [Luther] honored wives, he still did little to coutner the inherited understanding that the woman was subordinate to the man" (*Martin Luther* [New York: The Penguin Group, 2004], p. 108); yet in his will, in a significant break with tradition, Luther appointed only Katharina to oversee his estate (p. 110).
34. Lucy Hutchinson, *Memoir of the Life of Colonel Hutchinson*, ed. N. H. Keeble (London: J. M. Dent, 1995), p. 51.
35. Warnicke, *Women of the English Renaissance*, p. 22.
36. Kirsi Stjerna, *Women and the Reformation* (Malden, MA: Blackwell Publishing, 2009), p. 45.
37. Heide Wunder, *He Is the Sun, She Is the Moon: Women in Early Modern Germany*, trans. Thomas Dunlap (Cambridge, MA: Harvard University Press, 1998), p. 44.
38. Qtd. in Stjerna, *Women and the Reformation*, p. 78.
39. Stjerna, *Women and the Reformation*, p. 79.
40. See, for instance, Wendy Wall, *Staging Domesticity: Household Work and English Identity in Early Modern Drama* (Cambridge: Cambridge University Press, 2002), 19–25.
41. Thomas Middleton and Thomas Dekker, *The Roaring Girl*, ed. Paul Mulholland (Manchester: Manchester University Press, 1987, and New York: Palgrave, 1999), Act II, sc. I: 4.
42. In *The Working Life of Women in the Seventeenth Century* (first published in 1919 by George Routledge & Sons, reissued in 1985, and in 1992 with an introduction by Amy Erickson), Alice Clark offered extensive documentation and argument to demonstrate that capitalism had a deleterious effect on women's economic lives; however, the debate over whether economic change had a positive or negative impact on women has continued unabated since then.
43. Excerpted in *The Earthly Republic: Italian Humanists on Government and Society*, ed. and trans. Benjamin G. Kohl and Ronald G. Witt (Philadelphia: University of Pennsylvania Press, 1978), p. 216.
44. Joseph Swetnam, *The Arraignment of Lewd, Idle, Froward and Unconstant Women* (London, 1615), pp. 7–8, 15.

45. Merry Wiesner, *Working Women in Renaissance Germany*, (New Brunswick, NJ: Rutgers University Press, 1986), p. 3.
46. Heinrich Kramer and James Sprenger, *Malleus Maleficarum*, trans. Montague Summers (London: Anchor Books, 1971), p. 6.
47. Isabella Whitney, *A Sweet Nosgay, or Pleasant Posy* (London: R. Jones, 1573), d2.
48. "To her Sister, Mistress A. B.," in *A Sweet Nosgay*, d2r.
49. Wunder, *He is the Sun, She is the Moon*, p. 31.
50. Phillippa Berry, *Of Chastity and Power: Elizabethan Literature and the Unmarried Queen* (New York: Routledge, 1989).
51. Gail Kern Paster, *The Body Embarrassed: Drama and the Disciplines of Shame in Early Modern England* (Ithaca: Cornell University Press, 1993), pp. 23–63.
52. Michelle M. Dowd, *Women's Work in Early Modern English Literature and Culture* (New York: Palgrave, 2009).
53. Dowd notes that the eighteenth-century marriage fable became more essential precisely because real opportunities for marriage disappeared for female servants—particularly marriages that trended up the social scale (*Women's Work*, p. 54).

Chapter 1

1. William Shakespeare, *The Complete Works*, 5th ed., ed. David Bevington (New York: Pearson, 2004), 2.7.138–65. References to this text are by act, scene, and line numbers.
2. Elizabeth Sears, *The Ages of Man: Medieval Interpretations of the Life Cycle* (Princeton: Princeton University Press, 1986), pp. 78–79, 109, 132, 135–40.
3. P.J.P. Goldberg, "Life and Death: The Ages of Man," in *A Social History of England, 1200–1500*, ed. Rosemary Horrox and Mark W. Ormrod (Cambridge: Cambridge University Press, 2006), pp. 413–14; Philippa Maddern and Stephanie Tarbin, "Life Cycle," in *A Cultural History of Childhood and Family in the Early Modern Age*, ed. Sandra Cavallo and Sylvia Evangelisti (Oxford and New York: Berg, 2010), p. 116.
4. Sears, *Ages of Man*, p. 153, plate 98.
5. Shakespeare, *Complete Works*, 5.1.184.
6. John Amos Comenius, *Orbis Sensualium Pictus* (London: Printed for J. Kirton, 1659), 76–77.
7. Kim M. Phillips, "Maidenhood as the Perfect Age of Woman's Life," in *Young Medieval Women*, ed. Katherine J. Lewis, Noel James Menuge, and Kim M. Phillips (New York: St. Martin's Press, 1999), pp. 1–24.
8. Thomas Tusser, *Fiue Hundreth Pointes of Good Husbandrie* (London, 1585), p. 142.
9. Ralph A. Houlbrooke, *The English Family, 1400–1700* (New York: Longman, 1984), pp. 132, 150.
10. Maddern and Tarbin, "Life Cycle," p. 123.
11. Muriel St. Clare Byrne, ed., *The Lisle Letters: An Abridgement* (Chicago: University of Chicago Press, 1981, 1983), p. 248; D.J.H. Clifford, ed., *The Diaries of Lady Anne Clifford* (Phoenix Mill: Alan Sutton Publishing, 1990), p. 55.

12. Lynnea Brumbaugh-Walter, "Selections from the Gesta Romanorum," in *Medieval Literature for Children*, ed. Daniel T. Kline (New York and London: Routledge, 2003), p. 33.
13. Kate Aughterson, ed., *Renaissance Woman: A Sourcebook* (New York: Routledge, 1995), p. 28.
14. Ann Jones and Peter Stallybrass, *Renaissance Clothing and the Materials of Memory* (Cambridge: Cambridge University Press, 2000), p. 235. T. E. also remarks, "If a woman taketh more Appareell when her husband dyteth then is necessarily for her degree, it makes her Executrix de son tort demesne."
15. Samuel Rowlands, *'Tis Merry When Gossips Meet* (London, 1609), p. 15.
16. Thomas Becon, *The Principles of Christian Religion* (London, 1552), sig. J6.
17. Recounted in Aki C. L. Beam, "'Should I as Yet Call You Old?' Testing the Boundaries of Female Old Age in Early Modern England," in *Growing Old in Early Modern Europe: Cultural Representations*, ed. Erin Campbell (Aldershot and Burlington, VT: Ashgate, 2006), pp. 95–116, p. 97.
18. For more on Shrewsbury's pearls, see Karen Raber, "Chains of Pearls: Gender, Property, Identity," in *Ornamentalism: The Art of Renaissance Accessories*, ed. Bella Mirabella (Ann Arbor: University of Michigan Press, 2011), pp. 159–81.
19. Eucharius Roeslin, *The Byrth of Mankynde, newly translated out of Laten into Englisshe*, by Thomas Raynalde (London, 1540), fols liii–lvi.
20. Comenius, *Orbis Sensualium Pictus*, p. 76.
21. John Pound, ed., *The Norwich Census of the Poor, 1570* (Norfolk: Norfolk Record Society, XL, 1971), p. 25. K. J. Allison, "An Elizabethan Village Census," *Bulletin of the Institute of Historical Research* 36, no. 93 (1963): 91–103; see also John Webb, ed., *Poor Relief in Elizabethan Ipswich* (Ipswich: Suffolk Record Society, 9, 1966), which does not record sex.
22. Borthwick Institute of Historical Research [BIHR], CP.G.1521. Jane Vmfrey con. Thomas Peeres and Peeres con. Vmfrey. Even when the child's mother, Jane Vmfrey, recounted how she was moved with "motherly pittye" and begged her own mother to let the nurse enter the house "that she might se yt," the scribe recorded her words using neutral pronouns and terms ("her said child").
23. Mary Abbott, *Life Cycles in England 1560–1720: Cradle to Grave* (London and New York: Routledge, 1996), p. 52.
24. P.J.P. Goldberg, "Childhood and Gender in Later Medieval England," *Viator* 39, no. 1 (2008): 251–53.
25. Jaques Guillemeau, *Child-birth, or The happy deliuerie of woman* (London, 1612), pp. 8–11; Bartholomaeus Anglicus, *De Proprietatibus Rerum*, printed by Thomas Bertholet (London, 1535), fols 71v–72.
26. Aughterson, *Renaissance Woman*, pp. 120–21.
27. Patricia Crawford and Laura Gowing, eds., *Women's Worlds in Seventeenth-Century England: A Sourcebook* (London and New York: Routledge, 2000), p. 193.
28. Muriel St. Clare Byrne, ed., *The Lisle Letters: An Abridgement* (Chicago: University of Chicago Press, 1981, 1983), p. 203.
29. Sara Mendelson and Patricia Crawford, *Women in Early Modern England 1550–1720* (New York and Oxford: Oxford University Press, 1998), pp. 81–82.

30. E. A. Wrigley et al., *Population History of England, 1541–1871* (Cambridge: Cambridge University Press, 1989), p. 298.
31. Anne Laurence, *Women in England: A Social History, 1500–1760* (London, Weidenfeld and Nicholson, 1994), p. 30; Maddern and Tarbin, "Life Cycle," p. 118.
32. John M. Riddle, *Contraception and Abortion from the Ancient World to the Renaissance* (Harvard: Harvard University Press, 1992), pp. 11–13.
33. Goldberg, "Childhood and Gender in Later Medieval England," p. 257.
34. David Herlihy and Christiane Klapisch-Zuber, *Tuscans and Their Families: A Study of the Florentine Catasto of 1427* (New Haven and London: Yale University Press, 1985), pp. 133–37.
35. Philip Gavitt, *Charity and Children in Renaissance Florence: The Ospedale degli Innocenti, 1410–1536* (Ann Arbor: University of Michigan Press, 1990), pp. 210–11.
36. Gavitt, *Charity and Children*, pp. 212–14.
37. Ronald C. Finucane, *The Rescue of the Innocents: Endangered Children in Medieval Miracles* (Houndmills, Basingstoke: Macmillan, 1997), pp. 52, 98, 160–61. Others have interpreted the predominance of male children in the miracles as a result of the greater adventurousness of boys. See Eleanor C. Gordon, "Accidents Among Medieval Children as Seen from the Miracles of Six English Saints and Martyrs," *Medical History* 35 (1991): 149.
38. Louis Haas, *The Renaisance Man and His Children: Childbirth and Early Childhood in Florence, 1300–1600* (New York: St. Martin's Press, 1998), pp. 1–15. Haas responds to the argument of Philippe Ariès in *Centuries of Childhood: A Social History of Family Life*, trans. Robert Baldick (New York: Alfred A. Knopf, 1962), but also the many social historians swayed by his perspective; see also Linda Pollock, *Forgotten Children: Parent-Child Relations from 1500 to 1900* (Cambridge: Cambridge University Press, 1983).
39. Haas, *The Renaissance Man*, p. 1.
40. On the significance of "Odyllia," see Susanne Woods's introduction to *The Poems of Amelia Lanyer*, ed. Susanne Woods (New York, Oxford: Oxford University Press, 1993), p. xxv; she speculates that the name combines the word "ode" with "Amelia"; Clifford, *Diaries*, p. 105.
41. Nicholas Orme, *Medieval Children* (New Haven and London: Yale University Press, 2001), pp. 27–29.
42. Parents appointed another sponsor of the child's sex to attend the ceremony of confirmation before the bishop. R. Dyboski, ed., *Songs, Carols and other Miscellaneous Pieces from the Balliol MS. 354, Richard Hill's Commonplace Book*, Early English Text Society Extra Series 101 (London: Kegan Paul, Trench, Trubner and Co., 1907), pp. xiii–xiv; John Gough Nichols, ed., *The Diary of Henry Machyn, Citizen and Merchant-Taylor of London, from a.d. 1550 to a.d. 1563*, Camden Society, 42 (London: Camden Society, 1848), p. 153.
43. Mendelson and Crawford, *Women in Early Modern England*, p. 80.
44. Orme, *Medieval Children*, pp. 202–3.
45. Laurent Joubert, *Popular Errors*, ed. Gregory David de Rocher (Tuscaloosa: University of Alabama Press, 1989), p. 241.

46. Joubert, *Popular Errors*, pp. 242–44.
47. Juan Luis Vives, *Education of a Christian Woman: A Sixteenth Century Manual*, ed. Charles Fantazzi (Chicago: University of Chicago Press, 2000), p. 54.
48. William Caxton, *The Book of the Knight of the Tower*, ed. M. Y. Offord, Early English Text Society Supplementary Series 2 (London: Oxford University Press, 1971), p. 162; Vives, *Education of a Christian Woman*, p. 87; Aughterson, *Renaissance Woman*, p. 28.
49. Barbara Winchester, *Tudor Family Portrait* (London: J. Cape, 1955), p. 203.
50. Orme, *Medieval Children*, pp. 334–36.
51. Merry Wiesner, *Women and Gender in Early Modern Europe*, 2nd ed. (Cambridge: Cambridge University Press, 2000), p. 57; Barbara Hanawalt, *The Ties That Bound: Peasant Families in Medieval England* (New York: Oxford University Press, 1986), pp. 158–61, 272–73.
52. Anon., *A Glasse for Housholders, Wherin That They May Se, Both Howe to Rule Them Selfes & Ordre Their Housholde Verye Godly and Fruytfull* (London: Workshop of Richard Grafton, 1542), sig. F1v.
53. Cheshire and Chester Archives and Local Studies Services, Consistory Court Deposition Books, EDC 2/4/50–53. *Katherine Dutton v. Robert Busshell.*
54. Laurence, *Women in England*, p. 62.
55. Mendelson and Crawford, *Women in Early Modern England*, p. 77.
56. Shakespeare, *Complete Works*, I.2.13.
57. Laurence, *Women in England*, p. 32; the mean age at first marriage in England was twenty-six years; only 15 percent of married women were under twenty-four in the seventeenth century.
58. The National Archives, Chancery Petitions, C 1/1326/18–24. *William ANDERSON, gentleman, v. John MORLEY, esquire.*
59. "The Lady Falkland, Her Life," in Elizabeth Cary, *The Tragedy of Mariam, The Fair Queen of Jewry*, ed. Barry Weller and Margaret Ferguson (Berkeley: University of California Press, 1994), p. 188; it is not clear whether the marriage was consummated or not until Henry Cary returned from his travels, but the two did not have children for the first seven years of their marriage (p. 191).
60. Mendelson and Crawford, *Women in Early Modern England*, p. 124.
61. Aughterson, *Renaissance Woman*, p. 149.
62. Nicholas Culpeper, *A Directory for Midwives* (London, 1651), p. 50.
63. Qtd. in Patricia Crawford, "The Construction and Experience of Maternity in Seventeenth-Century England," in *Women as Mothers in Pre-Industrial England*, ed. Valerie Fildes (London and New York: Routledge, 1990), pp. 3–38, p. 6.
64. See, for instance, Mendelson and Crawford, *Women in Early Modern England*, pp. 149–50; they recount the example of Samuel Pepys, who was given a number of remedies for his wife's barrenness by a group of women, which suggests that infertility was not a taboo subject between the sexes (p. 150).
65. Jane Sharp, *The Midwives Book* (London, 1671), p. 93.
66. Laurence, *Women in England*, pp. 62–63; Robert Jutte, *Contraception: A History* (Cambridge: Polity Press, 2008), pp. 57–58.
67. Nicholas Culpeper, *A Directory for Midwives* (1651), p. 146.

68. Laurence, *Women in England*, p. 55–56.
69. Amy Froide, "Old Maids: The Lifecycle of Single Women in Early Modern England," in *Women and Ageing in British Society Since 1500*, ed. Lynn Botelho and Pat Thane (New York: Pearson, 2001), pp. 89–100, p. 90.
70. Froide, "Old Maids," p. 94; as Froide points out, civic authorities frequently simply ordered single women to live with someone else to ensure they were under the authority of a "normal," that is, patriarchal, family unit.
71. Beam, "'Should I as Yet Call You Old?'" p. 113.
72. Beam, "'Should I as Yet Call You Old?'" p. 112.
73. Erin J. Campbell, "'Unenduring' Beauty: Gender and Old Age in Early Modern Art and Aesthetics," in *Growing Old*, pp. 153–67.
74. Louise Gray, "The Experience of Old Age in the Narratives of the Rural Poor in Early Modern Germany," in *Power and Poverty: Old Age in the Pre-Industrial Past*, ed. Susannah R. Ottaway, L. A. Botelho, and Katharine Kittredge (Westport, CT: Greenwood Press, 2002), pp. 111–13.
75. Clifford, *Diaries*, pp. 231–68.
76. See, for instance, Lynne Botelho, "Images of Old Age in Early Modern Cheap Print: Women, Witches, and the Poisonous Female Body," in *Power and Poverty*, pp. 225–46.
77. Shakespeare, *Complete Works*, 4.4.116–17; 1.3.215.
78. Shakespeare, *Complete Works*, 1.1.4–6.
79. Mendelson and Crawford, *Women in Early Modern England*, p. 180. The association of old women and crime is mainly found in pamphlets on the underworld, and in their portrayal as bawds in plays.
80. Julia M. Walker, "Bones of Contention: Posthumous Images of Elizabeth and Stuart Politics," in *Dissing Elizabeth: Negative Representations of Gloriana*, ed. Julia M. Walker (Durham and London: Duke University Press, 1998), pp. 253–76, p. 267.
81. Mendelson and Crawford, *Women in Early Modern England*, p. 176.
82. Clifford, *Diaries*, pp. 105–6.

Chapter 2

1. Aristotle qtd. in Alcuin Blamires, ed., *Woman Defamed and Woman Defended: An Anthology of Medieval Texts* (Oxford: Clarendon Press, 1992), p. 40.
2. L. Lemnius, *The Touchstone of Complexions* (London, 1633), p. 69; Alexander Ross, *Arcana Microcosmi or The Hidden Secrets of Man's Body Disclosed* (London, 1651), p. 86; "A Homily on the State of Matrimony," in *Sexuality and Gender in the English Renaissance: An Annotated Edition of Contemporary Documents*, ed. Lloyd Davis (New York: Garland Publishing, Inc., 1998), p. 26; Helkiah Crooke, *Microcosmographia: A Description of the Body of Man* (London, 1615), p. 276.
3. Katherine Eisaman Maus, "A Womb of His Own: Male Renaissance Poets in the Female Body," in *Sexuality and Gender in Early Modern Europe: Institutions, Texts, Images*, ed. James Grantham Turner (Cambridge: Cambridge University Press, 1993), p. 268.

NOTES 217

4. William Shakespeare, *Othello*, in *The Riverside Shakespeare*, ed. G. Blakemore Evans (Boston: Houghton Mifflin Co., 1974), 3.4.38–39 (all subsequent references to Shakespeare's plays are from this edition and are cited parenthetically).
5. I gesture here toward the critical debates that followed the publication of Thomas Laqueur's *Making Sex: Body and Gender from the Greeks to Freud* (Cambridge: Harvard University Press, 1990). For the most notable responses, see Katherine Park and Robert Nye's book review "Destiny Is Anatomy," *The New Republic* 204, no. 7 (18 Feb. 1991): 53–57; Janet Adelman, "Making Defect Perfection: Shakespeare and the One-Sex Model," in *Enacting Gender on the English Renaissance Stage*, ed. Viviana Comensoli and Anne Russell (Urbana: University of Illinois Press, 1999), pp. 23–52; and Winfried Schleiner, "Early Modern Controversies about the One-Sex Model," *Renaissance Quarterly* 53, no. 1 (2000): 180–91.
6. Mary Douglas, *Purity and Danger: An Analysis of Concepts of Pollution and Taboo* (New York: Praeger, 1966), p. 15; Albert Tricomi, *Reading Tudor-Stuart Texts through Cultural Historicism* (Gainesville: University Press of Florida, 1996), p. 96; Mary E. Fissell, *Vernacular Bodies: The Politics of Reproduction in Early Modern England* (Oxford: Oxford University Press, 2004), p. 72.
7. See Jonathan Sawday, *The Body Emblazoned: Dissection and the Human Body in Renaissance Culture* (London: Routledge, 1995); and Katherine Park, *Secrets of Women: Gender, Generation, and the Origins of Human Dissection* (New York: Zone Books, 2006) for the history of early modern anatomy theaters and the growing vogue for anatomy texts.
8. Banister qtd. in Patricia Parker, "*Othello* and *Hamlet:* Dilation, Spying, and the 'Secret Place' of Women," *Representations* 44 (1993): 66.
9. Francis Beaumont and John Fletcher, *The Maid's Tragedy*, ed. T. W. Craik (Manchester: Manchester University Press, 1999), 4.1.108–9; John Taylor, "A common whore with all these graces grac'd" (London, 1625), sig. B8v; Philip Massinger, *The Renegado*, *The Dramatic Works of Massinger and Ford* (London: Edward Moxon, 1848), 3.1.14–16. For more on how the metaphor of text-as-body is constructed and utilized by printers and poets in the early modern era, see Wendy Wall, *The Imprint of Gender: Authorship and Publication in the English Renaissance* (Ithaca: Cornell University Press, 1993).
10. Eve Rachele Sanders, *Gender and Literacy on Stage in Early Modern England* (Cambridge: Cambridge University Press, 1998), p. 138.
11. T. E., *The Lawes Resolution of Womens Rights* (London, 1632), p. 6.
12. Crooke, *Microcosmographia*, p. 276.
13. For a fuller discussion of the contradictions found within and among the specific texts, see Marie Loughlin, *Hymeneutics: Interpreting Virginity on the Early Modern Stage* (Lewisburg: Bucknell University Press, 1997); and my "Frances Howard and Thomas Middleton and William Rowley's *The Changeling:* Trials, Tests, and the Legibility of the Virgin Body," in *The Single Woman in Medieval and Early Modern England: Her Life and Representation*, ed. Laurel Amtower and Dorothea Kehler (Tempe: Arizona Center for Medieval and Renaissance Studies, 2003), pp. 211–32.

14. Nicholas Culpeper, *A directory for midwives: or a guide for women in their conception*, 2nd ed. (London, 1656), p. 23.
15. Juan Luis Vives, *A very frutefull and pleasant boke Called the Instruction of a Christen Woman* (1523), trans. Richard Hyrde (London, 1529?), sig. Mv; Barnabe Rich, *The Excellency of good women* (London, 1613), sigs. D3-D3v; Barnabe Rich, *My Ladies Looking Glasse* (London, 1616), sig. Fv; Baldessar Castiglione, *The Book of the Courtier*, trans. Charles Singleton (New York: Anchor Books, 1959), p. 207.
16. Richard Brathwaite, *The English Gentlewoman, drawne out to the full body* (London, 1631), sig. GG2; Thomas Salter, *A Mirrhor mete for all Mothers, Matrones, and Maidens* (London, 1579), pp. 32–33; Thomas Tuke, *A Discourse Against Painting and Tincturing of Women* (London, 1616), sig. K2; Alexander Oldys, *The London Jilt: Or, The Politic Whore* (London, 1683), pp. 84–86; Philip Stubbes, *The Anatomie of Abuses* (London, 1595), sig. F4. See Frances Dolan, "Taking the Pencil Out of God's Hand: Art, Nature, and the Face-Painting Debate in Early Modern England," *PMLA* 108 (1993): 224–39, for more on the moral implications of female face-painting.
17. Ferrante Pallavicino, *The Whores Rhetorick* (London, 1683), p. 121; Tassie Gwilliam, "Female Fraud: Counterfeit Maidenheads in the Eighteenth Century," *Journal of the History of Sexuality* 6, no. 4 (1996): 520.
18. John Webster, *The White Devil*, ed. Christina Luckyj (London: A & C Black, 1998), 3.2.182 (all subsequent references are from this edition and are cited parenthetically).
19. Lara Bovilsky, "Black Beauties, White Devils: The English Italian in Milton and Webster," *ELH* 70, no. 3 (2003): 643.
20. Phyllis Rackin, "Foreign Country: The Place of Women and Sexuality in Shakespeare's Historical World," in *Enclosure Acts: Sexuality, Property, and Culture in Early Modern England*, ed. Richard Burt and John Michael Archer (Ithaca: Cornell University Press, 1994), p. 74. Rackin does note that prior to 1510 women's clothing was regulated. Peter Stallybrass writes that the absence of specific legislation regarding female dress "should be seen as a sign less of women's liberties than of the implicit assumption that women's bodies were already the object of policing by fathers and husbands" ("Patriarchal Territories: The Body Enclosed," in *Rewriting the Renaissance: The Discourses of Sexual Difference in Early Modern England*, ed. Margaret W. Ferguson, Maureen Quilligan, and Nancy J. Vickers [Chicago: University of Chicago Press, 1986], p. 126).
21. "A Homily Against Excesse of Apparel," in *Sexuality and Gender in the English Renaissance*, p. 20.
22. Rich, *My Ladies Looking Glasse*, sig. E3v; Wycherley qtd. in Will Pritchard, "Masks and Faces: Female Legibility in the Restoration Era," *Eighteenth-Century Life* 24, no. 3 (2000): 38. See David Cressy, "Gender Trouble and Cross-Dressing in Early Modern England," *Journal of British Studies* 35, no. 4 (1996): 438–65, for an examination of the historical record vis-à-vis the literary one.
23. John Dunton, *The Night-Walker: Or, Evening Rambles in search after Lewd Women* (London, 1696), p. 10.

24. Aphra Behn, *The Rover*, *The Rover and Other Plays*, ed. Jane Spencer (Oxford: Oxford University Press, 1995), 3.6.21 (all subsequent references are from this edition and are cited parenthetically).
25. Robert Herrick, "Delight in Disorder," *Works of Robert Herrick*, vol. I, ed. Alfred Pollard (London: Lawrence & Bullen, 1891), p. 32.
26. Stubbes, *The Anatomie of Abuses*, sig. G3; Stephen Gosson, *Plays Confuted in Five Actions* (London, 1582), sig. E5.
27. Thomas Middleton and Thomas Dekker, *The Roaring Girl*, ed. Elizabeth Cook (London: A & C Black, 1997), 1.1.98–99 (all subsequent references are from this edition and are cited parenthetically).
28. Stubbes, *The Anatomie of Abuses*, sig. G3; Ambroise Pare, *The Works of that Famous Chirugeon Ambrose Parey*, trans. Thomas Johnson (London, 1634), p. 975.
29. Laura Levine, *Men in Women's Clothing: Anti-theatricality and effeminization 1579–1642* (Cambridge: Cambridge University Press, 1994), p. 7; Ann Rosalind Jones and Peter Stallybrass, "Fetishizing Gender: Constructing the Hermaphrodite in Renaissance Europe," in *Body Guards: The Cultural Politics of Gender Ambiguity*, ed. Julia Epstein and Kristina Staub (New York: Routledge, 1991), p. 104.
30. Jenny C. Mann, "How to Look at a Hermaphrodite in Early Modern England," *SEL: Studies in English Literature 1500–1900* 46, no. 1 (2006): 68.
31. Edmund Spenser, *The Faerie Queene*, ed. Thomas P. Roche Jr. (New York: Penguin Books, 1978), 1.2.40 (all subsequent references are from this edition and are cited parenthetically).
32. Melinda Gough, "'Her filthy feature open showne' in Ariosto, Spenser, and *Much Ado about Nothing*," *SEL: Studies in English Literature 1500–1900* 39, no. 1 (1999): 50–51.
33. Anthony Munday, *A second and third blast of retrait from plaies and Theaters* (London, 1586), sig. D4v.
34. Sheila T. Cavanagh, *Wanton Eyes & Chaste Desires: Female Sexuality in The Faerie Queene* (Bloomington: Indiana University Press, 1994), p. 29.
35. Susanne Scholz, *Body Narratives: Writing the Nation and Fashioning the Subject in Early Modern England* (London: MacMillan Press, Ltd., 2000), p. 70; Colin Milbin, "Syphilis in Faerie Land: Edmund Spenser and the Syphilography of Elizabethan England," *Criticism* 46, no. 4 (2004): 610.
36. Nicholas de Blegny, *New and Curious Observations concerning the art of Curing the Venereal Disease*, trans. Walter Harris (London, 1676), p. 3; Kevin P. Siena, "Pollution, Promiscuity, and the Pox: English Venereology and the Early Modern Medical Discourse on Social and Sexual Danger," *Journal of the History of Sexuality* 8, no. 4 (1998): 563; Ulrich von Hutten, *Of the Wood Called Guaiacum, that Healeth the Frenche Pockes*, trans. Thomas Paynel (London, 1540), sigs. 4–4v; Winfried Schleiner, "Infection and Cure through Women: Renaissance Constructions of Syphilis," *Journal of Medieval and Renaissance Studies* 24 (1994): 499–517.
37. James Ferrand, *Erotomania or A Treatise discoursing of the essence, causes, symptoms, prognosticksm and cure of love*…(Oxford, 1640), sig. O3.

Chapter 3

1. Stuart Clark, *Thinking with Demons: The Idea of Witchcraft in Early Modern Europe* (Oxford: Oxford University Press, 1997), p. 31.
2. On early modern acceptance of the one-sex model of male and female and some of its implications, see Thomas Laqueur, *Making Sex: Body and Gender from the Greeks to Freud* (Cambridge and London: Harvard University Press, 1990).
3. Ian Maclean, *The Renaissance Notion of Woman: A Study in the Fortunes of Scholasticism and Medical Science in European Intellectual Life* (Cambridge: Cambridge University Press, 1980), pp. 3, 8.
4. Carolyn Walker Bynum, *Fragmentation and Redemption: Essays on Gender and the Human Body in Medieval Religion* (New York: Zone Books, 1991), pp. 98–100.
5. Peter Burke, *Popular Culture in Early Modern Europe* (New York: Harper and Row, 1978); Natalie Zemon Davis, *Society and Culture in Early Modern France* (Stanford: Stanford University Press, 1965); Robert Darnton, *The Great Cat Massacre and Other Episodes in French Cultural History* (New York: Random House, 1985).
6. Davis, *Society and Culture*, pp. 128–30.
7. Davis, *Society and Culture*, p. 105; Peter Burke defines "ritual" as "the use of action to express meaning, as opposed to more utilitarian actions and also to the expression of meaning through words or images" (Burke, *Popular Culture*, p. 180).
8. Davis, *Society and Culture*, pp. 98–100.
9. Burke, *Popular Culture*, p. 187.
10. Burke, *Popular Culture*, pp. 182–87, 190.
11. Laqueur, *Making Sex*, pp. 24–40.
12. Anthony Fletcher, *Gender, Sex and Subordination in England, 1500–1800* (New Haven: Yale University Press, 1995), p. xvii.
13. Clark, *Thinking with Demons*, pp. 113, 552.
14. Thomas Aquinas, *Summa Theologica*, 1, qu. 92, art. 1, ad. 1, quoted in Maclean, *The Renaissance Notion of Woman*, pp. 8–9.
15. Joseph Swetnam as Thomas Tel-troth, *The Arraignment of Lewde, Idle, Forward, and Unconstant Women* (London, 1615), pp. 33, 50.
16. Tertullian, *On the Apparel of Women*, trans. Rev. S. Thelwall, http://www.ccel.org/ccel/schaff/anf04.iii.iii.i.i.html (accessed December 2, 2010). Tertullian is considered one of the "fathers" of Latin Christianity (if not one of the four Fathers of the Latin Church).
17. Ruth Kelso, *Doctrine for the Lady of the Renaissance* (Urbana: University of Illinois Press, 1956). See also Suzanne W. Hull, *Chaste, Silent, and Obedient: English Books for Women, 1475–1640* (San Marino, CA: Huntingdon Library Press, 1982).
18. Maclean, *The Renaissance Notion of Woman*, pp. 15–19; John Flood, "A source for the depiction of Eve in the early-modern period: biblical Latin epic of the sixth and seventh centuries," in *Studies on Medieval and Early Modern Women: Pawns or Players?* ed. Christine Meek and Catherine Lawless (Dublin: Four Courts Press, 2003), pp. 18–19, 24–25.

19. Samantha J. E. Riches, "'Hyr wombe insaciate': The Iconography of the Feminised Monster," in *Pawns or Players?* pp. 180–82, at 182.
20. Marina Warner, *Alone of All Her Sex* (New York: Vintage Books, 1983, first published 1976), p. 68.
21. Warner, *Alone of All Her Sex*, p. 51.
22. Warner, *Alone of All Her Sex*, p. 77.
23. Helen M. Jewell, *Women in Late Medieval and Reformation Europe, 1200–1500* (Houndmills, Basingstoke: Palgrave Macmillan, 2007), p. 27.
24. Warner, *Alone of All Her Sex*, pp. 225–28.
25. Warner, *Alone of All Her Sex*, p. 57; Caroline Walker Bynum, *Fragmentation and Redemption: Essays on Gender and the Human Body in Medieval Religion* (New York: Zone Books, 1991), pp. 98–100, passim.
26. Karen A. Winstead, *Virgin Martyrs: Legends of Sainthood in Late Medieval England* (Ithaca and London: Cornell University Press, 1999), p. 5; Thomas J. Heffernan, *Sacred Biography: Saints and Their Biographers in the Middle Ages* (New York and Oxford: Oxford University Press, 1988), p. 186.
27. For example, the English Protestant polemicist John Bale saw female "saints" who abandoned their husbands in order to enter convents as guilty of violating St. Paul's proscriptions regarding marriage and sexual debt, all for the sake of their own harlotry (with convents described as whorehouses). See John Bale, *Actes of Englysh Votaryes* (London, 1560), pp. 19r, 34r, 42r–43r, passim.
28. While "Protestantism" denotes a variety of systems of belief, for the purposes of this chapter it is considered as referring to a broad early modern religious movement, with differences between different "Protestantisms" noted as necessary. Several essays cover historiography of the subject of the Reformation's impact on women and women's lives. See Susan C. Karant-Nunn, "The Reformation of Women," in *Becoming Visible: Women in European History*, ed. Renate Bridenthal, Susan Mosher Stuard, and Merry E. Wiesner, 3rd ed. (New York: Houghton Mifflin, 1998), pp. 175–202; Merry E. Wiesner, *Women and Gender in Early Modern Europe*, 2nd ed. (Cambridge: Cambridge University Press, 2000), esp. pp. 213–63; and recently, Merry Wiesner-Hanks, "Women, Gender and Sexuality," in *Palgrave Advances: The European Reformations*, ed. Alec Ryrie (Houndmills, Basingstoke: Palgrave Macmillan, 2006), pp. 253–72.
29. See, for example, G. M. Trevelyan, *England under the Stuarts* (London: Methuen, 1904); A. G. Dickens, *The English Reformation* (London: B. T. Batsford, 1964); Steven Ozment, *When Fathers Ruled: Family Life in Reformation Europe* (Cambridge, MA: Harvard University Press, 1983).
30. Lyndal Roper, *The Holy Household: Women and Morals in Reformation Augsburg* (Oxford: Clarendon Press, 1989), pp. 2, 15, 17, 57, 68–69, 203, passim.
31. Lyndal Roper, *Oedipus and the Devil: Witchcraft, Sexuality and Religion in Early Modern Europe* (London and New York: Routledge, 1994), p. 40.
32. Wiesner-Hanks, "Women, Gender and Sexuality," p. 260. See also Susan Karant Nunn, "Continuity and Change: Some Effects of the Reformation on the Women of Zwickau," *Sixteenth Century Journal* 13 (1982): 17–42.
33. Wiesner, *Women and Gender*, pp. 122–23.

34. Roper, *Holy Household*, p. 112.
35. Margaret King, *Women of the Renaissance* (Chicago and London: University of Chicago Press, 1991), pp. 138–39; Carole Levin and Patricia Sullivan, "Politics, Women's Voices, and the Renaissance: Questions and Context," in *Political Rhetoric, Power, and Renaissance Women*, ed. Carole Levin and Patricia Sullivan (Albany: SUNY Press, 1985), p. 6. The susceptibility of post-Reformation women to charges of whoredom provided a tool during the period associated with "gender crisis" (c. 1550–1650) for taking legal action against all sorts of "disorderly" women. As Laura Gowing has demonstrated, for example, the word "whore" was used as a broad term of insult against women in a context in which all women's honesty was defined by their sexuality. (Men's honesty and masculinity, conversely, depended on the honesty of women connected to them.) See Laura Gowing, *Domestic Dangers: Women, Words and Sex in Early Modern London* (Oxford: Clarendon Press, 1996), pp. 2, 7–8, 112. While, as Gowing has argued, the word "whore" was used as a popular form of insult appearing in a multitude of defamation cases in early modern London (mainly in church courts), it also frequently appears in the interrogations of women accused of heresy in reformation England. See Megan L. Hickerson, *Making Women Martyrs in Tudor England* (New York: Palgrave Macmillan, 2005), pp. 89–91.
36. John Bale, *Image of Both Churches* (1547), II, kiiii(r).
37. Susan Karant-Nunn, "The Masculinity of Martin Luther: Theory, Practicality and Humor," in *Masculinity in the Reformation Era*, ed. Scott H. Hendrix and Susan C. Karant-Nunn (Kirksville, MO: Truman State University Press, 2008), p. 169.
38. Merry E. Wiesner, "Luther and Women: The Death of Two Mary's," in *Feminist Theology: A Reader*, ed. Anne Loades (London: Society for the Promotion of Christian Knowledge, 1990), pp. 126–27.
39. The term "double subjection," relating to Calvin's soteriology, was coined by Richard Stauffer (*Dieu, la création et la Providence dans la predication de Calvin* [Bern: Peter Lang, 1978], p. 210), as discussed in John Lee Thompson, *John Calvin and the Daughters of Sarah: Women in Regular and Exceptional Roles in eh Exegesis of Calvin, His Predecessors, and His Contemporaries* (Geneva: Librairie Droz S. A., 1992), pp. 16–17. This construct is also clear in English Reformation discourse. See Patricia Crawford, *Women and Religion in Britain, 1500–1720* (London: Routledge, 1996), p. 9.
40. In his monumental history of the Church, for example, John Foxe deemphasizes the importance of their virginity in his versions of the stories of the "virgin" martyrs of the early Church. See Hickerson, *Women Martyrs*, pp. 114–19.
41. Flood, "A source," p. 23; Wiesner, "Two Marys," p. 129.
42. Roper, *Holy Household*, pp. 104–10, passim.
43. See Fletcher, *Gender, Sex and Subordination*, pp. 27–28; Susan D. Amussen, *An Ordered Society: Gender and Class in Early Modern England* (New York: Columbia University Press, 1988); Susan D. Amussen, "Gender, Family and the Social Order, 1560–1725," in *Order and Disorder in Early Modern England*, ed. Anthony Fletcher and John Stevenson (Cambridge: Cambridge University Press, 1985), p. 216; D. E. Underdown, "The Taming of the Scold: The Enforcement of

Patriarchal Authority in Early Modern England," in *Order and Disorder*, p. 116; Wiesner-Hanks, "Women, Gender and Sexuality," p. 264.
44. Francesca Medioli, "An unequal Law: the enforcement of *clausura* before and after the Council of Trent," in *Women in Renaissance and Early Modern Europe*, ed. Christine Meek (Dublin and Portland, OR: Four Courts Press, 2000), p. 143.
45. Mary Elizabeth Perry, *Gender and Disorder in Early Modern Seville* (Princeton, NJ: Princeton University Press, 1990), p. 13.
46. Perry, *Gender and Disorder*, pp. 13, 177–78.
47. Merry E. Wiesner, *Gender, Church and State in Early Modern Germany: Essays* (London: Longman, 1998), p. 78.
48. Roper, *Oedipus and the Devil*, pp. 40–46; also Roper, *Holy Household*. On the importance to Protestant polemicists of clerical celibacy as a mark of Antichrist, see Helen L. Parish, *Clerical Marriage and the English Reformation* (Aldershot: Ashgate, 2000), and Helen L. Parish, *Clerical Celibacy in the West: c. 1100–1700* (Burlington, VT: Ashgate, 2010).
49. Hickerson, *Women Martyrs*, 24–41.
50. See John Foxe, *Christus Triumphans* (1556), in *Two Latin Comedies by John Foxe the Martyrologist*, ed. J. H. Smith (Ithaca, NY, 1973).
51. Frances E. Dolan, *Whores of Babylon: Catholicism, Gender and Seventeenth-Century Print Culture* (Notre Dame, IN: University of Notre Dame Press, 1999), pp. 6–11.
52. Some scholars have looked for explanations to the effectiveness of increasingly rigid patriarchal social control during this period (responding to "crisis" in both Protestant and Catholic areas) in the development of the sovereign nation-state, contemporary to the Reformation and the splintering of "Christendom" accompanying it (see, for example, Christina Larner, *Enemies of God: The Witch Hunt in Scotland* [London: Chatto and Windus, 1981], p. 193); others emphasize the agency of local elites in managing the "hunts" (Brian Levack, "State-Building and Witch Hunting in Early Modern Europe," in *Witchcraft in Early Modern Europe: Studies in Culture and Belief*, ed. Jonathan Barry, Marianne Hester, and Gareth Roberts [Cambridge: Cambridge University Press, 1996], p. 99); while still others focus on neighborhood relationships and their breakdown in times of broad, social and economic difficulty (Robin Briggs, *Witches and Neighbors: The Social and Cultural Context of European Witchcraft* [London: Harper Collins, 1996]).
53. On "confessionalization," see William Monter, "Witch Trials in Continental Europe: 1560–1660," in *Witchcraft and Magic in Europe: The Period of the Witch Trials*, ed. Bengt Ankarloo and Stuart Clark, vol. 4 (University of Pennsylvania Press, 1999), p. 11.
54. Clark, *Thinking with Demons*, p. 552.
55. Heinrich Kramer and Jacob Sprenger, *Malleus Maleficarum* (1486), ed. Montague Summers (1928), http://www.malleusmaleficarum.org/?p=19 (accessed October 1, 2010).
56. Alexander Roberts, *A Treatise of Witchcraft* (1616), ed. and pub. Project Gutenberg (2005), http://infomotions.com/etexts/gutenberg/dirs/1/7/2/0/17209/17209.htm (accessed October 3, 2010).

57. Clark, *Thinking with Demons*, pp. 13–21, passim; Larner, *Enemies of God*, p. 9.
58. For discussion of anxieties about post-menopausal women informing accusations, see Lyndal Roper, "Witchcraft and Fantasy in Early Modern Germany," *History Workshop Journal* 32 (1991): 19–43.

Chapter 4

1. *Paracelsus: Selected Writings*, ed. Jolande Jacobi (Princeton: Princeton University Press, 1979), pp. 24–25.
2. See discussion of Paracelsus, *De Matrice*, in Hildegard Elisabeth Keller, "Paracelsus's Gendered Epistemology," in *Paracelsian Moments: Science, Medicine, & Astrology in Early Modern Europe*, ed. Gerhild Scholz Williams and Charles D. Gunnoe (Kirksville, MO: Truman State University Press, 2002), pp. 93–115, esp. pp. 94, 98, 104.
3. See Kate Aughterson, "Physiology," in *Renaissance Woman: Constructions of Femininity in England* (London: Routledge, 1995), pp. 41–66; and Merry E. Wiesner, *Women and Gender in Early Modern Europe* (Cambridge: Cambridge University Press, 1993), pp. 44–46.
4. Helkiah Crooke, *Microcosmographia* (London, 1618), pp. 270–72.
5. Crooke's account suggests he was familiar with and influenced by Paracelsus's descriptions of the sexes. Thomas Laqueur foregrounded the "one-sex" paradigm in *Making Sex: Body and Gender from the Greeks to Freud* (Cambridge, MA: Harvard University Press, 1990). Janet Adelman, "Making Defect Perfection: Shakespeare and the One-Sex Model," in *Enacting Gender on the English Renaissance Stage*, ed. Viviana Comensoli and Anne Russell (Chicago: Chicago University Press, 1999), has argued that it is difficult to imagine that the one-sex model of the body was as dominant as Laqueur maintains. Gail Kern Paster has argued that humoralism and other factors also contributed to the construction of gender in this period, see *The Body Embarrassed: Drama and the Disciplines of Shame in Early Modern England* (New York: Cornell University Press, 1993), and "The Unbearable Coldness of Being: Women's Imperfection and the Humoral Economy," *English Literary Renaissance* 28 (1998): 416–40, 418.
6. Jane Sharp, *The Midwives Book: or the whole art of midwifery discovered* (London, 1671), p. 40.
7. As Thomas Buckley and Alma Gottlieb point out, Mary Douglas linked menstrual pollution taboos with particular societies in which there was structural ambiguity surrounding women, see *Blood Magic: The Anthropology of Menstruation* (California: University of California Press, 1998), pp. 30–34.
8. From Anon., *Secrets of Women* (n.d.), qtd. in Danielle Jacquart and Claude Thomasset, *Sexuality and Medicine in the Middle Ages* (Cambridge: Polity Press, 1988), p. 76.
9. Qtd. in Aughterson, "Physiology," p. 35.
10. *The 1599 Geneva Bible* (Ozark, MO: L. L. Brown, Publishing, 1990), p. 45.
11. *The 1599 Geneva Bible*, p. 43.

12. See Patricia Crawford and Sara Mendelson, *Women in Early Modern England 1550–1720* (Oxford: Clarendon Press, 1996), p. 26; and Margaret Healy, *Fictions of Disease in Early Modern England: Bodies, Plagues and Politics* (Basingstoke: Palgrave, 2001), pp. 132–33. Syphilis emerged in Europe as a virulent, sexually transmitted disease in 1494.
13. Simon Kellwaye, *A Defensative against the Plague* (London, 1593), f 39r.
14. Anon., *Aristotle's Master-Piece* (London, 1690), p. 5.
15. John Sadler, *The Sicke Womans Private Looking-Glasse* (London, 1636), p. 13.
16. Anon., *Aristotle's Book of Problems* (London, 1764), p. 15.
17. Levinus Lemnius, *A Discourse touching Generation* (London, 1667), p. 268.
18. See Crawford and Mendelson, *Women in Early Modern England*, pp. 23–25.
19. William Shakespeare, *The Complete Works, Compact Ed.* (Oxford: Oxford University Press, 1988).
20. Stuart Clark, *Thinking with Demons: The Idea of Witchcraft in Early Modern Europe* (Oxford: Oxford University Press, 1997), p. 113.
21. See Buckley and Gottlieb, *Blood Magic*, pp. 26–47, 21.
22. Cornelius Agrippa, "De nobilitate et praecellentia sexus foeminei" (1529), qtd. in Wiesner, *Women and Gender*, p. 9.
23. Thomas Raynold, *The byrth of mankynde, otherwise named the womans booke* (London, 1545), f.44v.
24. Reginald Scot, *The discoverie of witchcraft* (London, 1584), pp. 278–79.
25. John Sadler, *The Sicke Womans Private Looking-Glasse* (London, 1636), pp. 8–10.
26. Jacobi, *Paracelsus*, p. 26.
27. Jacobi, *Paracelsus*, p. 26.
28. Jacobi, *Paracelsus*, p. 27.
29. Jacobi, *Paracelsus*, pp. 28–29.
30. Paracelsus, *Opus Paramirum*, I, qtd. in N. Goodrick-Clarke, ed., *Paracelsus: Essential Readings* (Berkeley: North Atlantic, 1991), p. 83.
31. Jacobi, *Paracelsus*, p. 26.
32. Holt T. Parker, "Women Doctors in Greece, Rome and the Byzantine Empire," in *Women Healers and Physicians: Climbing a Long Hill*, ed. Lilian R. Furst (Lexington, KY: University Press of Kentucky, 1997), pp. 131–51, 131.
33. Parker, "Women Doctors," p. 133.
34. Parker, "Women Doctors," pp. 134, 137.
35. Tacitus, *Germania*, described in Debra L. Stoudt, "Medieval Women and the Power of Healing," in *Women Healers*, pp. 13–43, 14.
36. Parker, "Women Doctors," p. 140.
37. Stoudt, "Medieval Women," p. 14.
38. Parker, "Women Doctors," p. 131.
39. Stoudt, "Medieval Women," p. 14.
40. Stoudt, "Medieval Women," 13; Michael Solomon, "Women Healers and the Power to Disease in Late Medieval Spain," in *Women Healers*, pp. 79–93, 79.
41. Victoria Sweet, "Hildegard of Bingen and the Greening of Medieval Medicine," *Bulletin of the History of Medicine* 73, no. 3 (1999): 381–403, 383.
42. Sweet, "Hildegard," pp. 388–89.

43. Stoudt, "Medieval Women," pp. 20–23.
44. Stoudt, "Medieval Women," p. 22.
45. Qtd. in Stoudt, "Medieval Women," p. 24.
46. Qtd. in Stoudt, "Medieval Women," p. 18.
47. Parker, "Women Doctors," p. 131.
48. Stoudt, "Medieval Women," p. 15.
49. Nancy P. Nenno, "Between Magic and Medicine: Medieval Images of the Woman Healer," in *Women Healers*, pp. 43–64, 59.
50. Sigrid Maria Brauner, "Frightened Shrews and Fearless Wives: The Concept of the Witch in Early Modern German Texts (1487–1560)" (Ph.D. diss., University of California, Berkeley, 1989), p. 393, qtd. in Nenno, "Between Magic and Medicine," pp. 59, 61.
51. Nenno, "Between Magic and Medicine," p. 59.
52. Nenno, "Between Magic and Medicine," p. 45.
53. Nenno, "Between Magic and Medicine," p. 46.
54. A Short Discoverie of the Unobserved Dangers, qtd. in Lynette Hunter, "Women and Domestic Medicine: Lady Experimenters 1570–1620," in *Women and Science, 1500–1700: Mothers and Sisters of the Royal Society*, ed. Lynette Hunter and Sarah Hutton (Stroud: Sutton Publishing, 1997), p. 99.
55. Mary Elizabeth Fissell, "Introduction: Women, Health, and Healing in Early Modern Europe," *Bulletin of the History of Medicine* 82, no. 1 (2008): 1–17, 1.
56. John Securis, *A Detection and Querimonie of the daily enormities and abuses committed in physick* (London, 1566), qtd. in Deborah E. Harkness, "A View from the Streets: Women and Medical Work in Elizabethan London," *Bulletin of Medical History* 82 (2008): 52–85, 53.
57. Harkness, "A View," p. 54.
58. Fissell, "Introduction," p. 3.
59. Fissell, "Introduction," p. 3.
60. Fissell, "Introduction," p. 14.
61. Fissell, "Introduction," p. 9.
62. William Kerwin, "Where Have you Gone, Margaret Kennix? Seeking the Tradition of Healing Women in English Renaissance Drama," in *Women Healers*, pp. 93–113, esp. p. 100.
63. Margaret Pelling and Charles Webster, "Medical Practitioners," in *Health, Medicine and Mortality in the Sixteenth Century*, ed. Charles Webster (London: Cambridge, 1979), p. 188.
64. Pelling and Webster, "Medical Practitioners," p. 188.
65. Harold J. Cook, *The Decline of the Old Medical Regime in Stuart London* (Ithaca: Cornell University Press, 1986), p. 32.
66. See Jean Donnison, *Midwives and Medical Men: A History of Inter-professional Rivalries and Women's Rights* (New York: Schocken Books, 1977).
67. See Webster, *Health, Medicine and Mortality*, p. 8.
68. Harkness, "A View," p. 55.
69. Margaret Pelling, "Thoroughly Resented: Older Women and the Medical Role in Early Modern London," in *Women and Science, 1500–1700*, pp. 63–88, 70.

70. Kerwin, "Seeking the Tradition," p. 111.
71. See Sweet, "Hildegard," pp. 398–99.
72. Sweet, "Hildegard," p. 399.
73. Francis McKee, "The Paracelsian Kitchen," in *Paracelsus: the Man and His Reputation, His Ideas and Their Transformation*, ed. Ole Peter Grell (Leiden: Brill, 1998), pp. 283–308.
74. McKee, "Paracelsian Kitchen," p. 287.
75. Paracelsus, "Of the Supreme Mysteries of Nature," qtd. in McKee, "Paracelsian Kitchen," p. 285.
76. Michael Maier, Emblem 22, *Atalanta Fugiens*, illustrates a woman cooking fish, for example. This led the wise observer to esoteric natural knowledge about boiling waters and vapors.
77. Fissell, "Introduction," p. 9.
78. McKee, "Paracelsian Kitchen," p. 296.
79. See the description of "The Margaret Manuscript" held in the Cumbria Record Office (MS WD/Hoth/A988/5) in Penny Bayer, "Lady Margaret Clifford's Alchemical Receipt Book and the John Dee Circle," *Ambix* 52, no. 3 (November 2005): 271–84. This manuscript may have been produced partly with the help of Christopher Taylour, an alchemist who was associated with the Dee-Kelley circle in Mortlake, London.
80. Bayer, "Lady Margaret," p. 274.
81. *Historical Memoirs of the House of Russell*, in *Redeeming Eve: Women Writers of the English Renaissance*, by Elaine V. Beilin (Princeton: Princeton University Press, 1990), p. 192.
82. Bayer, "Lady Margaret," p. 377; see also Jayne Archer, "Women and Alchemy in Early Modern England" (Ph.D. diss., University of Cambridge, Newnham College, 1999), chap. 2.
83. See Kerwin, "Seeking the Tradition," p. 110.
84. Lady Margaret Hoby, *The Private Life of an Elizabethan Lady: The Diary of Lady Margaret Hoby, 1599–1605*, ed. Joanna Moody (Stroud: Sutton Publishing, 2001), p. 112.
85. Qtd. in McKee, "Paracelsian Kitchen," p. 301.
86. Elaine Leong, "Making Medicines in the Early Modern Household," *Bulletin of Medical History* 82 (2008): 145–68.
87. Leong, "Making Medicines," p. 153.
88. Leong, "Making Medicines," p. 157.
89. Leong, "Making Medicines," p. 161.

Chapter 5

1. This passage is discussed in Margaret J. M. Ezell, "Afterword: Critical Distance," in *Early Modern Women and Transnational Communities of Letters*, ed. Julie D. Campbell and Anne R. Larsen (Aldershot: Ashgate, 2009). William Gouge, *A Funerall Sermon* (London, 1646).

2. Lancelot Andrewes, *Pattern of Catechistical Doctrine* (London, 1650, first published 1630), p. 345.
3. King James Version; Latin quotation from the Vulgate, Titus 2.5, http://www.latinvulgate.com/verse.aspx?t=1&b=17&c=2 (accessed December 16, 2010).
4. See my "Gender and the Inculcation of Virtue: The Book of Proverbs and Early Modern Exemplarity," in *Biblical Women and Early Modern Literary Culture*, ed. Victoria Brownlee and Laura Gallagher (Aldershot: Ashgate, forthcoming).
5. See, in particular, Amy Louise Erickson, *Women and Property in Early Modern England* (New York: Routledge, 1993), and Wendy Wall, *Staging Domesticitiy: Household Work and English Identity in Early Modern Drama* (Cambridge: Cambridge University Press, 2002). A good overview of women's lives can be found in Sara Mendelson and Patricia Crawford, *Women in Early Modern England* (Oxford University Press, 1998).
6. Wall, *Staging Domesticity*, p. 17.
7. John Dod and William Hinde, *Bathshebaes Instructions* (1614), p. 26. This refers to verses 10–12, "The scope & drift of these verses is…to set forth unto us the vertues of a good wife."
8. John Milton, *Paradise Lost*, ed. Gordon Teskey (New York: W.W.Norton, 2005), IX, 214–15.
9. Lorna Hutson, *The Usurer's Daughter: Male Friendship and Fictions of Women in Sixteenth Century England* (New York and London: Routledge, 1994), p. 22.
10. John Dod and Robert Cleaver, *A godlie forme of householde government* (London, 1598), pp. 170–71.
11. Hutson, *Usurer's Daughter*, p. 21.
12. Hutson, *Usurer's Daughter*, p. 21.
13. One might reasonably see here an echo or a refraction of the key marital and dynastic crisis of the sixteenth century, namely the desire of Henry VIII to divorce Katherine of Aragon; numerous texts play with the consequences arising from second marriages, most famously, of course, *Hamlet*. It is also worth noting that second marriages were very common in early modern England.
14. *Three Tragedies by Renaissance Women*, ed. Diane Purkiss (Harmondsworth: Penguin, 1998), 5.1.119–30.
15. Rayna Kalas, *Frame, Glass, Verse: The Technology of Poetic Invention in the English Renaissance* (Ithaca: Cornell University Press, 2007).
16. John King, *Vitis Palatina* (1614), p. 11.
17. Edmund Tilney, *The Flower of Friendship: A Renaissance Dialogue Contesting Marriage*, ed. Valerie Wayne (Ithaca: Cornell University Press, 1992), p. 138.
18. John Gataker, *A good Wife Gods Gift: and, A Wife Indeed* (1623), p. 13.
19. See Walter Benjamin, "The Work of Art in an Age of Mechanical Reproduction," in *Illuminations*, ed. Hannah Arendt (New York: Sprocken Books, 1968), pp. 211–44.
20. Joan Kelly, "Did Women Have a Renaissance?" in *Women, History and Theory: The Essays of Joan Kelly* (Chicago: University of Chicago Press, 1984), pp. 21–22.
21. David Cressy, *Birth, Marriage and Death: Ritual, Religion, and the Life-Cycle in Tudor and Stuart England* (Oxford: Oxford University Press, 1997); see also

Fiona McNeil, *Poor Women in Shakespeare* (Cambridge: Cambridge University Press, 2007).
22. Cressy, *Birth, Marriage and Death*, p. 287.
23. See, for example, the career of Edward Coke, in *Oxford Dictionary of National Biography*, http://www.oxforddnb.com.eproxy.ucd.ie/view/article/5826?docPos=4 (accessed March 13, 2011).
24. See chapter 2 of my *Language, Gender and Discourse, 1500–1700: Articulating the Feminine* (Aldershot: Ashgate, 2013).
25. *Collected Works of Mary Sidney Herbert*, ed. Margaret P. Hannay, Noel J. Kinnamon, and Michael G. Brennan, 2 vols (Oxford: Clarendon Press, 1998), pp. 49–52.
26. Anne Wheathill, *Handfull of Holesome (though Homelie) Hearbs* (1584), p. 51.
27. Elaine V. Beilin, *Redeeming Eve: Women Writers of the English Renaissance* (Princeton: Princeton University Press, 1990), p. 53.
28. See Lena Cowen Orlin, *Locating Privacy in Tudor London* (Oxford: Oxford University Press, 2008); Helen Smith, *Grossly Material Things: Women and Book Production in Early Modern England* (Oxford: Oxford University Press, 2012).
29. *A Christian Directory* (London, 1673), pp. 432–33. See also Adam Fox, *Oral and Literate Culture in England, 1500–1700* (Oxford: Clarendon Press, 2000), and Mary Ellen Lamb and Karen Bamford, eds., *Oral Traditions and Gender in Early Modern Literary Texts* (Aldershot: Ashgate, 2008).
30. Edward Gosynhill, *Scholehouse of women* (1560), sig. A4r.
31. Bernard Capp, *When Gossips Meet: Women, Family, and Neighbourhood in Early Modern England* (Oxford: Oxford University Press, 2003), p. 273.
32. Capp, *When Gossips Meet*, chap. 7.
33. See Laura Gowing, *Domestic Dangers: Women, Words, and Sex in Early Modern London* (Oxford: Oxford University Press, 1996).
34. See Alan Stewart, "The Voices of Anne Cooke, Lady Anne and Lady Bacon," in *"This Double Voice": Gendered Writing in Early Modern England*, ed. Danielle Clarke and Elizabeth Clarke (New York: Macmillan, 2000), pp. 88–102, and Lynne Magnusson, "Imagining a National Church: Election and Education in the Works of Anne Cooke Bacon," in *The Intellectual Culture of Puritan Women, 1558–1680*, ed. Johanna Harris and Elizabeth Scott-Baumann (New York: Palgrave, 2011), pp. 42–56.
35. See James Daybell, *Women Letter-Writers in Tudor England* (Oxford: Oxford University Press, 2006), and Marie-Louise Coolahan, *Women, Writing, and Language in Early Modern Ireland* (Oxford: Oxford University Press, 2010).
36. Lawrence Manley, *Literature and Culture in Early Modern London* (Cambridge: Cambridge University Press, 2005).
37. The attempts of Elizabeth I to reconcile these contradictions have been extensively considered in recent criticism.
38. Queen Elizabeth to Sir Amyas Paulet, c. May 1579, no. 44, in *Elizabeth I: Collected Works*, ed. Leah S. Marcus, Janel Mueller, and Mary Beth Rose (Chicago: University of Chicago Press, 2000), p. 234.
39. Queen Elizabeth to Monsieur, December 19, 1579, no. 45, in *Elizabeth I*, pp. 238–39.

40. Speech at the Close of the Parliamentary Session, March 15, 1576, no. 13, in *Elizabeth I*, p. 168.
41. Speech at the Close of the Parliamentary Session, March 15, 1576, no. 13, in *Elizabeth I*, p. 168.
42. Speech at the Close of the Parliamentary Session, March 15, 1576, no. 13, in *Elizabeth I*, p. 169.
43. Speech at the Close of the Parliamentary Session, March 15, 1576, no. 13, in *Elizabeth I*, p. 170.
44. A telling early example of the real effects of such proscriptions—and the ways in which they might be read against the grain—can be found in the case of Anne Askew; see *The Examinations of Anne Askew*, ed. Elaine V. Beilin (Oxford: Oxford University Press, 1996), pp. 29–30.
45. Barbara J. Harris, "Women and Politics in Early Tudor England," *Historical Journal* 33 (1990): 259–81.
46. Danielle Clarke, ed. *Renaissance Women Poets* (New York: Penguin Classics, 2000), pp. 47–50.
47. See Edith Snook, *Women, Reading, and the Cultural Politics of Early Modern England* (Aldershot: Ashgate, 2005), pp. 87–89.
48. See Francis Barker, *The Tremulous Private Body: Essays on Subjection* (Ann Arbor: University of Michigan Press, 1995), pp. 1–63.

Chapter 6

1. It is very difficult to establish any reliable or meaningful figures about literacy rates in early modern Europe. Literacy was inflected by nationality, geography (i.e., urban or rural, village or discrete farms), religion, class, and gender. Urban, elite men were more likely to be able to read than women of similar social standing, but those women were far more likely to be able to read than, for instance, rural male peasants. Even if the data existed to compute an average figure, that average would be, for all practical purposes, useless for understanding a particular country or even city. The most literate group would have been urban men working in trades that demanded literacy or working as secretaries; perhaps 50–75 percent of them could read. Only 10–15 percent of urban day laborers would have been able to read, and even fewer rural agricultural laborers; probably less than 2 percent of rural women of the servant class were literate. H. G. Koenigsberger, George L. Mosse, and G. Q. Bowler, *Europe in the Sixteenth Century*, 2nd ed. (London: Longman, 1968), p. 80. In the Renaissance, reading and writing were taught as separate skills, and though all of the professional scribes and secretaries of the era were male, some girls did take instruction from writing masters.
2. Qtd. in Howard Adelman, "The Literacy of Jewish Women in Early Modern Italy," in *Women's Education in Early Modern Europe*, ed. Barbara J. Whitehead (New York: Garland, 1999), p. 133.
3. Adelman, "The Literacy of Jewish Women," pp. 135, 137.
4. Merry E. Wiesner, *Women and Gender in Early Modern Europe*, 2nd ed. (New York: Cambridge University Press, 2000), p. 146.

5. Jane Stevenson, "Women and Classical Education in the Early Modern Period," in *Pedagogy and Power: Rhetorics of Classical Learning*, ed. Yun Lee Too and Niall Livingstone (New York: Cambridge University Press, 1998), p. 94.
6. Margaret J. Mason, "Nuns and Vocations of the Unpublished Jerningham Letters: Charlotte Bedingfield, Augustinian Canoness (1802–1876), Louisa Jerningham, Franciscan Abbess (1808–1893), and Clementina Jerningham, Marquise de Ripert-Monclar (1810–1864)," *Recusant History* 21 (1993): 503–55.
7. Caroline Bowden, "'For the Glory of God': A Study of the Education of English Catholic Women in Convents in Flanders and France in the First Half of the Seventeenth Century," *Paedagogica Historica* Supplementary Series 5 (1999): 86.
8. The collect for the Second Sunday of Advent, *The Book of Common Prayer*.
9. Adelman, "The Literacy of Jewish Women," p. 137.
10. Adelman, "The Literacy of Jewish Women," pp. 141–42.
11. Sharon T. Strocchia, "Learning the Virtues: Convent Schools and Female Culture in Renaissance Florence," in *Women's Education in Early Modern Europe*, pp. 3–46.
12. Qtd. in Margaret L. King and Albert Rabil Jr., trans. and eds., *Her Immaculate Hand: Selected Works by and about the Women Humanists of Quattrocento Italy* (Asheville, NC: Pegasus Press, 2000), p. 83.
13. King and Rabil Jr., *Her Immaculate Hand*, p. 59.
14. W. H. Woodward, ed., *Vittorino da Feltre and Other Humanist Educators* (Cambridge: Cambridge University Press, 1921), pp. 119–33.
15. Peter Davidson, "The *Theatrum* for the Entry of Claudia de' Medici and Federigo Ubaldo della Rovere into Urbino, 1621," in *Court Festivals of the European Renaissance: Art, Politics and Performance*, ed. J. R. Mulryne and Elizabeth Goldring (Aldershot: Ashgate, 2002), pp. 331–34.
16. Paul F. Grendler, *Schooling in Renaissance Italy: Literacy and Learning 1300–1600* (Baltimore: The Johns Hopkins University Press, 1989), pp. 88–89.
17. Mary Ellen Lamb, "Margaret Roper, the Humanist Political Project, and the Problem of Agency," in *Opening the Borders: Inclusivity in Early Modern Studies: Essays in Honor of James V. Mirollo*, ed. Peter C. Herman (Newark: University of Delaware Press, 2001), pp. 83–108.
18. Qtd. in Phyllis Stock, *Better Than Rubies: A History of Women's Education* (New York: Capricorn, 1978), p. 62.
19. Qtd. in Stock, *Better Than Rubies*, p. 66.
20. Juan Luis Vives, *A very frutful and pleasant boke called the Instruction of a christen woman, made fyrst in latyne, by the right famous clerke mayster Lewes Viues, and tourned out of latyne into Englishe by Rycharde Hyrde* (London, 1585), pp. 4, 5, chap. 2. Hyrde's translation of Vives is available through EEBO, http://eebo.chadwyck.com, and in Foster Watson, ed., *Vives and the Renascence Education of Women* (New York: Longmans, Green, 1912).
21. Vives, *A very frutful and pleasant boke*, p. 21.
22. Vives, *A very frutful and pleasant boke*, pp. 27, 28.
23. Vives, *A very frutful and pleasant boke*, pp. 31–41.
24. Vives, *A very frutful and pleasant boke*, p. 64.
25. Wiesner, *Women and Gender in Early Modern Europe*, p. 160.

26. Qtd. in Stock, *Better Than Rubies*, pp. 83–84.
27. Makin's work is widely available: on the Internet through EEBO, http://eebo.chadwyck.com; through the website *Sunshine for Women*, http://www.pinn.net/~sunshine/book-sum/makin1.html; and in two modern editions, including most recently that edited by Frances N. Teague, *Bathsua Makin, Woman of Learning* (Lewisburg, PA: Bucknell University Press, 1998).
28. Qtd. in Teague, *Bathsua Makin*, p. 43.
29. Mary Ward, letter to Winifred Bedingfeld, July 16, 1627, in James Walsh, S. J., introduction to *Till God Will: Mary Ward Through Her Writings*, ed. M. Emmanuel Orchard, IBVM (London: Darton, Longman and Todd, 1985), p. 96.
30. Mary Ward, letter to Winifred Wigmore, Oct. 10, 1667, in Walsh, introduction, *Till God Will*, p. 97. Walsh also demonstrates Ward's extensive training in the forms of classical rhetoric and the way in which her prose follows the rhythms of the Vulgate and incorporates many Latin phrases.
31. Qtd. in Orchard, *Till God Will*, p. 37.
32. Material on Ward's life not otherwise cited comes from M. Immolate Wetter, IBMV, *Mary Ward: In Her Own Words* (Rome: Istituto Beata Vergine Maria, 1999); Henriette Peters, *Mary Ward: A World in Contemplation* (Leominster, UK: Gracewing, 1994); and Christina Kenworthy-Browne, CJ, e-mail communication with the author.
33. Baldassare Castiglione, "Of the Chief Conditions and Qualities in a Waiting Gentlewoman," in *The Book of the Courtier*, trans. Thomas Hoby (London, 1561), z.r iii. Hoby's translation is available through EEBO, http://eebo.chadwyck.com.
34. Brathwaite's *English Gentleman* and his *English Gentlewoman* were published together in one volume in 1641. All three books are available through EEBO, http://eebo.chadwyck.com.

Chapter 7

1. Elizabeth I, as qtd. in Carole Levin, *Heart and Stomach of a King: Elizabeth I and the Politics of Sex and Power* (Philadelphia: University of Pennsylvania Press, 1994), p. 144.
2. Caterina Sforza, as qtd. in Sharon Jansen, *The Monstrous Regiment of Women: Female Rulers in Early Modern Europe* (New York, Palgrave, 2002), p. 5.
3. Theresa Earenfight, "Absent Kings: Queens as Political Partners in the Medieva Crown of Aragon," in *Queenship and Political Power in Medieval and Early Modern Spain*, ed. Earenfight (Aldershot, UK: Ashgate, 2005), p. 40.
4. Committee of Seventeen Reformers, as qtd. in Natalie Tomas, *The Medici Women* (Aldershot: Ashgate, 2003), p. 168.
5. Christine de Pisan, *The Treasure of the City of Ladies*, trans. Sarah Lawson (London: Penguin, 1985), p. 51.
6. Pisan, as qtd. in Sharon Jansen, *Debating Women, Politics and Power in Early Modern Europe* (New York: Palgrave, 2008), p. 127.
7. Margaret of Austria, as qtd. in Jansen, *Debating Women*, p. 95.

8. Christine de Pisan, *The Book of the City of Ladies*, trans. Earl Jeffrey Richards (New York: Persea Books, 1982), p. 32.
9. John Knox, as qtd. in Jansen, *Debating Women*, p. 15.
10. Elaine Kruse, "The Blood-stained Hands of Catherine de Médicis," in *Political Rhetoric, Power, and Renaissance Women*, ed. Carole Levin and Patricia A Sullivan (Albany: State University of New York Press, 1995), pp. 139–56.
11. Lucrezia Marinelli, *The Nobility and Excellence of Women, and the Defects and Vices of Men*, trans. Letizia Panizza (Chicago: University of Chicago Press, 1999), p. 79.
12. Baldessare Castiglione, *The Book of the Courtier* (New York: Penguin, 1967), p. 216.
13. Castiglione, *Courtier*, p. 238.
14. John Calvin, as qtd. in Jansen, *Debating Women*, pp. 40–41; Filippo Strozzi qtd. in Tomas, *Medici Women*, p. 167.
15. Julia Hairston, "Skirting the Issue: Machiavelli's Caterina Sforza," *Renaissance Quarterly* 53 (2000): 694, 691.
16. John Sanderson, as qtd. in Leslie Peirce, *The Imperial Harem: Women and Sovereignty in the Ottoman Empire* (Oxford: Oxford University Press, 1993), p. 224.
17. Tomas, *Medici Women*, p. 49.
18. Francesco Barbaro, "On Wifely Duties," trans. Benjamin Kohl, in *The Earthly Republic: Italian Humanists on Government and Society*, ed. Benjamin Kohl and Ronald Witt (Philadelphia: University of Pennsylvania Press, 1991), p. 216.
19. Barbara Harris, *English Aristocratic Women, 1450–1550: Marriage and Family, Property and Careers* (Oxford: Oxford University Press, 2002), p. 160.
20. Lady Berkeley, as qtd. in Harris, *Aristocratic Women*, p. 162.
21. Nicolo Mudazzo, as qtd. in Stanley Chojnacki, *Women and Men in Renaissance Venice* (Baltimore: Johns Hopkins University Press, 2000), p. 99.
22. As qtd. in Roy Strong, *Portraits of Queen Elizabeth I* (Oxford: Clarendon Press, 1963), p. 10.
23. Juan Luis Vives, *Education of a Christian Woman*, ed. Charles Fantazzi (Chicago: University of Chicago Press, 2000), p. 311.
24. As qtd. in Lyndal Roper, *The Holy Household: Women and Morals in Reformation Augsburg* (Oxford: Clarendon Press, 1989), p. 222.
25. Jacob Burkhardt, *The Civilization of the Renaissance in Italy* (New York: Penguin, 1990), p. 250.
26. Joan Kelly, "Did Women Have a Renaissance?" in *Women, History and Theory: The Essays of Joan Kelly* (Chicago: University of Chicago Press, 1984), pp. 22, 47.
27. Sharon Kettering, "Patronage Power of Early Modern French Noblewomen," *History Journal* 32 (1989): 818.

Chapter 8

1. Paolo Buffa, ed., *Sofonisba Anguissola e le sue sorelle*, exhibitions in Vienna and Washington, 1994–95 (Milan: Leonardo, 1994); Caroline P. Murphy, *Lavinia Fontana: A Painters and Her Patrons in Sixteenth-Century Bologna* (New Haven and London: Yale University Press, 2003); Frederika H. Jacobs, *Defining the Renaissance "Virtuosa"* (Cambridge: Cambridge University Press, 1997).

2. Sheryl E. Reiss and David G. Wilkins, eds., *Beyond Isabella: Secular Women Patrons of Art in Early Renaissance Italy* (Kirksville, MO: Truman State University Press, 2001); Catherine King, *Renaissance Women Patrons: Wives and Widows in Italy c. 1300–1550* (Manchester: Manchester University Press, 1998); Anabel Thomas, *Art and Piety in the Female Religious Communities of Renaissance Italy: Iconography, Space, and the Religious Woman's Perspective* (Cambridge: Cambridge University Press, 2003); Allison Levy, ed., *Widowhood and Visual Culture in Early Modern Europe* (Aldershot: Ashgate, 2003).
3. Marta Ajmar-Wollheim and Flora Dennis, eds., *At Home in Renaissance Italy* (London: Victoria and Albert Museum, 2006); Andrea Bayer, ed., *Art and Love in Renaissance Italy* (New York: Metropolitan Museum, 2008).
4. Margaret L. King, *Women of the Renaissance* (Chicago: University of Chicago Press, 1991), p. 238.
5. Good general studies are in Nicolas Mann and Luke Syson, *The Image of the Individual: Portraits in the Renaissance* (London: British Museum, 1998); and Lorne Campbell, Miguel Falomir, Jennifer Fletcher, and Luke Syson, eds., *Renaissance Faces: Titian to Van Dyck* (London: National Gallery Company, 1998).
6. This claim that the rise of portraiture formed part of a general rediscovery of human individuality was made in J. Pope-Hennessy, *The Portrait in the Renaissance* (New York: Bollingen Foundation, 1966), p. 3, although the importance of Flemish portraits for Italian portraits is later conceded.
7. Stylistic considerations date the Campin and the Rogier van der Weyden *Portrait of a Lady* (Staatliche Museen, Berlin) to the 1430s; the year 1439 is inscribed on Jan van Eyck's *Portrait of Margareta van Eyck* (Bruges, Groeningemuseum).
8. Notably by Patricia Simons, "Women in Frames: The Gaze, the Eye, the Profile in Renaissance Portraiture," *History Workshop* 25 (Spring 1988): 4–30; see also Alison Wright, *The Pollaiuolo Brothers. The Arts of Florence and Rome* (New Haven and London: Yale University Press, 2005), pp. 117–29.
9. Alessandra Macinghi negli Strozzi, *Selected Letters of Alessandra Strozzi*, trans. and intro. Heather Gregory (Berkeley and Los Angeles: University of California Press, 1997), letters of 1447 and 1465–66.
10. Letters of July 26, August 17, and September 13, 1465, in *Selected Letters*, pp. 148–151, 154–55, 156–61.
11. For more on these treatises on marriage and the family, see Ruth Kelso, *Doctrine for the Lady of the Renaissance* (Urbana: University of Illinois Press, 1956), pp. 38–35; see also Benjamin G. Kohl and Ronald G. Witt, *The Earthly Republic: Italian Humanists on Government and Society* (Manchester: Manchester University Press, 1978); G. Griffiths, J. Hankins, and D. Thompson, eds., *The Humanism of Leonardo Bruni* (Binghampton, NY: Medieval and Renaissance Texts and Studies, 1987), pp. 306–17; and Rudolph M. Bell, *How to Do It: Guides to Good Living for Renaissance Italians* (Chicago and London: University of Chicago Press, 1999), pp. 208–36.
12. Francesco Barbaro, *De re uxoria*, trans. A. Lollio, in *Prudentissimi et gravi documenti circa la elettion della moglie* (Venice: Giolito, 1548); excerpts in Kohl and Witt, *The Earthly Republic*, pp. 179–228.

13. Leon Battista Alberti, *The Family in Renaissance Florence*, ed. and trans. R. Neu Watkins (Columbus: University of South Carolina Press, 1969), Book II, pp. 114–20, on choosing a wife; Book III, pp. 207–29, on the training of the wife.
14. Notions of the "natural" character of women, derived from the Greek intellectual tradition of their Greek sources, Aristotle, Xenophon, and Plutarch, are stated in, for example, Alberti, *The Family in Renaissance Florence*, Book III, p. 207.
15. Vespasiano da Bisticci, *Le vite*, ed. A. Greco, 2 vols. (Florence: Istituto Palazzo Strozzi, 1970–76).
16. Juan Luis Vives's *Education of a Christian Woman* appeared in several Italian translations, starting with that by Pietro Lauro, as *De l'istituzione de la femina Christiana* (Venice: Vaugris, 1546); see also Lodovico Dolce, *Dialogo della institution delle donne* (Venice: Giolito, 1547, 1553).
17. Laura Pagnotta, *Bartolomeo Veneto: l'opera completa* (Florence: Centro Di, 1997), cat. 39, pp. 253–54.
18. Caroline P. Murphy, "Lavinia Fontana and Female Life Cycle Experience in Late Sixteenth-Century Bologna," in *Picturing Women in Renaissance and Baroque Italy*, ed. Geraldine A. Johnson and Sara F. Matthew Grieco (Cambridge: Cambridge University Press, 1997), pp. 113–19.
19. This is most strongly stated in Simons, "Women in Frames."
20. A.W.B. Randolph, "Performing the Bridal Body in Fifteenth-Century Florence," *Art History* 21 (June 1998): 182–200.
21. In a wedding of 1448, clothing for the bride took four years of work, involving five different professions. Evelyn Welch, *Shopping in the Renaissance* (New Haven and London: Yale University Press, 2005), p. 229; see also Roberta Orsi Landini and Mary Westerman Bulgarella, "Costumes of Fifteenth-Century Florentine Portraits of Women," in *Virtue and Beauty: Leonardo's "Ginevra de' Benci" and Renaissance Portraits of Women*, ed. David Alan Brown, exhibition catalogue, National Gallery, Washington, D.C., 2001–2 (Princeton: Princeton University Press, 2001), pp. 90–97.
22. Letters of July 26, 1465, and August 24, 1447, in *Selected Letters*, pp. 150–51, 30–31.
23. Letters of January 1, 1466, in *Selected Letters*, pp. 190–91.
24. As Vespasiano da Bisticci describes Alessandra de' Bardi, when she was still unmarried, dextrously and gracefully serving Emperor Sigismund and his retinue. See Vespasiano, *Le vite*, vol. 2, pp. 478–79; references to other such accounts appear in Judith Bryce, "Performing for Strangers: Women, Dance and Music in Quattrocento Florence," *Renaissance Quarterly* 54, no. 4 (2001): 1074–1107.
25. Illustrated in John Garton, *Grace and Splendour* (London: Harvey Miller, 2008), plate 10. Garton contextualizes some types of female portraits treated in this chapter. Several essays by Stanley Chojnacki deal with dowry inflation in Venice and its possible effects on family relationships and the position of women at an earlier period. See Stanley Chojnacki, *Women and Men in Renaissance Venice* (Baltimore and London: The Johns Hopkins University Press, 2000).
26. Argued by Jacqueline Marie Musacchio in Bayer, *Art and Love*, pp. 33–34.
27. See, especially, Gabrielle Langdon, *Medici Women: Portraits of Power, Love and Betrayal* (Toronto: University of Toronto Press, 2006), pp. 59–97.

28. Licinio's paintings of families, such as that at Hampton Court, apparently show members of the artisan classes, the classes to which he himself belonged.
29. A good northern example is Martin van Heemskerk's c. 1530 *Portrait of a Lady with a Spindle and Distaff*, in the Thyssen Museum, Madrid; illustration in Campbell, Falomir, Fletcher, Syson, eds., *Renaissance Faces*, no. 25, p. 131. Numerous examples of women spinning, or giving maternal care, can be found in seventeenth-century Dutch genre painting, as discussed in Wayne Franits, *Paragons of Virtue: Women and Domesticity in Seventeenth-Century Dutch Art* (Cambridge: Cambridge University Press, 1993).
30. I have argued in Mary Rogers, "An Ideal Wife in the Villa Maser: Veronese, the Barbaros and Renaissance Theorists of Marriage," *Renaissance Studies* 7, no. 4 (1993): 379–97, that the image of Marcantonio Barbaro's wife in the villa at Maser conveys her supervision of and maintenance of order in her household.
31. A useful overview of recent work on widows is by Allison Levy, in *Widowhood and Visual Culture in Early Modern Europe*, pp. 1–7.
32. See, especially, King, *Renaissance Women Patron*, pp. 129–99; and Caroline Valone, "Roman Matrons as Patrons: Various Views of the Cloister Wall," in *The Crannied Wall: Women Religion and the Arts in Early Modern Europe*, ed. Craig A. Monson (Ann Arbor: University of Michigan Press, 1992), pp. 49–73, esp. fig. 9.
33. Allison Levy, "Mourning, Gender and Portraiture in Early Modern Florence," in *Widowhood and Visual Culture*, pp. 211–31.
34. See Vespasiano, *Le vite*, vol. 2, pp. 490–99, on the conduct of the widowed Alessandra de' Bardi, or conduct treatises such as Vives's *De l'istituzione de la femina Christiana*, Book III, which is closely followed in Dolce's *Dialogo della institution delle donne*; Bell, *How to Do It*, pp. 258–78.
35. Levy, *Widowhood and Visual Culture*, pp. 225–26.
36. See the full discussion by Elizabeth Cropper in Brown, *Virtue and Beauty*, pp. 208–12.
37. For Italian Renaissance education, see Paul Grendler, *Schooling in Italy: Literacy and Learning, 1300–1600* (Baltimore: The Johns Hopkins University Press, 1989); and for women's education, see Mary Rogers and Paola Tinagli, *Women in Italy, 1350–1650* (Manchester: Manchester University Press, 2005), pp. 101–6.
38. Margaret King and Alfred Rabil Jr., *Her Immaculate Hand* (Binghampton, NY: Medieval and Renaissance Texts Society, 1983).
39. For English translation, see Griffiths, Hankins, and Thompson, eds., *The Humanism of Leonardo Bruni*, pp. 240–51.
40. Giovanni Boccaccio, *Famous Women*, ed. and trans. Virginia Brown (Cambridge, MA: Harvard University Press, 2001), pp. 156–58.
41. For Isabella d'Este's interest in emblems, see Giancarlo Malacarne, "Il Segno di Isabella: stemmi, motti, imprese," in *Isabella d'Este: la primadonna del Rinascimento*, ed. Daniele Bini (Modena: Il Bulino, 2001), pp. 185–201.
42. Conor Fahy, "The 'De Mulieribus admirandi' of Antonio Cornazzano," *La Bibliofilia* 52 (1960): 144–74; Vittorio Zaccaria, "La fortuna del 'De mulieribus claris' del Boccaccio nel secolo XV: Giovanni Sabbadino degli Arienti. Iacopo Filippo

Foresti e le loro biografie femminili (1490–1497)," in *Il Boccaccio nelle culture e literature nazionali*, ed. F. Mazzini (Florence: Olschki, 1978), pp. 519–45. Spanish adaptations of Boccaccio, of possible relevance to the Aragonese princesses of Naples who will be mentioned shortly, are briefly noted in Chrysa Damianaki, *I busti femminili di Francesco Laurana tra realtà e finzione* (Verona: Cierre, 2008), pp. 106–7.

43. Giovanni Sabadino degli Arienti, *Gynevera de le clare donne*, ed. C. Ricci and A. Bacchi della Lega (Bologna: Romagnoli-Dall'Acqua, 1888).
44. Giuseppe Betussi, *Libro de M. Giovanni Boccaccio delle donne illustri…* (Venice: de gl'Imperatori, 1558).
45. Sabadino, *Gynevera*, p. 339; see also King and Rabil Jr., *Her Immaculate Hand*, pp. 20–21, 44–48; and Bryce, "Performing for Strangers," p. 1074, for Ippolita's public oration in Florence.
46. Sabadino, *Gynevera*, pp. 265, 290–91.
47. Jacobs, in *Defining the Renaissance "Virtuosa,"* traces attempts to account for talented women within the framework of Renaissance notions of female capabilities, culminating in Torquato Tasso, *Discorso della virtù feminile, e donnesca* (1582), ed. Maria Luisi Doglio (Palermo: Sellerio, 1997).
48. See, in particular, W. R. Valentiner, "Laurana's Busts of Women,"*Art Quarterly* 5 (1942): 272–99; and, more recently, Damianaki, *I busti femminili di Francesco Laurana*.
49. For recent commentary on the bust of Beatrice, see Nancy Edwards in Bayer, *Art and Love*, no. 119, pp. 256–59, with bibliography. See also Langdon, *Medici Women*, pp. 117–20, on aristocratic betrothal portraits.
50. Damianaki, *I busti femminili di Francesco Laurana*, pp. 217–40, argues that the Berlin bust, whose head can still be examined carefully, is a nineteenth-century fake, but, in line with most scholars, sees the Frick bust as an authentic Laurana and a likeness of Ippolita Sforza, though one made posthumously, after her death in 1488. This dating is hard to accept, as the sitter looks much younger than her early forties.
51. Sabadino, *Gynevera*, pp. 336–52.
52. Sabadino, *Gynevera*, pp. 344–45.
53. Damianaki has pointed out that incised dress patterns were not a feature of Laurana's authentic busts.
54. Sabadino, *Gynevera*, pp. 288–312; Betussi, *Libro de M. Giovanni Boccaccio*, fol. 176v–178. See also Cecil H. Clough, "Daughters and Wives of the Montefeltro: Outstanding Bluestockings of the Quattrocento,"*Renaissance Studies* 10, no. 1 (1996): 31–55.
55. See Deborah Parker, *Bronzino: Renaissance Painter as Poet* (Cambridge: Cambridge University Press, 2000), pp. 96–104.
56. See Rogers and Tinagli, *Women in Italy*, pp. 317–18, for the two women's words on their hunger for knowledge.
57. For the self-portraits of Sofonisba Anguissola, see J. Woods-Marsden, *Renaissance Self-Portraiture: The Visual Construction of Identity and the Social Status of the Artist* (New Haven and London: Yale University Press, 1998), pp. 187–213; and

Mary D. Garrard, "Here's Looking at Me! Sophonisba Anguissola and the Problem of the Woman Artist,"*Renaissance Quarterly* 47 (1994): 556–622.
58. Virginia Cox, *Women's Writing in Italy, 1400–1650* (Baltimore: The Johns Hopkins University Press, 2008), esp. pp. 64–79.
59. See Woods-Marsden, *Renaissance Self-Portraiture*, p. 212, for illustrations.
60. Annibal Guasco, *Discourse to Lady Lavinia His Daughter* (1586), ed. and trans. Peggy Osborn (Chicago: University of Chicago Press, 2003), pp. 70–77.
61. The most detailed recent study is Charles Dempsey, *The Portrayal of Love: Botticelli's "Primavera" and Humanist Culture at the Time of Lorenzo the Magnificent* (Princeton: Princeton University Press, 1992); see also Elizabeth Cropper, "On Beautiful Women: Parmigianino, *Petrarchismo*, and the Vernacular Style," *Art Bulletin* 58, no. 3 (1976): 374–95; David Hemsoll, "Beauty as an Aesthetic Ideal in Late Fifteenth-Century Florence," in *Concepts of Beauty in Renaissance Art*, ed. Francis Ames-Lewis and Mary Rogers (Aldershot: Ashgate, 1998), pp. 66–76; and the essays and bibliographies in Brown, *Virtue and Beauty*.
62. Angelo Poliziano, *Poesie italiane*, ed. M. Luzi and S. Orlando (Milan: Rizzoli, 1976), pp. 53–55.
63. Eleonora Luciano in Brown, *Virtue and Beauty*, pp. 162–64; Mary D. Garrard, "Who Was Ginevra de' Benci? Leonardo's Portrait and Its Sitter Reconceptualised," *Artibus et historiae* 53 (2006): 23–56.
64. David Alan Brown in Brown, *Virtue and Beauty*, pp. 182–85.
65. "The utmost grace in the shadows and the lights is added to the faces of those who sit in the darkened doorways of their dwelling"; "In women and young girls there must be no actions where the legs are raised or too far apart, because that would indicate boldness and a general lack of shame." See Martin Kemp and Margaret Walker, eds. and trans., *Leonardo on Painting* (New Haven and London: Yale University Press, 1989), pp. 215, 152.
66. As, famously, by Aby Warburg, for which see E. H. Gombrich, *Aby Warburg: An Intellectual Biography* (Oxford: Phaidon, 1986), pp. 61–66, 105–27, 312. On the problem of movement in Renaissance art, see Sharon Fermor, "Movement and Gender in Sixteenth-Century Italian Painting," in *The Body Imaged: The Human Form and Visual Culture since the Renaissance*, ed. Kathleen Adler and Marcia Pointon (Cambridge: Cambridge University Press, 1993), pp. 129–45.
67. Pietro Bembo, *Gli Asolani*, in *Opere in volgare*, ed. Mario Marti (Florence: Sansoni, 1961), pp. 100–103.
68. Agnolo Firenzuola, *On the Beauty of Women* (1541), ed. Konrad Eisenbichler and Jaqueline Murray (Philadelphia: University of Pennsylvania Press, 1992); see also Cropper, "On Beautiful Women"; Mary Rogers, "The Decorum of Woman's Beauty: Trissino, Firenzuola, Luigini and Renaissance Representations of Women in Sixteenth-Century Art," *Renaissance Studies* 2, no. 1 (1988): 47–88.
69. Elizabeth Cropper, "The Beauty of Women: Problems in the Rhetoric of Renaissance Portraiture," in *Rewriting the Renaissance: The Discourses of Sexual Difference in Early Modern Europe*, ed. Margaret W. Ferguson, Maureen Quilligan, and Nancy J. Vickers (Chicago and London: University of Chicago Press, 1986), p. 190.

70. See Kirkham, *Bronzino*, pp. 98–104, for the triangular exchange between Battiferra, Bronzino, and Grazzini.
71. For texts referring to assumed names and to costume changes, see Rogers and Tinagli, *Women in Italy*, pp. 277–78.
72. For example, praise for the cultivated Imperia by Bandello, in Rogers and Tinagli, *Women in Italy*, pp. 279–80; see also Mary Rogers, "Fashioning Identities for the Renaissance Courtesan," in *Fashioning Identities in Renaissance Art*, ed. M. Rogers (Ashgate: Aldershot, 2000), pp. 91–103.

BIBLIOGRAPHY

Abbott, Mary. 1996. *Life Cycles in England 1560–1720: Cradle to Grave.* London: Routledge.
Adelman, Howard. 1999. "The Literacy of Jewish Women in Early Modern Italy." In *Women's Education in Early Modern Europe,* ed. Barbara J. Whitehead, 23–52. New York: Garland.
Ajmar-Wollheim, Marta, and Flora Dennis, eds. 2006. *At Home in Renaissance Italy.* London: Victoria and Albert Museum.
Alberti, Leon Battista. 1969. *The Family in Renaissance Florence [Della Famiglia],* trans. and intro. R. Neu Watkins. Columbia: University of South Carolina Press.
Allison, K. J. 1963. "An Elizabethan Village Census." *Bulletin of the Institute of Historical Research* 36 (93): 91–103.
Ames-Lewis, Francis, and Mary Rogers, eds. 1998. *Concepts of Beauty in Renaissance Art.* Aldershot: Ashgate.
Amussen, Susan D. 1985. "Gender, Family and the Social Order, 1560–1725." In *Order and Disorder in Early Modern England,* ed. Anthony Fletcher and John Stevenson. Cambridge: Cambridge University Press.
Anderson, Jaynie. 1997. *Giorgione: The Painter of "Poetic Brevity."* New York: Flammarion.
Andrewes, Lancelot. 1650. *Pattern of Catechistical Doctrine.* London.
Anglicus, Bartholomaeus. 1535. *De Proprietatibus Rerum.* London: Printed by Thomas Bertholet.
Anon. 1542. *A Glasse for Housholders, Wherin That They May Se, Both Howe to Rule Them Selfes & Ordre Their Housholde Verye Godly and Fruytfull.* London: Workshop of Richard Grafton.
Anon. 1690. *Aristotle's Master-Piece.* London.
Anon. 1764. *Aristotle's Book of Problems.* London.
Archer, Jane. 1999. "Women and Alchemy in Early Modern England." Ph.D. diss. University of Cambridge, Newnham College.

Ariès, Philippe. 1962. *Centuries of Childhood: A Social History of Family Life*, trans. Robert Baldick. New York: Alfred A. Knopf.

Askew, Anne. 1996. *The Examinations of Anne Askew*, ed. Elaine V. Beilin. Oxford: Oxford University Press.

Aughterson, Kate. 1995. *Renaissance Woman: Constructions of Femininity in England*. London: Routledge.

Bale, John. 1560. *Actes of Englysh Votaryes*. London.

Bale, John. 1547. *Image of Both Churches*.

Bamber, Linda. 1982. *Comic Women, Tragic Men: A Study of Gender and Genre in Shakespeare*. Stanford: Stanford University Press.

Barbaro, Francesco. 1548. *Prudentissimi et gravi documenti circa la elettion della moglie [De re uxoria]*. Venice: Giolito.

Barker, Francis. 1995. *The Tremulous Private Body: Essays on Subjection*. Ann Arbor: University of Michigan Press.

Battiferra degli Ammanati, Laura. 2006. *Laura Battiferra and Her Literary Circle*, ed. and trans. V. Kirkham. Chicago: University of Chicago Press.

Bayer, Andrea, ed. 2009. *Art and Love in Renaissance Italy*. New York: Metropolitan Museum.

Bayer, Penny. 2005. "Lady Margaret Clifford's Alchemical Receipt Book and the John Dee Circle." *Ambix* 52 (3): 271–84.

Beam, Aki C. L. 2006. "'Should I as Yet Call You Old?' Testing the Boundaries of Female Old Age in Early Modern England." In *Growing Old in Early Modern Europe: Cultural Representations*, ed. Erin Campbell, 95–116. Aldershot: Ashgate.

Beaumont, Francis, and John Fletcher. 1999. *The Maid's Tragedy*, ed. T. W. Craik. Manchester: Manchester University Press.

Becon, Thomas. 1552. *The Principles of Christian Religion*. London.

Behn, Aphra. 1995. *The Rover: The Rover and Other Plays*, ed. Jane Spencer. Oxford: Oxford University Press.

Beilin, Elaine V. 1990. *Redeeming Eve: Women Writers of the English Renaissance*. Princeton: Princeton University Press.

Bell, Rudolph M. 1999. *How to Do It: Guides to Good Living for Renaissance Italians*. Chicago: University of Chicago Press.

Bembo, Pietro. 1961. *Gli Asolani*. In *Opere in volgare*, ed. Mario Marti. Florence: Sansoni.

Benjamin, Walter. 1992. "The Work of Art in an Age of Mechanical Reproduction." In *Illuminations*, ed. Hannah Arendt, 211–44. London: Fontana.

Berry, Phillippa. 1989. *Of Chastity and Power: Elizabethan Literature and the Unmarried Queen*. New York: Routledge.

Betussi, Giuseppe. 1558. *Libro de M. Giovanni Boccaccio delle donne illustri...* Venice: de gl'Imperatori.

Bible. King James Version. Available at: http://www.latinvulgate.com/verse.aspx?t=1& b=17&c=2. Accessed December 16, 2010.

Bible. 1990. *The 1599 Geneva Bible*. Ozark, MO: L. L. Brown Publishing.

Bini, Daniele, ed. 2001. *Isabella d'Este: la prima Donna del Rinascimento*. Modena: Il Bulino.

Blamires, Alcuin, ed. 1992. *Woman Defamed and Woman Defended: An Anthology of Medieval Texts.* Oxford: Clarendon Press.

Boccaccio, Giovanni. 2001. *Famous Women,* ed. and trans. Virginia Brown. Cambridge and London: Harvard University Press.

Borthwick Institute of Historical Research [BIHR], CP.G.1521.

Botelho, Lynne. 2002. "Images of Old Age in Early Modern Cheap Print: Women, Witches, and the Poisonous Female Body." In *Power and Poverty: Old Age in the Pre-Industrial Past,* ed. Susannah R. Ottaway, L. A. Botelho, and Katharine Kittredge, 225–46. Westport, CT: Greenwood Press.

Bovilsky, Lara. 2003. "Black Beauties, White Devils: The English Italian in Milton and Webster." *ELH* 70 (3): 625–51.

Bowden, Caroline. 1999. "'For the Glory of God': A Study of the Education of English Catholic Women in Convents in Flanders and France in the First Half of the Seventeenth Century." *Paedagogica Historica* Supplementary Series 5: 78–95.

Brathwaite, Richard. 1631. *The English Gentlewoman, drawne out to the full body.* London.

Brathwaite, Richard. 1641. *The English Gentleman and The English Gentlewoman.* London.

Brauner, Sigrid Maria. 1989. "Frightened Shrews and Fearless Wives: The Concept of the Witch in Early Modern German Texts, 1487–1560." Ph.D. diss., University of California at Berkeley.

Briggs, Robin. 1996. *Witches and Neighbors: The Social and Cultural Context of European Witchcraft.* London: Harper Collins.

Brink, Jean R. 1980. *Female Scholars: A Tradition of Learned Women before 1800.* Montréal: Eden Press Women's Publications.

Broad, Jacqueline, and Karen Green. 2009. *A History of Women's Political Thought in Europe, 1400–1700.* Cambridge: Cambridge University Press.

Brown, David Alan. 1990. "Leonardo and the Ladies with an Ermine and Book." *Artibus et Historiae* 11: 47–61.

Brown, David Alan. 1998. *Leonardo da Vinci: Origins of a Genius.* New Haven, CT: Yale University Press.

Brown, David Alan, ed. 2001. *Virtue and Beauty: Leonardo's "Ginevra de' Benci" and Renaissance Portraits of Women.* Exhibition catalogue. National Gallery, Washington, D.C. 2001–2. Princeton: Princeton University Press.

Brumbaugh-Walter, Lynnea. 2003. "Selections from the Gesta Romanorum." In *Medieval Literature for Children,* ed. Daniel T. Kline, 33. New York and London: Routledge.

Bryce, Judith. 2001. "Performing for Strangers: Women, Dance and Music in Quattrocento Florence." *Renaissance Quarterly* 54 (4): 1074–1107.

Buckley, Thomas, and Alma Gottlieb. 1998. *Blood Magic: The Anthropology of Menstruation.* Berkeley: University of California Press.

Buffa, Paolo, ed. 1994. *Sofonisba Anguissola e le sue sorelle.* Exhibitions in Vienna and Washington, D.C., 1994–95. Milan: Leonardo.

Burckhardt, Jacob. 1904. *The Civilisation of the Renaissance in Italy,* trans. S.G.C. Middlemore. New York: MacMillan.

Burke, Peter. 1978. *Popular Culture in Early Modern Europe.* New York: Harper and Row.
Bynum, Carolyn Walker. 1991. *Fragmentation and Redemption: Essays on Gender and the Human Body in Medieval Religion.* New York: Zone Books.
Byrne, Muriel St. Clare, ed. 1983. *The Lisle Letters: An Abridgement.* Chicago: University of Chicago Press.
Campbell, Erin J. 2006. " 'Unenduring' Beauty: Gender and Old Age in Early Modern Art and Aesthetics." In *Growing Old in Early Modern Europe: Cultural Representations,* ed. Erin Campbell, 153–67. Aldershot: Ashgate.
Campbell, Lorne, Miguel Falomir, Jennifer Fletcher, and Luke Syson, eds. 2008. *Renaissance Faces. Van Eyck to Titian.* London: National Gallery Company.
Capp, Bernard. 2003. *When Gossips Meet: Women, Family, and Neighbourhood in Early Modern England.* Oxford: Oxford University Press.
Cary, Elizabeth. 1994. "The Lady Falkland, Her Life." In *The Tragedy of Mariam, The Fair Queen of Jewry,* ed. Barry Weller and Margaret Ferguson. Berkeley: University of California Press.
Castiglione, Baldassare. 1561. *The Book of the Courtier,* trans. Thomas Hoby. London.
Castiglione, Baldessar. 1959. *The Book of the Courtier,* trans. Charles Singleton. New York: Anchor Books.
Castiglione, Baldassar. 1981. *Il Libro del Cortegiano,* ed. Amedeo Quondam. Milan: Garzanti.
Castiglione, Baldassare. 1994. *The Book of the Courtier,* trans. Sir Thomas Hoby. London: J. M. Dent.
Cavanagh, Sheila T. 1994. *Wanton Eyes & Chaste Desires: Female Sexuality in The Faerie Queene.* Bloomington: Indiana University Press.
Caxton, William. 1971. *The Book of the Knight of the Tower,* ed. M. Y. Offord. Early English Text Society Supplementary Series 2. London: Oxford University Press.
Cheshire and Chester Archives and Local Studies Services. Consistory Court Deposition Books. EDC 2/4/50–53. *Katherine Dutton v. Robert Busshell.*
Chojnacka, Monica. 1998. "Women, Charity and Community in Early Modern Venice: The Casa delle Zitelle." *Renaissance Quarterly* 51 (1): 68–92.
Chojnacki, Stanley. 2000. *Women and Men in Renaissance Venice.* Baltimore: Johns Hopkins University Press.
Cholakian, Patricia, and Rouben Cholakian. 2006. *Marguerite de Navarre: Mother of the Renaissance.* New York: Columbia University Press.
Ciapelli, G., and P. Rubin. 2000. *Art, Memory and Family in Renaissance Florence.* Acts of the conference, Courtauld Istitute of Art, London, July 1996. Cambridge: Cambridge University Press.
Clark, Alice. 1919. *The Working Life of Women in the Seventeenth Century.* New York: George Routledge and Sons.
Clark, Stuart. 1997. *Thinking with Demons: The Idea of Witchcraft in Early Modern Europe.* Oxford: Oxford University Press.
Clarke, Danielle, ed. 2000. *Renaissance Women Poets.* New York: Penguin Classics.
Clarke, Danielle. 2013. *Language, Gender and Discourse, 1500–1700: Articulating the Feminine.* Aldershot: Ashgate.

Clarke, Danielle. Forthcoming. "Gender and the Inculcation of Virtue: The Book of Proverbs and Early Modern Exemplarity." In *Biblical Women and Early Modern Literary Culture,* ed. Victoria Brownlee and Laura Gallagher. Aldershot: Ashgate.

Clifford, Anne. 1990. *The Diaries of Lady Anne Clifford,* ed. D.J.H. Clifford. Phoenix Mill: Alan Sutton Publishing.

Clough, Cecil H. 1996. "Daughters and Wives of the Montefeltro: Outstanding Bluestockings of the Quattrocento." *Renaissance Studies* 10 (1): 31–55.

Comenius, John Amos. 1659. *Orbis Sensualium Pictus.* London: Printed for J. Kirton.

Cook, Harold J. 1986. *The Decline of the Old Medical regime in Stuart London.* Ithaca: Cornell University Press.

Coolahan, Marie-Louise. 2010. *Women, Writing, and Language in Early Modern Ireland.* Oxford University Press.

Cox, Virginia. 2008. *Women's Writing in Italy, 1400–1650.* Baltimore: The Johns Hopkins University Press.

Crawford, Katherine. 2000. "Catherine de Medicis and Performance of Political Motherhood." *Sixteenth Century Journal* 31: 643–673.

Crawford, Patricia. 1990. "The Construction and Experience of Maternity in Seventeenth-century England." In *Women as Mothers in Pre-Industrial England,* ed. Valerie Fildes, 3–38. London: Routledge.

Crawford, Patricia. 1996. *Women and Religion in Britain, 1500–1720.* London: Routledge.

Crawford, Patricia, and Laura Gowing, eds. 2000. *Women's Worlds in Seventeenth-Century England: A Sourcebook.* London: Routledge.

Crawford, Patricia, and Sara Mendelson. 1996. *Women in Early Modern England 1550–1720.* Oxford: Clarendon Press.

Cressy, David. 1997. *Birth, Marriage and Death: Ritual, Religion, and the Life-Cycle in Tudor and Stuart England.* Oxford: Oxford University Press.

Crooke, Helkiah. 1615. *Microcosmographia: A Description of the Body of Man.* London.

Crooke, Helkiah. 1618. *Microcosmographia.* London.

Cropper, Elizabeth. 1976. "On Beautiful Women: Parmigianino, Petrarchismo, and the Vernacular Style." *Art Bulletin* 58: 374–94.

Cropper, Elizabeth. 1986. "The Beauty of Women: Problems in the Rhetoric of Renaissance Portraiture." In *Rewriting the Renaissance: The Discourses of Sexual Difference in Renaissance Europe,* ed. M. W. Ferguson, M. Quilligan, and N. J. Vickers, 175–90. Chicago and London: University of Chicago Press.

Cruz, Anne, and Mihoko Suzuki. 2009. *The Rule of Women in Early Modern Europe.* Urbana: University of Illinois Press.

Culpeper, Nicholas. 1651. *A Directory for Midwives.* London.

Culpeper, Nicholas. 1656. *A Directory for Midwives: Or a Guide for Women in Their Conception.* 2nd ed. London.

Damaniaki, Chrysa. 2008. *I busti femminili di Francesco Laurana tra realità e finzione.* Verona: Cierre.

Darnton, Robert. 1985. *The Great Cat Massacre and Other Episodes in French Cultural History.* New York: Random House.

Davidson, Peter. 2002. "The *Theatrum* for the Entry of Claudia de' Medici and Federigo Ubaldo della Rovere into Urbino, 1621." In *Court Festivals of the European Renaissance: Art, Politics and Performance,* ed. J. R. Mulryne and Elizabeth Goldring, 331–34. Aldershot: Ashgate.

Davis, Natalie Zemon. 1965. *Society and Culture in Early Modern France.* Stanford, CA: Stanford University Press.

Daybell, James. 2006. *Women Letter-Writers in Tudor England.* Oxford: Oxford University Press.

Dean, Trevor, and K.J.P. Lowe. 1998. *Marriage in Italy, 1300–1650.* Cambridge: Cambridge University Press.

de Blegny, Nicholas. 1676. *New and Curious Observations Concerning the art of Curing the Venereal Disease,* trans. Walter Harris. London.

Dempsey, Charles. 1992. *The Portrayal of Love. Botticelli's "Primavera" and Humanist Culture at the Time of Lorenzo the Magnificent.* Princeton: Princeton University Press.

Dickens, A. G. 1964. *The English Reformation* London: B. T. Batsford.

Dixon, Annette, ed. 2002. *Women Who Ruled: Queens, Goddesses, Amazons in Renaissance and Baroque Art.* London: Merrell.

Dod, John, and Robert Cleaver. 1598. *A Godlie Forme of Householde Government.* London.

Dolan, Frances E. 1999. *Whores of Babylon: Catholicism, Gender and Seventeenth-Century Print Culture.* Notre Dame, IN: University of Notre Dame Press.

Dolce, Lodovico. 1547. *Dialogo della institution delle donne.* Venice: Giolito.

Donnison, Jean. 1977. *Midwives and Medical Men: A History of Inter-professional Rivalries and Women's Rights.* New York: Schocken Books.

Douglas, Mary. 1966. *Purity and Danger: An Analysis of Concepts of Pollution and Taboo.* New York: Praeger.

Dowd, Michelle M. 2009. *Women's Work in Early Modern English Literature and Culture.* New York: Palgrave.

Doyle, Daniel. 2000. "The Sinews of Hapsburg Governance in the Sixteenth Century: Mary of Hungary and Political Patronage." *Sixteenth Century Journal* 31: 349–60.

Dunton, John. 1696. *The Night-Walker: Or, Evening Rambles in search after Lewd Women.* London.

Dusinberre, Juliet. 1979. *Shakespeare and the Nature of Women.* London: MacMillan.

Dyboski, R., ed. 1907. *Songs, Carols and Other Miscellaneous Pieces from the Balliol MS. 354, Richard Hill's Commonplace Book.* Early English Text Society Extra Series 101. London: Kegan Paul, Trench, Trubner and Co.

Earenfight, Theresa, ed. 2005. *Queenship and Political Power in Medieval and Early Modern Spain.* Aldershot: Ashgate.

Eichberger, Dagmar, and Lisa Beaven. 1995. "Family Members and Political Allies: The Portrait Collection of Margaret of Austria." *Art Bulletin* 77: 225–48.

Elizabeth I. 2002. *Elizabeth I: The Collected Works,* ed. Leah Marcus, Janel Mueller, and Mary Beth Rose. Chicago: University of Chicago Press.

Erickson, Amy Louise. 1993. *Women and Property in Early Modern England*. New York: Routledge.

Ezell, Margaret J. M. 2009. "Afterword: Critical Distance." In *Early Modern Women and Transnational Communities of Letters*, ed. Julie D. Campbell and Anne R. Larsen. Aldershot: Ashgate.

Fahy, Conor. 1960. "The 'De Mulieribus admirandi' of Antonio Cornazzano." *La Bibliofilia* 52: 144–74.

Ferguson, Margaret, Maureen Quilligan, and Nancy Vickers, eds. 1986. *Rewriting the Renaissance: The Discourses of Sexual Difference in Early Modern Europe*. Chicago: University of Chicago Press.

Fermor, Sharon. 1993. "Movement and Gender in Sixteenth-Century Italian Painting." In *The Body Imaged: The Human Form and Visual Culture since the Renaissance*, ed. Kathleen Adler and Marcia Pointon, 129–45. Cambridge: Cambridge University Press.

Ferrand, James. 1640. *Erotomania or A Treatise discoursing of the essence, causes, symptoms, prognosticksm and cure of love....* Oxford.

Filmer, Robert. 1680. *Patriarcha, or the Natural Power of Kings*. London.

Finucane, Ronald C. 1997. *The Rescue of the Innocents: Endangered Children in Medieval Miracles*. Houndmills, Basingstoke: Macmillan.

Firenzuola, Agnolo. 1992. *On the Beauty of Women*, trans. and ed. Konrad Eisenbichler and Jacqueline Murray. Philadelphia: Philadelphia University Press.

Fissell, Mary E. 2004. *Vernacular Bodies: The Politics of Reproduction in Early Modern England*. Oxford: Oxford University Press.

Fissell, Mary Elisabeth. 2008. "Introduction: Women, Health, and Healing in Early Modern Europe." *Bulletin of the History of Medicine* 82 (1): 1–17.

Fletcher, Anthony. 1995. *Gender, Sex and Subordination in England, 1500–1800*. New Haven, CT: Yale University Press.

Flood, John. 2003. "A Source for the Depiction of Eve in the Early-Modern Period: Biblical Latin Epic of the Sixth and Seventh Centuries." In *Studies on Medieval and Early Modern Women: Pawns or Players?* ed. Christine Meek and Catherine Lawless, 18–19, 24–25. Dublin: Four Courts Press.

ffolliott, Sheila. 1986. "Catherine de' Medici as Artemisia: Figuring the Powerful Widow." In *Rewriting the Renaissance: The Discourses of Sexual Difference in Early Modern Europe*, ed. Margaret Ferguson, Maureen Quilligan, and Nancy Vickers, 227–41. Chicago: University of Chicago Press,

Fonte, Moderata. 1997. *The Worth of Women*, ed. and trans. Virginia Cox. Chicago: University of Chicago Press.

Fox, Adam. 2000. *Oral and Literate Culture in England, 1500–1700*. Oxford: Clarendon Press.

Foxe, John. [1556] 1973. "Christus Triumphans." In *Two Latin Comedies by John Foxe the Martyrologist*, ed. J. H. Smith. Ithaca, New York.

Franits, Wayne. 1993. *Paragons of Virtue: Women and Domesticity in Seventeenth-Century Dutch Art*. Cambridge: Cambridge University Press.

Freedberg, S. J. 1970. *Painting in Italy 1500 to 1600*. Harmondsworth: Penguin.

Froide, Amy. 2001. "Old Maids: The Lifecycle of Single Women in Early Modern England." In *Women and Ageing in British Society since 1500*, ed. Lynn Botelho and Pat Thane, 89–100. New York: Pearson.

Garrard, Mary D. 1994. "Here's Looking at Me! Sophonisba Anguissola and the Problem of the Woman Artist." *Renaissance Quarterly* 47: 556–622.

Garrard, Mary D. 2006. "Who Was Ginevra de' Benci? Leonardo's Portrait and Its Sitter Reconceptualised." *Artibus et historiae* 53: 23–56.

Garton, John. 2008. *Grace and Grandeur: The Portraiture of Paolo Veronese*. London: Harvey Miller.

Gataker, John. 1623. *A Good Wife Gods Gift: and, A Wife Indeed*.

Gavitt, Philip. 1990. *Charity and Children in Renaissance Florence: The Ospedale degli Innocenti, 1410–1536*. Ann Arbor: University of Michigan Press.

Goffen, Rona. 1997. *Titian's Women*. New Haven, CT: Yale University Press.

Goldberg, P.J.P. 2006. "Life and Death: The Ages of Man." In *A Social History of England, 1200–1500*, ed. Rosemary Horrox and Mark W. Ormrod. Cambridge: Cambridge University Press.

Goldberg, P.J.P. 2008. "Childhood and Gender in Later Medieval England." *Viator* 39 (1): 251–53.

Gombrich, E. H. 1986. *Aby Warburg: An Intellectual Biography*. Oxford: Phaidon.

Goodrick-Clarke, N., ed. 1991. *Paracelsus: Essential Readings* Berkeley: North Atlantic.

Gordon, Eleanor C. 1991. "Accidents among Medieval Children as Seen from the Miracles of Six English Saints and Martyrs." *Medical History* 35: 149.

Gosson, Stephen. 1582. *Plays Confuted in Five Actions*. London.

Gosynhill, Edward. 1560. *Scholehouse of women*.

Gouge, William. 1634. *Of Domesticall Duties: Eight Treatises*. 3rd ed. London.

Gough, Melinda. 1999. "'Her Filthy Feature Open Showne' in Ariosto, Spenser, and *Much Ado about Nothing*." *SEL: Studies in English Literature 1500–1900* 39 (1): 41–67.

Gowing, Laura. 1996. *Domestic Dangers: Women, Words and Sex in Early Modern London* Oxford: Clarendon Press.

Gray, Louise. 2002. "The Experience of Old Age in the Narratives of the Rural Poor in Early Modern Germany." In *Power and Poverty: Old Age in the Pre-Industrial Past*, ed. Susannah R. Ottaway, L. A. Botelho, and Katharine Kittredge, 111–13. Westport, CT: Greenwood Press.

Grendler, Paul F. 1989. *Schooling in Renaissance Italy: Literacy and Learning 1300–1600*. Baltimore: The Johns Hopkins University Press.

Griffiths, G., J. Hankins, and D. Thompson, eds. 1987. *The Humanism of Leonardo Bruni: Selected Texts*. Binghamton, NY: Medieval and Renaissance Texts and Studies.

Guasco, Annibal. [1586] 2003. *Discourse to Lady Lavinia his Daughter*, ed. and trans. Peggy Osborn. Chicago: University of Chicago Press.

Guillemeau, Jaques. 1612. *Child-birth, or The happy deliuerie of woman*. London.

Gundersheimer, Werner. 1980. "Eleonora of Aragon and the Court of Ferrara." In *Beyond Their Sex: Learned Women of the European Past*, ed. Patricia Labalme, 43–65. New York: New York University Press.

Gwilliam, Tassie. 1996. "Female Fraud: Counterfeit Maidenheads in the Eighteenth Century." *Journal of the History of Sexuality* 6 (4): 518–48.

Haas, Louis. 1998. *The Renaisance Man and His Children: Childbirth and Early Childhood in Florence, 1300–1600.* New York: St. Martin's Press.
Hanawalt, Barbara. 1986. *The Ties That Bound: Peasant Families in Medieval England.* New York: Oxford University Press.
Harkness, Deborah E. 2008. "A View from the Streets: Women and Medical Work in Elizabethan London." *Bulletin of Medical History* 82: 52–85.
Harris, Barbara J. 1990. "Women and Politics in early Tudor England." *Historical Journal* 33: 259–81.
Harris, Barbara. 2002. *English Aristocratic Women, 1450–1550: Marriage and Family, Property and Careers.* Oxford: Oxford University Press.
Healy, Margaret. 2001. *Fictions of Disease in Early Modern England: Bodies, Plagues and Politics.* Basingstoke: Palgrave.
Heffernan, Thomas J. 1988. *Sacred Biography: Saints and Their Biographers in the Middle Ages.* New York: Oxford University Press.
Hemsoll, David. 1998. "Beauty as an Aesthetic and Artistic Ideal in Late Fifteenth-Century Florence." In *Concepts of Beauty in Renaissance Art,* ed. Francis Ames-Lewis and Mary Rogers, 66–79. Aldershot: Ashgate.
Herlihy, David, and Christiane Klapisch-Zuber. 1985. *Tuscans and Their Families: A Study of the Florentine Catasto of 1427.* New Haven, CT: Yale University Press.
Herrick, Robert. 1891. "Delight in Disorder." In *Works of Robert Herrick.* Vol. 1, ed. Alfred Pollard, 32. London: Lawrence & Bullen.
Hickerson, Megan L. 2005. *Making Women Martyrs in Tudor England.* New York: Palgrave Macmillan.
Hoby, Lady Margaret. 2001. *The Private Life of an Elizabethan Lady: The Diary of Lady Margaret Hoby, 1599–1605,* ed. Joanna Moody. Stroud: Sutton Publishing.
"A Homily Against Excess of Apparel." 1998. In *Sexuality and Gender in the English Renaissance: An Annotated Edition of Contemporary Documents,* ed. Lloyd Davis, 16–24. New York: Garland Publishing.
"A Homily on the State of Matrimony." 1998. In *Sexuality and Gender in the English Renaissance: An Annotated Edition of Contemporary Documents,* ed. Lloyd Davis, 24–34. New York: Garland Publishing.
Hull, Suzanne. 1988. *Chaste, Silent, and Obedient, English Books for Women 1475–1640.* San Marino, CA: Huntington Library Press.
Hunt, Margaret. 1996. *The Middling Sort: Commerce, Gender, and the Family in England, 1680-1780.* Berkeley: University of California Press.
Hunter, Lynette. 1997. "Women and Domestic Medicine: Lady Experimenters 1570–1620." In *Women and Science, 1500–1700: Mothers and Sisters of the Royal Society,* ed. Lynette Hunter and Sarah Hutton. Stroud: Sutton Publishing.
Hurlburt, Holly S. 2006. *The Dogaressa of Venice, 1200–1500: Wife and Icon.* New York: Palgrave.
Hurlburt, Holly S. 2006. "Women, Gender and Rulership in Medieval Italy." *History Compass* 4: 528–35.
Hurlburt, Holly S. 2009. "Body of Empire: Caterina Corner in Venetian History and Iconography." *Early Modern Women: An Interdisciplinary Journal* 4: 61–99.

Hutchinson, Lucy. 1995. *Memoir of the Life of Colonel Hutchinson,* ed. N. H. Keeble. London: J. M. Dent.

Hutson, Lorna. 1994. *The Usurer's Daughter: Male Friendship and Fictions of Women in Sixteenth-Century England.* New York: Routledge.

Jacobs, Frederika H. 1997. *Defining the Renaissance "Virtuosa."* Cambridge: Cambridge University Press.

Jacquart, Danielle, and Claude Thomasset. 1988. *Sexuality and Medicine in the Middle Ages.* Cambridge: Polity Press.

James I. 1918. *The Political Works of James I,* ed. Charles McIlwain. Cambridge, MA: Harvard University Press.

Jansen, Sharon. 2002. *The Monstrous Regiment of Women: Female Rulers in Early Modern Europe.* New York: Palgrave.

Jansen, Sharon. 2008. *Debating Women, Politics and Power in Early Modern Europe.* New York: Palgrave.

Jewell, Helen M. 2007. *Women in Late Medieval and Reformation Europe, 1200–1500.* Houndmills, Basingstoke: Palgrave Macmillan.

Jones, Ann Rosalind, and Peter Stallybrass. 1991. "Fetishizing Gender: Constructing the Hermaphrodite in Renaissance Europe." In *Body Guards: The Cultural Politics of Gender Ambiguity,* ed. Julia Epstein and Kristina Staub, 80–111. New York: Routledge.

Jones, Ann, and Peter Stallybrass. 2000. *Renaissance Clothing and the Materials of Memory.* Cambridge: Cambridge University Press.

Joubert, Laurence. 1989. *Popular Errors,* ed. Gregory David de Rocher. Tuscaloosa: University of Alabama Press.

Jutte, Robert. 2008. *Contraception: A History.* Cambridge: Polity Press.

Kalas, Rayna. 2007. *Frame, Glass, Verse: The Technology of Poetic Invention in the English Renaissance.* Ithaca, NY: Cornell University Press.

Karant-Nunn, Susan C. 1998. "The Reformation of Women." In *Becoming Visible: Women in European History,* 3rd ed., ed. Renate Bridenthal, Susan Mosher Stuard and Merry E. Wiesner, 175–202. New York: Houghton Mifflin.

Karant Nunn, Susan. 1982. "Continuity and Change: Some Effects of the Reformation on the Women of Zwickau." *Sixteenth Century Journal* 13: 17–42.

Karant-Nunn, Susan. 2008. "The Masculinity of Martin Luther: Theory, Practicality and Humor." In *Masculinity in the Reformation Era,* ed. Scott H. Hendrix and Susan C. Karant-Nunn. Kirksville, MO: Truman State University Press.

Keller, Hildegard Elisabeth. 2002. "Paracelsus's Gendered Epistemology." In *Paracelsian Moments: Science, Medicine, and Astrology in Early Modern Europe,* ed. Gerhild Scholz Williams and Charles D. Gunnoe, 93–115. Kirksville, MO: Truman State University Press.

Kellwaye, Simon. 1593. *A Defensative against the Plague.* London.

Kelly, Joan. 1984. "Did Women Have a Renaissance?" In *Women, History and Theory: The Essays of Joan Kelly.* Chicago: University of Chicago Press.

Kelso, Ruth. 1956. *Doctrine for the Lady of the Renaissance.* Urbana: University of Illinois Press.

Kemp, Martin, and Margaret Walker, eds. and trans. 1989. *Leonardo on Painting.* New Haven, CT: Yale University Press.

Kerwin, William. 1997. "Where Have you Gone, Margaret Kennix? Seeking the Tradition of Healing Women in English Renaissance Drama." In *Women Healers and Physicians: Climbing a Long Hill,* ed. Lilian R. Furst, 93–111. Lexington, KY: University Press of Kentucky.

Kettering, Sharon. 1989. "Patronage Power of Early Modern French Noblewomen." *History Journal* 32: 817–41.

King, Catherine. 1998. *Renaissance Women Patrons: Wives and Widows in Italy c. 1300–1550.* Manchester: Manchester University Press.

King, John. 1614. *Vitis Palatina.*

King, Margaret. 2005. "Mothers of the Renaissance." In *Humanism, Venice and Women: Essays on the Italian Renaissance,* 211–37. Aldershot: Ashgate Variorum.

King, Margaret L. 1991. *Women of the Renaissance.* Chicago: University of Chicago Press.

King, Margaret L., and Albert Rabil Jr. 1983. *Her Immaculate Hand: Selected Works by and about the Women Humanists of Quattrocento Italy.* Binghamton, NY: Medieval and Renaissance Texts and Studies.

King, Margaret L., and Albert Rabil Jr., trans. and eds. 2000. *Her Immaculate Hand: Selected Works by and about the Women Humanists of Quattrocento Italy.* Asheville, NC: Pegasus Press.

Klapisch-Zuber, Christiane. 1985. *Women, Family and Ritual in Renaissance Italy.* Chicago: University of Chicago Press.

Koenigsberger, H. G., George L. Mosse, and G. Q. Bowler. 1968. *Europe in the Sixteenth Century.* 2nd ed. London: Longman.

Kohl, Benjamin, and Ronald G. Witt, eds. and trans. 1978. *The Earthly Republic: Italian Humanists on Government and Society.* Philadelphia: University of Pennsylvania Press.

Kramer, Heinrich, and Jacob Sprenger. 1971. *Malleus Maleficarum,* trans. Montague Summers. London: Anchor Books.

Labalme, Patricia H., ed. 1984. *Beyond Their Sex: Learned Women of the European Past.* New York: New York University Press.

Lamb, Mary Ellen. 2001. "Margaret Roper, the Humanist Political Project, and the Problem of Agency." In *Opening the Borders: Inclusivity in Early Modern Studies: Essays in Honor of James V. Mirollo,* ed. Peter C. Herman, 83–108. Newark: University of Delaware Press.

Lamb, Mary Ellen, and Karen Bamford, eds. 2008. *Oral Traditions and Gender in Early Modern Literary Texts.* Aldershot: Ashgate.

Langdon, Gabrielle. 2006. *Medici Women. Portraits of Power, Love and Betrayal from the Court of Duke Cosimo I.* Toronto: University of Toronto Press.

Lanyer, Amelia. 1993. *The Poems of Amelia Lanyer,* ed. Susanne Woods. New York: Oxford University Press.

Laqueur, Thomas. 1990. *Making Sex: Body and Gender from the Greeks to Freud.* Cambridge: Harvard University Press.

Larner, Christina. 1981. *Enemies of God: The Witch Hunt in Scotland.* London: Chatto and Windus.

Laurence, Anne. 1994. *Women in England: A Social History, 1500–1760.* London: Weidenfeld and Nicholson.

Lefeldt, Elizabeth. 2000. "Ruling Sexuality: Political Legitimacy of Isabel of Castile." *Renaissance Quarterly* 53: 31–56.
Lefeldt, Elizabeth. 2005. *Religious Women in Golden Age Spain.* Aldershot: Ashgate.
Lemnius, L. 1633. *The Touchstone of Complexions.* London.
Lemnius, Levinus. 1667. *A Discourse touching Generation.* London.
Leong, Elaine. 2008. "Making Medicines in the Early Modern Household." *Bulletin of Medical History* 82: 145–68.
Levack, Brian. "State-Building and Witch Hunting in Early Modern Europe." In *Witchcraft in Early Modern Europe: Studies in Culture and Belief,* ed. Jonathan Barry, Marianne Hester, and Gareth Roberts. Cambridge: Cambridge University Press, 1996.
Levin, Carole. 1994. *The Heart and Stomach of a King: Elizabeth I and the Politics of Sex and Power.* Philadelphia: University of Pennsylvania Press.
Levin, Carole. 2000. "St. Frideswide and St. Uncumber: Changing Images of Female Saints in England." In *Women, Writing, and the Reproduction of Culture in Tudor and Stuart England,* ed. Mary Elizabeth Burke, Jane Donawerth, Linda L. Love, and Karen Nelson, 223–37. Syracuse: University of Syracuse Press.
Levin, Carole, and Patricia A. Sullivan, eds. 1995. *Political Rhetoric, Power, and Renaissance Women.* Albany: State University of New York Press.
Levin, Carole, and Robert Bucholz, eds. 2009. *Queens and Power in Medieval and Early Modern England.* Lincoln: University of Nebraska Press.
Levine, Laura. 1994. *Men in Women's Clothing: Anti-theatricality and effeminization 1579–1642.* Cambridge: Cambridge University Press.
Levy, Alison, ed. 2003. *Widowhood and Visual Culture in Early Modern Europe.* Aldershot: Ashgate.
Liss, Peggy. 2004. *Isabel the Queen: Life and Times.* Philadelphia: University of Pennsylvania Press.
MacDonald, Deanna. 2002. "Collecting a New World: The Ethnographic Collections of Margaret of Austria." *Sixteenth Century Journal* 33: 649–63.
Maclean, Ian. 1980. *The Renaissance Notion of Woman: A Study in the Fortunes of Scholasticism and Medical Science in European Intellectual Life.* Cambridge: Cambridge University Press.
Magnusson, Lynne. 2011. "Imagining a National Church: Election and Education in the Works of Anne Cooke Bacon." In *The Intellectual Culture of Puritan Women, 1558–1680,* ed. Johanna Harris and Elizabeth Scott-Baumann, 42–56. New York: Palgrave.
Malacarne, Giancarlo. 2001. "Il Segno di Isabella: stemmi, motti, imprese." In *Isabella d'Ete: la primadonna del Rinacimento,* ed. Daniele Bini, 185–201. Modena: Il Bulino.
Manley, Lawrence. 2005. *Literature and Culture in Early Modern London.* Cambridge University Press.
Mann, Jenny C. 2006. "How to Look at a Hermaphrodite in Early Modern England." *SEL: Studies in English Literature 1500–1900* 46 (1): 67–91.
Mann, N., and L. Syson. 1998. *The Image of the Individual: Portraits in the Renaissance.* London: British Museum.

Marty, Martin. 2004. *Martin Luther.* New York: The Penguin Group.
Mason, Margaret J. "Nuns and Vocations of the Unpublished Jerningham Letters: Charlotte Bedingfield, Augustinian Canoness 1802–1876, Louisa Jerningham, Franciscan Abbess 1808–1893, and Clementina Jerningham, Marquise de Ripert-Monclar 1810–1864." *Recusant History* 21 (1993): 503–55.
Massinger, Philip. 1848. *The Renegado. The Dramatic Works of Massinger and Ford.* London: Edward Moxon.
Maus, Katherine Eisaman. 1993. "A Womb of His Own: Male Renaissance Poets in the Female Body." In *Sexuality and Gender in Early Modern Europe: Institutions, Texts, Images,* ed. James Grantham Turner, 266–88. Cambridge: Cambridge University Press.
McIver, Katherine. 2006. *Women, Art, and Architecture in Northern Italy, 1520–1850.* Aldershot: Ashgate.
McKee, Francis. 1998. "The Paracelsian Kitchen." In *Paracelsus: The Man and His Reputation, His Ideas and their Transformation,* ed. Ole Peter Grell, 283–308. Leiden: Brill.
McNeil, Fiona. 2007. *Poor Women in Shakespeare.* Cambridge: Cambridge University Press.
Medioli, Francesca. 2000. "An Unequal Law: The Enforcement of *Clausura* before and after the Council of Trent." In *Women in Renaissance and Early Modern Europe,* ed. Christine Meek. Dublin: Four Courts Press.
Mendelson, Sara, and Patricia Crawford. 1998. *Women in Early Modern England 1550–1720.* New York: Oxford University Press.
Middleton, Thomas, and Thomas Dekker. 1997. *The Roaring Girl,* ed. Elizabeth Cook. London: A & C Black.
Middleton, Thomas, and Thomas Dekker. 1999. *The Roaring Girl,* ed. Paul Mulholland. New York: Palgrave.
Milbin, Colin. 2004. "Syphilis in Faerie Land: Edmund Spenser and the Syphilography of Elizabethan England." *Criticism* 46 (4): 597–632.
Milton, John. [1667] 2005. *Paradise Lost,* ed. Gordon Teskey. New York: W. W. Norton.
Monson, Craig A. 1992. *The Crannied Wall. Women, Religion and the Arts in Early Modern Europe.* Ann Arbor: University of Michigan Press.
Monter, William. 1999. "Witch Trials in Continental Europe: 1560–1660." In *Witchcraft and Magic in Europe: The Period of the Witch Trials,* ed. Bengt Ankarloo and Stuart Clark, vol. 4. Philadelphia: University of Pennsylvania Press.
Moryson, Fynes. [1903] 1967. *Shakespeare's Europe: A Survey of the Conditions of Europe at the End of the Sixteenth Century Being unpublished chapters of Fynes Moryson's Itinerary 1617,* intro. and ed. Charles Hughes. New York: Benjamin Bloom.
Moryson, Fynes. 1908. *The Itinerary of Fynes Moryson.* Vol. 4. Glasgow: Hames MacLehose and Sons.
Munday, Anthony. 1586. *A Second and Third Blast of Retrait from Plaies and Theaters.* London.
Murphy, Caroline P. 1997. "Lavinia Fontana and Female Life Cycle Experience in Late Sixteenth-Century Bologna." In *Picturing Women in Renaissance and Baroque*

Italy, ed. Geraldine A. Johnson and Sara F. Matthew Grieco, 113–38. Cambridge: Cambridge University Press.

Murphy, Caroline P. 2003. *Lavinia Fontana: A Painter and Her Patrons in Sixteenth-Century Bologna*. New Haven, CT: Yale University Press.

Musacchio, Jacqueline Marie. 1999. *The Art and Ritual of Childbirth in Renaissance Italy*. New Haven, CT: Yale University Press.

Musacchio, Jacqueline Marie. 2009. "Wives, Lovers and Art in Italian Renaissance Courts." In *Art and Love in Renaissance Italy*, ed. Andrea Bayer, 29–41. New York: Metropolitan Museum.

Nelson, Jonathan, ed. 2000. *Suor Plautilla Nelli 1523–1588: The First Woman Painter of Florence*. Proceedings of Symposium, Florence-Fiesole. May 27, 1998. Fiesole: Cadmo.

Nenno, Nancy P. 1997. "Between Magic and Medicine: Medieval Images of the Woman Healer." In *Women Healers and Physicians: Climbing a Long Hill*, ed. Lilian R. Furst, 43–64. Lexington, KY: University Press of Kentucky.

Nichols, John Gough, ed. 1848. *The Diary of Henry Machyn, Citizen and Merchant-Taylor of London, from A.D. 1550 to A.D. 1563*. Camden Society 42. London: Camden Society.

Oldys, Alexander. 1683. *The London Jilt: Or, The Politic Whore*. London.

Orlin, Lena Cowen. 2008. *Locating Privacy in Tudor London*. Oxford: Oxford University Press.

Orme, Nicholas. 2001. *Medieval Children*. New Haven, CT: Yale University Press.

Orsi Landini, Roberta, and Mary Westerman Bulgarella. 2001. "Costumes of Fifteenth-Century Florentine Portraits of Women." In *Virtue and Beauty: Leonardo's "Ginevra de' Benci" and Renaissance Portraits of Women*, ed. David Alan Brown, 90–97. Exhibition catalogue. National Gallery, Washington, D.C. 2001–2002. Princeton: Princeton University Press.

Overbury, Thomas. 1622. *His Wife, with Additions of New Characters*. London: Laurence Lisle.

Owen Hughes, Diane. 1986. "Representing the Family: Portraits and Purposes in Early Modern Italy." *Journal of Interdisciplinary History* 17: 7–38.

Ozment, Steven. 1983. *When Fathers Ruled: Family Life in Reformation Europe*. Cambridge, MA: Harvard University Press.

Pagnotta, Laura. 1997. *Bartolomeo Veneto: l'opera completa*. Florence: Centro Di.

Pallavicino, Ferrante. 1683. *The Whores Rhetorick*. London.

Panizza, Letizia, ed. 2000. *Women in Italian Renaissance Culture and Society*. Oxford: Legenda.

Paracelsus: Selected Writings. 1979. Ed. Jolane Jacobi. Princeton: Princeton University Press.

Pare, Ambroise. 1634. *The Works of that Famous Chirugeon Ambrose Parey*, trans. Thomas Johnson. London.

Parish, Helen L. 2000. *Clerical Marriage and the English Reformation: Precedent, Policy, Practice*. Aldershot: Ashgate.

Parish, Helen L. 2010. *Clerical Celibacy in the West: c. 1100–1700*. Burlington, VT: Ashgate.

Parker, Deborah. 2000. *Bronzino: Renaissance Painter as Poet.* Cambridge: Cambridge University Press.
Parker, Holt T. 1997. "Women Doctors in Greece, Rome and the Byzantine Empire." In *Women Healers and Physicians: Climbing a Long Hill,* ed. Lilian R. Furst, 131–51. Lexington, KY: University Press of Kentucky.
Parker, Patricia. 1993. "*Othello* and *Hamlet:* Dilation, Spying, and the 'Secret Place' of Women." *Representations* 44: 60–95.
Paster, Gail Kern. 1993. *The Body Embarrassed: Drama and the Disciplines of Shame in Early Modern England.* Ithaca, NY: Cornell University Press.
Paster, Gail Kern. 1998. "The Unbearable Coldness of Being: Women's Imperfection and the Humoral Economy." *English Literary Renaissance* 28: 416–40.
Pearson, Andrea, ed. 2008. *Women and Portraits in Early Modern Europe: Gender, Agency, Identity.* Aldershot: Ashgate.
Peirce, Leslie. 1993. *The Imperial Harem: Women and Sovereignty in the Ottoman Empire.* New York: Oxford University Press.
Pelling, Margaret. 1997. "Thoroughly Resented: Older Women and the Medical Role in Early Modern London." In *Women and Science, 1500–1700: Mothers and Sisters of the Royal Society,* ed. Lynette Hunter and Sarah Hutton. Stroud: Sutton Publishing.
Pelling, Margaret, and Charles Webster. 1979. "Medical Practitioners." In *Health, Medicine and Mortality in the Sixteenth Century,* ed. Charles Webster. London: Cambridge.
Perlingieri, Ilya Sandra. 1992. *Sophonisba Anguissola: The First Great Woman Artist of the Renaissance.* New York: Rizzoli International Publications.
Perry, Mary Elizabeth. 1990. *Gender and Disorder in Early Modern Seville.* Princeton, NJ: Princeton University Press.
Peters, Henriette. 1994. *Mary Ward: A World in Contemplation.* Leominster, UK: Gracewing.
Phillips, Kim M. 1999. "Maidenhood as the Perfect Age of Woman's Life." In *Young Medieval Women,* ed. Katherine J. Lewis, Noel James Menuge, and Kim M. Phillips, 1–24. New York: St. Martin's Press.
Pisan, Christine de. 1982. *The Book of the City of Ladies,* trans. Earl Jeffrey Richards. New York: Persea Books.
Pisan, Christine de. 1985. *The Treasure of the City of Ladies,* trans. Sarah Lawson. London: Penguin.
Poliziano, Angelo. 1976. *Poesie italiane,* ed. Mario Luzi and Saverio Orlando. Milan: Rizzoli.
Pollock, Linda. 1983. *Forgotten Children: Parent-Child Relations from 1500 to 1900.* Cambridge: Cambridge University Press.
Pope-Hennessy, J. 1966. *The Portrait in the Renaissance.* New York: Bollingen Foundation.
Pound, John, ed. 1971. *The Norwich Census of the Poor, 1570.* Norfolk: Norfolk Record Society, XL.
Pritchard, Will. 2000. "Masks and Faces: Female Legibility in the Restoration Era." *Eighteenth-Century Life* 24 (3): 31–52.
Raber, Karen. 2001. "Chains of Pearls: Gender, Property, Identity." In *Ornamentalism: The Art of Renaissance Accessories,* ed. Bella Mirabella, 159–81. Ann Arbor: University of Michigan Press.

Rackin, Phyllis. 1994. "Foreign Country: The Place of Women and Sexuality in Shakespeare's Historical World." In *Enclosure Acts: Sexuality, Property, and Culture in Early Modern England,* ed. Richard Burt and John Michael Archer, 68–95. Ithaca: Cornell University Press.

Radke, Gary. 2001. "Nuns and their Art: The Case of San Zaccaria in Renaissance Venice." *Renaissance Quarterly* 54: 430–59.

Randolph, A.W.B. 1998. "Performing the Bridal Body in Fifteenth-Century Florence." *Art History* 21 (June): 182–200.

Raynold, Thomas. 1545. *The byrth of mankynde, otherwise named the womans booke.* London.

Reiss, Sheryl E., and David G. Wilkins, eds. 2001. *Beyond Isabella: Secular Women Patrons of Art in Early Renaissance Italy.* Kirksville, Missouri: Truman State University Press.

Rich, Barnabe. 1613. *The Excellency of good women.* London.

Rich, Barnbe. 1616. *My Ladies Looking Glasse.* London.

Riches, Samantha J. E. 2003. "'Hyr wombe insaciate': The Iconography of the Feminised Monster." In *Studies on Medieval and Early Modern Women: Pawns or Players?* ed. Christine Meek and Catherine Lawless, 180–82. Dublin: Four Courts Press.

Riddle, John. 1992. *Contraception and Abortion from the Ancient World to the Renaissance.* Cambridge, MA: Harvard University Press.

Roberts, Alexander. [1616] 2005. *A Treatise of Witchcraft,* ed. and pub. Project Gutenberg. Available at: http://infomotions.com/etexts/gutenberg/dirs/1/7/2/0/17209/17209.htm. Accessed October 3, 2010.

Roeslin, Eucharius. 1540. *The Byrth of Mankynde, newly translated out of Laten into Englisshe by* Thomas Raynalde. London.

Rogers, Mary. 1988. "The Decorum of Woman's Beauty Trissino, Firenzuola, Luigini and the Representation of Women in Sixteenth-Century Painting." *Renaissance Studies* 2 (1): 47–88.

Rogers, Mary. 1993. "An Ideal Wife in the Villa Maser: Veronese, the Barbaros and Renaissance Theorists of Marriage." *Renaissance Studies* 7 (4): 379–97.

Rogers, Mary. 2000. "Fashioning Identities for the Renaissance Courtesan." In *Fashioning Identities in Renaissance Art,* ed. M. Rogers, 91–103. Aldershot: Ashgate.

Rogers, Mary, and Paola Tinagli. 2005. *Women in Italy, 1350–1650.* Manchester: Manchester University Press.

Roper, Lyndal. 1989. *The Holy Household: Women and Morals in Reformation Augsburg.* Oxford: Clarendon Press.

Roper, Lyndal. 1991. "Witchcraft and Fantasy in Early Modern Germany." *History Workshop Journal* 32: 19–43.

Roper, Lyndal. 1994. *Oedipus and the Devil: Witchcraft, Sexuality and Religion in Early Modern Europe.* London: Routledge.

Rosenthal, Margaret. 1992. *The Honest Courtesan: Veronica Franco, Citizen and Writer in Sixteenth-Century Venice.* Chicago: University of Chicago Press.

Ross, Alexander. 1651. *Arcana Microcosmi or The Hidden Secrets of Man's Body Disclosed.* London.

Sabadino degli Arienti, Joanne. 1888. *Gynevera de le clare donne,* ed. C. Ricci and A. Bacchi della Lega. Bologna: Romagnoli-Dall'Acqua.

Sadler, John. 1636. *The Sicke Womans Private Looking-Glasse.* London.

Salter, Thomas. 1579. *A Mirrhor mete for all Mothers, Matrones, and Maidens.* London.

Sanders, Eve Rachele. 1998. *Gender and Literacy on Stage in Early Modern England.* Cambridge: Cambridge University Press.

San Juan, Rose Marie. 1991. "The Court Lady's Dilemna: Isabella D'Este and Art Collecting in the Renaissance." *Oxford Art Journal* 14: 67–78.

Schleiner, Winfried. 1994. "Infection and Cure through Women: Renaissance Constructions of Syphilis." *Journal of Medieval and Renaissance Studies* 24: 499–517.

Scholz, Susanne. 2000. *Body Narratives: Writing the Nation and Fashioning the Subject in Early Modern England.* London: MacMillan Press.

Scot, Reginald. 1584. *The discoverie of witchcraft.* London.

Sears, Elizabeth. 1986. *The Ages of Man: Medieval Interpretations of the Life Cycle.* Princeton: Princeton University Press.

Securis, John. 1566. *A Detection and Querimonie of the daily enormities and abuses committed in physick.* London.

Shakespeare, William. 1974. *The Riverside Shakespeare,* ed. G. Blakemore Evans. Boston: Houghton Mifflin.

Shakespeare, William. 1988. *The Complete Works, Compact Edition.* Oxford: Oxford University Press.

Shakespeare, William. 2004. *The Complete Works,* ed. David Bevington. 5th ed. New York: Pearson.

Sharp, Jane. 1671. *The Midwives Book: Or the Whole Art of Midwifery Discovered.* London.

Siena, Kevin P. 1998. "Pollution, Promiscuity, and the Pox: English Venereology and the Early Modern Medical Discourse on Social and Sexual Danger." *Journal of the History of Sexuality* 8 (4): 553–74.

Simons, Patricia. 1988. "Women in Frames: The Gaze, the Eye, the Profile in Renaissance Portraiture." *History Workshop* 25 (Spring): 4–30.

Smith, Lesley, and Jane H. M. Taylor, eds. 1997. *Women and the Book: Assessing the Visual Evidence.* London: The British Library.

Snook, Edith. 2005. *Women, Reading, and the Cultural Politics of Early Modern England.* Aldershot: Ashgate.

Solomon, Michael. 1997. "Women Healers and the Power to Disease in Late Medieval Spain." In *Women Healers and Physicians: Climbing a Long Hill,* ed. Lilian R. Furst, 79–93. Kentucky: University Press of Kentucky.

Spenser, Edmund. 1978. *The Faerie Queene,* ed. Thomas P. Roche Jr. New York: Penguin Books.

Stallybrass, Peter. 1986. "Patriarchal Territories: The Body Enclosed." In *Rewriting the Renaissance: The Discourses of Sexual Difference in Early Modern England,* ed. Margaret W. Ferguson, Maureen Quilligan, and Nancy J. Vickers, 123–42. Chicago: University of Chicago Press.

Stauffer, Richard. 1978. *Dieu, la création et la Providence dans la predication de Calvin.* Bern: Peter Lang.

Stevenson, Jane. 1998. "Women and Classical Education in the Early Modern Period." In *Pedagogy and Power: Rhetorics of Classical Learning,* ed. Yun Lee Too and Niall Livingstone, 83–109. New York: Cambridge University Press.

Stewart, Alan. 2000. "The Voices of Anne Cooke, Lady Anne and Lady Bacon." In *"This Double Voice": Gendered Writing in Early Modern England,* ed. Danielle Clarke and Elizabeth Clarke, 88–102. New York: Macmillan.

Stjerna, Kirsi. 2009. *Women and the Reformation.* Malden, MA: Blackwell Publishing.

Stock, Phyllis. 1978. *Better Than Rubies: A History of Women's Education.* New York: Putnam.

Strocchia, Sharon T. 1999. "Learning the Virtues: Convent Schools and Female Culture in Renaissance Florence." In *Women's Education in Early Modern Europe,* ed. Barbara J. Whitehead, 3–46. New York: Garland.

Strocchia, Sharon. 2009. *Nuns and Nunneries in Renaissance Florence.* Baltimore: Johns Hopkins University Press.

Strozzi, Alessandra Macinghi. 1997. *Selected Letters of Alessandra Strozzi,* ed. Heather Gregory. Berkeley: University of California Press.

Stubbes, Philip. 1595. *The Anatomie of Abuses.* London.

Swain, Elisabeth. 1986. "'My Excellent and Most Singular Lord': Marriage in a Noble Family of Fifteenth-Century Italy." *Journal of Medieval and Renaissance Studies* 16: 171–95.

Sweet, Victoria. 1999. "Hildegard of Bingen and the Greening of Medieval Medicine." *Bulletin of the History of Medicine* 73 (3): 381–403.

Swetnam, Joseph. 1615. *The Arraignment of Lewde, Idle, Forward, and Unconstant Women.* London.

"Syphilis." 1994. *Journal of Medieval and Renaissance Studies* 24: 499–517.

Taylor, John. 1625. "A Common Whore with All These Graces Grac'd." London.

Teague, Frances N. 1998. *Bathsua Makin, Woman of Learning.* Lewisburg, PA: Bucknell University Press.

T. E. 1632. *The Lawes Resolution of Womens Rights.* London.

Tertullian. *On the Apparel of Women,* trans. Rev. S. Thelwall.

Thomas, Anabel. 2003. *Art and Piety in the Female Religious Communities of Renaissance Italy: Iconography, Space, and the Religious Woman's Perspective.* Cambridge: Cambridge University Press.

Thompson, John Lee. 1992. *John Calvin and the Daughters of Sarah: Women in Regular and Exceptional Roles in the Exegesis of Calvin, His Predecessors, and His Contemporaries.* Geneva: Librairie Droz S. A.

Tilney, Edmund. 1992. *The Flower of Friendship: A Renaissance Dialogue Contesting Marriage,* ed. Valerie Wayne. Ithaca, NY: Cornell University Press.

Tomas, Natalie. 2003. *Medici Women: Gender and Power in Renaissance Florence.* Aldershot: Ashgate.

Trevelyan, G. E. 1904. *England under the Stuarts.* London: Methuen.

Tricomi, Albert. 1996. *Reading Tudor-Stuart Texts Through Cultural Historicism.* Gainesville: University Press of Florida.

Tuke, Thomas. 1616. *A Discourse Against Painting and Tincturing of Women.* London.

Tusser, Thomas. 1585. *Fiue Hundreth Pointes of Good Husbandrie.* London.

Underdown, D. E. 1985. "The Taming of the Scold: The Enforcement of Patriarchal Authority in Early Modern England." In *Order and Disorder in Early Modern England,* ed. Anthony Fletcher and John Stevenson. Cambridge: Cambridge University Press.

Valentiner, W. R. 1942. "Laurana's Busts of Women." *Art Quarterly* 5: 272–92.

Valone, Caroline. 1992. "Roman Matrons as Patrons: Various Views of the Cloister Wall." In *The Crannied Wall: Women Religion and the Arts in Early Modern Europe,* ed. Craig A. Monson, 49–73. Ann Arbor: University of Michigan Press.

Venereal Disease. 1676. Trans. Walter Harris. London.

Vespasiano da Bisticci. 1970–76. *Le vite,* ed. A. Greco. 2 vols. Florence: Istituto Palazzo Strozzi.

Vives, Juan Luis. 1529? *A very frutefull and pleasant boke Called the Instruction of a Christen Woman,* trans. Richard Hyrde. London.

Vives, Juan Luis. 1546. *De l'istituzione de la femina Christiana,* trans. Pietro Lauro. Venice: Vaugris.

Vives, Juan Luis. 1585. *A very frutful and pleasant boke called the Instruction of a christen woman, made fyrst in latyne, by the right famous clerke mayster Lewes Viues, and tourned out of latyne into Englishe by Rycharde Hyrde.* London.

Vives, Juan Luis. 2000. *Education of a Christian Woman: A Sixteenth Century Manual,* ed. Charles Fantazzi. Chicago: University of Chicago Press.

von Hutten, Ulrich. 1540. *Of the Wood Called Guaiacum, that Healeth the Frenche Pockes,* trans. Thomas Paynel. London.

Walker, Julia M. 1998. "Bones of Contention: Posthumous Images of Elizabeth and Stuart Politics." In *Dissing Elizabeth: Negative Representations of Gloriana,* ed. Julia M. Walker, 253–76. Durham, NC: Duke University Press.

Wall, Wendy. 2002. *Staging Domesticity: Household Work and English Identity in Early Modern Drama.* Cambridge: Cambridge University Press.

Walsh, James, S. J. 1985. *Till God Will: Mary Ward through Her Writings,* ed. M. Emmanuel Orchard. London: Darton, Longman and Todd.

Warner, Marina. 1983. *Alone of All Her Sex.* New York: Vintage Books.

Warnicke, Retha M. 1983. *Women of the English Renaissance and Reformation.* Westport, CT: Greenwood Press.

Watson, Foster, ed. 1912. *Vives and the Renascence Education of Women.* New York: Longmans, Green.

Webb, John, ed. 1966. *Poor Relief in Elizabethan Ipswich.* Ipswich: Suffolk Record Society 9.

Webster, John. 1998. *The White Devil,* ed. Christina Luckyj. London: A & C Black.

Welch, Evelyn. 2000. "Women as Patrons and Clients in the Courts of Quattrocento Italy." In *Women in Italian Renaissance Culture and Society,* ed. Letizia Panizza, 18–34. Oxford: Legenda.

Welch, Evelyn. 2005. *Shopping in the Renaissance. Consumer Cultures in Italy 1400–1600.* New Haven, CT: Yale University Press.

Wetter, M. 1999. Immolate. In *Mary Ward: In Her Own Words.* Rome: Istituto Beata Vergine Maria.

Whitehead, Barbara J., ed. 1999. *Women's Education in Early Modern Europe: A History, 1500–1800.* New York: Garland.

Whitney, Isabella. 1573. *A Sweet Nosgay, or Pleasant Posy* London: R. Jones.
Wiesner, Merry. 1986. *Working Women in Renaissance Germany.* New Brunswick, NJ: Rutgers University Press.
Wiesner, Merry E. 1990. "Luther and Women: The Death of Two Mary's." In *Feminist Theology: A Reader,* ed. Anne Loades, 126–27. London: Society for the Promotion of Christian Knowledge.
Wiesner, Merry E. 1998. *Gender, Church and State in Early Modern Germany: Essays.* London: Longman.
Wiesner, Merry E. 2000. *Women and Gender in Early Modern Europe.* 2nd ed. Cambridge: Cambridge University Press.
Wiesner-Hanks, Marry. 2006. "Women, Gender and Sexuality." In *Palgrave Advances: The European Reformations,* ed. Alec Ryrie, 253–72. Houndmills, Basingstoke: Palgrave Macmillan.
Winchester, Barbara. 1955. *Tudor Family Portrait.* London: J. Cape.
Winstead, Karen A. 1999. *Virgin Martyrs: Legends of Sainthood in Late Medieval England.* Ithaca, NY: Cornell University Press.
Woods-Marsden, J. 1998. *Renaissance Self-Portraiture. The Visual Construction of Identity and the Social Status of the Artist.* New Haven, CT: Yale University Press.
Woodward, W. H., ed. 1921. *Vittorino da Feltre and Other Humanist Educators.* Cambridge: Cambridge University Press.
Wright, Alison. 2005. *The Pollaiuolo Brothers: The Arts of Florence and Rome.* New Haven, CT: Yale University Press.
Wrigley, E. A., et al. 1989. *Population History of England, 1541–1871.* Cambridge: Cambridge University Press.
Wunder, Heidi. 1998. *He Is the Sun, She Is the Moon: Women in Early Modern Germany,* trans. Thomas Dunlap. Cambridge, MA: Harvard University Press.
Zaccaria, Vittorio. 1978. "La fortuna del 'De mulieribus claris' del Boccaccio nel secolo XV: Giovanni Sabbadino degli Arienti. Iacopo Filippo Foresti e le loro biografie femminili 1490–1497." In *Il Boccaccio nelle culture e literature nazionali,* ed. F. Mazzini, 519–45. Florence: Olschki.

CONTRIBUTORS

Mara I. Amster is Associate Professor of English at Randolph College (formerly Randolph-Macon Woman's College) and the editor of the two-volume facsimile edition, *Seventeenth-Century Texts on Prostitution: Essential Works for the Study of Early Modern Englishwomen* (2007). She is currently working on "The Purchase of Pleasure: Representing Prostitution and the Early Modern Market," a study of gender and economic anxiety in early modern prostitute texts.

Meg Lota Brown is Professor of English at the University of Arizona, and the author of *Donne and the Politics of Conscience in Early Modern England* (1994); she is also coauthor, with Kari Boyd McBride, of *Women's Roles in the Renaissance* (2005). She is a contributing editor of the Donne Variorum and author of numerous articles on the poetry, prose, and drama of the English Renaissance.

Danielle Clarke is Professor of English Renaissance Language and Literature at University College Dublin. She has published widely on gender in the early modern period, and her most recent book is *Teaching the Early Modern Period* (2011), edited with Derval Conroy.

Margaret Healy is Reader in English at the University of Sussex. She teaches many aspects of Renaissance literature, and is particularly interested in the cultural history of the body and the interfaces between literature, medicine, science, and art. She is the author of *Shakespeare, Alchemy and the Creative*

Imagination: The Sonnets and A Lover's Complaint (2011); *Fictions of Disease in Early Modern England: Bodies, Plague and Politics* (2001); *Richard II* (1998); and the co-editor of *Renaissance Transformations: The Making of English Writing 1500–1650* (2009). She edits the new British medical journal *Medical Humanities*.

Megan L. Hickerson is Associate Professor History at Henderson State University in Arkansas. The principal focus of her research is the intersection of religious ideas with ideas about women and gender in early modern England. She is the author of article-length publications on women and religion appearing in journals such as *Sixteenth Century Journal, Gender and History,* and *Journal of British Studies,* as well as of a monograph, *Making Women Martyrs in Tudor England* (Palgrave Macmillan, 2005), which considers the presentation of women as martyrs in popular Tudor martyrology, most importantly John Foxe's *Acts and Monuments (Book of Martyrs)*. She has a continuing interest in popular literature rising out of religious division in Reformation England, especially texts produced by and about those considered to be religious martyrs; thus, along with also currently working on representations of Henry VIII in popular culture, she is developing a follow up to her first book, which will consider adaptations of Tudor stories about women martyrs in post-Tudor polemical literature.

Holly Hurlburt is Associate Professor of History and Women's Studies at Southern Illinois University Carbondale. Her first book, *The Dogaressa of Venice, Wife and Icon,* appeared in the Palgrave New Middle Ages series in 2006. She is currently working on a monograph about Caterina Corner, Queen of Cyprus.

Kari Boyd McBride is Associate Professor of Gender and Women's Studies at the University of Arizona. She is the author of *Country House Discourse in Early Modern England: A Cultural Study of Landscape and Legitimacy* (2001), editor of *Domestic Arrangements in Early Modern England* (2002), and coauthor with Meg Lota Brown of *Women's Roles in the Renaissance* (2005). She is currently working on a study of women and education in early modern England, 1500–1700.

Karen Raber is Professor of English at the University of Mississippi. She is author of *Dramatic Difference: Gender, Class and Genre in the Early Modern Closet Drama* (2001), and editor of *Elizabeth Cary*, Vol. 4, *Ashgate Critical Essays on Women Writers in England, 1550–1700* (2009). She has also co-edited volumes on horses, Shakespeare, and ecostudies, and written numerous articles on women writers, gender, horses and horsemanship, and animals in the Renaissance.

Mary Rogers has published mainly on the relationships between representations of women in the visual arts and in the writing of the Italian Renaissance, especially of the Veneto. Her books include the anthologies of translated Italian texts *Women in Italy, 1350–1650* and *Women and the Visual Arts in Italy c. 1400–1650* (both coauthored with Paola Tinagli, 2005 and 2012). She hopes to work in future on writing on art and artifacts by women in sixteenth-century Italy.

Stephanie Tarbin is Lecturer in History at the University of Western Australia. With Susan Broomhall she edited *Women, Identities and Communities in Early Modern Europe* (2008), and has written essays on children, emotion, and domestic life and the family in early modern England.

INDEX

Agrippa, Cornelius, 102
Alberti, Leon Battista, 186
anatomy, 217n7
Andrewes, Launcelot, *Pattern of Catechistical Doctrine,* 116
Anguissola, Elena, 6
Anguissola, Sophonisba, 1–3, 9, 198, 200
   artistic training, 211n1
   relationship to family, 211n2
   Portrait of the Artist, 199
Antoniano, Silvio, 151–53
Aquinas, Thomas, *Summa Theologica,* 72
Aragon, Beatrice of, 195
Aragon, Catherine of, Queen of England, 154
Aragon, Eleonora of, 195
Aragon, Isabella of, 195
Aragon, Juana, Queen of, 165
Arienti, Giovanni Sabadino degli, 194, 198
Ariés, Philippe, 214n38
   "Ariés thesis," 35
Aristotle, 67–68
   De Generationae Animalium, 45
Askew, Anne, 14
   Examinations, 129
   see also Bale, John

Assheton, Nicholas, 33
Austria, Margaret of, 10, 166, 167, 175, 177, 179
Aylmer, John, 169

Babel and Bethel, 85–87
Bacchiacca, Francesco, *Portrait of a Lady with Music Book,* 203–4, *204*
Bacon, Anne Cooke, trans. (John Jewel) *Apologia eccesiae anglicanae,* 133
Badoer, Agnesina, 174
Baillet, Anne, 172
Baldovinetti, Alesso, *Portrait of a Lady,* 184, *185*
Bale, John, 78, 82, 85, 221n27
   Examinations of Anne Askew, 14
Bamber, Linda 5
Banister, John, *Historie of Man,* 48
Barbaro, Francesco, 172, 173, 186
   Of Wifely Duties, 16
Barker, Francis, 141
Baxter, Richard, 131
Beam, Aki, 40
Beaufort, Margaret, 170, 171
Beaumont, Francis and John Fletcher, *The Maid's Tragedy,* 49
Becon, Thomas, 31
   Catechism, 31

Behn, Aphra, *The Rover,* 57–58
Beilin, Elaine, 130
Bembo, Pietrao, *Gli Asolani,* 203
Bentivoglio, Ginevra Sforza of
    Bologna, 169
Bentley, Thomas, *Monument of*
    Matrons, 33
Betussi, Guiseppe, 194
Bible
    Corinthians, 119
    Genesis, 116
    Pauline letters, 116
    Proverbs, 116–18
    Timothy, 162
    women figures in, 138
Bingen, Hildegard von, 106
Blount, Katherine, 171
blushing, 51–53
Boccaccio, Giovanni
    daughter's death, 35
    Decameron, 31
    De Claris Mulieribus, 49
    Life of Camilla, 193–94
    On Famous Women, 168
Boniface VIII, Pope, 80
book as body, metaphor, 217n9
Borad, Jacqueline, 11
Botticelli, Sandro, *Tragedy of*
    Lucretia, 49
Botticelli, Simonetta, 205
Brandenburg, Barbara of, 166
Brathwaite, Richard, *The English*
    Gentlewoman, 52, 161
Brauner, Sigrid Maria, 108
Breu, Jorg, *Nine Ages of Man,* 26
Bruni, Leonardo, 150–52, 193
Buckley, Thomas and Alma Gotlieb, 101
Burckhardt, Jacob, 3–4, 127, 181, 184
Burgundy, Mary of, 164
Burke, Peter, 68

Calenda, Costanza, 107–108
Calvin, John, 79, 153, 169
Campbell, Erin, 41
Capp, Bernard, 132

Carnival, or Feast of Fools, 69–71
Cary, Elizabeth, 38
    marriage to Henry Cary, 14, 215n59
    The Tragedy of Mariam, 124–26
Castiglione, Baldassare, 8–9, 20, 51
    Il Cortegiano (Book of the Courtier),
    160–61, 169, 195, 200, 203–204
Castiglione, Fra Sabba, 152
Castile, Isabel of, 163–64, 166, 179
Castile, María of, 165
Cellier, Elizabeth, 112
Cereta, Laura 11, 148–49, 198
Channel, Elinor, *Message from God,* 129
Chapman, George and John Marston,
    Eastward Ho, 57
Charivari, 69–71, 91
Charles I, King of England, 10
Charles II, King of England, 85, 87
Chaucer, Geoffrey, *Legend of Good*
    women, 49
children, male and miracles, 214n37
Clark, Alice, 211n42
Clark, Stuart, 71, 101
Clarke, Samuel, *Ten Eminent*
    Divines, 116
classification, dualist systems of, 67–69
Clement, Margaret, 146
Cleves, Catherine of, 179
Clifford, Anne, 9, 20, 29–30, 35, 41,
    43, 112
Clifford, Lady Margaret, 112
Clinton, Elizabeth, 112
clothing, 54–58, 218n20
    and jewels, in portraiture, 186–88
    for marriage, 235n1
Comenius, Jan, 154
Comenius, John Amos, *Orbis Sensualium*
    Pictus, 27
Córdoba, Martin, *Jardín des nobles*
    doncellas, 166
Cornazzano, Antonio, *De mulieribus*
    admirandis, 194
Cornazzano, Antonio, *Del modo di*
    regere e di regnare, 166
Corner, Caterina, 165

Cosimo, Piero di, 205
cosmetics, 52–53
Council of Trent, 80
Cranach, Lucas, *Whore of Bablyon*, 83
Crawford, Patricia and Sarah Mendelson, 37
Cressy, David, 127–28
Crooke, Helkiah, *Microcosmographia*, 96–98
Culpeper, Nicholas, *A directory for midwives*, 39, 50

da Vinci, Leonardo, 177
  Bella Simonetta, 201
  Cecilia Gallerani, 202
  drawing of Isabella d'Este, 200, *201*
  Ginevra de'Benci, 201
  Lady with an Ermine, 190, *191*
  Madonna and Child with Saint Anne, 202
  on position of the body, 238n65
Darnton, Robert, 68
Davis, Natalie Zemon 4, 69
Dekker, Thomas, 7
de León, Lucrecia, 181
Deloney, Thomas, *Jack of Newbury*, 41
del Sarto, Andrea, *Woman with a Basket of Spindles*, 190
de Medici, Catherine, 9, 165, 170, 171, 172, 174
Denmark, Christina of, 174
d'Este, Isabella, 165, 175, 177, 200, 202
D'Ewes, Lady Anne, 33, 38
Dod and Cleaver, *A godlie forme of householde government*, 121–22
Dod, John and William Hinde, *Bathshebaes Instructions*, 118
Dolan, Frances, 85
Donati, Lucrezio, 200
Donato, Marina, 180
Donnington, Margaret, 174
Douglas, Mary, 47
Dowd, Michell, 20, 212n53
Dunton, John, 57

Duplessis-Mornay, Phillippe, 11
Durer, Albrecht
  Apocalypse, 83
  Three Witches, 93–94
  The Witch, 92–93
Dusinberre, Juliet, 4

Eliezer, Rabbi, 144
Elizabeth I, Queen of England, 9, 12–13, 30–31, 42–43, 109, 134, 163
  cult of virginity, 164, 177
  marriage of, 134–37
English Civil War, 141, 142, 145
Erasmus, Desiderius, 153

Fedele, Cassandra, 176
Ferrara, Eleonora, Duchess of, 171
Ferrara, Renee of France, 181
Ficino, Marsilio, 200
Filmer, Robert, 10
Firenzuola, Agnolo, 203
Fissell, Mary Elizabeth, 109
Foscari, Elena, 180
Foscarini, Ludovico, 149
Foxe, John
  Book of Martyrs, 133
  Christus Triumphans, 82, 83, 85
France, Anne of, 166
Franco, Veronica, 179
Freke, Elizabeth, 113
Froide, Amy, 40

Gallerani, Cecilia, 202–203
gender, imagery in religion, 82–84
  see also women and religion
Gentileschi, Artemesia, *Lucretia*, 49
Giorgione, *La Vecchia*, 31, 40
Gonzaga, Cecilia, 173, 193
Gonzaga, Elisabetta, 9
  see also Castiglione, Baldassare, *Il Corteggiano*
Gonzaga, Paola Malatesta, 179
Goodman, Nicholas, *Hollands Leaguer*, 7
gossip, or gossiping, 118, 131–32
Gosson, Stephen, 58

Gouge, William, *Of Domestical Duties,* 38
  funeral sermon on Mrs. Margaret Ducke, 115
Gowing, Laura, 132
Grafton, Richard, *Advice for Housholders,* 37
Gray, Lady Jane, 169
Gray, Louise, 41
Green, Karen, 11
Grey, Elizabeth, Countess of Kent, *A Choice Manual of Rare and Select Secrets,* 112
Grien, Hans Baldung
  "Bewitched Groom," 91
  The Seven Ages of Woman, 29
  Three Ages of Woman and Death, 27
Grumbach, Argula von, 14
Guise, Mary of, 168
Gwilliam, Tassie, 53–54

Halkett, Lady Anne, 112
Hall, John, 109
Hameln, Glückel of, 148
Hardwick, Elizabeth, Countess of Shrewsbury, 10, 20, 32, 43
Harkness, Deborah, 109, 110–12
Harman, Thomas, 7
Harris, Barbara, 138
Harvey, Mary, Lady Dering, 145
Henrietta Maria, Queen of England, 112
Henry VII, King of England, 170
Henry VIII, King of England, 9, 134
  divorce, 228 n13
Hoby, Lady Margaret, 112
Holbein, Hans the Younger, 164
"Homily Against Excesse of Apparel," 55
household
  and order, 118–21
  and women's labor, 119–22
Howard, Katherine, 172
Hull, Suzanne, 6
humanism, 3, 5, 14
  and portraiture, 193
  see also women, education of
humoral theory, 71

Hungary, Beatrice Queen of, 176
Hungary, Mary of, 166
Hutchinson, Lucy, 14
Hutson, Lorna, 120, 122–23

infertility, 215 n64
Innocent VIII, Pope, 89

James I, King of England, 10
Jonson, Ben, *Bartholomew Fair,* 20, 57
Joubert, Laurent, 36

Karant-Nunn, Susan, 78
Kellwaye, Simon, 99
Kelly, Joan (Gadol), "Did Women Have a Renaissance," 4–5, 127, 181
Kempe, Margery, 13
Kennix, Margaret, 109
Kerwin, William, 109
Kettering, Sharon, 182
Klapisch-Zuber, Christiane, 5
  and Herlihy, 34
Knox, John, 8, 153
  First blast of the trumpet, 168
Kramer, Heinrich and Jacob Sprenger
  see Malleus Maleficarum

Lanyer, Amelia, 35
Laquer, Thomas, 217 n5, 220 n2, 224 n5
Laurana, Francesco, 195, 237 n50
  Bust of Battista Sforza 195–98
Lawes, Henry, 145
Leong, Elaine, 113
Lestrange, Anne, 172, 173
Levy, Allison, 192
literacy, rates of, 230 n1
London, city of, 130–31
Luther, Martin, 13, 14, 153
  and women, 211 n33

Makin, Bathsua, 156–58
Malleus Maleficarum, 18, 89, 91, 108
Marinelli, Lucrezia, 169
marriage
  clothing for, 235 n21
  dowry, 235 n25

INDEX

in portraits, 186–89
as private, 121
see also women and marriage
Marston, John, *The Dutch Courtesan*, 55–56
Mary Magdalene, 74
Mary Stuart, Queen of Scotland, 9, 168
Massinger, Philip, *The Renegado*, 49
McKee, Francis, 111, 112
Medici, Catherine de *see* de Medici, Catherine
Medioli, Francesca, 81
Middleton, Thomas, *A Chaste Maid in Cheapside*, 57
Middleton, Thomas and Thomas Dekker
The Roaring Girl, 16, 59–61
The Honest Whore, 57
Mildmay, Lady Grace, 111
Milton, John, *Paradise Lost*, 119–21
Modena, Fioretta of, 146
Modena, Rabbi Aaron Berechiah, 146
Modena, Rabbi Leon, 144
Montefeltro, Battista Malatesta da, 150, 193
Moroni, Giovanni Battista, *Portrait of a Lady in Red*, 200
Moryson, Fynes, 6
movement, depiction in art, 238 n66
Mudazzo, Nicolo, 174
Musgrave, Lady Elizabeth, 171

Navarre, Margaret of, 167, 172, 175, 181
Heptameron, 12
Nenno, Nancy, 108
Nogarola, Isotta, 11, 149, 195
Norwich, Julian of, 13
Nurbanu Sultan, 171

Oldys, Alexander, *The London Jilt*, 53
Orsini, Alfonsina, 166, 169, 173, 175
Overbury, Thomas, 7–8

Pallavicina-Sanserverina, Ippolita, 175
Paracelsus, 95
and Paracelsian medicine, 103–105, 111

Paré, Ambroise, 50
Parker, Holt, 105–106
Parker, Patricia, 48
Parma, Margaret of, 166
Parr, Katherine, 172
Paster, Gail Kern, 20
patriarchy, crisis of, 80, 223 n52
Pelling, Margaret, 111
Perry, Mary Elizabeth, 81
Petrarch, influence on art, 202
Philips, Katherine, 130
Pia, Emilia, 9
see also Castiglione, Baldassare, *Il Corteggiano*
Piccolomini, Caterina, 175
Pisan, Christine de, 11, 167–69, 176
Book of the City of Ladies, 49
Pisanello, Antonio, medal of Cecilia Gonzaga, 193, *194*
Pius V, Pope, 81
Plat, Sir Hugh, *The Jewell House of Art and Nature*, 112, 133
Poole, Elizabeth, 11
"Popish Plot," 85
portraits, style of, 184
Portugal, Isabella of, 166
Protestantism, definition of, 221 n28
see also reformation; women and religion
public vs. private, boundaries, 117–42
Purcell, Henry, 145

querelle des femmes, 71

Raphael (Raphaello Sanzio da Urbino), *La Gravida*, 190
Ratke, Wolfgang, *The New Method*, 154
Raynolds, Thomas, 102
Reade, Alice, 32
Reformation, 76–80
see also Protestantism; women and religion
Rich, Barnabe, 51, 56
Roberts, Alexander, 90
Romana, Francesca de, 106
Rondinelli, Scholastica, 180

Roper, Lyndal, 77–78
Roper, Margaret More, 153
Rowlands, Samuel, 31

Sadler, John, *The Sicke Woman's Private Looking-Glasse,* 99–100, 102
Safiye, 171
Sanders, Eve Rachele, 49
San Jerónimo, Magdalena de, 181
Savoldo, Girolamo, *Portrait of a Lady with the Attributes of St. Margaret,* 205, 207
Savoy, Bona, 172
Savoy, Louise of, 9, 10, 166, 167, 179
Schurman, Anna Maria van, 156
Scot, Reginald, *The discoverie of witchcraft,* 102
Senecan drama, 124
Sevigné, Marquise de, Marie de Rabutin-Chantal, 158
Sforza, Battista, 195
Sforza, Caterina, 164–65
Sforza, Ippolita, 167, 168
Shakespeare, William
  All's Well that Ends Well, 110
  As You Like It, 25–26, 59
  Cymbeline, 59, 65
  Hamlet, 51
  King John, 49
  Macbeth, 100–101
  Measure for Measure, 8, 15, 27, 50
  Merchant of Venice, 59
  A Midsummer Night's Dream, 41–42
  Much Ado About Nothing, 51–54
  Othello, 47
  Rape of Lucrece, 49
  Richard III, 41
  Romeo and Juliet, 38
  Twelfth Night, 20, 59
Sharp, Jane, *The Midwives Book,* 39, 50, 98
Sidney, Mary (Herbert), Countess of Pembroke, 124, 129, 138–39
Sidney, Sir Philip, 135
Sophocles, 25

Spenser, Edmund, *The Faerie Queene,* 61–65
Strozzi, Alessandra Macinghi, 170, 185, 188, 189
Stubbes, John, *Discoverie of a Gaping Gulf,* 135
Stubbes, Philip, 58
Sweet, Victoria, 106
Swetnam, Joseph, *Arraignment of Lewd…Women,* 16–17, 20

T. E., *Lawes Resolution of Womens Rights,* 9–10
Tacitus, 105
Tertullian, 73
Toledo, Eleonora of, 178
  portrait of by Bronzino, 190
Trye, Mary, 112
Tuke, Thomas, 53
Turner, William, *Herbal,* 111
Tusser, *Book of Huswiferie,* 28

Varano, Costanza, 152, 176
Vecchio, Palma, *Blonde Woman,* 205, 206
Veneto, Bartolomeo, *Portrait of a Lady,* 186–187
Verroccio, *Lady with the Flowers,* 201
Vesalius, Andreas, 47
Vespucci, Simonetta, 200
Virgin Mary, 22, 71–76
  versus Eve, 71–76
Visconti, Bianca Maria, 195
Visconti, Maria, 195
Visitacion, María de la, 181
Vivaldi, Antonio, 145
Vives, Juan Luis, 36, 51
  Instruction of a Christian Woman, 154–56, 180
Vivonne, Catherine de, 158
von Bora, Katharina, 13–14
von Gorlitz, Elizabeth, 10
Voreagine, Jacobus, *Legendum Aurea,* 76

Wall, Wendy, 117
Ward, Mary, 159–60

Warner, Marina, 74
Warnicke, Retha 5
Webster, John, *The White Devil,* 54–55
Whately, William, 98–99
Wheathill, Anne, 130
Whitney, Isabella, 19
  poems, 133–34
Whore of Babylon, 82–84
  see also Durer, Albrecht
Wiesner, Merry, 17, 78–79
woman, ages of, 25–28
women
  in art, 183–207
  attitudes toward, in Roman Catholicism, 80–81
  and Catholicism, 139
  character of derived from classical texts, 235 n14
  and conscience, 128–29
  education of, 14, 143–62
  Galenic theory of reproduction, 47
  as healers, 105–13
  and humanism, 148, 177
  and humoral theory, 45–46
  imperfection of, 72
  infancy and childhood, 30–36
  Jewish, 23, 106, 144, 146
  legal status, 8–11
  literacy, 143
  literacy as religious requirement for, 146
  and marriage, 37–39
  and marriage among servants, 212 n53
  medical knowledge of, 45–47, 95–113
  menstruation, 98–100, 224 n7
  as mothers, 170–71, 236 n30
  in mother-son portraits, 177–78
  musical education of, 145–46
  and old age, 40–43
  old age associated with crime, 216 n79
  in the Ottoman Empire, 171
  and patriarchy, 10
  as patrons, 174–75
  and politics, 11
  portraits of, 183–207
  and power, 163–82
  and privacy, 10–11, 115–42
  as property in marriage, 139
  and prostitution, 7–8, 16, 57, 74–76, 222 n35
  and religion, 6, 11, 13–15
  roles, 3–4, 15
  as rulers, 164–79
  as saints, 210 n12
  salic law, 9
  virginity and chastity, 50–51, 217 n13, 222 n40
  as widows, 173–4, 190–92
  as witches, and witchcraft, 87–92, 102
  and work, 15–21
  writers, 129–30, 132–33
Woolley, Hannah, *The Ladies Directory,* 112
Worcester, Elizabeth Countess of, 171
Wroth, Lady Mary, 129
Wycherley, William, *The Plain Dealer,* 56

York, Elizabeth, Queen of, 171–72

Zuniga, María de, 179